VALUATION

OF

LIFE INSURANCE
LIABILITIES

Establishing Reserves for Life Insurance Policies and Annuity Contracts

Fourth Edition

Louis J. Lombardi, FSA, MAAA

D1211631

ACTEX Publications, Inc., Winsted, Connecticut

Printed in the United States of America

10 9 8 7 6 5 4 3 2

Cover design by Christine Phelps

Library of Congress Cataloging-in-Publication Data

Lombardi, Louis J., 1954-
  Valuation of life insurance liabilities : establishing reserves for life insurance policies and annuity contracts /
Louis J. Lombardi. -- 4th ed.
      p. cm.
  Rev. ed. of: Valuation of life insurance liabilities / Mark A.
Tullis. 3rd ed. 1997.
  ISBN-13: 978-1-56698-560-4
  ISBN-10: 1-56698-560-9
  1. Insurance, Life--Valuation--United States. 2. Insurance, Life--Valuation--Canada. I. Tullis, Mark A.
Valuation of life insurance liabilities. II. Title.

  HG8951.T85 2006
  368.3'201--dc22
                                                                                    2006011205

ISBN 13: 978-1-56698-560-4
ISBN 10: 1-56698-560-9

✧ PREFACE

The fourth edition of this book is being published at a time when valuations of individual life and annuity liabilities under statutory accounting principles are undergoing a significant shift from "formula-based" to "principle-based." Given the complexity of the types of products sold by the life insurance industry, this is a necessary and important change. However, it is a complex undertaking and will require a significant amount of education and training. Part of this education is an understanding of the "old" and the "new" methods. This is a primary goal of this book.

Those of you who are familiar with the third edition will barely recognize the fourth edition. This is because the fourth edition has undergone a significant rewrite. Important changes are:

1. New chapters on the statutory annual statement, the valuation process, and risk-based capital and;

2. Extensive modification to the chapters covering universal life, deferred annuities and cash flow testing.

Equally important are Excel workbooks contained on the CD-ROM associated with chapters 4-11, chapter 13 and 16. When reading these chapters, it may be helpful to have the Excel Workbook open to follow along with the text.

First, I want to thank Phil Polkinghorn and Mark Tullis for suggesting me as the author of the fourth edition. As a practitioner, I found the previous editions extremely helpful and I hope that this fourth edition lives up to the standard they have set. Second, I want to thank Gail Hall for encouraging me to write the fourth edition and the significant amount of support she gave during the editing process. Third, I want to thank Richard May for writing the material on Canadian valuation. Finally, I want to thank the following reviewers, some of which provided very constructive comments: Bruce Bohlman, Andy Boyer, Byron Corner, Mike DuBois, John Engelhardt, Mike Hale, Mike Harrington, Ed Jarrett, Charlie Linn, Link Richardson, Lyle Semchyshyn, Keith Sharp, and Don Skokan.

I also appreciate the editorial and design contributions made by the staff at ACTEX Publications, especially Marilyn J. Baleshiski for her manuscript editing and Christine Phelps for the textbook cover.

Louis J. Lombardi, FSA, MAAA
March 27, 2006

✧ Table of Contents

CHAPTER 3 THE VALUATION PROCESS

CHAPTER 4 VALUATION ASSUMPTIONS

CHAPTER 16 RISK-BASED CAPITAL

APPENDIX

To Hope, Scott, and Mark

1 ✧ Overview of VALUATION REQUIREMENTS

1.1 INTRODUCTION

At the end of 2004 approximately 167.7 million individual life insurance policies[1] were in force. The mortality tables used at the time most of these policies were sold assumed the insured would not live past his or her 100th birthday. Each year, several hundred of these insureds reach their 100th birthday. In some circumstances, the policies covering these insureds were issued over fifty years ago. This development illustrates three important facets of individual life insurance and annuity products. First, when the owners of these policies paid their first premium, the life insurance company that underwrote these risks and accepted the premium entered into a long term contractual commitment to pay certain benefits and provide certain services. Second, this relationship is based on events whose timing and occurrence are uncertain. Third, the long-term fiduciary responsibilities of the life insurance company have led to the development of specialized accounting and actuarial principles that involve a considerable degree of training, estimation and judgment.

Furthermore, a significant amount of the liabilities of a typical life insurance company are policy reserves. These liabilities are mostly devoted to the cost of future benefits and services. The magnitude of these reserves is such that a relatively small change in their unit value could significantly affect both the surplus and the earnings of the company in the period of the change. Consequently, the determination of these liabilities is among the more important actuarial functions of a life insurance company.

Reserves are liabilities for amounts an insurance company is obligated to pay in accordance with a life insurance policy or annuity contract[2]. The amounts are usually uncertain as to the exact amount and the time of payment. Some reserves are held because the event insured against has already happened, but the amount of claim is not known by the insurance company since the claim has not yet been reported to the company, or insufficient information has been furnished. Most reserves are held because the event insured against has not yet happened, but the company is obligated to pay if the event does happen. The first category is often called *claim reserves* or *loss reserves*, and the latter is often called *policy reserves*.

This book primarily addresses policy reserves for life insurance policies and annuity contracts, including miscellaneous benefits that are often included in such policies. The term *actuarial reserves* is used in this book to refer to those policy reserves. Actuarial reserves are determined using an *actuarial valuation*.

1.2 ROLE OF RESERVES[3]

Most life insurance policies and annuity contracts are characterized by the payment of a level or single premium by the policy owner, even though the cost of the benefits and services is not level over the term of the

---

[1] *2006 Life Insurers Fact Book,* Table 7.1 [7]

[2] In this book, policy and contract have the same meaning. Policy is typically used to identify a life insurance contract and contract is typically used to refer to an annuity contract.

[3] Some of the concepts discussed in Section 1.2 and Section 1.3 reflect concepts addressed in Chapter 8 of the *AICPA Audit* and *Accounting Guide for Life and Health Insurance Entities* [8].

policy. This creates a timing problem that is often described as a mismatch between revenue and costs. For example, in the early years of a block[4] of whole life policies, the premiums collected by the insurance company usually exceed the cost of benefits and services provided during those years. In contrast, the cost of benefits and services provided in the later years typically exceeds the premiums collected in those years. This relationship is demonstrated in Figure 1.1.

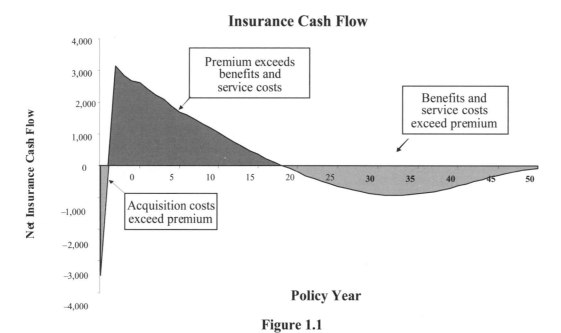

Figure 1.1

To properly match revenues and costs, reserves are established during the early policy years to provide for the excess cost of benefits and services over the corresponding premium in the later policy years.

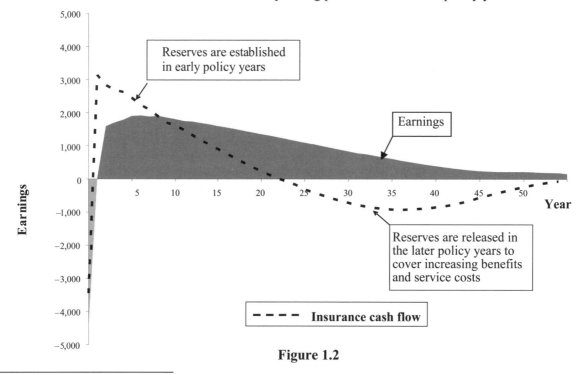

Figure 1.2

---

[4] A block of policies will usually mean a fairly large number of policies issued in a particular calendar year with fairly homogeneous risk characteristics.

As the above graph in Figure 1.2 shows, the establishment of reserves in the early policy years causes earnings to be lower than on a cash or "pay as you go" basis. In the later policy years, the opposite relationship holds. In fact, cash shortfall is avoided as the invested assets held in support of the reserves are sold to provide for the amount by which the benefit payments and service costs exceed the premium collected plus the investment earnings on these assets.

1.3 ACTUARIAL ASSUMPTIONS

When a life insurance company enters into an insurance contract, it does not know precisely when the benefits and service costs will occur or how much they will be. Accordingly, the reserving process requires the use of various assumptions, estimates and judgments about the future. The primary assumptions are expenses, investment returns, mortality, morbidity, voluntary terminations (i.e., expiries, lapses, surrenders and withdrawals) and taxes. These assumptions are usually based on the company's past experience, industry studies, regulatory requirements and judgments about the future, and are often called ***actuarial assumptions***.

The actuarial assumptions used in the determination of policy reserves affect the timing of reported earnings. If the assumptions are too optimistic, earnings will be overstated in the early policy years and understated in the later policy years. Conversely, if the assumptions are unduly pessimistic, the opposite will occur.

Results of an actuarial valuation can vary widely, not only because of the legitimately wide range of possible assumptions, but also the purpose of the valuation. Thus, it is important for the actuary to have a thorough awareness of the customary valuation methodologies available and the context in which they are used.

Policy reserves are determined using financial modeling techniques that project revenue, benefits, and service costs over the term of the life insurance policy, which could be 100 years or more. The predictability of these projections depends on, among other factors, how well the assumptions and estimates represent actual experience in the future. Furthermore, these actual values are subject to a variety of internal influences (underwriting criteria, product features, and premium rates) that are under the control of the life insurance company, and external influences (competitive, demographic, economic, political, and social) that are beyond the control of the life insurance company. In addition, it is the nature of these values, especially over the long projection period used in an actuarial valuation, to be inherently volatile, and random fluctuations will occur that will affect the predictability of these projections. Accordingly, what may initially have been thought to be conservative may ultimately prove to have been too optimistic or too pessimistic (e.g., assuming everyone dies by age 100).

Finally, since reserves are calculated using probabilities of future events (for example, the probability that a male age 35 will die between the ages 45 and 46), they are subject to the Law of Large Numbers. In particular, reserves have true significance only for blocks (or groups) of policies. Although as a practical matter, a reserve may be calculated for an individual policy, resulting in a real liability to the insurance company, the theory behind reserves only holds for a large number of policies, and not at the individual policy level.

In addition, many life insurance and annuity products are exposed to market risk. This type of risk is often not possible to eliminate through diversification.[5]

---

[5] Mortality is an example of a diversifiable risk. A variable product with guarantees is exposed to market risk and is an example of a non-diversifiable risk (i.e., selling a large number of these type of policies does not reduce the risk).

1.4   ACCOUNTING PRINCIPLES

Financial statements provide information to a variety of users who often have very different uses for this information. For example, insurance regulators, who represent the interests of policyholders, are concerned with the ability of the life insurance company to honor its commitments in accordance with the terms of the life insurance policy or annuity contract. Shareholders of stock life insurance companies, on the other hand, are more interested in understanding the earnings of the life insurance company and its growth prospects. Regulators and shareholders are important users of financial statements, but their interests are significantly different. Accordingly, different accounting principles have been developed to serve the needs of these different groups.

1.4.1   STATUTORY ACCOUNTING PRINCIPLES

Statutory accounting principles (SAP) are the principles prescribed or permitted by the insurance laws and regulations of the state or country in which the insurance company is incorporated[6]. The primary reason for preparing financial statements in accordance with statutory accounting principles is to help insurance regulators assess the ability of the life insurance company to satisfy their contractual obligations to policyholders. In other words, the emphasis is on ***solvency***. With this emphasis on solvency, the primary focus of statutory financial statements centers on the balance sheet – in particular, the level of statutory capital and surplus[7].

In the United States, statutory accounting principles can vary from state to state. Although there is a desire to minimize these variations and variations have been reduced in recent years, differences do exist. The ***National Association of Insurance Commissioners (NAIC)*** assists the state insurance officials with the development and maintenance of statutory accounting principles. One of the objectives of the NAIC is to provide a standard against which exceptions will be measured and disclosed[8].

1.4.2   GENERALLY ACCEPTED ACCOUNTING PRINCIPLES (GAAP)

When a company issues securities on a United States exchange (e.g., New York Stock Exchange) it must prepare a registration statement for approval with the Securities and Exchange Commission (SEC). This statement must include financial statements prepared in accordance with ***generally accepted accounting principles (U.S. GAAP)***. The Financial Accounting Standards Board (FASB) is the primary accounting standards body responsible for establishing accounting standards under U.S. GAAP.

Financial statements prepared in accordance with generally accepted accounting principles have a more diverse group of interested users. Shareholders, bondholders, banks and rating agencies are examples of users interested in financial statements prepared in accordance with GAAP. Although these groups have different needs, they share a common interest in understanding the earnings of the life insurance company. Accordingly, under generally accepted accounting principles, the emphasis switches to the matching of current revenue with current costs[9]. Large initial expenses are, therefore, generally deferred and amortized over the expected life of the block of policies. With this switch in emphasis, the income statement becomes the primary focus – in particular, the emergence of earnings of a block of business from accounting period to accounting period. Underlying this matching concept is the assumption that the life insurance company is a viable going concern.

---

[6] The term, ***domestic life insurance companies***, refers to the life insurance companies incorporated in a particular state within the United States.

[7] Statutory capital and surplus is the amount of assets in excess of liabilities.

[8] NAIC constitution [19].

[9] With the adoption of several standards since the early 1990's, FASB began also placing increasing emphasis on the balance sheet.

1.4.3 INTERNATIONAL ACCOUNTING STANDARDS (IAS)

With the growth of financial markets around the world, there has been an increasing need to enhance the consistency of global financial reporting standards. The International Accounting Standards Board (IASB) is an international standards body based in London, England. The IASB mission is to develop a set of *International Accounting Standards (IAS)* that would require transparency and comparability in general purpose financial statements[10].

Due to the importance of United States capital markets, a large number of multi-national companies have shares listed on one of the United States stock exchanges. Accordingly, they prepare one set of financial statements in accordance with U.S. GAAP and another set of financial statements in accordance with accepted accounting standards in the country where they are domiciled. The International Accounting Standards Board is working with the Securities and Exchange Commission and regulators in other countries to achieve a consistent set of accounting standards around the world. Their goal is for regulatory bodies of these countries to recognize statements prepared in accordance with International Accounting Standards to be in compliance with their local GAAP standards. If the IAS achieves this goal, multi-national companies would be able to avoid preparing financial statements under multiple general purpose accounting standards.

1.4.4 TAX BASIS ACCOUNTING

Generally, a life insurance company is taxed under the same federal income tax laws that are used to tax other taxable corporations. However, because of the unique accounting requirements of life insurance companies, there are sections of the Internal Revenue Code (IRC) that apply specially to life insurance companies.

In 1984, the United States Congress passed the Deficit Reduction Act of 1984 (DEFRA). Similar to regulations affecting other corporations, DEFRA defines the taxable income of a life insurance company as gross income less deductions. A significant deduction is the net annual increase in policy reserves. However, DEFRA requires that policy reserves, when used in the determination of taxable income, must be computed using federally prescribed standards. Policy reserves computed using such standards are called *Federally Prescribed Tax Reserves (FPTRs) or tax reserves*.

Another important piece of tax legislation was the Revenue Reconciliation Act of 1990. This Act also contained a provision that affected the determination of taxable income for a life insurance company. This provision is referred to as the DAC tax. Similar to GAAP principles, the concept was that certain expenses (for example, commissions and underwriting and issue expenses) should be deferred and amortized to produce a better matching of revenue with costs. The DAC tax significantly increased the taxable income of life insurance companies and, as a result, the amount of tax paid.

1.4.5 FAIR VALUE ACCOUNTING

In 1993, FASB adopted Statement of Financial Accounting Standards No. 115, *"Accounting for Certain Investment in Debt and Equity Securities"* (SFAS 115). The adoption of this standard resulted in a significant change in GAAP that had been under consideration by IAS and FASB since the early 1980s. SFAS 115 required that unrealized capital gains on certain assets be reported in the balance sheet as if they had been realized. This statement was a preliminary step toward fair value accounting.

Prior to SFAS 115, the balance sheet prepared in accordance with U.S. GAAP was primarily based on historical cost accounting principles. For example, if a bond was bought at a premium, the value of this bond was reported on the balance sheet at amortized cost. In other words, the premium was amortized in earnings from the date the bond was purchased to the maturity date of the bond. If the insurance company was to sell this

---

[10] IASB mission statement [15].

bond before the maturity date, the **market value** would likely have been significantly different than the **book value** (the amount reported on the balance sheet). If interest rates had risen since the company bought the bond, the market value of the bond would probably have been lower then the book value, and the company would have reported a realized capital loss. Conversely, if interest rates had fallen since the company bought the bond, the market value of the bond would probably have been higher than the book value, and the company would have reported a realized capital gain.

Fair value accounting would report assets and liabilities at their fair value, which is defined "as the price at which an asset or liability could be exchanged in a current transaction between knowledgeable, unrelated willing parties."[11] When an asset or liability actively trades on one of the exchanges, the fair value of this asset or liability would be the market price. When an asset does not actively trade on one of the exchanges, both FASB and IAS define a hierarchy of valuation methods for determining their value:

(1)   Market value when available;

(2)   Market value of similar instruments, with appropriate adjustment; and

(3)   Present value of projected cash flows.

The determination of the fair value of certain life insurance policies and annuity contracts are often based on the third method.

1.5 TYPES OF VALUATIONS

The methodology and assumptions underlying the determination of policy reserves depend upon whether the financial statements are being prepared in accordance with statutory accounting principles, generally accepted accounting principles (GAAP), tax basis accounting or other purposes. Accordingly, there are several different types of valuations.

1.5.1 STATUTORY VALUATIONS

Statutory valuations are performed to help insurance regulators assess the ability of the life insurance company to pay future benefits and service costs. Because the emphasis is on this ability to pay these long term contractual commitments, policy reserves established under a statutory valuation utilize conservative methodologies and assumptions. Accordingly, the liabilities are generally larger than if less conservative methodologies and assumptions had been used.

In the United States, the methodologies and assumptions are prescribed in a fairly precise manner by insurance laws and regulations and include significant provisions for adverse experience or deviations. For example, even though the life insurance company might be earning 7.5% on the assets supporting the policy reserves, insurance regulations require that it use a much lower interest rate such as 4% to establish the reserve. In addition, a significant portion of the costs incurred acquiring a policy are expensed when incurred since the assets used to pay for these costs are no longer available to provide for future benefits and service costs.

By expensing acquisition costs when incurred and using conservative assumptions in determining the reserves, a statutory valuation results in a conservative reporting of earnings in the early policy years. In particular, in the first policy year, statutory earnings of a block of life insurance policies or annuity contracts are usually negative because of the high acquisition costs. In the later policy years, however, statutory earnings are usually high as the conservatism in the reserves is released.

---

[11] *Proposed Statement of Financial Accounting Standards Fair Value Measurements*, [12] page 14-24.

Many of the insurance laws and regulations were written before the introduction of computers. Accordingly, many of the required techniques were based on practical considerations, such as not explicitly specifying all the actuarial assumptions in the determination of the policy reserve. For example, when determining reserves for whole life policies under the net level premium method, a mortality table and interest rate are explicitly specified. However, there are no explicit assumptions for expenses and lapse rates. These assumptions are implicitly provided through conservatism in the mortality tables, the interest rate and the reserve method.

In the United States, reliance is increasingly being placed upon the valuation actuary. Starting in the 1980s and continuing to today, there is a trend away from viewing policy reserves as "cookbook" items, and toward the view that the actuary must seriously consider whether these liabilities make good and sufficient provision for all unmatured obligations of the life insurance company for the guarantees under the terms of its policies. This has naturally led the actuary to consider the type of assets held in support of these liabilities and how the asset cash flows and the insurance cash flows relate under a wide range of scenarios.

In Canada, much more responsibility is placed on the appointed actuary. Unlike the United States law, Canadian law does not require specific mortality tables or interest rates to be used in determining reserve liabilities. Rather, these assumptions are chosen by the actuary. Furthermore, as we shall see later, Canadian statutory valuations tend to more realistically reflect future liabilities under the contracts, with less emphasis placed on conservatism. Canadian actuaries must explicitly recognize the impact of lapses and expenses, and use of the prescribed reserving method (the Canadian Asset Liability Method or CALM) can even sometimes produce negative reserves.

1.5.2 GAAP VALUATIONS

The methodologies under GAAP valuations are less prescriptive and the assumptions are generally based on company experience with more modest provisions for adverse experience. Furthermore, GAAP valuations incorporate explicit recognition of all actuarial assumptions that are considered material[12].

Another significant difference between statutory valuation principles and GAAP is the treatment of acquisition costs. To achieve a better matching of revenue with costs, GAAP requires that the costs incurred acquiring a policy are deferred and amortized in relation to the future revenue expected to be generated by the sale. This deferral process gives rise to an intangible asset called the deferred acquisition cost asset (DAC asset) which is often a significant portion of the GAAP equity of most life insurance companies.

1.5.3 TAX RESERVE VALUATIONS

Tax reserve valuations are used in order to calculate the policy reserve for purposes of determining taxable income. Policy reserves determined by a tax reserve valuation are often called *tax reserves*[13]. In the United States, tax reserves have historically been related to statutory reserves. From 1958 to 1984, tax reserves were based on the statutory reserves of the company, adjusted for some items. Because established companies frequently used more conservative reserving methods than new or growing companies, the prior law allowed restatement of tax reserves to a more conservative reserve method, using either exact or approximate methods. Also, an approximation formula was used to adjust the underlying reserve interest rate.

Congress perceived that this system was subject to abuse, compounded by the fact that the approximate recalculation methods specified in the law became less accurate as interest rates rose in the 1970's. Beginning in 1984 with the passage of DEFRA, the law was changed to require use of Federally Prescribed Tax Reserves

---

[12] Materiality addresses the question "Is this item large enough for users of the information to be influenced by it?" It is important that the actuary discuss materiality with those who make accounting decisions, generally within the accounting department. See Section VI in the Preamble of the NAIC *Accounting Practices and Procedures Manual* [18] for a more thorough discussion of materiality.

[13] This term should be used with caution since tax specialists use this term for other purposes.

(FPTRs) in the calculation of taxable income. Federally Prescribed Tax Reserves are determined using the methodology and assumptions which the company uses to calculate statutory reserves, with adjustments, the most significant of which are:

(1)   The Commissioners Reserve Valuation Method (CRVM) must be used for life insurance policies and the Commissioners Annuity Reserve Valuation Method (CARVM) must be used for annuity contracts;[14]

(2)   The interest rate must be equal to the larger of (a) and (b), where:

   (a)   is the ***Applicable Federal Interest Rate (AFIR)***; and
   (b)   is the prevailing state assumed interest rate, which is defined as the interest rate that at least 26 states permit in the determination of statutory reserves;

(3)   The mortality table must be the prevailing Commissioners standard mortality table that at least 26 states permit in the determination of statutory reserves;

In addition to these adjustments, federally prescribed standards specify additional adjustments in the determination of tax reserves.

In Canada, Policy reserves for income tax purposes underwent significant change in 1978, 1988 and then again in 1996. The 1988 changes were accompanied by transitional measures introduced to lessen the immediate impact on life insurers. For 1996, the new taxes rules retained the same tax reserves ("old rules") for policies issued prior to January 1, 1996. For policies issued after December 31, 1995 a new set of tax reserves ("new rules") were developed.

For ordinary life insurance policies issued prior to January 1, 1996, the maximum reserve permitted is calculated on the one and one-half year preliminary term basis,[15] with a cash surrender value floor. Generally, this produces a lower reserve than both the net level premium method[16] (which applied prior to 1978) and the one-year preliminary term method[17] (which applied from 1978 to 1987) because effectively the reserve does not commence until about the mid-point of the second year. This methodology is in rough recognition of the fact that the cost of acquiring the policy may be written off immediately. Interest and mortality assumptions are those used in setting the premiums, except for participating life insurance policies with guaranteed cash surrender values (other than annuities) where the assumptions are those used in computing the cash surrender value. For group term policies with coverage not exceeding 12 months, there is an unearned premium reserve determined by apportioning the net premium over the policy period.

For policies issued after December 31, 1995, the maximum reserve permitted is the lesser of the insurer's "reported reserves" and its "policy liabilities." The reported reserve is the amount included in the insurer's financial statements and the policy liability is the positive or negative amount of the insurer's liability in respect of the policy as determined in accordance with accepted actuarial practice. Both reserves are calculated without reference to income or capital taxes. Tax reserves for group term policies remain the same as for pre-1996 policies.

1.5.4 GROSS PREMIUM VALUATIONS

Gross premium valuations are generally performed when it is desirable to produce a "best estimate" value of the liabilities of the company. Gross premium valuations may be appropriate when it is necessary to deter-

---

[14] These reserve methods are defined in Chapter 5.
[15] Ibid
[16] Ibid
[17] Ibid

mine the value of a company, such as in the case of an acquisition or merger, or when a company is being examined in order to determine solvency.

As with GAAP, gross premium valuations explicitly recognize all actuarial assumptions that are considered material. However, gross premium valuations are generally performed with assumptions that have little or no provision for conservatism (i.e., "best estimate" assumptions). In most cases, the reserves are calculated as the present value of future benefits and expenses less the present value of future gross premiums.

1.5.5 EMBEDDED VALUE

A relatively new and increasingly popular performance measurement system is ***embedded value***[18]. Financial performance of the life insurance company is measured by the change in embedded value of the life insurance company over a specified time period. Under this measurement system, embedded value is the sum of the following two items:

(1)   Value of in force business; and

(2)   Adjusted net worth.

The value of in force business is the present value of projected after-tax statutory earnings minus the change in ***required capital***[19] of the blocks of in force policies that the company has sold. The earnings are discounted using the cost of capital. The ***cost of capital*** is the rate of return offered by investments with similar or equivalent characteristics. The cost of capital is often determined using the ***Capital Asset Pricing Model (CAPM)***[20]. Under CAPM, the cost of capital rate of return is the sum of the risk-free rate of return and a risk premium.

Adjusted net worth is the market value of assets supporting statutory surplus plus the present value of the cost of capital for holding required capital. Required capital is the minimum amount of capital and surplus the life insurance company must maintain to remain a going concern and to be in compliance with the covenants of debt obligations.

1.6   EFFECTS OF STATUTORY VALUATION REQUIREMENTS

The level of statutory reserves has many effects on a life insurance company other than the obvious direct financial implications.

1.6.1 GROSS PREMIUM LEVELS

Although statutory reserve requirements do not directly affect the gross premiums charged by the company, they do have an indirect impact. Generally, guaranteed premium rates for whole life and term policies and guaranteed fund accumulation rates for universal life policies are set at a level so as to avoid holding additional reserves. Also, when setting gross premium rates, companies must take into account the cost of establishing statutory reserves.

---

[18] Embedded value is not a liability valuation method, but a performance measure.
[19] See Chapter 16 for further discussion of required capital.
[20] See Brealey, Myers, and Allen [9] for a more complete discussion.

1.6.2 PRODUCT DESIGN

Aside from the design features inherent in the choice of guarantees as discussed above, statutory requirements often make otherwise desirable product features difficult or costly to reserve. Because of statutory reserve considerations, guaranteed cost of insurance rates for Universal Life policies are almost never less than mortality rates used to determine the policy reserve under a statutory valuation. Term policies often feature guaranteed premium rates higher than those actually charged, primarily to avoid deficiency reserves[21]. As a final example, interest guarantee structures of annuities can be influenced by Commissioners Annuity Reserve Valuation Method reserve levels.

1.6.3 FEDERAL INCOME TAXES

In the United States, federal income taxes are fairly insensitive to the actual statutory reserve level, as Federally Prescribed Tax Reserves are defined separately in the tax code. However, the choice of a statutory reserve basis still has several minor effects on tax reserves. Items unspecified in the tax code, such as whether tax reserves are calculated on a continuous or curtate basis, should follow the statutory practice for the plan in question. Also, in the United States, tax reserves for a policy may not exceed statutory reserves. Thus, the choice of a statutory basis which results in lower reserves than would be required on the Federally Prescribed basis would result in lower tax reserves than if a more conservative basis were used.

1.6.4 DIVIDENDS TO POLICYHOLDERS

There are many techniques used by companies to calculate policyholder dividends, but many companies use two- or three-factor formula methods using the statutory reserve as an input item in the calculation of the interest and mortality components. Where this is the case, the choice of the statutory reserve basis will have a significant effect on how dividends are distributed among the various classes of policyholders. Even if a company uses another method to calculate dividends, choice of a statutory reserve basis will enter into the calculation and allocation of surplus, thereby indirectly affecting distribution of dividends.

1.6.5 STATUTORY EARNINGS

The fact that statutory reserves affect statutory earnings is obvious in itself, but it leads to several interesting corollaries. In the United States, the amount of money which may be paid out as dividends to stockholders is generally limited by the accumulated statutory earnings of the company. This makes the realistic projection of statutory earnings the basis of determining the appraisal value of a life company, since the economic value of the company is most directly related to the present value of distributable earnings. It also means that the incidence of statutory earnings, and hence the appraisal value of the company, will be affected by the statutory reserve basis.

1.6.6 IMPORTANT INDICATORS

Several important indicators used by regulators, rating agencies, investment analysts and various marketing organizations to measure the strength of companies are based in part upon statutory financial measures. Many companies manage their business, including the selection of the statutory reserve basis, so that these indicators are as favorable as possible.

It is important to remember that the reserving method and basis do not directly affect the total profitability of a policy over its lifetime, only the emergence of profit by year. It can be shown that if two alternative sets of reserves for a policy grade together at the maturity date, the pre-tax profits produced by the two will have the same present value at issue, assuming the interest rate used to discount is the same rate at which investment

---

[21] Deficiency reserves will be discussed in Chapter 7.

income is calculated. However, if a higher interest rate is used to discount, the set of reserves which are generally lower will produce the largest present value of profits.

1.7 STATUTORY VALUATION REQUIREMENTS IN CANADA[22]

1.7.1 INSURANCE COMPANIES ACT

A significant rewrite of the federal Insurance Companies Act (ICA) was implemented in 1992 redefining the regulation of insurance companies and more specifically creating the role of Appointed Actuary. Several revisions to the ICA have been implemented since, but have not affected the defined responsibilities of the actuary. The appointed actuary has been given broad roles and responsibilities similar in concept to those of the appointed actuary in the United Kingdom:

(1)   Appointments will be made and terminated by the board of directors, and the actuary will have access to the board.

(2)   The actuary will value and report on actuarial and other policy benefit liabilities.

(3)   The actuary will report annually to the board of directors on the current financial position of the company. For foreign branches, the actuary reports to the Chief Agent.

(4)   The actuary may be directed by regulation to report on the future financial condition of the company.

(5)   The actuary is to have access to all necessary company records and information required in the performance of assigned duties.

(6)   If the actuary becomes aware of any circumstances that may have a material impact on the ability of the company to meet its obligations and which require rectification, he or she must bring the matter to the attention of management and the board.

(7)   If satisfactory action is not taken to correct the situation within a reasonable period of time, the actuary will have a statutory obligation to send a copy of his or her report to the Superintendent of Financial Institutions and so advise the board of directors.

(8)   The actuary is to render an opinion to the board on the administration of the company dividend policy prior to any distributions.

1.7.2 STANDARDS OF PRACTICE FOR THE APPOINTED ACTUARY

The Canadian Institute of Actuaries (CIA) is the national organization of the actuarial profession in Canada. Member driven, the Institute is dedicated to serving the public through the provision, by the profession, of actuarial services and advice of the highest quality. Its Guiding Principles are:

> To ensure that services are provided by qualified individuals, the Institute maintains publicly visible programs and procedures for the attainment and maintenance of professional qualification by its members.

> The Institute develops standards of professional practice and codes of conduct and, through its disciplinary process, ensures their compliance by its members.

> The Institute promotes the development of a body of expert actuarial knowledge and practice relevant to Canadian social and economic needs. It encourages actuarial research and scholarly

---

[22] This section was written by Richard May, FSA, FCIA.

activity and the dissemination of the results among its members. It encourages the application of actuarial science and technique to new areas where these are relevant.

The Institute cooperates with governments and public bodies and makes timely and relevant contributions to public policy issues.

To assure a continuing supply of qualified professionals, the Institute encourages the recruitment and training of new actuaries.

The Institute serves the professional needs of all Canadian actuaries regardless of area of practice, language, or geographic region.

To assist its members in their professional activities, the Institute develops technical support including collection and analysis of statistical data, and the publication of actuarial handbooks and texts.

The Institute represents Canadian actuaries internationally and cooperates with other national actuarial bodies in areas of mutual interest.

The Institute provides opportunities for the professional development of its members.

In conjunction with the new defined role of appointed actuary, the CIA developed and implemented new standards of practice for the appointed actuary of an insurance company which govern the conduct of the actuary in such matters as appointment, access to information, management reporting, board reporting and financial statements. The evolution of new products and new techniques has led to the development of further guidance and additional clarification.

In May, 2002, the Canadian Institute of Actuaries issued the "Consolidated Standards of Practice – General Standards" applicable to all Fellows and Associates of the Canadian Institute of Actuaries. In December, 2002, the Consolidated Standards of Practice – Practice Specific Standards for Insurers were issued. The consolidation of the Standards of Practice (SOP) was primarily a re-write of existing recommendations in a format and presentation that was more cohesive and consistent. The standards were to ensure that actuarial information be properly determined and fully disclosed, and that such information and disclosure be judged by peers as good actuarial practice and merit the respect and acceptance by the public and regulators. They consist of recommendations and other guidance intended to amplify the recommendations or to illustrate their application. The recommendations deal with the verification of valuation data, the development of appropriate assumptions, the choice of valuation method, and the text and implications of the reports accompanying the published financial statements and government statement. They also touch on documentation of the valuation actuary's work, the use of approximations, and judgment regarding materiality. Information on the Standards of Practice and other CIA materials is publicly available on the Institute's website, www.actuaries.ca.

While the recommendations provide sound general guidance for the practicing valuation actuary, they are most easily and directly interpreted in the context of traditional ordinary life insurance. However, there is a wide range of types of policies included in a typical valuation today. They present a variety of technical problems that are difficult to resolve by a straightforward interpretation of professional standards. To assist the valuation actuary in applying the Standards of Practice, the CIA has issued a number of publications. The following is a list of the current Canadian Institute of Actuaries Standards of Practice, Research Papers, Educational and Guidance Notes applicable to the valuation of individual insurance products:

205122   Consolidated Standards of Practice – General Standards

205060   Consolidated Standards of Practice – Practice Specific Standards for Insurers

205111   Educational Note: Valuation of Segregated Fund Investment Guarantees

205007	Educational Note: Margins for Adverse Deviations
205004	Educational Note: Best Estimate Assumption for Expenses
204054	Educational Note: Approximations to Canadian Asset Liability Method (CALM)
203106	Educational Note: Selection of Interest Rate Models
203083	Educational Note: Aggregation and Allocation of Policy Liabilities
202065	Educational Note: Future Income and Alternative Taxes
202037	Educational Note: Expected Mortality: Fully Underwritten Canadian Individual Life Insurance Policies
9803	Educational Note: Disclosure of Actuarial Information By Life Insurance Companies
9721	Research Paper: C-1 Risk
9634	Educational Note: Nature and Use of Derivatives
9633	Educational Note: Asset and Mortgage-Backed Securities
9627	Educational Note: Management, Risks, Regulations and Accounting of Derivatives
9626	Educational Note: Liquidity Risk Management
9543	Educational Note: Measurement of Exposure to Interest Rate Risk
9430	Guidance Notes: An Overview of an Investment Policy Statement in an Asset/Liability Management Context

In addition to the above, the CIA Committee on Life Insurance Financial Reporting (CLIFR) annually prepares a letter to actuaries on "Guidance for the Current Year's Valuation of Policy Liabilities of Life Insurers" and the federal Office of the Superintendent of Financial Institutions (OSFI) distributes an annual "Memorandum to the Appointed Actuary on the Report on the Valuation of Life Insurance Policy Liabilities." These two documents provide current advice, guidance and requirements with respect to preparing and reporting on valuations for the current year end.

As a regulator, OSFI can impose its own requirements on the performance of the actuary's work. In addition to the above standards of practice, OSFI has implemented requirements to periodically perform an "External Review of the Actuary's Work." The purpose of the External Review is to:

- Maintain and strengthen confidence in the work of the Appointed Actuary by the public, by insurance company management and directors, and by supervisory authorities,
- Narrow the range of practice by Appointed Actuaries
- Improve the quality of the Appointed Actuary's work
- Provide significant professional education for the Appointed Actuary

The CIA has also developed standards of practice for the external review process. These measures are a key component of the continual development process for actuaries and supplement the Standards for the Continuing Professional Development of the Actuary.

1.7.3 THE CANADIAN ASSET LIABILITY METHOD

The current statutory reporting basis for reserves in Canada is the *Canadian Asset Liability Method* (CALM). CALM is a prospective method of valuation which uses

(1)   the full gross premium for the policy,

(2)   the estimated expenses and obligations under the policy (without arbitrary limitations),

(3)   current expected experience assumptions plus a margin for adverse deviations, and

(4)   scenario testing (deterministic or stochastic) to assess interest rate risks and market risks (particularly for segregated fund or variable annuity guarantees)

The CALM valuation method will be discussed in more detail in Chapter 14.

1.7.4 MINIMUM CONTINUING CAPITAL AND SURPLUS REQUIREMENTS

The calculation of actuarial liabilities serves a dual purpose: to provide for future obligations on the balance sheet and to appropriately charge income in the income statement. Canadian statutory valuations had in the past been performed primarily to meet the concerns of regulators that companies remain solvent. This is why prescribed Canadian valuation methods and assumptions were conservative.

The movement in Canada to make actuarial liabilities appropriate for both statutory and GAAP purposes has necessitated a fresh look at how management and regulators can be assured that a company will remain solvent.

In Canada, the guarantee association *Assuris* protects Canadian life insurance policyholders against loss of benefits due to the insolvency of a member company. Every life insurance company authorized to sell insurance policies in Canada is required, by the federal, provincial and territorial regulators, to be a member of Assuris.

Assuris does not cancel policies or pay cash compensation; Assuris facilitates the transfer of the policy to a solvent company and ensures the continuity of covered benefits under the original terms of the policy. To hasten this process and reduce losses, Assuris seeks to identify risks in both individual companies and the industry and works closely with the regulators on timely intervention.

Assuris is a not-for-profit organization funded by assessments of its members. Key elements of its governance include:

(1)   A Board of Directors, each of whom must be independent of members,

(2)   An Industry Advisory Committee that provides advice to the Board on coverage, the assessment system, and emerging issues,

(3)   The right of each of the participating jurisdictions (federal, provincial and territorial) to object to any change in Assuris' By-laws or Memorandum of Operations.

(4)   Member voting on By-law changes and Memorandum changes affecting costs.

The assessment base for each member is its Capital Required according to the Minimum Continuing Capital and Surplus Requirements (MCCSR) that operate for companies in Canada in much the same way that Risk Based Capital (RBC) operates for companies in the U.S. This measure is set by the primary regulators and is an important, risk-related component of life insurance supervision in Canada.

While Assuris maintains a liquidity fund in excess of $100 million, the costs of an actual insolvency will be assessed on the continuing members after the insolvency. Assessments for an insolvency may continue indefinitely at the rate of 1.33% of Capital Required, and other short-term assessments are available. The total present value of Assuris' assessment capacity is in excess of $3.5 billion.

1.7.5 DYNAMIC CAPITAL ADEQUACY TESTING

The Canadian Institute of Actuaries created a Committee on Solvency Standards to study the actuarial aspects of corporate solvency and to provide guidance to actuaries practicing in this area. Accordingly, a standard of practice was adopted which requires the actuary to examine not only the company's current financial position, but also its financial condition, including its ability to withstand future threats to solvency.

The actuary's annual investigation of the company's solvency considers the past, present and future financial positions of the company and the sensitivity of   surplus to changes in various experience factors and management policies. In addition to the base scenario normally underlying the company's business plan, a variety of other scenarios are suggested for investigation (worse than expected mortality, morbidity, withdrawals, expenses, changing investment yields, and so on), as well as any additional or integrated scenarios which the actuary considers appropriate to the circumstances. Investigations should include both the business in force and anticipated new business. Finally, the actuary should provide a written report to the board of directors each year outlining the investigation performed and presenting the significant findings and conclusions.

1.7.6 JOINT POLICY STATEMENT

An insurance company's auditor relies on the actuary for many items in the balance sheet and year-to-year changes in these liabilities implicit in the income statement. The actuary may in turn rely upon the auditor's verification of data on which the policy valuation is based.

A Joint Policy Statement was issued by the Canadian Institute of Actuaries and the Canadian Institute of Chartered Accountants in 1991 to address how the actuary and auditor should interact in meeting their professional responsibilities and how their roles should be disclosed to readers of financial statements.

The Joint Policy Statement recognizes that either the actuary or the auditor could be using the specialized work of the other, and outlines the following four aspects of the work that should be considered when preparing a report relying on such work:

(1)   The specialist professional's qualifications, competence, integrity, and objectivity.

(2)   The specialist professional's appointment to do the work.

(3)   Whether the specialist professional has followed the standards of his or her profession in carrying out the work.

(4)   The appropriateness of the specialist professional's findings and opinions.

In addition to the report of the auditor and the report of the actuary, the new legislation requires a statement of management describing the respective roles of the auditor and the actuary. The Canadian Institute of Chartered Accountants revised its Assurance and Related Sevices Guideline AuG-15, Audit of Actuarial Liabilities of Life Insurance Enterprises in December 2005. It requires the auditor to confirm and independently assess the policy liabilities. This may mean that the Joint Policy Statement will need to be revised.

This project will result in revisions to Assurance and Related Services Guideline AuG-15, Audit of Actuarial Liabilities of Life Insurance Enterprises, to more closely reflect current best practice.

1.8 Statutory Valuation Requirements in the United States

In 1994, the NAIC devoted a significant amount of resources to codification of statutory accounting principles (SAP). The purpose of codification was "to produce a comprehensive guide to SAP for use by insurance departments, insurers, and auditors."[23] A consistent and comprehensive guide to statutory accounting principles did not exist prior to codification. Accordingly, life insurance companies were sometimes uncertain about what principles to apply and regulators were not always familiar with the statutory accounting principles used in other states.

This comprehensive guide was first published in 1998 and is called the *"Accounting Practices and Procedures Manual"* (NAIC Manual). This manual has three major parts:

(1)   Preamble;

(2)   Statements of Statutory Accounting Principles (SSAPs); and

(3)   Appendices.

This manual does not preempt state laws and regulations. Instead, the objective of the NAIC is that this manual will be the foundation of a state's statutory accounting practices and will be subject to modification by a state's insurance commissioner.

It is important that an actuary who is responsible for the calculation of statutory reserves for individual life insurance and annuity contracts has a sound understanding of the following sections of this manual:

- Statement of Statutory Accounting Principles No. 50, *"Classifications and Definitions of Insurance or Managed Care Contracts In Force"* (SSAP No. 50);

- Statement of Statutory Accounting Principles No. 51, *"Life Contracts"* (SSAP No. 51);

- Appendix A-820, *"Minimum Life And Annuity Reserve Standards"* (A-820); and

- Appendix A-822, *"Asset Adequacy Analysis Requirements"* (A-822);

In addition, the actuary should have a sound understanding of the actuarial guidelines found in Appendix C of the NAIC manual and the *Actuarial Standards of Practice* promulgated by the Actuarial Standards Board of the American Academy of Actuaries that pertain to the particular type of life insurance policies and annuity contracts for which statutory reserves are being established. Finally, the actuary should be familiar with the concepts underlying **Risk Based Capital**,[24] how it is determined and how it is used.

1.8.1 SSAP No. 50

SSAP No. 50 provides a general framework for classifying insurance contracts into four broad categories:

(1)   Life Contracts

(2)   Accident and Health Contracts

(3)   Property and Casualty Contracts

(4)   Deposit-type Contracts

---

[23] See [18], Paragraph 12 of Preamble
[24] See Chapter 16 for a thorough discussion of Risk Based Capital.

These classifications reflect that the premium payment pattern and the protection provided are "fundamentally different and, therefore, require different income recognition and reserving methods."[25] Product classification is important because it determines the recognition of revenue and costs and the methodologies and assumptions used to determine policy reserves.

1.8.2 SSAP No. 51

SSAP No. 51 establishes statutory accounting principles for income recognition and policy reserves for all contracts classified as life contracts in accordance with SSAP No. 50. In particular, Paragraph 5 of SSAP No. 51 states that "premiums shall be recognized on a gross basis (amount charged the policyholder) when due from policyholder under the terms of the insurance contracts." Additionally, Paragraph 14 of SSAP No. 51 states "Statutory policy reserves shall be established for all unmatured contractual obligations of the reporting entity arising out of the provisions of the insurance contract." Finally, Paragraph 15 of SSAP No. 51 states "The reserving methodologies and assumptions used in computation of policy reserves shall meet the provisions of Appendices A-820 and A-822 and the actuarial guidelines found in Appendix C of this manual." Furthermore, SSAP No. 51 requires that policy reserves shall be in compliance with those Actuarial Standards of Practice promulgated by the Actuarial Standards Board.

1.8.3 APPENDICES A-820 AND A-822

Appendices A-820 and A-822 contain excerpts of the NAIC model *Standard Valuation Law* (SVL) and the model *Actuarial Opinion and Memorandum Regulation*, respectively. The Standard Valuation Law and Actuarial Opinion and Memorandum Regulation are the two most important model regulations governing a statutory valuation.

The Standard Valuation Law states:

> *"Every life insurance company doing business in this state shall annually submit the opinion of a qualified actuary as to whether the reserves and related actuarial items held in support of the policies and contracts are computed appropriately, are based on assumptions which satisfy contractual provisions, are consistent with prior reported amounts, and comply with applicable laws of this state. The commissioner by regulation shall define the specifics of this opinion and add any other items deemed to be necessary to its scope."[26]*

The qualified actuary mentioned above is appointed by the Board of Directors of the life insurance company and is called the ***appointed actuary***.

The Actuarial Opinion and Memorandum Regulation requires that the appointed actuary issue a ***statement of actuarial opinion***. Within this actuarial opinion, the appointed actuary must attest to being "familiar with valuation requirements applicable to life and health insurance companies" and that the reserves are "at least as great as the minimum aggregate amounts required by the state in which this statement is filed."

The statement of actuarial opinion should list the items and amounts for which the actuary expresses an opinion. There may be separate opinions for separate blocks of business; for example one actuary may sign an opinion relating to group insurance, while another signs an opinion relating to individual life insurance, and a third actuary signs an opinion relating to individual health insurance. Note, however that the opinion is on the adequacy of reserves in aggregate, and that it is possible for deficiencies in individual components of the reserves to be offset by margins in other components.

---

[25] See [18], Paragraph 4 of SSAP No. 50
[26] See [4], Standard Valuation Law Paragraph A of Section 3.

The statement of actuarial opinion frequently indicates reliance on others. For example, it may indicate reliance on others within the life insurance company for the accuracy and completeness of the underlying policy records, and reliance on actuaries with other companies for items such as reinsurance assumed. The statement of actuarial opinion should indicate the relationship of the actuary with the company, and the scope of the actuary's work and any reliances.

In addition, Actuarial Standard of Practice No. 22, *Statements of Opinion Based on Asset Adequacy Analysis by Actuaries for Life or Health Insurers* (ASOP N0. 22),[27] contains requirements with the key provisions of Section 3 paraphrased below:

Section 3.1
When performing an asset adequacy analysis, the actuary should review and apply applicable law and applicable actuarial standards of practice, such as ASOP No. 7, *Analysis of Life, Health, or Property/Casualty Insurer Cash Flows*[28]. The actuary should be aware of the Actuarial Guidelines published by the NAIC and make a reasonable effort to be aware of generally distributed interpretations of each regulatory authority.

Section 3.2
The actuary should determine that he or she meets the requirements of the Qualification Standards for Prescribed Statements of Actuarial Opinion, promulgated by the American Academy of Actuaries. The appointment should be in writing, from the board of directors or its designee, citing the applicable law. If the appointment as an entity's appointed actuary is required by applicable law, the actuary should accept or withdraw from such an appointment in conformance with the applicable law. Acceptance of or withdrawal from the position should be in writing.

Section 3.3
The form, content, and recommended language of the statement of opinion may be specified by applicable law. The actuary should include in the opinion a statement on the adequacy of reserves and other liabilities based on an asset adequacy analysis, the details of which are contained in the supporting memorandum.

Section 3.4
The actuary should use appropriate analysis methods when forming an opinion with respect to asset adequacy. In judging whether the results from the asset adequacy analysis are satisfactory, the actuary should use professional judgment.

To assist the appointed actuary, the American Academy of Actuaries, in conjunction with the Society of Actuaries, publishes the *Life & Health Valuation Law Manual*.[29] This annual publication is designed to help the appointed actuaries comply with the Standard Valuation Law and Actuarial Opinion and Memorandum Regulation.

---

[27] See [2].
[28] See [1].
[29] See [4].

1.9 EXERCISES

1.9.1 KEY TERMS

claim reserves	loss reserves
policy reserves	actuarial reserves
actuarial valuation	actuarial assumptions
statutory accounting principles	generally accepted accounting principles
solvency	NAIC
IAS	Federally Prescribed Tax Reserves
market value	book value
fair value accounting	tax reserves
Applicable federal interest rate	CAPM
appointed actuary	actuarial opinion

1.9.2 QUESTIONS

a. With what is this book primarily concerned?

b. What is the role of reserves?

c. What are the primary actuarial assumptions?

d. What is the emphasis of statutory accounting?

e. What is the primary emphasis of generally accepted accounting principles?

f. What is the hierarchy for determining the fair value of an asset?

g. Briefly describe the major types of valuation.

h. What are some of the effects of statutory valuation requirements?

i. What was the purpose of codification?

2 ✧ NAIC ANNUAL STATEMENT

2.1 STATUTORY ANNUAL STATEMENT

Each year a life insurance company is required to submit financial statements in accordance with statutory accounting principles to the insurance department of each state in which the life insurance company has issued an insurance policy that is still in force. These financial statements are collectively called a *statutory annual statement* and must comply with the statutory accounting standards as adopted by that state.

The general format and content of the statutory annual statement is specified by the NAIC. However, several states have additional requirements and the statutory annual statement filed with these states must reflect their modifications. Since many life insurance companies have policies in force in all fifty states, not to mention the District of Columbia, American Samoa, Guam, Puerto Rico and the Virgin Islands, they must file several different statutory annual statements.

The statements as presented in this book were in place for calendar year 2005. Minor changes are made from time to time, but any changes subsequent to 2005 would be incidental to the concepts presented in this book.

2.1.1 PRIMARY FINANCIAL STATEMENTS

The primary financial statements contained in the statutory annual statement are:

(1) Balance Sheet
(2) Summary of Operations
(3) Capital and Surplus Account
(4) Cash Flow Statement
(5) Analysis of Operations by Lines of Business

The primary objective of this chapter is to illustrate the content of these statements and to give a brief description of their purpose.

2.1.2 PRIMARY ACTUARIAL SCHEDULES AND EXHIBITS

The statutory annual statement also includes numerous exhibits, schedules and supplemental reports that provide additional information in support of the primary financial statements. Many of these supplemental financial statements have entries that are determined using actuarial techniques. The primary schedules and exhibits that contain individual life and annuity information and that require the assistance of an actuary to complete are:

(1) Analysis of Increase in Reserves During the Year

(2) Exhibit 1 – Part 1 – Premiums and Annuity Considerations

(3) Exhibit 5 – Aggregate Reserve For Life Policies and Contracts

(4)   Exhibit 8 – Policy and Contract Claims

(5)   Exhibit of Life Insurance

(6)   Exhibit of Number of Policies, Contracts, Certificates, Income Payable and Account Values in Force for Supplementary Contracts, Annuities, Accident & Health and Other Policies

Following the brief description of the primary financial statements, this chapter will also give a brief description of these primary actuarial schedules and exhibits.

2.1.3 SUCCESSIVE EQUATION

Several of these financial statements share a common purpose.

Each of them demonstrate how the value of a particular balance sheet entry or inventory item changed from one accounting date to a subsequent accounting date. This demonstration is based on the following *successive equation*:

$$Value\,(E) \;=\; Value\,(B) + Increases - Decreases$$

where

> (E) denotes the end of the accounting period; and
> (B) denotes the beginning of the accounting period (or the end of the prior accounting period).

The statements and exhibits that feature this property are:

(1)   Capital and Surplus Account

(2)   Cash Flow Statement

(3)   Analysis of Increase in Reserves During the Year

(4)   Exhibit of Life Insurance

(5)   Exhibit of Number of Policies, Contracts, Certificates, Income Payable and Account Values In Force for Supplementary Contracts, Annuities, Accident & Health and Other Policies

For example, the Capital and Surplus Account demonstrates how surplus changed from the end of the prior accounting period to the end of the current accounting period. This demonstration is based on the following successive equation:

$$Surplus(E) \;=\; Surplus(B) + Net\,Income + Other\,Changes$$

where

> $Surplus\,(E) \;=\;$ surplus at the end of accounting period; and
> $Surplus\,(B) \;=\;$ surplus at the beginning of the accounting period.

This successive equation shows an important relationship between the balance sheet and income statement. It also captures the cyclical nature of the financial reporting process and reflects that the balance sheet is as of a particular point in time, while the summary of operations spans a period of time.

This book will detail several statements which contain successive equations. These successive equations will be used to develop various controls and analytical procedures to assist the actuary with a statutory valuation.

2.2 BALANCE SHEET

The **balance sheet** summarizes the assets, liabilities and surplus (i.e., statutory equity) of the life insurance company as of a particular point in time. Under generally accepted accounting principles, the balance sheet is based on the following equation:

$$assets \ = \ liabilities + equity$$

where equity measures the net worth of the owners of the life insurance company.

The first chapter indicated that the balance sheet is the primary focus of the statutory accounting principles because of the emphasis on solvency. Accordingly, under statutory accounting principles, this equation is more appropriately written as:

$$surplus \ = \ assets - liabilities$$

stressing that the level of surplus (in relation to risk based capital) is the primary measure of the solvency of the life insurance company.

2.2.1 ASSETS

Illustration 2-1 presents an abridged version of the asset portion of the balance sheet[1]. This illustrates an important aspect of the life insurance industry. Specifically, the life insurance industry has almost $3 trillion of invested assets under management[2] and performs an important role as a financial intermediary. Because of this role and the critical relationship between the assets and liabilities, the balance sheet and supporting schedules show a significant amount of detail with regards to the types of assets held by the life insurance company.

ILLUSTRATION 2-1

Assets		
	1 **Current Year**	2 **Prior Year**
Cash and Invested Assets		
Bonds		
Stocks		
Preferred stocks		
Common stocks		
Mortgage loans on estate		
Real estate		
Cash		
Contract loans		
Other invested asset		
Total **Cash and Invested Assets**		
Investment income due and accrued		
Premium and considerations:		
Uncollected premiums		
Deferred premiums		
Other assets (excluding separate accounts)		
Separate accounts assets		
Total **Assets**		

[1] To focus on certain key concepts, the illustrations of financial statements from the statutory annual statement have been abridged to eliminate accounting entries not addressed in this book.

[2] *2006 Life Insurers Fact Book,* Table 2.1 [7].

2.2.2 LIABILITIES AND SURPLUS

Illustration 2-2 presents an abridged version of the liability and surplus portion of the balance sheet. Most of the liabilities of a typical life insurance company are the policy reserves (i.e., aggregate reserves).

ILLUSTRATION 2-2

Liabilities, Surplus and Other Funds		
	1 **Current Year**	2 **Prior Year**
Liabilities		
Aggregate reserve for life contracts		
Aggregate reserve for accident and health contracts		
Liability for deposit-type contracts		
Contract claims:		
Life		
Accident and health		
Policyholders' dividend due and unpaid		
Provision for policyholders' dividends payable in the following year		
Premium and considerations received in advance		
Contract liabilities not included elsewhere		
Other liabilities (excluding separate accounts)		
Separate accounts liabilities		
Total **Liabilities**		
Surplus		
Total **Liabilities and Surplus**		

The primary purpose of this book is to describe the methodologies and assumptions used to determine many of the entries shown in this illustration and the financial statements that support these entries.

2.3 SUMMARY OF OPERATIONS

The *Summary of Operations* is the statutory annual statement equivalent of the income statement under generally accepted accounting principles. This statement presents the operating results of a life insurance company for a period of time (usually one year). Illustration 2-3 presents an abridged version of the Summary of Operations.

ILLUSTRATION 2-3

Summary of Operations		
	1 **Current Year**	**2** **Prior Year**
Revenue		
Premium and annuity considerations		
Net investment income		
Amortization of interest maintenance reserve		
Separate accounts net gain, excluding unrealized gains and losses		
Other income		
Total **Revenue**		
Costs		
Death benefits		
Matured endowments		
Annuity benefits		
Disability benefits and benefits under accident and health contracts		
Surrender benefits and withdrawals for life contracts		
Interest on deposit-type contracts		
Payments on supplementary contracts with life contingencies		
Increase in aggregate reserves for life, and accident and health contracts		
Subtotal, **Benefit Costs**		
Commissions on premiums, annuity considerations and deposit-type contracts		
General insurance expenses		
Insurance taxes, licenses and fees, excluding federal income taxes		
Increase in loading on deferred and uncollected premiums		
Net transfers to or (from) separate accounts		
Other costs		
Total **Costs**		
Net gain from operations before dividends and FIT[1]		
Dividend to policyholders		
Net gain from operations after dividends and before FIT		
Federal income taxes, excluding taxes on capital gains		
Net gain from operations after dividends and FIT and before realized capital gains		
Net realized capital gains less capital gains taxes		
Net Income		

[1] Dividends means dividends to policyholders and FIT means federal income taxes

It is based on the following equations:

$$net\ gain\ =\ revenue - costs$$

and

$$net\ income\ =\ net\ gain + realized\ capital\ gains \text{ (after taxes)}$$

The major revenue items are premium and annuity considerations and net investment income. The major cost items are benefit payments, increase in reserves, commissions and expenses.

2.4 CAPITAL AND SURPLUS ACCOUNT

Illustration 2-4 presents an abridged version of the *Capital and Surplus Account*. The Capital and Surplus Account shows how surplus changed from one accounting date to a subsequent accounting date.

ILLUSTRATION 2-4

Capital and Surplus Account		
	1 Current Year	2 Prior Year
Capital and Surplus, December 31, prior year Net Income Change in unrealized gains Change in reserve in account of change in valuation basis Dividend to stockholders Other changes **Capital and surplus, December 31, current year**		

This statement centers around the following equation:

$$Surplus(E) \ = \ Surplus(B) + Net\ Income - Dividends + Other\ Changes$$

where

Surplus (E)	=	surplus at the end of accounting period;
Surplus (B)	=	surplus at the beginning of the accounting period;
Net Income	=	the net income for the period;
Dividends	=	dividends to shareholders; and
Other Changes	=	credits and charges for the current accounting period that did not flow through the summary of operations.

This account is the first example of the successive equation discussed at the beginning of this chapter and shows an important relationship between the balance sheet and income statement. In particular, the Capital and Surplus Account shows that the most important contributor to the change in surplus is net income. In order for surplus to grow at a desired rate, net income less dividends to shareholders must exceed this specified growth rate times the surplus at the beginning of the period. There will be accounting periods where other changes significantly affect the change in surplus, but over a long time period net income is the primary source by which surplus grows.

2.5 CASH FLOW STATEMENT

Illustration 2-5 presents an abridged version of a *Cash Flow Statement*. This statement shows a reconciliation of cash and short-term investments from one accounting date to a subsequent accounting date. It is comprised of two major sections. The first section demonstrates the three primary sources and uses of cash flow, which are:

(1)   cash from operations;

(2)   cash from investment activities; and

(3)   cash from financing activities.

ILLUSTRATION 2-5

Summary of Operations		
	1 **Current Year**	**2** **Prior Year**
Cash from Operations		
Premium collected net of reinsurance		
Net investment income		
Miscellaneous income		
Sub-total		
Net transfers to (from) separate accounts		
Commissions, expenses and other deductions		
Dividend to policyholders		
Federal income taxes		
Sub-total		
Net cash from operations		
Cash from Investments		
Proceeds from investments sold, matured or repaid		
Cost of investments acquired (long-term only)		
Net increase in (decrease in) policy loans and premium notes		
Net cash from investments		
Cash from Financing and Miscellaneous Sources		
Net Cash from Financing and Miscellaneous Sources		
Reconciliation of Cash and Short-Term Investments		
Net change in cash and short-term investments		
Cash and short-term investments:		
Beginning of year		
End of period		

The last section demonstrates another version of the successive equation. In this statement, the successive equation takes on the following form:

$$Cash(E) = Cash(B) + Cash\ from\ operations + Cash\ from\ investments + Cash\ from\ financing$$

where

Cash (E) = cash and short-term investments at the end of accounting period; and
Cash (B) = cash and short-term investments at the beginning of the accounting period.

It shows how the liquidity of the life insurance company changed during the accounting period and why it changed.

2.6 ANALYSIS OF OPERATIONS BY LINES OF BUSINESS

Analysis of Operations by Lines of Business shows the gain from operations for the major business segments of a life insurance company. Illustration 2-6 presents an abridged version of an Analysis of Operations by Lines of Business.

ILLUSTRATION 2-6

Analysis of Operations by Lines of Business			
	Ordinary		
	3	4	5
	Life Insurance	Individual Annuities	Supplementary Contracts
Revenue			
Premium and annuity considerations			
Net investment income			
Amortization of interest maintenance reserve			
Separate account net gain, excluding unrealized gains and losses			
Other income			
Total **Revenue**			
Costs			
Death benefits			
Matured endowments			
Annuity benefits			
Disability benefits and benefits under accident and health contracts			
Surrender benefits and withdrawals for life contracts			
Interest of deposit-type contracts			
Payments on supplementary contracts with life contingencies			
Increase in aggregate reserves for life and accident and health contracts			
Subtotal, **Benefit Costs**			
Commissions on premiums, annuity considerations and deposit-type contracts			
General insurance expenses			
Insurance taxes, licenses and fees, excluding federal income taxes			
Increases in loading on deferred and uncollected premiums			
Net transfers to (or from) separate accounts			
Other costs			
Total **Costs**			
Net gain from operations before dividends and FIT[1]			
Dividends to policyholders			
Net gain from operations after dividends and before FIT			
Federal income taxes, excluding taxes on capital gains			
Net gains from operations after dividends and FIT and before realized capital gains			

[1]Dividends means dividends to policyholders and FIT means federal income taxes

The primary purpose of the Analysis of Operations by Lines of Business is to provide information to do an analysis of the profitability under statutory accounting principles of the major product lines of the life insurance company. In fact, this exhibit is also called the Gain and Loss Exhibit.

2.7 ANALYSIS OF INCREASE IN RESERVES DURING THE YEAR

Illustration 2-7 presents an abridged version of the *Analysis of Increase in Reserves During the Year.* This Analysis shows how the policy reserve changed from one accounting date to a subsequent accounting date.

ILLUSTRATION 2-7

Analysis of Increase in Reserves During the Year			
	Ordinary		
	3	4	5
	Life Insurance	Individual Annuities	Supplementary Contracts
Reserve December 31, prior year			
Tabular net premiums or considerations			
Tabular interest			
Tabular cost			
Reserves released by death			
Reserves released by other terminations (net)			
Other changes			
Reserve December 31, current year			

This statement centers around the following successive equation:

$$Reserve(E) = Reserve(B) + Net\ Premium + Tabular\ Interest - Tabular\ Cost + Other\ Changes$$

where

Reserve (E)	=	reserve at the end of the accounting period;
Reserve (B)	=	reserve at the beginning of the accounting period;
Net Premium	=	net premium used in the determination of the reserve for the period;
Tabular Interest	=	interest used in the determination of the reserve for the period;
Tabular Cost	=	expected claims used in the determination of the reserve for the period;
Other Changes	=	other reserve increases and decreases for the current accounting period such as reserves released on death.

In later chapters, the fundamental concepts underlying this exhibit and how it can be used in conjunction with the Analysis of Operations by Lines of Business to develop some important analytical ratios will be discussed more fully.

2.8 EXHIBIT 1 – PART 1: PREMIUMS AND ANNUITY CONSIDERATIONS

Illustration 2-8 presents an abridged version of *Exhibit I – Part 1 – Premiums and Annuity Considerations*. Premium is the major source of revenue for most life insurance companies. Accordingly, Exhibit 1 – Part 1: Premiums and Annuity Considerations shows how the premium in the Summary of Operations has been adjusted from a cash basis to an accrual basis. It also shows the effect of reinsurance and splits total premium into (1) premium earned on policies in the first policy year (an indication of sales), (2) single premium (an indication of nonrecurring premium) and (3) premium earned on policies after the first policy year (renewal premium).

ILLUSTRATION 2-8

Exhibit 1 – Part 1 **Premiums and Annuity Considerations for Life and Accident and Health Policies and Contracts**			
		Ordinary	
	3 **Life Insurance**	4 **Individual Annuities**	5 **Supplementary Contracts**
First Year (other than single)			
Deferred and accrued			
Direct			
Reinsurance assumed			
Reinsurance ceded			
Net			
Advance			
Collected during year:			
Direct			
Reinsurance assumed			
Reinsurance ceded			
Net			
Prior year (uncollected + deferred and accrued – advance)			
First year premiums and considerations:			
Direct			
Reinsurance assumed			
Reinsurance ceded			
Net			
Single			
Single premiums and consideration:			
Direct			
Reinsurance assumed			
Reinsurance ceded			
Net			
Renewal			
Deferred and accrued			
Direct			
Reinsurance assumed			
Reinsurance ceded			
Net			
Advance			
Collected during year:			
Direct			
Reinsurance assumed			
Reinsurance ceded			
Net			
Prior year (uncollected + deferred and accrued - advance)			
Renewal premiums and considerations:			
Direct			
Reinsurance assumed			
Reinsurance ceded			
Net			
Total			
Total premiums and considerations:			
Direct			
Reinsurance assumed			
Reinsurance ceded			
Net			

This exhibit is based on the following two equations:

$$Premium = Direct\ Premium + Reinsurance\ Assumed - Reinsurance\ Ceded$$

and

$$Direct\ Premium = Collected\ Premium + \Delta Deferred\ Premium - \Delta Advanced\ Premium$$

where

Direct premium	=	premium due from policies issued by the life insurance company;
Reinsurance assumed	=	premium due from policies assumed under a reinsurance contract;
Reinsurance ceded	=	premium due on policies ceded to another company under a reinsurance contract;
Collected premium	=	premium collected during the current reporting period;
ΔDeferred Premium	=	change in deferred premium asset; and
ΔAdvanced Premium	=	change in advance premium liability.

The *deferred premium* reflects the frequency of premium payments assumed in the determination of policy reserves and the actual frequency of premium payments required by the life insurance policy. For example, a life insurance policy may state that the premium is payable monthly, but the policy reserve is determined assuming the premium is paid annually at the beginning of the policy year. This assumption results in an overstatement of the policy reserve for this particular policy (i.e., the entire annual premium has not been collected until the last month of the policy year). A *deferred premium asset* is established to reflect this overstatement. Deferred premiums will be discussed more fully in Chapter 5.

Advanced premiums are premiums "that have been received by the reporting entity prior to the valuation date but which are due on or after the next policy anniversary."[3] For example, consider a policy with a premium of $1,000 with a due date[4] of January 15th of each year. If the end of the current accounting period is December 31, 2005 and the policyholder paid the $1,000 that was due on January 15th 2006 to the life insurance company on December 15, 2005 (i.e., the life insurance company "collected" this premium), then the advance premium would be $1,000.

2.9 EXHIBIT 5 – AGGREGATE RESERVE FOR LIFE POLICIES AND CONTRACTS

Illustration 2-9 presents an abridged version of *Exhibit 5 – Aggregate Reserve For Life Policies and Contracts*. This exhibit is one of the most important actuarial exhibits in the statutory annual statement. It shows policy reserves for the current period by major product line and *valuation standard*.

---

[3]See [18], Paragraph 25 of SSAP No. 51.

[4] The due date is the date the policyholder must pay the premium in order for the policy to remain fully in force.

ILLUSTRATION 2-9

Exhibit 5	
Aggregate Reserve for Life Policies	
1 Valuation Standard	4 Ordinary
Section A: LIFE INSURANCE:	
Section B: ANNUITIES (excluding supplementary contracts with life contingencies):	
Section C: SUPPLEMENTARY CONTRACTS WITH LIFE CONTINGENCIES:	
Section D: ACCIDENTAL DEATH BENEFITS:	
Section E: DISABILITY – ACTIVE LIVES:	
Section F: DISABILITY – DISABLED LIVES:	
Section G: MISCELLANEOUS RESERVES:	

Valuation standard indicates the methodology and assumptions used to determine the policy reserves summarized in this exhibit. Subsequent chapters will describe the various valuation standards for the major product lines shown in this exhibit.

2.10 EXHIBIT 8 – POLICY AND CONTRACT CLAIMS

Illustration 2-10 presents an abridged version of part one of *Exhibit 8 – Policy and Contract Claims*. Similar to Exhibit 1, this exhibit shows how certain benefit payments in the Summary of Operations have been adjusted from a cash basis to an accrual basis. These accrual adjustments reflect that certain claims have been (1) reported but not paid, (2) in course of settlement or (3) incurred but not reported.

ILLUSTRATION 2-10

Exhibit 8 – Claims for Life and Accident and Health Contracts Part 1 – Liability End of Current Year			
	Ordinary		
	3 Life Insurance	4 Individual Annuities	5 Supplementary Contracts

Due and Unpaid
  Direct
  Reinsurance assumed
  Reinsurance ceded
  Net			

In course of settlement:
  Direct
  Reinsurance assumed
  Reinsurance ceded
  Net			

Incurred but unreported
  Direct
  Reinsurance assumed
  Reinsurance ceded
  Net			

Totals
  Direct
  Reinsurance assumed
  Reinsurance ceded
  Net			

2.11 EXHIBIT OF LIFE INSURANCE

Illustration 2-11 presents an abridged version of *Exhibit of Life Insurance*. This exhibit shows the number of policies and the amount of insurance in force. It also demonstrates how these values changed from one accounting date to a subsequent accounting date.

Illustration 2-11

Exhibit of Life Insurance		
	Ordinary	
	Number of Policies	Amount of Insurance
In force end of prior year		
Issued during year		
Other increases		
Total **Increases**		
Death		
Maturity		
Disability		
Expiry		
Surrender		
Lapse		
Conversion		
Other decreases		
Total **Decreases**		
In force end of year		

This exhibit is based on the following successive equation:

$$Inforce(E) \ = \ Inforce(B) + Issues - Deaths - Other\ Terminations + Other\ Changes$$

where

Inforce (E)   =   in force at the end of accounting period; and
Inforce (B)   =   in force at the beginning of the accounting period.

This is a very useful exhibit. Similar to The Analysis of Increase in Reserves During the Year, the Exhibit of Life Insurance exhibit will be used to develop some important analytical ratios that will be discussed more fully in later chapters.

2.12 EXHIBIT OF ANNUITIES

Exhibit of Number of Policies, Contracts, Certificates, Income Payable and Account Values In Force for Supplementary Contracts, Annuities, Accident & Health and Other Policies has a similar purpose as the Exhibit of Life Insurance. Illustration 2-12 presents an abridged version of the annuity section of this exhibit.

ILLUSTRATION 2-11

Annuities		
	Ordinary	
	Immediate	Deferred
In force end of prior year		
Issued during year		
Other increases		
Total **Increases**		
Decreased (net)		
Other decreases		
Total **Decreases**		
In force end of year		
Amount in income payable		
Account Balance		

This book will refer to this section of Exhibit of Number of Policies, Contracts, Certificates, Income Payable and Account Values In Force for Supplementary Contracts, Annuities, Accident & Health and Other Policies as the *Exhibit of Annuities*.

2.13 EXERCISES

2.13.1 KEY TERMS

statutory annual statement

balance sheet

summary of operations

cash flow statement

analysis of increase in reserves during the year

deferred premium

Exhibit 5

Exhibit of Life Insurance

successive equation

income statement

capital and surplus account

analysis of operations by line of business

Exhibit I

advance premium

Exhibit 8

Exhibit of Annuities

2.13.2 QUESTIONS

a. What are the primary financial statements?

b. What are the primary actuarial schedules and exhibits?

c. What is the successive equation for the following financial statements:

(1) Capital and Surplus Account

(2) Cash Flow Statement

(3) Analysis of Increase in Reserves During the Year

(4) Exhibit of Life Insurance

(5) Exhibit of Number of Policies, Contracts, Certificates, Income Payable and Account Values In Force for Supplementary Contracts, Annuities, Accident & Health and Other Policies

d. The summary of operations is equivalent to what statement under generally accepted accounting principles?

3 ✧ THE VALUATION PROCESS

3.1 INTRODUCTION

It is not uncommon for a statutory valuation to be performed on several million policies with several thousand different plan designs. Accordingly, a statutory valuation utilizes a significant amount of data and resources. The *valuation process* refers to the computer systems, procedures and personnel used to perform a statutory valuation. Although valuation actuaries do not need extensive training in computer science, it is important that they have a general understanding of the entire valuation process, including the computer systems used. This general understanding is necessary in order to:

(1)   communicate with Information Technology professionals;

(2)   understand how a new product design or regulation will affect the valuation process;

(3)   implement appropriate controls to ensure an accurate valuation of all inforce policies; and

(4)   document appropriately the results of a statutory valuation.

This chapter will give an overview of the valuation process. It will also give an overview of financial information systems and the role the valuation process performs within these systems.

3.2 VALUATION SYSTEMS

The major steps performed during the valuation process are data gathering, assumption setting, modeling, analyzing and reporting. How these steps are performed depends on the particular requirements of the valuation systems. A *valuation system* refers to the computer software used in the valuation process.

The following diagram is a flow chart of a typical valuation system. This flow chart divides the valuation system into five major parts:

(1)   Extract process;

(2)   Plan description and valuation criteria;

(3)   Calculation modules;

(4)   Valuation results; and

(5)   Reports.

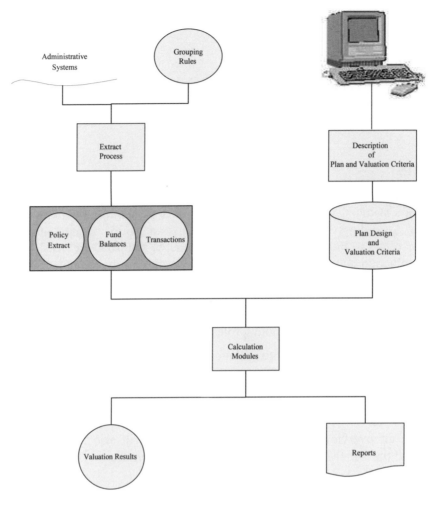

Figure 3.1

The next several sections will describe the major activities performed within each of these segments.

3.2.1 POLICY EXTRACT

The primary purpose of the extract process is to retrieve information from the policy administrative systems that is needed to perform a statutory valuation for all in force policies. This information is stored in computer files or databases. Typically, there are three types of files created during this process: policy extract, fund file and transaction file. The policy extract contains information about the insured obtained during the underwriting process such as gender, issue age and smoking habit. It also identifies the plan of insurance, the amount of insurance coverage and the current status of the policy. The following is an example of the type of information that is stored for each policy in a policy extract:

Policy Extract	
Policy Number	A123456789
Plan Code	VUL12345
Policy Status	Active
Underwriting Criteria	Standard
Extract Date	12/31/2005
Issue Date	7/1/2000
Maturity Date	7/1/2040
Issue Age	60
Gender	Male
Smoking Criteria	Nonsmoker
Gross Premium	35,000
Premium Payment Period	40 Years
Face Amount	1,000,000

For universal life, variable life, and annuities, a fund file is needed to provide additional information about the fund value such as the type of investments chosen by the policy owner, whether any the investments chosen are in a fixed account[1] with a guaranteed interest rate and, if so, for how long this interest rate is guaranteed. The following is an example of the type of information that is stored in the fund file:

Fund File					
Policy Number	Fund ID	Fund Type	Interest Rate	Guarantee Date	Balance
A123456789	F05	Fixed	5.00%	7/1/2010	15,000
A123456789	V01	Equity			60,000
A123456789	V02	Bond			20,000
A123456789	V03	Money Market			10,000

The death benefit, surrender benefit and expense charge often depend on the amount and timing of premium payments. In addition, certain deductions from the fund balance are not fully earned as of the valuation date and a liability must be established for the unearned amount. A transaction file contains debits and credits needed during the valuation process. The following is an example of the type of information that is stored in a transaction file:

Transaction File					
Policy Number	Transaction ID	Transaction Code	Transaction Date	Amount	Description
A123456789	T001	TC01	6/1/2005	35,000	Premium Payment
A123456789	T002	TC02		700	Premium Load
A123456789	T003	TC03		1,000	COI

In most circumstances, these files will contain a large amount of data. For instance, it is not uncommon for the policy extract to have several million records and each record in the policy extract might have 25 or more fields. To reduce the size of these files and the amount of time to perform a statutory valuation, many life insurance companies group similar policies into representative cells. The rules used to group these files must

---

[1] Fixed account refers to an investment that does not fluctuate with the market value of a segment of assets.

be chosen carefully in order to accurately determine policy reserves. The grouped file should produce the same total reserve as the seriatim file (i.e., ungrouped file).

3.2.2 PLAN DESCRIPTION FILE

In order to calculate the policy reserve for an in force policy that is contained in the policy extract, the plan design, valuation method and assumptions must be specified. The primary purpose of this part of the valuation process is to gather this information and store it in a database. This database is often called a *rates and values file* or *plan description file*[2]. The following is the type of information that is stored in a rates and values file:

- Valuation basis
- Premium rates
- Cash value scales
- Reserve factors
- Dividend scales

The following is the type of information that is stored in a plan description file:

- Valuation codes
- Mortality tables
- Interest rate tables

These files must be updated each time a new plan is designed or statutory reserve assumptions have changed.

3.2.3 CALCULATION MODULES

The calculation modules perform three major functions. First, they calculate the policy reserve. Second, they store the policy reserve and other information in a valuation file. Third, they produce various reports.

Prior to the introduction of universal life and accumulation annuities, death benefits and cash values from the issue date to the maturity date could be determined at the time the policy was issued. Accordingly, most calculation modules for whole life and term policies use the *factor method* to determine the policy reserve. Under the factor method, the reserve per unit of insurance, or *reserve factor,* is determined for all possible combinations (e.g., gender, smoking classification, issue ages, policy durations, etc.) when the plan is first designed. These factors are then stored in a rates and values file.

Starting with the first policy in the policy extract, the calculation module would determine the policy reserve in the following steps:

(1) Information about the policy is retrieved from the policy extract;

(2) A reserve factor is retrieved from the rates and values file based on the information retrieved from the policy extract;

(3) This reserve factor is multiplied times the number of units of insurance to determine the policy reserve;

(4) This policy reserve is added to a running total; and

(5) The policy reserve is then stored in a valuation file.

---

[2] A "rates and values" file is usually used to identify this file in older valuation systems, and "plan description file" is used to identify this file in newer valuation systems.

This process is repeated sequentially for each policy or policy group in the policy extract. After the last policy has been processed, a number of reports are produced.

With the introduction of universal life and accumulation annuities, death benefits and cash values could not be determined from the issue date to the maturity date at the time the policy was issued. Accordingly, the factor method was difficult, if not impossible, to apply. The only solution was to program the underlying formulas into the calculation modules. These types of calculation modules are said to be based on *first principles.*

Rather than store reserve factors in a rates and values file, a valuation system based on first principles stores the following information in the plan description file:

- codes that identify particular reserve formulas that have been programmed in the calculation modules;
- codes identifying a particular mortality table and interest rate table;
- valuation mortality tables; and
- valuation interest rates.

Starting with the first policy in the policy extract, the calculation module would determine the policy reserve in the following steps:

(1)   Information about the policy is retrieved from the policy extract;

(2)   Codes identifying a particular set of formulas and tables are retrieved from the plan description file based on the information retrieved from the policy extract;

(3)   Using the codes determined in the previous step, the mortality table and interest rate table are retrieved from the plan description file;

(3)   The appropriate reserve formulas in the calculation module are identified and the policy reserve is determined using the assumptions from the tables retrieved in the previous step;

(4)   This policy reserve is added to a running total; and

(5)   The results are then stored in the valuation file.

This process is repeated sequentially for each policy in the policy extract. After the last policy has been processed, a number of reports are produced.

3.2.4 VALUATION FILE

The *valuation file* contains the policy reserves and additional information needed to complete the statutory annual statement and provide support in an audit. At a minimum, this file should contain the following information:

- Plan code
- Valuation basis or codes
- Policy number
- Valuation Date
- Extract Date
- Issue Date
- Face amount
- Reserve amount

Regulations require that the valuation files used in preparation of the statutory annual statement be retained for at least seven years.

3.2.5 REPORTS

A critical part of the valuation process is the generation of reports to document the results of the statutory valuation. The following diagram is a high level flow chart of the types of reports a valuation system should produce:

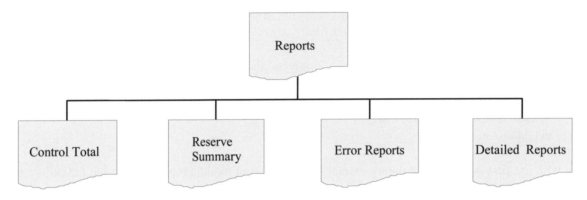

Figure 3.2

A *control report* contains critical date information and *control totals.* Control totals are simply the sum of certain critical fields that help determine if all in force policies have been extracted and processed correctly throughout the entire valuation process. The following is an example of a control report:

Control Report	
Valuation Date	12/31/2005
Extract Date	12/31/2005
Run Date	1/6/2006
Total Face Amount	100,000,000,000
Total Cash Value	10,000,000,000
Total Statutory Reserves	12,500,000,000
Total Number of Policies	1,000,000
Total Number of Records Processed	1,000,000
No errors or warnings	1,000,000
Warnings	0
Errors	0
Total	1,000,000

At a minimum, the total face amount and number of policies should be compared to a reliable and independently determined set of controls to confirm that all in force policies have been extracted.

A *reserve summary* summarizes the reserves by valuation standard in order to complete Exhibit 5 of the statutory annual statement. An *error report* lists the policies where the valuation process encountered a problem trying to determine the policy reserve. This list would contain the policy number and a brief description or error code indicating the type of problem encountered. Finally, *detailed reports* would provide enough information to show exactly how the policy reserve for a particular policy was calculated. This is particularly important for calculation modules that are based on first principles.

3.3 FINANCIAL INFORMATION SYSTEMS

Over the life cycle of a life insurance policy or annuity contract, a life insurance company will have a large number of computer systems that are responsible for generating and maintaining some portion of the data utilized during the financial reporting process. For example, a life insurance company that has been operating for fifty years or longer will most likely have over a hundred computer systems supporting particular functions such as underwriting, policy issue, agent compensation, policy administration, investment accounting and claims processing.

A *Financial Information System* encompasses all the data and computer systems, including the valuation process, that perform a critical role during the financial reporting process. The primary goal of a financial information system is to provide the management of the life insurance company with the information that they need to make informed decisions in a timely and confident manner. At a minimum, this requires that the system contains:

- Accurate, complete and up-to-date data
- Analytical and reporting tools that are flexible and easy to use
- Multiple views of the data
- Sufficient response time to support ad hoc analysis
- Helpful documentation

3.3.1 DATA WAREHOUSE

Consider a life insurance company that has one policy administrative system to administer whole life policies and another policy administrative system to administer universal life policies. The whole life policy administrative system uses the codes '1' and '2' to identify the gender of the insured as male or female, respectively. The universal life policy administrative system uses the codes 'M' and 'F' to identify the insured of the policy as male or female, respectively. One of the goals of a financial information system is to extract this information from the various sources, translate it into a consistent format and store it in a data warehouse. A *data warehouse* is a large centralized database that integrates data from various sources with a variety of formats, and stores this data in a standardized format. Thus, the individuals who use this data need only know that 'M' denotes male and 'F' denotes female.

Figure 3.3 demonstrates the process for creating the data warehouse.

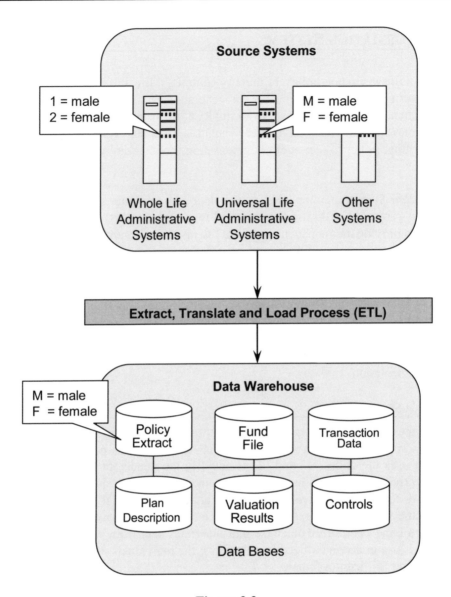

Figure 3.3

3.3.2 EXTRACT, TRANSLATE AND LOAD PROCESS

The process of extracting this information from the various sources, translating it into a consistent format and storing it in a data warehouse is referred to as an Extract, Translate and Load Process (ETL process). Such specialized computer software is often referred to as ETL software. As demonstrated in Figure 3.4, ETL software is also used to extract the information needed during the valuation process from the data warehouse, reformat this data in accordance with the requirements of the valuation system and send it to a data staging area where it can be accessed by the valuation systems.

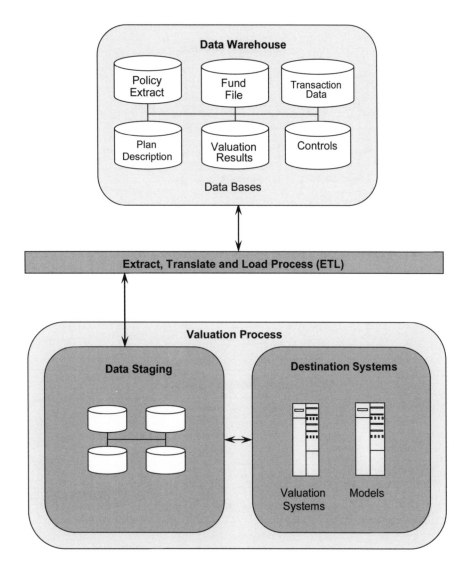

Figure 3.4

The valuation system receives this information, calculates the policy reserves and sends the results back to the data staging area. The ETL software retrieves the data from the data staging area and updates the data warehouse with the new valuation results.

3.3.3 ANALYTICAL AND REPORTING PROCESS

Online Analytical Processing (OLAP) is a computer software package that is designed to assist with the analysis and reporting process. OLAP software lets the users retrieve data stored in a database, analyze this data and write reports.

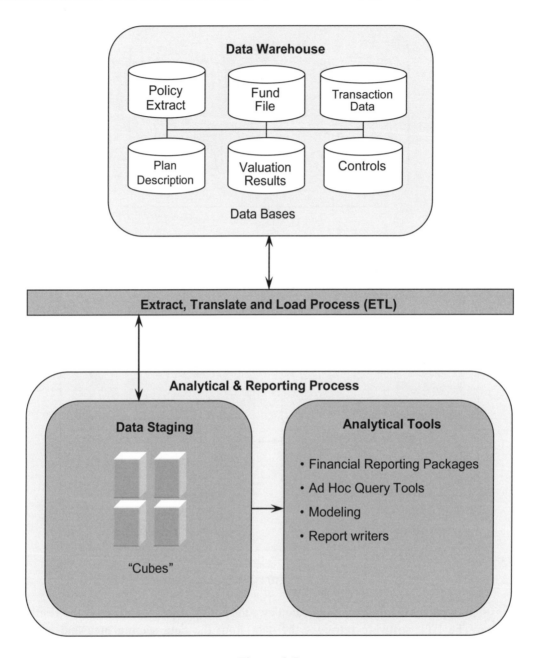

Figure 3.5

On a regular basis, the large volume of data in the data warehouse is condensed and stored in "cubes" as shown in Figure 3.5. A cube summarizes the data along various dimensions such as plan, issue age and policy duration. If the cubes have been designed correctly, analyzing the data can be fairly straightforward and intuitive. For example, the default view of the statutory annual statement exhibit, Analysis of Increase in Reserves During the Year, might appear as follows:

Analysis of Increase in Reserves During the Year			
	Ordinary		
	3 Life Insurance	4 Individual Annuities	5 Supplementary Contracts
Reserves December 31, prior year	10,000,000,000	25,000,000,000	100,000,000
Tabular net premiums or considerations	250,000,000	1,000,000,000	2,500,000
Tabular Interest	40,000,000	1,250,000,000	5,000,000
Tabular cost	75,000,000	5,000,000	750,000
Reserves released by death	25,000,000	100,000,000	250,000
Reserves released by other terminations (net)	50,000,000	250,000,000	500,000
Other changes	5,000,000	10,000,000	50,000
Reserve December 31, current year	10,145,000,000	26,905,000,000	106,050,000

The cubes should be designed so that the valuation actuary could easily "drill-down" to analyze the product lines within the life insurance line of business as follows:

Analysis of Increase in Reserves During the Year			
	Life Insurance		
	Whole Life	Universal Life	Total
Reserves December 31, prior year	9,000,000,000	1,000,000,000	10,000,000,000
Tabular net premiums or considerations	225,000,000	25,000,000	250,000,000
Tabular Interest	36,000,000	4,000,000	40,000,000
Tabular cost	67,500,000	7,500,000	75,000,000
Reserves released by death	22,500,000	2,500,000	25,000,000
Reserves released by other terminations (net)	45,000,000	5,000,000	50,000,000
Other changes	4,500,000	500,000	5,000,000
Reserve December 31, current year	9,130,500,000	1,014,500,000	10,145,000,000

Within this view of the data, the valuation actuary should be able to "drill-down" further by "filtering" only universal life data and expanding the issue year dimension as follows:

Analysis of Increase in Reserves During the Year			
	Universal Insurance		
	2000	2001 ⋯	Total
Reserves December 31, prior year	150,000,000	200,000,000	1,000,000,000
Tabular net premiums or considerations	3,750,000	5,000,000	25,000,000
Tabular Interest	600,000	800,000	4,000,000
Tabular cost	1,125,000	1,500,000	7,500,000
Reserves released by death	375,000	500,000	2,500,000
Reserves released by other terminations (net)	750,000	1,000,000	5,000,000
Other changes	75,000	100,000	500,000
Reserve December 31, current year	152,175,000	202,900,000	1,014,500,000

A well designed financial information system takes several years to design and implement. It also takes a variety of professionals with different skills to determine how this system should be designed, tested and implemented. Actuaries involved with the financial reporting process should be willing and active participants in the development effort.

3.4 Testing, Controls and Analytical Procedures

3.4.1 Testing

When introducing a new product or installing a new valuation system, it is very important that you establish a very thorough test plan. This test plan should include at least twenty-five to fifty test policies, some of which should be randomly selected, and others should be specifically chosen to test the more popular options or potentially complicated situations. These test policies should be used to test the entire valuation process. In particular, the testing should address the following:

(1)   Was information in the plan description coded correctly?
(2)   Is the information from the policy administrative system being extracted accurately?
(3)   Is the valuation process reading the plan description file and policy extracts correctly?
(4)   Are the policy reserves being calculated correctly?
(5)   Are the policy reserves being written to the valuation file correctly?
(6)   Are the control reports and summary reports accurate?

When significant modifications are made to the valuation system (e.g., assumptions are updated or the code has been modified), similar testing procedures should be used.

3.4.2 Controls and Analytical Procedures

Another very important part of the valuation process is the controls and analytical procedures. Control procedures should be in place to make sure that every major step of the valuation process included all inforce policies. In addition, all errors in the error report must be reviewed and appropriate adjustments made to the final reserve entries.

Analytical procedures are very helpful for identifying trends and potential problems. The successive formula discussed in Chapter 2 is a good starting point for establishing analytical procedures. For example, the Exhibit of Life Insurance can be used to establish the following analytical report:

	Exhibit of Life Insurance				
	2000	**2001**	**2002**	**2003**	**2004**
In force end of prior year	100,000	100,300	101,823	104,786	109,439
Issued during year	10,000	11,500	13,225	15,209	17,490
Deaths	400	404	408	412	416
Lapses and surrenders	9,000	9,270	9,548	9,835	10,130
Other terminations	300	303	306	309	312
Inforce end of year	100,300	101,823	104,786	109,439	116,071
Deaths	400	404	408	412	416
÷ Average inforce	100,150	101,062	103,304	107,112	112,755
= Mortality ratio (per 1000)	3.99	4.00	3.95	3.85	3.69
Lapses and surrenders	9,000	9,270	9,548	9,835	10,130
÷ Average inforce	100,150	101,062	103,304	107,112	112,755
= Lapse and surrender ratio (per 100)	8.99	9.17	9.24	9.18	8.98

Similarly, the Analysis of Increase in Reserves can be used to establish the following analytical report:

Analysis of Increase in Reserves During the Year					
	2000	**2001**	**2002**	**2003**	**2004**
Reserve December 31, prior year	100,000	101,000	101,722	102,133	102,196
Tabular net premiums	9,000	9,882	10,850	11,914	13,081
Tabular interest	4,000	4,040	4,080	4,121	4,162
Tabular cost	3,000	3,300	3,630	3,993	4,392
Reserves released by death	1,000	1,100	1,210	1,331	1,464
Reserves released by other terminations (net)	8,000	8,800	9,680	10,648	11,713
Reserve December 31, current year	101,000	101,722	102,133	102,196	101,870
Tabular net premiums or considerations	9,000	9,882	10,850	11,914	13,081
÷ Premium*	10,000	11,000	12,100	13,310	14,641
= Net Premium Ratio	90.00%	89.84%	89.67%	89.51%	89.35%
Tabular interest	4,000	4,040	4,080	4,121	4,162
÷ Average reserve	100,500	101,361	101,927	102,164	102,033
= Interest Ratio	3.98%	3.99%	4.00%	4.03%	4.08%
Death benefits* less reserves released on death	1,200	1,302	1,413	1,533	1,663
÷ Tabular cost	3,000	3,300	3,630	3,993	4,392
= Death benefit ratio	40.00%	39.45%	38.92%	38.39%	37.86%

* From Analysis of Operations by Line of Business

3.5 EXERCISES

3.5.1 KEY TERMS

valuation process	valuation system
policy extract	fund file
transaction file	rates and values file
plan description file	factor method
reserve factor	first principles
valuation file	control totals
Financial Information System	data warehouse
ETL	OLAP

3.5.2 QUESTIONS

a. Why is it important for the valuation actuary to have a general understanding of the entire valuation process?

b. What are the major steps that are performed during the valuation process?

c. Draw a flow chart of a typical valuation system.

d. Briefly describe the following major parts of a valuation system:
   (1) Extract process;
   (2) Plan description and valuation criteria;
   (3) Calculation modules;
   (4) Valuation results; and
   (5) Reports.

e. What are the major steps that are used to determine the policy reserve under a factor based valuation system?

f. What are the major steps that are used to determine the policy reserve under a first principles based valuation system?

g. Briefly describe the primary purpose of the following types of reports:
   (1) Control report;
   (2) Reserve summary;
   (3) Error report; and
   (4) Detailed reports

h. What is a financial information system?

i. What role should an actuary play in the design and ongoing maintenance of a financial information system? Why?

j. How would you justify the cost of developing and maintaining a financial information system?

k. Briefly describe a testing plan you would use to determine if the reserves for a new product are being determined correctly.

l. In addition to the two analytical reports discussed in this chapter, what other types of analytical reports would you use?

4 ✧ Valuation Assumptions

4.1 Product Classification

As was mentioned in the first chapter, SSAP No. 50 provides a general framework for classifying insurance contracts into four broad categories, with one of these categories being life contracts. An insurance contract is classified as a ***life contract*** if the distinguishing characteristic is that the primary coverage provided is for the risk of loss due to death anytime during an extended period. SSAP No. 50 contains the following list of representative life contracts:

(1) Whole life contracts

(2) Endowment contracts

(3) Term life contracts

(4) Supplementary contracts

(5) Group life contracts

(6) Franchise life contracts

(7) Universal life type contracts

(8) Variable life contracts

(9) Limited payment contracts

(10) Credit life contracts

(11) Annuity contracts

Paragraphs 10 through 20 of SSAP No. 50 define these representative life contracts. The Appendix of this book contains extracts of these definitions for the major types of individual life insurance and annuity contracts discussed in this book.

Product classification is important because it determines: (1) how revenue and costs associated with a insurance contract are reported in the income statement; (2) the methodologies and assumptions used to determine policy reserves; and (3) the supporting information which must be provided in exhibits, schedules and supplemental reports of the statutory annual statement.

Since the methodologies and assumptions used to determine policy reserves are significantly different for the major types of individual life insurance and annuity contracts, separate chapters will discuss the valuation standards for:

- Whole life contracts[1] (including limited payment and endowment contracts)
- Term life contracts

---

[1] In this book, whole life contracts, limited payment contracts and endowment contracts will often be collectively referred to as whole life contracts when a distinction among the differences between these contracts is not necessary.

- Universal life type contracts
- Variable life contracts
- Annuities

This chapter and the next chapter discuss the basic principles underlying a statutory valuation.

4.2 VALUATION STANDARDS

Valuation standard indicates the methodology and assumptions used to determine the policy reserves under a statutory valuation. In the United States, the valuation standard is determined by the state valuation laws in effect as of the issue date of the policy. While specific valuation requirements can vary from state to state, all states have adopted some form of the model Standard Valuation Law (SVL)[2] developed by the National Association of Insurance Commissioners.

4.2.1 STANDARD VALUATION LAW

The Standard Valuation Law has consistently defined minimum reserves in terms of a net premium valuation. This law also sets forth the minimum standards for mortality and interest that may be used in calculating statutory reserves.

Since it was initially drafted, the Standard Valuation Law has been amended several times. The three most recent significant amendments were in 1976, 1980 and 1990. The most significant change in the 1976 Amendments was the inclusion of the Commissioners Annuity Reserve Valuation Method (CARVM) as the minimum reserve standard for annuities.[3] The 1980 Amendment introduced dynamic valuation interest rates and adopted the 1980 Commissioner Standard Ordinary Mortality Table (1980 CSO Mortality Table) as the minimum standard for mortality. Finally, the 1990 Amendments added the requirement that an Actuarial Opinion of Reserves be filed annually.

4.2.2 ACTUARIAL GUIDELINES

Often an unusual product design feature or situation not anticipated by the Standard Valuation Law is encountered. To assist the state insurance departments and to promote uniformity, the Life and Health Actuarial Task Force of the National Association of Insurance Commissioners will issue *actuarial guidelines*[4,5] to provide guidance on how the Standard Valuation Law should be applied to these occurrences. For example, since the 1976 Amendments, the number of annuity contracts sold each year has grown significantly. This growth has led to a wide variety of annuity plan designs that were not envisioned in 1976 when the Commissioners' Annuity Reserve Valuation Method was first adopted. Accordingly, the Life and Health Actuarial Task Force issued Actuarial Guidelines XIII, XXXIII, XXXIV and XXXV with regards to the application of the Commissioners' Annuity Reserve Valuation Method to various kinds of annuities.

---

[2] Both Appendix A-820 of *Accounting Practices and Procedures Manual* [18] and the *Life and Health Valuation Law Manual* [4] contain a copy of the *Standard Valuation Law*.

[3] This method is discussed further in Chapter 10.

[4] Both Appendix C of the *Accounting Practices and Procedures Manual* [18] and the *Life and Health Valuation Law Manual* [4] contain copies of these guidelines.

[5] As stated in Appendix C, these guidelines "are not intended to be viewed as statutory revisions but merely a guide in applying a statute."

4.3 VALUATION ASSUMPTIONS

Valuation assumptions refer to the explicit assumptions used to determine the policy reserve. There are two explicit assumptions - the mortality table and interest rate. Acquisition expenses are recognized in the choice of the reserve method (i.e., net level premium method versus modified reserve method). Other assumptions such as maintenance expenses and voluntary withdrawal rates are recognized implicitly by the valuation margin incorporated in the mortality table and interest rate.

4.3.1 MORTALITY TABLES

During the 1900's insured mortality improved approximately 2% per annum. To reflect this improvement and other factors, a new mortality table to be used as the minimum standard for valuation mortality is developed approximately every twenty years. The following lists the prevailing[6] commissioners' standard mortality tables for ordinary contracts[7] by issue year:

Prevailing Commissioners' Standard Mortality Tables for Ordinary Contracts	
Issue Year	**Mortality Table**
1948-60	1941 CSO
1961-79	1958 CSO (a)
1980-82	1958 CSO (b)
1983-85	1980 CSO (c)
1986-?	1980 CSO (d)
?	2001 CSO

(a)   Female mortality rates are equal to males three years younger with gender distinct rates for ages younger than 15.

(b)   Female mortality rates are equal to males six years younger with gender distinct rates for ages younger than 20.

(c)   The 1980 CSO Mortality Table may be used with or without select mortality factors. Distinct female and male rates are available at all ages.

(d)   The 1980 CSO Mortality Table smoker/nonsmoker distinct may be used if desired, in lieu of the original 1980 CSO Mortality Table, on a plan-by-plan basis.

Prior to the 1980 Amendments to the Standard Valuation Law, minimum standards of valuation mortality for life policies were stated in terms of attained age mortality tables with age setbacks used to reflect differences in mortality between males and females. With the adoption of the 1980 Commissioner Standard Ordinary Mortality Table (1980 CSO Mortality Table) as specified in the 1980 Amendments, the situation is more complicated. For example, in a number of states, the valuation actuary has a choice of the following tables for life products:

(1)   The regular 1980 CSO Mortality Table, both male and female versions.

(2)   Smoker and nonsmoker versions of the 1980 CSO Mortality Table for each sex.

---

[6] Prevailing means that the insurance laws of at least 26 states have been amended to recognize a particular mortality table as the minimum standard. At press time, this threshold had not yet been reached for the 2001 CSO table.

[7] Ordinary life contracts include whole life, limited payment life, endowment, term life, universal life and variable life. It excludes industrial policies, which have separate valuation mortality tables.

(3)   Unisex versions of the 1980 CSO Mortality Table.

(4)   Unisex smoker and nonsmoker versions of the 1980 CSO Mortality Table.

All of the above tables are also available in both age last and age nearest birthday versions. Additionally, all may be modified by use of optional 10-year select factors.

It should be noted that the 1980 Amendments to the Standard Valuation Law prescribe different minimum standards of mortality for males and females, except when unisex tables are allowed. Although unisex tables are allowed in all states for nonforfeiture purposes, most states require reserves for unisex products to be calculated using separate mortality for males and females.

Prior to the 1980 Amendments, the Standard Valuation Law allowed only a three year age setback for female issues prior to 1977, and a six year age setback for female issues thereafter. In developing the 1980 CSO Mortality Table, it was noted that the actual theoretical age setback varied by age and that use of a single age setback could be inappropriate in certain circumstances. Also, more and more insurance was being sold to female lives, providing both a greater need for a separate table and more experience upon which such a table could be based. These facts led to the development of a separate version of the 1980 CSO Mortality Table for females.

In 2002, the Life and Health Task Force adopted the 2001 Commissioners' Standard Ordinary Mortality Table (2001 CSO Mortality Table) as the new minimum standard of valuation mortality for life policies. Like the 1980 CSO Mortality Table, this table refers to multiple tables that vary by gender, smoking status and select periods. However, the 2001 CSO Mortality Table increased the maximum age from 99 to 120 and increased the select period from 10 years to 25 years.

4.3.2 Interest Rates

Since the 1980 Amendments, the Standard Valuation Law has used *dynamic valuation interest rates* that are meant to adjust valuation interest rates for changes in market interest rates more quickly than was previously possible. Prior to the 1980 Amendments, a change in the maximum valuation interest rate would have required each state to pass an amendment to their version of the Standard Valuation Law. Since this is an involved and time-consuming process, the valuation interest rate changed rather infrequently. Accordingly, valuation interest rates were not very responsive to changes in market interest rates. For example, the following graph compares the yield on long-term government bonds[8] with the valuation interest rate for life insurance over the past fifty years. Between 1947 and 1974, most states used a 3.5% valuation interest rate in defining the minimum valuation standard for all classes of insurance and annuities.

---

[8] See [14].

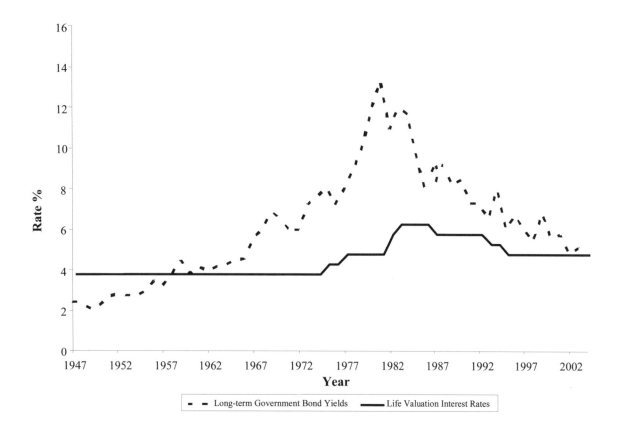

The average net investment rate earned by life insurance companies reached historic lows in the 1940's and was below this 3.5% rate. During this period, many companies strengthened reserves on old blocks of business voluntarily by decreasing the valuation interest rates, and valuation interest rates of 2% to 3% for new business were not uncommon. Later, as market interest rates increased and net investment rates of life insurance companies increased, companies began to use higher valuation interest rates but were constrained by the legal maximum of 3.5%.

Eventually, competition forced companies to reflect the higher available investment earnings in their premium rates even though they were unable to reflect these higher earnings in their reserve calculations. As a result, annual premium products often required deficiency reserves,[9] and single premium products were sold at premium rates lower than the reserves required at issue. In response, the NAIC adopted more liberal valuation bases in line with the higher interest earnings. It is important to note that the changes made at that time began to reflect the differing investment risks associated with different product lines, as well as the increasing importance of annuities in the marketplace. For example, the maximum statutory valuation rate for group annuities and single premium immediate annuities was increased to 6% but the maximum statutory valuation interest rate for life insurance and deferred annuities was increased only to 4%. Previously, the maximum valuation interest rate was identical for all lines of business.

In December of 1976, the NAIC further changed the model Standard Valuation Law and even higher valuation interest rates were adopted with the rate for life insurance raised to 4.5%. Also, a provision in the Standard Valuation Law that would otherwise have required statutory valuation interest rates to revert to 3.5% on January 1, 1986 was removed.

---

[9] Deficiency reserves are defined in Chapter 7.

4.4 Dynamic Valuation Interest Rates

The 1980 Amendments to the Standard Valuation Law contain *dynamic maximum valuation interest rates*. Rather than specifying a maximum valuation interest rate, this amendment specified a formula to determine the maximum statutory valuation interest rate for each calendar year. This formula is a function of the following criteria:

- reference rate;
- product classification;
- guarantee duration;
- existence of cash settlement options;
- existence of future interest guarantees;
- plan type; and
- issue year method versus change in fund method.

These criteria were chosen so that the interest rate would reflect the characteristics of the assets held in support of the liabilities. Each is now discussed separately.

4.4.1 Dynamic Valuation Interest Rate Formula

The description of the dynamic valuation interest rate formula in the Standard Valuation Law is rather involved, but algebraically it can be expressed succinctly as follows:

$$i_{CY} = 0.03 + w_1 \cdot (r_{CY}^1 - 0.03) + 0.50 \cdot w_2 \cdot (r_{CY}^2 - 0.09)$$

where

CY	=	calendar year;
i_{CY}	=	maximum valuation interest rate in calendar year CY;
w_1, w_2	=	weighting factors;
r_{CY}	=	reference interest rate in calendar year CY;
r_{CY}^1	=	$Min(r_{CY}, 0.09)$; and
r_{CY}^2	=	$\begin{cases} Max(r_{CY}, 0.09) & \text{if product classification is other annuities} \\ 0 & \text{otherwise} \end{cases}$

4.4.2 Reference Rate

Depending on criteria listed above and discussed below, the *reference rate* in the above formula is determined using either (1) or (2), where:

(1) is the lesser of (a) and (b), where:

    (a) is the monthly average over a thirty-six months period of the composite yield on seasoned corporate bonds, as published by Moody's Investors Service; and

    (b) is the monthly average over a twelve months period of the composite yield on seasoned corporate bonds, as published by Moody's Investors Service; and

(2) is the monthly average over a twelve months period of the composite yield on seasoned corporate bonds, as published by Moody's Investors Service.

4.4.3 PRODUCT CLASSIFICATION

For purposes of determining the maximum statutory valuation interest rate, individual life and annuity contracts are classified into three broad categories:

- life insurance;
- single premium immediate annuities; and
- other annuities.

The interest rate formula for single premium immediate annuities is the most straightforward, resulting in maximum statutory valuation interest rates that vary only by calendar year of issue.

4.4.4 GUARANTEE DURATION

For life insurance and other annuities, the maximum statutory valuation interest rate also depends on guarantee duration. For life insurance, the guarantee duration is the maximum number of years the life insurance can remain in force on a guaranteed basis. For other than single premium immediate annuities, the guarantee duration is the number of years that the contract guarantees an interest rate in excess of the calendar year statutory valuation interest rates for life insurance policies with a guarantee duration in excess of twenty years.

For example, consider an annuity issued in 2000 that had the following guaranteed interest rates:

Contract Year	Guaranteed Interest Rate
1-5	7%
6-10	6
11 & later	3

Since in 2000 the valuation interest rate for life insurance policies with a guarantee duration in excess of twenty years was 4.5%, the guarantee duration for this annuity is 10 years.

4.4.5 CASH SETTLEMENT OPTIONS AND FUTURE INTEREST GUARANTEES

For other annuities, the maximum statutory valuation interest rate also depends on the type of settlement options offered and future interest rate guarantees. If the annuity contract permits the contract owner to surrender the contract prior to the maturity date and receive cash as one of the forms of settlement, a lower maximum statutory valuation interest rate will result than if a cash option was not offered. Similarly, if the annuity contract guarantees interest rates on deposits received after the first year that are in excess of the calendar year statutory valuation interest rate for life insurance policies with guarantee duration in excess of twenty years, a lower interest rate will result than if this guarantee was not offered.

4.4.6 PLAN TYPE

For other annuities, the maximum statutory valuation interest rate also depends on the *plan type*. Plan type reflects the level of disintermediation risk. The Standard Valuation Law defines three plan types:

Plan Type A
At any time the policyholder may withdraw funds only (1) with an adjustment to reflect changes in interest rates or asset values since receipt of the funds by the insurance company, or (2) without an adjustment but in installments over five years or more, or (3) as an immediate life annuity, or (4) no withdrawal permitted.

Plan Type B

Before expiration of the interest rate guarantee, policyholder may withdraw funds only (1) with an adjustment to reflect changes in interest rates or asset values since receipt of the funds by the insurance company, or (2) without an adjustment but in installments over five years or more, or (3) no withdrawal permitted. At the end of the interest rate guarantee, funds may be withdrawn without an adjustment in a single sum or installments over less than five years.

Plan Type C

Policyholder may withdraw funds before expiration of the interest rate guarantee in a single sum or installments over less than five years either (1) without adjustment to reflect changes in interest rates or asset values since receipt of the funds by the insurance company, or (2) subject only to a fixed surrender charge stipulated in the contract as a percentage of the fund.

4.4.7 ISSUE YEAR VERSUS CHANGE IN FUND

For other annuities, the maximum statutory valuation interest rate also depends on whether the statutory reserve is be calculated using the *issue year method* or *change in fund method*. The issue year method uses a valuation interest rate based on when the annuity contract was issued. The change in fund method uses valuation interest rates that vary by calendar year. In the first contract year, the maximum valuation interest rate for that calendar year is associated with the fund balance at the end of the calendar year. In the next calendar year, the maximum valuation interest rate for that calendar year is associated with the change in the fund balance during the calendar year, and so on. The following table illustrates these two methods for an annuity issued in 2000:

| | | | Valuation Interest Rate | |
| | | | Issue Year | Change in |
Year	Fund Value	Change in Fund Value	Method	Fund Method
2000	50,000	50,000	7.00%	7.75%
2001	70,000	20,000	7.00	7.50
2002	85,000	15,000	7.00	7.25
2003	90,000	10,000	7.00	6.50
2004	95,000	5,000	7.00	6.00

For the change in fund method, the 7.75% valuation interest rate would be applied to the $50,000 fund value at the end of 2000. The 7.50% would be applied to the $20,000 increase in 2001, and so forth. The change in fund method generally is more responsive to changes in the interest rates, but is considerably more difficult to implement in practice.

4.4.8 EXAMPLE

Associated with this chapter is an Excel workbook, Chapter 4.xls, that shows how the maximum valuation interest rate is determined. The first worksheet in this workbook is named "Parameters" and appears as follows:

Parameters		
Product Classification	Other Annuities	▼
Guarantee duration.........................		10 years
Other Annuities:		
Cash settlement option?	Yes	▼
Future interest guarantee?	Yes	▼
Plan Type	A	▼
Method	Issue Year	▼
	Calculate	Print

These are the criteria discussed above upon which the formula for the maximum valuation interest rate is based. After the parameters have been selected, press the "Calculate" button and the workbook calculates the maximum valuation interest rate using the dynamic valuation interest rate formula.

The second worksheet in this workbook is named "Weights" and appears as follows:

Weights		w_1	w_2
	Product Classification	1.0000	0.0000
$\times$	Guarantee duration[1]...	0.7500	0.0000
	Other Annuities[1]:		
$\times$	Cash settlement option	1.0000	0.0000
$+$	Future interest guarantee	0.0000	0.0000
$+$	Method	0.0000	0.0000
$=$	Weight..	0.7500	0.0000

[1] For other annuities, reflects plan type

w_1 and w_2 are the weights identified in the dynamic valuation interest rate formula. This is a useful worksheet because it shows how these weights are affected by the criteria specified in the Parameters worksheet. For example, if the method is "change in fund" as opposed to "issue year," then the sheet above would change as follows:

Weights		
	w_1	w_2
Product Classification	1.0000	0.0000
× Guarantee duration[1]..	0.7500	0.0000
Other Annuities[1]:		
× Cash settlement option	1.0000	0.0000
+ Future interest guarantee	0.0000	0.0000
+ Method	0.1500	0.0000
= Weight..	0.9000	0.0000

[1] For other annuities, reflects plan type

The third worksheet in this workbook is named "Reference Rate" and appears as follows:

Reference Rate		
	Moody's Rolling Averages		
Year	12 Month	36 Month	Reference Rate
1981	13.71	11.57	13.71
1982	15.70	13.64	15.70
1983	13.39	14.26	13.39
1984	13.22	14.10	13.22
1985	13.01	13.21	13.01
1986	10.75	12.33	10.75
1987	9.40	11.05	9.40
1988	10.32	10.15	10.32
1989	10.09	9.93	10.09
1990	9.52	9.97	9.52
1991	9.63	9.74	9.63
1992	8.88	9.34	8.88
1993	8.13	8.88	8.13
1994	7.52	8.18	7.52
1995	8.42	8.03	8.42
1996	7.55	7.83	7.55
1997	7.74	7.90	7.74
1998	7.11	7.47	7.11
1999	6.96	7.27	6.96
2000	7.93	7.33	7.93
2001	7.72	7.54	7.72
2002	7.44	7.70	7.44
2003	6.71	7.29	6.71
2004	6.26	6.80	6.26
2005	5.78	6.25	5.78

Based on the criteria selected in the Parameters worksheet, this sheet displays the reference rate using the formula discussed in Section 4.4.2. For example, for the Product Classification chosen in this example, the 36-month rolling average is not used.

Using the dynamic valuation interest rate formula, the weights from the "Weights" worksheet and the reference rate from the "Reference Rate" worksheet, the worksheet "Valuation Interest Rates" shows how the statutory maximum valuation interest rates for the criteria chosen (e.g., the parameters of the Issue Year method noted above) were determined:

Statutory Maximum Valuation Interest Rates									
(1)	(2)	(3)	(4)	(5)	(6)	(7)	(8)	(9)	(10)
Year	i_{CY} =	.03 +	w_1 ×	$(r^1$ −	.03) +	.50 ×	w_2 ×	$(r^2$ −	.09)
1981	11.0000	.0300	.7500	.1371	.0300	.5000	.0000	.0000	.0900
1982	12.5000	.0300	.7500	.1570	.0300	.5000	.0000	.0000	.0900
1983	10.7500	.0300	.7500	.1339	.0300	.5000	.0000	.0000	.0900
1984	10.7500	.0300	.7500	.1322	.0300	.5000	.0000	.0000	.0900
1985	10.5000	.0300	.7500	.1301	.0300	.5000	.0000	.0000	.0900
1986	8.7500	.0300	.7500	.1075	.0300	.5000	.0000	.0000	.0900
1987	7.7500	.0300	.7500	.0940	.0300	.5000	.0000	.0000	.0900
1988	8.5000	.0300	.7500	.1032	.0300	.5000	.0000	.0000	.0900
1989	8.2500	.0300	.7500	.1009	.0300	.5000	.0000	.0000	.0900
1990	8.0000	.0300	.7500	.0952	.0300	.5000	.0000	.0000	.0900
1991	8.0000	.0300	.7500	.0963	.0300	.5000	.0000	.0000	.0900
1992	7.5000	.0300	.7500	.0888	.0300	.5000	.0000	.0000	.0900
1993	6.7500	.0300	.7500	.0813	.0300	.5000	.0000	.0000	.0900
1994	6.5000	.0300	.7500	.0752	.0300	.5000	.0000	.0000	.0900
1995	7.0000	.0300	.7500	.0842	.0300	.5000	.0000	.0000	.0900
1996	6.5000	.0300	.7500	.0755	.0300	.5000	.0000	.0000	.0900
1997	6.5000	.0300	.7500	.0774	.0300	.5000	.0000	.0000	.0900
1998	6.0000	.0300	.7500	.0711	.0300	.5000	.0000	.0000	.0900
1999	6.0000	.0300	.7500	.0696	.0300	.5000	.0000	.0000	.0900
2000	6.7500	.0300	.7500	.0793	.0300	.5000	.0000	.0000	.0900
2001	6.5000	.0300	.7500	.0772	.0300	.5000	.0000	.0000	.0900
2002	6.2500	.0300	.7500	.0744	.0300	.5000	.0000	.0000	.0900
2003	5.7500	.0300	.7500	.0671	.0300	.5000	.0000	.0000	.0900
2004	5.5000	.0300	.7500	.0626	.0300	.5000	.0000	.0000	.0900
2005	5.0000	.0300	.7500	.0578	.0300	.5000	.0000	.0000	.0900

Notes:
1. Maximum valuation interest rate is rounded to nearest 0.25%.
2. For life insurance, if $ABS(i(cy+1) - i(cy)) < 0.5$, then $i(cy+1) = i(cy)$.

4.5 EXERCISES

4.5.1 KEY TERMS

life contract

Standard Valuation Law

valuation assumptions

plan type

change in fund method

valuation standard

actuarial guidelines

dynamic valuation interest rates

issue year method

reference rate

4.5.2 QUESTIONS

a. What is the distinguishing characteristic of life contracts?

b. Why is the product classification important?

c. What are some examples of representative life contracts?

d. What does the valuation standard indicate?

e. Why is the Standard Valuation Law so important?

f. Why does the Life and Health Actuarial Task Force issue actuarial guidelines?

g. What are the two explicit assumptions specified by the Standard Valuation Law?

h. What assumptions are implicitly provided for by the explicit assumptions specified by the Standard Valuation Law?

i. How are acquisition expenses recognized by the Standard Valuation Law?

j. Why was the Standard Valuation Law modified to incorporate dynamic valuation interest rates?

k. What are the primary criteria needed to determine the maximum dynamic valuation interest rate for a particular plan of insurance?

4.5.3 PROBLEMS

a. Using the Excel workbook, Chapter 4.xls,

(1) Determine the maximum dynamic valuation interest rates from 1981 to 2004 for a whole life policy sold to a 45 year old male.

(2) Determine the maximum dynamic valuation interest rates from 1981 to 2004 for the following deferred annuity policy using the issue year method:

Guaranteed Credited Interest:	Policy Year	Interest Rate
	1	7.0%
	2	7.0
	3	7.0
	4	7.0
	5	7.0
	6 and later	3.0

Cash settlement option: cash surrender at book value less surrender charge

Surrender Charge:

Policy Year	Percent of Fund
1	7%
2	6
3	5
4	4
5	3
6	2
7	1
8 and later	0

Free Partial withdrawals: 10% of fund value, after first contract year

(3) Determine the maximum dynamic valuation interest rates from 1981 to 2004 for the above deferred annuity policy using the change in fund method.

(4) Why are the maximum dynamic valuation interest rates for the whole life policy the lowest?

(5) Why are the maximum dynamic valuation interest rates for the change in fund method the highest?

b. For which time periods from 1981 to 2005, would using the issue year method versus the change in fund method have resulted in a higher reserve for the deferred annuity contract in Problem a. (Assume the fund value increases $10,000 each year and matures 10 years after issue)?

5 ✧ Valuation Methodologies and Approximations

5.1 Valuation Methodologies

Valuation methodology refers to the particular net premium method used to determine the policy reserve. The two most common net premium reserve methods for life insurance in the United States are the *net level premium method (NLP)* and *Commissioners Reserve Valuation Method (CRVM)*. Other methods are permitted provided they produce reserves that equal or exceed minimum reserve standards.

5.2 Notation

5.2.1 Key Dates

Issue date is the date that the primary coverage of the life insurance policy or annuity contract becomes effective and *maturity date*[1] is the date that the primary coverage of the life insurance policy or annuity contract ends.

The policy is generally not in force until the first premium has been received by the life insurance company (i.e., the life insurance company does not have to pay the death benefit if the insured dies during the underwriting process). Because of the length of time it takes to receive and review all the medical information during the underwriting process, it is a common occurrence that the first premium payment may not be received until after the issue date. A policy reserve would only have to be established under these circumstances if a conditional receipt or temporary term was in place until the underwriting process was completed.

Valuation date is the date on which the policy reserve is measured. This is an important date and must be the same date as the end of the financial reporting period if valuation is being performed as part of the financial statements preparation process.

Most life insurance companies stop processing business on the last business day of the fiscal year to facilitate the financial statement preparation process. The valuation actuary must coordinate with the accounting and information technology departments to determine when the policy extract is created "as of" so that it is in synch with the other accounting systems. Additionally, the policy reserves may have to be adjusted to recognize that the policy extract is not as of the end of the financial reporting period.

5.2.2 Time Periods

The following time diagram shows some of the time periods that will be used in the description of the methodologies.

---

[1] The maturity date for some forms of insurance such as term life insurance is more appropriately called the expiry date.

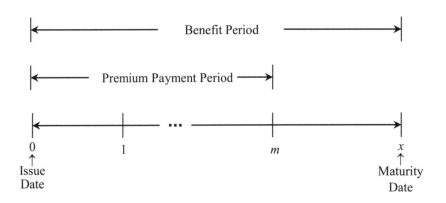

The benefit period is the number of years from the issue date to the maturity date. The ***premium payment period*** is the number of years from the issue date to the end of the period over which premium payments may be made. ***Policy duration*** or ***duration*** will be the number of years from the issue date to a specific valuation date, rounded down to the nearest whole year, and ***policy year*** will be the number of years from the issue date to a specific valuation date, rounded up to the nearest whole year. For example, if the issue date is July 1, 2000, then on December 31, 2005 the policy duration is five years and the policy is in the sixth policy year.

5.2.3 SYMBOLS

The following symbols will be used in this book:

$[x]$ = issue age;

t = policy duration;

n = number of years from the issue date to the maturity date; and

m = number of years from the issue date to the end of the premium payment period.

Other symbols will be defined as they are introduced in the description of a particular formula.

5.2.4 EXAMPLE

Similar to Chapter 4, associated with this chapter is an Excel workbook, Chapter 5.xls. This workbook will be used to demonstrate several of the concepts discussed in this chapter. The policy used for illustration purposes will be a 10 payment, 15 year endowment issued on September 1, 2000. The insured is a 50 year old male. This information is captured in the first worksheet, called "Parameters," in this workbook:

Parameters	
Issue Date	9/1/2000
Maturity Date	9/1/2015
Valuation Date................................	12/31/2005
Issue Age.......................................	50
Gender	Male ▼
Gross Premium	10,000
Premium Payment Mode......................	10 years
Premium Payment Period....	Quarterly ▼
Paid-to-Date	12/1/2006
Face Amount...................................	100,000
Endowment Amount	100,000
Statutory Valuation Standard:	
Mortality Table	1980 CSO ▼
Interest Rate	5.00%
Method	NLP ▼
Function	Curtate ▼
Age Rule	ANB ▼
Smoking Class	Nonsmoker ▼
Select Period...............................	Aggregate ▼
Deferred Premium Method	Before Codification ▼

Calculate

5.3 COMMON METHODOLOGIES

5.3.1 NET LEVEL PREMIUM METHOD (NLP)

The net level premium reserve method uses the net premium method to provide only for future death benefits and endowment benefits. No explicit recognition for any expenses or other benefits is made. For an m payment, n year endowment, the net level premium reserve is defined by the following prospective formula:

$$_t^mVB_{[x]:\overline{n}|} = AB_{[x]+t:\overline{n-t}|} - {}_mPB_{[x]:\overline{n}|} \cdot \ddot{a}_{[x]+t:\overline{m-t}|}$$

where

$\quad _t^mVB_{[x]:\overline{n}|} \quad$ = net level premium reserve at duration t;

$\quad AB_{[x]+t:\overline{n-t}|} \quad$ = present value of future benefits at duration t;

$\quad _mPB_{[x]:\overline{n}|} \quad$ = net level premium in the first policy year;

$$\quad\quad\quad\quad = \frac{AB_{[x]:\overline{n}|}}{\ddot{a}_{[x]:\overline{m}|}} \text{ ; and}$$

$\quad \ddot{a}_{[x]+t:\overline{m-t}|} \quad$ = present value of annuity due at duration t.

Using the valuation mortality table and interest rate, the present value of future benefits as of duration t is defined by the following formula:

$$AB_{[x]+t:\overline{n-t}|} = \left(\sum_{s=0}^{n-t-1} v^{s+1} \cdot {}_sp_{[x]+t} \cdot q_{[x]+t+s} \cdot BD_{[x]+t+s} \right) + \left(v^{n-t} \cdot {}_{n-t}p_{[x]+t} \cdot BM_{[x]+n} \right)$$

where

v = discount factor;

= $\dfrac{1}{1+i}$;

${}_sp_{[x]+t}$ = probability that the insured who survived to duration t will survive to duration $t+s$;

= $\displaystyle\prod_{r=0}^{s-1}(1-q_{[x]+t+r})$;

$q_{[x]+t+s}$ = valuation mortality rate for attained age $x+t+s$;

$BD_{[x]+t}$ = death benefit amount[2] between durations t and $t+1$ and assumed to be paid at duration $t+1$;

and

$BM_{[x]+n}$ = maturity benefit amount paid on the maturity date.

The term "net level" denotes that the net premiums are a constant percentage of the gross premiums and not necessarily a level amount. In order for the net premiums to be a constant percentage of the gross premiums, the pattern of gross premiums is reflected in the formula for the present value of an annuity as follows:

$$\ddot{a}_{[x]+t:\overline{m-t}|} = \sum_{s=0}^{m-t-1} v^s \cdot {}_sp_{[x]+t} \cdot \eta_{[x]+t+s}^{GP}$$

where

$\eta_{[x]+t+s}^{GP}$ = gross premium ratio;

= $\dfrac{GP_{[x]+t+s}}{GP_{[x]}}$; and

$GP_{[x]+t+s}$ = annual gross premium[3] due at duration $t+s$.

Finally, the net level premium at duration t is determined using the following formula:

$$_mPB_{[x]+t:\overline{n}|} = \begin{cases} \dfrac{AB_{[x]:\overline{n}|}}{\ddot{a}_{[x]:\overline{m}|}} & \text{if } t=0 \\[2mm] \eta_{[x]+t}^{GP} \cdot {}_mPB_{[x]:\overline{n}|} & \text{if } 0 < t < m \\[2mm] 0 & \text{if } m \le t < n \end{cases}$$

where

$_mPB_{[x]+t:\overline{n}|}$ = net level premium at duration t

The net level premium reserve method typically produces the highest reserves of any of the methods discussed in this book. Unlike most other reserving methods, the net level method typically requires a significant first-year reserve and is therefore avoided by surplus-conscious companies.

---

[2] This is the death benefit for the primary or base coverage of the policy. In most circumstances, it will be the face amount of the policy.

[3] This is the annual premium payable in its entirety at the beginning of the policy year for the primary coverage of the policy. It excludes the policy fee and any extra charges.

5.3.2 EXAMPLE (CONTINUED)

The fourth worksheet in the workbook is named "PV" and shows how $AB_{[x]+t:\overline{n-t}|}$ and $\ddot{a}_{[x]+t:\overline{m-t}|}$ were determined as of the issue date of the policy:

					**Present Values**							
(1)	(2)	(3)	(4)	(5)	(6)	(7)	(8)	(9)	(10)	(11)	(12)	(13)
x	t	$v(t)$	$\cdot\ p(t)$	$\cdot\ CRAGP(t)$	$\cdot\ RGP(t)$	$=\ PVRGP(t)$	$v(t+1)$	$\cdot\ p(t)$	$\cdot\ q(t)$	$\cdot\ CRABD(t)$	$\cdot\ [BD(t)+BM(t)]$	$=\ PVB(t)$
50	0	1.00000	1.00000	1.0000	1.0000	1.00000	.95238	1.00000	.00491	1.00000	100,000	468
51	1	0.95238	0.99509	1.0000	1.0000	0.94770	.90703	0.99509	.00535	1.00000	100,000	483
52	2	0.90703	0.98977	1.0000	1.0000	0.89775	.86384	0.98977	.00586	1.00000	100,000	501
53	3	0.86384	0.98397	1.0000	1.0000	0.84999	.82270	0.98397	.00643	1.00000	100,000	521
54	4	0.82270	0.97764	1.0000	1.0000	0.80431	.78353	0.97764	.00709	1.00000	100,000	543
55	5	0.78353	0.97071	1.0000	1.0000	0.76058	.74622	0.97071	.00782	1.00000	100,000	566
56	6	0.74622	0.96312	1.0000	1.0000	0.71869	.71068	0.96312	.00863	1.00000	100,000	591
57	7	0.71068	0.95481	1.0000	1.0000	0.67856	.68684	0.95481	.00949	1.00000	100,000	613
58	8	0.67684	0.94574	1.0000	1.0000	0.64012	.64461	0.94574	.01042	1.00000	100,000	635
59	9	0.64461	0.93589	1.0000	1.0000	0.60328	.61391	0.93589	.01147	1.00000	100,000	659
60	10	0.61391	0.92515	1.0000	1.0000	0.00000	.58468	0.92515	.01264	1.00000	100,000	684
61	11	0.58468	0.91346	1.0000	1.0000	0.00000	.55684	0.91346	.01394	1.00000	100,000	709
62	12	0.55684	0.90073	1.0000	1.0000	0.00000	.53032	0.90073	.01542	1.00000	100,000	737
63	13	0.53032	0.88684	1.0000	1.0000	0.00000	.50507	0.88684	.01711	1.00000	100,000	766
64	14	0.50507	0.87166	1.0000	1.0000	0.00000	.48102	0.87166	.01902	1.00000	100,000	41,929
						$\ddot{a}(0)\ =\ 7.90097$					$AB(0)\ =\ 50,404$	

The fifth worksheet in the workbook is named "SR" and shows how $^{m}_{t}VB_{[x]:\overline{n}|}$ was determined using the prospective formula $^{m}_{t}VB_{[x]:\overline{n}|} = AB_{[x]+t:\overline{n-t}|} - {_m}PB_{[x]:\overline{n}|} \cdot \ddot{a}_{[x]+t:\overline{m-t}|}$:

					Statutory Reserves					
(1)	(2)	(3)	(4)	(5)	(6)	(7)	(8)	(9)	(10)	(11)
x	t	$AB(t)$	$-\ PB(0)\ \cdot$	$\ddot{a}(t)$	$=\ VB(t)$	$PE(0)\ \cdot$	$\ddot{a}(t)$	$=\ VE(t)$	$P(t) = PB(t){-}PE(t)$	$V(t) = VB(t){-}VE(t)$
50	0	50,404	6,379	7.90097	0	0	7.90097	0	6,379	0
51	1	52,692	6,379	7.28178	6,238	0	7.28178	0	6,379	6,238
52	2	55,086	6,379	6.63134	12,782	0	6.63134	0	6,379	12,782
53	3	57,592	6,379	5.94776	19,649	0	5.94776	0	6,379	19,649
54	4	60,216	6,379	5.22877	26,859	0	5.22877	0	6,379	26,859
55	5	62,964	6,379	4.47192	34,436	0	4.47192	0	6,379	34,436
56	6	65,845	6,379	3.67425	42,405	0	3.67425	0	6,379	42,405
57	7	68,869	6,379	2.83240	50,800	0	2.83240	0	6,379	50,800
58	8	72,047	6,379	1.94246	59,655	0	1.94246	0	6,379	59,655
59	9	75,393	6,379	1.00000	69,014	0	1.00000	0	6,379	69,014
60	10	78,921	0	0.00000	78,921	0	0.00000	0	0	78,921
61	11	82,648	0	0.00000	82,648	0	0.00000	0	0	82,648
62	12	86,593	0	0.00000	86,593	0	0.00000	0	0	86,593
63	13	90,781	0	0.00000	90,781	0	0.00000	0	0	90,781
64	14	95,238	0	0.00000	95,238	0	0.00000	0	0	95,238
65	15	100,000								

5.3.3 Modified Reserves

A *modified reserve* method is a net premium reserve method that contains an expense allowance or expense adjustment. An *expense allowance* is used to reflect the fact that most life insurance sales involve large first year expenses which are intended to be recovered from future margins. The expense allowance is an offset to the reserve for future benefits and is amortized over the premium payment period.

A modified reserve can generally be thought of as a net level premium reserve less an *unamortized expense allowance*[4] as shown in the following formula:

$$ {}^{m}_{t}V^{Mod}_{[x]:\overline{n}|} \ =\ {}^{m}_{t}VB_{[x]:\overline{n}|} - {}^{m}_{t}VE_{[x]:\overline{n}|} $$

where

$\quad\quad {}^{m}_{t}V^{Mod}_{[x]:\overline{n}|} \ =\ $ modified reserve at duration t; and

$\quad\quad {}^{m}_{t}VE_{[x]:\overline{n}|} \ =\ $ unamortized expense allowance at duration t.

---

[4] The deferred acquisition cost asset established under U.S. GAAP is essentially equivalent to an unamortized expense allowance.

In the above formula, the unamortized expense allowance would be determined as follows:

$$ {}^m_t VE_{[x]:\overline{n}|} = {}_m PE_{[x]} \cdot \ddot{a}_{[x]+t:\overline{m-t}|} $$

where

$$ {}_m PE_{[x]:\overline{n}|} = \text{portion of the premium used to amortize expense allowance;} $$

$$ = \frac{{}_m EA_{[x]:\overline{n}|}}{\ddot{a}_{[x]:\overline{m}|}} \text{; and} $$

$$ {}_m EA_{[x]:\overline{n}|} = \text{expense allowance.} $$

Finally, the net premium[5] at duration t is determined using the following formula:

$$ {}_m P_{[x]+t} = \begin{cases} {}_m PB_{[x]} + {}_m PE_{[x]} - {}_m EA_{[x]} & \text{if } t = 0 \\ \eta^{GP}_{[x]+t} \cdot \left({}_m PB_{[x]} + {}_m PE_{[x]} \right) & \text{if } 0 < t < m \\ 0 & \text{if } m \le t < n \end{cases} $$

where ${}_m P_{[x]+t}$ = net premium at duration t.

5.3.4 FULL PRELIMINARY TERM (FPT) RESERVE METHOD

The *full preliminary term (FPT) reserve method* is a modified reserve method that defines the expense allowance as follows:

$$ {}_m EA^{FPT}_{[x]:\overline{n}|} = \frac{AB_{[x]+1:\overline{n-1}|}}{\ddot{a}_{[x]+1:\overline{m-1}|}} - c_{[x]} $$

where

$$ {}_m EA^{FPT}_{[x]:\overline{n}|} = \text{expense allowance under the full preliminary term method;} $$

$$ c_{[x]} = \text{first year cost of insurance;} $$

$$ = v \cdot q_{[x]} \cdot BD_{[x]}. $$

At the end of the first policy year, the full preliminary term reserve is zero. The proof is left as an exercise.

---

[5] Under a modified method, the first year net premium is often denoted as α_x and the renewal net premium as β_x.

5.3.5 Example (continued)

Switching the reserve method on the "Parameters" worksheet to full preliminary term and pressing the calculate button, the "SR" worksheet changes to the following:

					Statutory Reserves						
(1)	(2)	(3)	(4)	(5)	(6)	(7)	(8)	(9)	(10)	(11)	
x	t	$AB(t)$	$- PB(0) \cdot$	$\ddot{a}(t)$	$= VB(t)$	$PE(0) \cdot$	$\ddot{a}(t)$	$= VE(t)$	$P(t) = PB(t){-}PE(t)$	$V(t) = VB(t){-}VE(t)$	
50	0	50,404	6,379	7.90097	0	857	7.90097	6,769	468	0	
51	1	52,692	6,379	7.28178	6,238	857	7.28178	6,238	7,236	0	
52	2	55,086	6,379	6.63134	12,782	857	6.63134	5,681	7,236	7,101	
53	3	57,592	6,379	5.94776	19,649	857	5.94776	5,095	7,236	14,553	
54	4	60,216	6,379	5.22877	26,859	857	5.22877	4,479	7,236	22,380	
55	5	62,964	6,379	4.47192	34,436	857	4.47192	3,831	7,236	30,605	
56	6	65,845	6,379	3.67425	42,405	857	3.67425	3,148	7,236	39,258	
57	7	68,869	6,379	2.83240	50,800	857	2.83240	2,426	7,236	48,373	
58	8	72,047	6,379	1.94246	59,655	857	1.94246	1,664	7,236	57,991	
59	9	75,393	6,379	1.00000	69,014	857	1.00000	857	7,236	68,157	
60	10	78,921	0	0.00000	78,921	0	0.00000	0	0	78,921	
61	11	82,648	0	0.00000	82,648	0	0.00000	0	0	82,648	
62	12	86,593	0	0.00000	86,593	0	0.00000	0	0	86,593	
63	13	90,781	0	0.00000	90,781	0	0.00000	0	0	90,781	
64	14	95,238	0	0.00000	95,238	0	0.00000	0	0	95,238	
65	15	100,000									

Notice that the full preliminary term reserve is zero at the end of the first policy year or duration one (i.e., $t = 1$).

5.3.6 Commissioners Reserve Valuation Method (CRVM)

The reserve method producing the smallest reserves allowed by the Standard Valuation Law is the ***Commissioners Reserve Valuation Method (CRVM)***. The Commissioners Reserve Valuation Method limits the expense allowance to the smaller of (a) and (b), where:

(a)   is the expense allowance under the full preliminary term method for the given plan of insurance; and

(b)   is the expense allowance under the full preliminary term method for a 20-pay limited payment life contract.

In the case of a policy with non-level death benefits, Actuarial Guideline XVII states that the expense allowance for a 20-pay limited payment life contract in the above definition must be calculated assuming a level death benefit equal to the arithmetic average of the death benefits at the beginning of policy years 2 through 10, inclusive.

Reflecting Actuarial Guideline XVII, the formula for the expense allowance under the Commissioners Reserve Valuation Method is as follows:

$$_m EA^{CRVM}_{[x]:\overline{n}|} = \begin{cases} _m EA^{FPT}_{[x]:\overline{n}|} & \text{if} \quad _m EA^{FPT}_{[x]} < {}_{20} EA^{FPT}_{[x]:\overline{n}|} \\ _{20} EA^{FPT}_{[x]:\overline{n}|} & \text{if} \quad _m EA^{FPT}_{[x]} \geq {}_{20} EA^{FPT}_{[x]:\overline{n}|} \end{cases}$$

where

$_m EA_{[x]:\overline{n}|}^{CRVM}$ = expense allowance under the Commissioners Reserve Valuation Method;

$_m EA_{[x]:\overline{n}|}^{FPT}$ = expense allowance under full preliminary term method; and

$_{20} EA_{[x]}^{FPT}$ = expense allowance under the full preliminary term method for a 20-pay limited

payment life contract with a level death benefit equal to $\dfrac{\sum\limits_{t=1}^{9} BD_{[x]+t}}{9}$.

For life contracts that have an increasing premium pattern, the expense allowance can become negative when the slope is steep. This happens when the first year cost of insurance exceeds the first year net premium. In these circumstances, Actuarial Guideline XXI states for policies issued on or after January 1, 1987 a negative expense allowance should be set to zero. When this occurs, the reserve methodology reverts to the net level premium method.

As the above formulas indicate, the net premiums are dependent on the slope of the gross premium scale. However, except in situations where deficiency reserves[6] are required or when the expense allowance under the full preliminary term method is negative, the magnitude of the gross premiums does not affect the level of net premiums or reserves. The Commissioners Reserve Valuation Method produces a first-year terminal reserve of zero for a large number of policies, thus reducing the statutory surplus strain associated with the sale of new business.

5.3.7 EXAMPLE (CONTINUED)

Switching the reserve method on the "Parameters" worksheet to the Commissioners Reserve Valuation Method and pressing the calculate button, the "SR" worksheet changes to the following:

Statutory Reserves										
(1) (2)		(3)	(4)	(5)	(6)	(7)	(8)	(9)	(10)	(11)
x	t	$AB(t)$	$- PB(0)$ ·	$\ddot{a}(t)$	$= VB(t)$	$PE(0)$ ·	$\ddot{a}(t)$	$= VE(t)$	$P(t) = PB(t) - PE(t)$	$V(t) = VB(t) - VE(t)$
50	0	50,404	6,379	7.90097	0	277	7.90097	2,192	4,465	0
51	1	52,692	6,379	7.28178	6,238	277	7.28178	2,020	6,657	4,218
52	2	55,086	6,379	6.63134	12,782	277	6.63134	1,840	6,657	10,942
53	3	57,592	6,379	5.94776	19,649	277	5.94776	1,650	6,657	17,999
54	4	60,216	6,379	5.22877	26,859	277	5.22877	1,450	6,657	25,409
55	5	62,964	6,379	4.47192	34,436	277	4.47192	1,241	6,657	33,195
56	6	65,845	6,379	3.67425	42,405	277	3.67425	1,019	6,657	41,386
57	7	68,869	6,379	2.83240	50,800	277	2.83240	786	6,657	50,014
58	8	72,047	6,379	1.94246	59,655	277	1.94246	539	6,657	59,116
59	9	75,393	6,379	1.00000	69,014	277	1.00000	277	6,657	68,736
60	10	78,921	0	0.00000	78,921	0	0.00000	0	0	78,921
61	11	82,648	0	0.00000	82,648	0	0.00000	0	0	82,648
62	12	86,593	0	0.00000	86,593	0	0.00000	0	0	86,593
63	13	90,781	0	0.00000	90,781	0	0.00000	0	0	90,781
64	14	95,238	0	0.00000	95,238	0	0.00000	0	0	95,238
65	15	100,000								

Notice that the CRVM reserve is no longer zero at the end of the first policy year or duration one (i.e., $t = 1$). This is because of the nineteen-pay whole life expense allowance limitation.

---

[6] Deficiency reserves are discussed in Chapter 6.

5.3.8 OTHER METHODS

Other modified reserve methods are in use. One of the more common alternatives is a method in which reserves grade from CRVM to net level at some duration. A major reason for such a method is that many companies want to offer products with 20th year cash values that are higher than minimum cash values yet not greater than the reserve held.

5.4 COMMON APPROXIMATIONS

It is not uncommon for a statutory valuation to be performed on several million policies with several thousand different plan designs. Accordingly, a statutory valuation utilizes a significant amount of data and resources. Prior to the introduction of computers, several approximations were used to simplify the valuation process. Although modern computers can handle complex computations, these approximations are still used, partly because of historical precedent and partly for simplicity.

5.4.1 TERMINAL RESERVES

To illustrate the rationale for some of these approximations, assume the policy reserve was being determined for a whole life policy under the following conditions:

(1) the valuation date is December 31, 2005;

(2) the policy was issued on January 1, 2001;

(3) premiums are paid annually at the beginning of each policy year; and

(4) the valuation method is the net level premium method.

The policy reserve on December 31, 2005 would be the terminal reserve at the end of the 5th policy year. It would be determined correctly by the following formula:

$$_5VB_{[x]} = AB_{[x]+5} - PB_{[x]} \cdot \ddot{a}_{[x]+5}$$

Terminal reserves are policy reserves computed at the end of each policy year.

If, however, the policy were issued on December 31, 2001, the policy reserve on December 31, 2005 would be the initial reserve at the beginning of the 5th policy year, just after the premium due date. It would be determined correctly by the following formula:

$$_4VB_{[x]} + PB_{[x]+t}$$

The ***initial reserve*** is the terminal reserve at the end of the previous policy year plus the net premium for the current policy year.

For most policies, the valuation date will not coincide with either the end of the policy year or the beginning of the policy year. Accordingly, some form of interpolated reserve is computed as of the valuation date. The two most common interpolated reserve approximations are ***mean reserves*** and ***mid-terminal reserves***.

5.4.2 MEAN RESERVES

In general, for a policy issued a fraction h of the year after the beginning of the valuation year, the ***interpolated mean reserve*** is defined by

$$(1-h) \cdot ({}_{t}^{m}V_{[x]:\overline{n}|} + {}_{m}P_{[x]+t:\overline{n}|}) + h \cdot {}_{t+1}^{m}V_{[x]:\overline{n}|} \quad \text{if} \quad t < m$$

and

$$(1-h) \cdot {}_{t}^{m}V_{[x]:\overline{n}|} + h \cdot {}_{t+1}^{m}V_{[x]:\overline{n}|} \qquad\qquad \text{if} \quad t \geq m$$

The correct reserve would fall on the line segment in the following graph that begins with the point denoted as initial reserve and ends with the point denoted as terminal reserve.

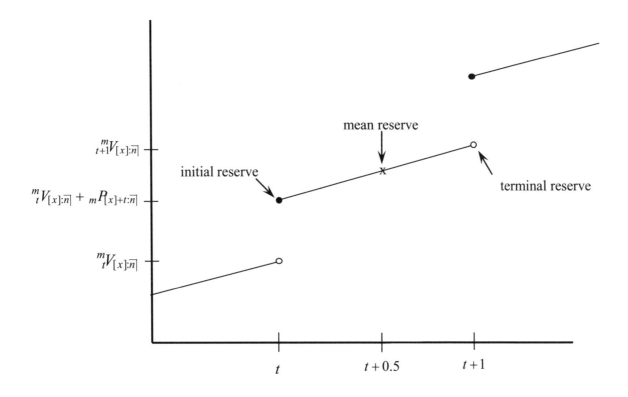

Figure 5.1

To simplify calculations and to make the results easier to check, most companies assume that all policies of a given duration were issued six months prior to the date of valuation. This allows the company to calculate the reserves for a group of similar policies issued in the same policy year as the total face amount for the group times a mean reserve factor. A ***mean reserve factor*** is the mean of the initial and terminal reserves. It is equal to the interpolated mean reserve with $h = 0.5$, and is given by

$$_{t+1}^{m}MV_{[x]:\overline{n}|} = \frac{({}_{t}^{m}V_{[x]:\overline{n}|} + {}_{m}P_{[x]+t:\overline{n}|}) + {}_{t+1}^{m}V_{[x]:\overline{n}|}}{2} \quad \text{if} \quad t < m$$

and

$$_{t+1}^{m}MV_{[x]:\overline{n}|} = \frac{{}_{t}^{m}V_{[x]:\overline{n}|} + {}_{t+1}^{m}V_{[x]:\overline{n}|}}{2} \qquad\qquad \text{if} \quad t \geq m$$

Although the example assumed that the valuation took place on December 31, the principles are equally applicable to valuations on other dates.

5.4.3 DEFERRED PREMIUMS

Suppose, as is typically the case, the block of policies being valued contains a mix of various premium payment modes, such as annual, quarterly or monthly. One approach would be to apply the above factors only to the annual mode policies, and to develop separate factors for each other mode. However, to simplify calculations, companies using the above methods almost universally apply the factors based on annual premiums to the entire block, and then make adjustments for the policies with other premium payment modes.

The mean reserve, $_t MV_{[x]}$, is developed by assuming that the entire premium for the tth policy year was paid at the beginning of that policy year. In reality, for a policy with a quarterly premium mode, the mean reserve factor is overstated by the amount of quarterly net premiums for the tth policy that have not yet become due.

Deferred premiums are modal premiums that are due after the valuation date but before the next policy anniversary. For example, in the following diagram the fourth quarterly premium for a whole life policy with a quarterly premium mode is due on February 1, 2006 which is after the valuation date of December 31, 2005. In this circumstance, the deferred premium for this policy is $\dfrac{P_{[x]}^{(4)}}{4}$.

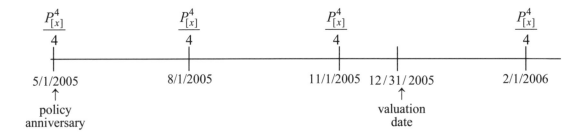

Deferred premiums are set up either as an asset (in the United States) or a negative liability (in Canada) to adjust for the fact that mean reserves based on an annual net premium payment at the beginning of the policy year overstate reserves in the case of more frequent modes of premium payment.

The usual practice is to determine deferred premiums by taking an inventory of the policy premium payment records, and to set up a deferred premium based on the exact number of modal premiums not yet due for each individual policy. The deferred premiums used must be net premiums, because the mean reserves are based on net premiums.

5.4.4 MID-TERMINAL RESERVES

Instead of mean reserves with deferred premiums, some companies use an alternative approach. In general, for a policy issued a fraction h of the year after the beginning of the valuation year, the ***interpolated terminal reserve*** is defined by:

$$(1-h) \cdot {}_t^m V_{[x]:\overline{n}|} + h \cdot {}_{t+1}^m V_{[x]:\overline{n}|}$$

The correct reserve would fall on the dashed line segment in the following graph:

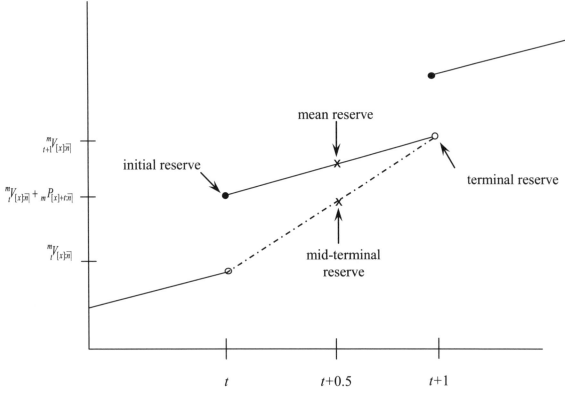

Figure 5.2

Companies that use this approach generally assume once again that all policies of a given duration were issued six months prior to the date of valuation. Based on this assumption, the ***mid-terminal reserve*** for duration t is defined by:

$$\frac{^{m}_{t}V_{[x]:\overline{n}|} + ^{m}_{t+1}V_{[x]:\overline{n}|}}{2}$$

It has been common practice to use mean reserve factors for ordinary business, and mid-terminal factors for weekly premium industrial and long-term disability. However, some companies use mid-terminal factors for ordinary business.

5.4.5 UNEARNED PREMIUM LIABILITY

Mid-terminal reserves understate the policy reserve unless premiums are payable very frequently, such as weekly. This can be seen in the above graph by comparing the mid-terminal reserve to the mean reserve. The mean reserve exceeds the mid-terminal by $\frac{1}{2}{}_{m}P_{[x]+t:\overline{n}|}$, yet we had previously determined that the mean reserve is appropriate for annual premium policies.

To offset this understatement, an unearned premium liability is set up as an adjustment. The unearned premium liability is, in practice, calculated on either a gross or net basis. However, most companies calculate unearned premiums for ordinary life policies on a net basis.

The usual practice is to determine the unearned premium liability by taking one-half of the sum of one modal premium for each policy in force. If the modal premiums are listed by mode and latest month paid, the actual number of months unearned can be reflected as in the following formula:

$$\frac{k}{m'} \cdot {}_m P^{(m')}_{[x]+t:\overline{n}|}$$

where

$$k \quad = \quad \text{the number of months to the next premium due date;}$$

$$m' \quad = \quad \text{the number of months between successive premium due dates; and}$$

$${}_m P^{(m')}_{[x]+t:\overline{n}|} \quad = \quad \text{annualized modal net premium at policy duration } t.$$

5.4.6 EXAMPLE (CONTINUED)

Using the original parameters, but changing to the Commissioners Reserve Valuation Method, the "Summary" worksheet shows the values for many of the terms discussed above:

Summary	
Premium Payment Period	10
Benefit Period	15
Policy Duration	5
Net Level Premium	6,379.48
Expense Allowance	2,191.71
Net Premium – Alpha	4,465.17
Net Premium – Beta	6,656.88
Terminal Reserve – Prior Duration	33,195.15
Terminal Reserve – Current Duration	41,386.26
Mean Reserve	40,619.14
Mid-terminal Reserve	37,290.70
Advance (Uncollected) Premium	7,500.00
Deferred Premium	5,000.00
Unearned Premium	1,666.67

Print

5.4.7 IMMEDIATE PAYMENT OF CLAIMS RESERVE

Prior formulas implied the use of curtate functions, which are based on the assumptions that (a) annual net premiums are payable at the beginning of each policy year, and (b) death benefits are payable at the end of the policy year of death. In practice, most companies use curtate reserves for their basic reserve factors.

Although the assumption as to annual payment of premiums may be accurate in a particular situation, the assumption that death benefits are payable at the end of the policy year of death has no basis in fact for modern life insurance contracts, and is made to make the formulas simpler, which was a primary consideration before the computer age. Curtate reserves are so widely used that it is a common misconception of actuaries and non-actuaries alike that "standard actuarial practice" is to assume that annual premiums are payable at the beginning of the year and death benefits at the end. However, in many situations these may be inappropriate, non-actuarial assumptions. In particular, when performing a realistic model office projection, as in the case of an appraisal valuation or a financial projection, it is never appropriate to assume deaths at year-end.

Because death benefits are actually paid near the time of death instead of at the end of the year, an additional reserve, the ***immediate payment of claims reserve***, is traditionally held in addition to the basic curtate reserve. The immediate payment of claims reserve is often developed using relatively crude techniques. Actuarial Guideline XXXII requires that an immediate payment of claims reserve be established, if the basic reserves have been calculated using curtate factors, as follows:

(1) If the contract provides for payment of death claims immediately upon receipt of due proof of death, without interest from the date of death, Actuarial Guideline XXXII requires an immediate payment of claims reserve of one-third of the valuation interest rate times the death portion of the basic reserve (e.g. $A^1_{[x]:\overline{n}|}$ for an n-year endowment contract); and

(2) If the policy contract calls for payment of interest on the death proceeds from the date of death to the date of payment, Actuarial Guideline XXXII requires an immediate payment of claims reserve of one-half of the valuation interest rate times the death portion of the basic reserve.

No immediate payment of claims reserve is required for policies which provide for payment of death claims at the end of the policy year of death, or if the basic reserve factors are semicontinuous, fully continuous or discounted continuous.

5.4.8 CONTINUOUS RESERVES

Semicontinuous reserves are explicitly calculated under the assumption that death benefits are payable at the moment of death and that net premiums are payable annually at the beginning of the year. A number of companies use this approach for their basic reserve factors, eliminating the need for immediate payment of claims reserves.

For a given plan and issue age, the net level premium semicontinuous reserve is defined by the following prospective formula:

$$ {}^m_t V(\overline{A})_{[x]:\overline{n}|} = \overline{A}_{[x]+t:\overline{n-t}|} - {}_m P(\overline{A})_{[x]:\overline{n}|} \cdot \ddot{a}_{[x]+t:\overline{m-t}|} $$

where

$\quad {}^m_t V(\overline{A})_{[x]:\overline{n}|} \quad = \quad$ semicontinuous net level premium reserve at duration t;

$\quad \overline{A}_{[x]+t:\overline{n-t}|} \quad = \quad$ present value of future benefits at duration t under the assumption that death benefits are payable at the moment of death; and

$\quad {}_m P(\overline{A})_{[x]:\overline{n}|} \quad = \quad$ semicontinuous net level premium in the first policy year.

The present value of future benefits as of duration t under the assumption that death benefits are payable at the moment of death is determined using the following formula:

$$ \overline{A}_{[x]+t:\overline{n-t}|} = CRABD(t) \cdot \left[\sum_{s=0}^{n-t-1} v^{s+1} \cdot {}_s p_{[x]+t} \cdot q_{[x]+t+s} \cdot BD_{[x]+t+s} \right] + v^{n-t} \cdot {}_{n-t} p_{[x]+t} \cdot BM_{[x]+n} $$

where

$\quad CRABD(t) \quad = \quad$ continuous reserve adjustment; and

$$ \qquad\qquad\quad = \quad \frac{i}{\delta}. $$

δ = the interest rate compounded continuously (i.e., force of interest) that is equivalent to i;

= $\ln(1+i)$;

The semicontinuous net level premium in the first policy year is determined using the following formula:

$$_m P(\overline{A})_{[x]:\overline{n}|} = \frac{\overline{A}_{[x]:\overline{n}|}}{\ddot{a}_{[x]:\overline{m}|}}$$

Fully continuous reserves are those which would result from the assumption that premiums are payable continuously throughout the year and death benefits are payable at the moment of death. Again, the assumption that premiums are payable continuously throughout the year has been made for the sake of convenience only, and does not necessarily have a basis in fact, as continuous reserves may be used for policies with any mode of premium payment. The assumption that death benefits are payable at the moment of death does, however, accurately reflect modern policies. No immediate payment of claims reserve is needed if the basic reserve factors are fully continuous.

For a given plan and issue age, the continuous net level premium reserve is defined by the following prospective formula:

$$_t^m \overline{V}_{[x]:\overline{n}|} = \overline{A}_{[x]+t:\overline{n-t}|} - _m \overline{P}_{[x]:\overline{n}|} \cdot \overline{a}_{[x]+t:\overline{m-t}|}$$

where

$_t^m \overline{V}_{[x]:\overline{n}|}$ = semicontinuous net level premium reserve at duration t;

$\overline{A}_{[x]+t:\overline{n-t}|}$ = present value of future benefits at duration t under the assumption that death benefits are payable at the moment of death; and

$_m \overline{P}_{[x]:\overline{n}|}$ = continuous net level premium in the first policy year.

The present value of a continuous annuity at duration t is determined using the following formula:

$$\overline{a}_{[x]+t:\overline{m-t}|} = \sum_{s=0}^{m-t-1} v^s \cdot {}_s p_{[x]+t} \cdot r_{[x]+t+s}^{GP} \cdot CRA_{[x]+t+s}^{GP}$$

where

$CRA_{[x]+t+s}^{GP}$ = continuous reserve adjustment to reflect the assumption that premiums are payable continuously;

$$= \frac{\delta - d}{\delta^2} + \frac{i - \delta}{\delta^2} \cdot \frac{\left(1 - q_{[x]+t+s}\right)}{1+i};$$

d = discount rate that is equivalent to i;

$$= \frac{i}{1+i}$$

Finally, the continuous net level premium in the first policy year is determined using the following formula:

$$_m\overline{P}_{[x]:\overline{n}|} = \frac{\overline{A}_{[x]:\overline{n}|}}{\overline{a}_{[x]:\overline{m}|}}$$

Since premiums are assumed to be payable continuously throughout the year, mean reserves cannot really be used under continuous assumptions. Accordingly, fully continuous reserves have largely given way in practice to ***discounted continuous reserves***, which are also calculated on the assumption that death benefits are payable at the moment of death. Net premiums are assumed to be payable annually at the beginning of the year with a refund of the unearned portion of the current year's premium at death. Terminal reserves are identical to those on a fully continuous basis.

The mean reserves reflect the discounted continuous premium payable at the beginning of the year (discounted with interest only). The ***discounted continuous premium*** payable at the beginning of the policy year is determined using the following formula:

$$_m\overline{P}_{[x]+t:\overline{n}|} \cdot \overline{a}_{\overline{1}|}$$

and the corresponding mean reserve is determined using the following formula:

$$_{t+1}MV_{[x]:\overline{n}|} = \begin{cases} \dfrac{_t^m\overline{V}_{[x]:\overline{n}|} + {}_m\overline{P}_{[x]+t:\overline{n}|} \cdot \overline{a}_{\overline{1}|} + {}_{t+1}^m\overline{V}_{[x]:\overline{n}|}}{2} & \text{if } t < m \\[4ex] \dfrac{_t^m\overline{V}_{[x]:\overline{n}|} + {}_{t+1}^m\overline{V}_{[x]:\overline{n}|}}{2} & \text{if } t \geq m \end{cases}$$

where

$\overline{a}_{\overline{1}|}$ = present value of a one-year continuous annuity certain.

Discounted continuous reserves are in widespread use as most companies which hold "continuous reserves" actually use this method. This is because the assumption that premiums are paid annually at the beginning of the policy year enables the use of traditional mean reserve methodology and computer systems, and also because the Society of Actuaries has published continuous monetary values using this technique.

The differences between fully continuous and discounted continuous reserves can be summarized as follows:

(1)   Fully continuous reserves are based on net premiums payable continuously throughout the year. Reserve factors are mid-terminals and an unearned premium reserve must be set up for net premiums paid beyond the valuation date.

(2)   Discounted continuous terminal reserves are equal to fully continuous terminals. However, mean reserves are calculated assuming an annual net premium equal to the continuous net premium discounted with interest only. A deferred premium asset is calculated if the mode is other than annual.

5.4.9 EXPENSE ALLOWANCE UNDER CONTINUOUS ASSUMPTIONS

Larger net premiums and expense allowances are produced with the semicontinuous and the two continuous methods than with curtate assumptions. Whether these larger expense allowances should be permitted under the Standard Valuation Law was historically a matter of some controversy, since the Society of Actuaries had published monetary values for discounted continuous reserves based on curtate expense allowances. Thus, the formula for the published Commissioners Reserve Valuation Method discounted continuous renewal premium for a whole life policy was based on the following formula:

$$EA = \frac{AB_{[x]+1}}{\ddot{a}_{[x]+1}} - c_{[x]}$$

rather than

$$EA = \frac{\overline{A}_{[x]+1}}{\overline{a}_{[x]+1}} - \overline{c}_{[x]}$$

which would result from strict application of preliminary term methodology.

In December 1986 the National Association of Insurance Commissions adopted Actuarial Guideline XVIII, which allows use of expense allowances calculated on the same basis as the reserves. Therefore, the second equation is the correct expense allowance in the example above.

It is relatively easy to derive the formulas for CRVM reserves, based on the choice of the appropriate expense allowance as discussed above. For more information, the paper "Relationships among the Fully Continuous, the Discounted Continuous, and the Semicontinuous Reserve Bases for Ordinary Life Insurance" by Edward Scher in Transactions XXVI, Part I [7] is an excellent source.

5.4.10 NONDEDUCTION RESERVE

When curtate or semicontinuous reserves are held, a theoretical error is introduced in the basic reserve calculation, which assumes that full annual premiums will be collected each year. This is incorrect because the remaining modal premiums will not be collected in the year of death. It is customary to provide for this understatement by setting up a reserve for the nondeduction of deferred fractional premiums at death, more simply called the **nondeduction reserve**. This reserve is, in theory, equal to that for term insurance of an amount equal to the average number of remaining deferred premiums at the date of death under the policy. For an m-payment, n-year endowment life policy, the terminal reserve for this amount is

$$\frac{m'-1}{2m'} \cdot {}_{m}P_{[x]:\overline{n}|}^{(m')} \cdot {}_{t}^{m}V_{x:\overline{n}|}^{1}$$

where $m' = $ number of premium payments per year.

[7] See [23].

5.4.11 REFUND RESERVE

It is common practice for many companies to refund the amount of any gross premiums at death which represents payment for periods beyond the date of death. The reasoning behind this practice is to avoid "penalizing" the policyholder who could have switched to a more frequent mode just prior to the date of death and paid less for coverage in that year. For policies with this provision, the terminal reserve factor to cover both the refund of premium provision and the nondeduction of deferred premiums is

$$\frac{1}{2} \cdot {}_m P^{(m')}_{[x]:\overline{n}|} \cdot {}^{m}_t V_{x:\overline{n}|}$$

where

$$_m P^{(m')}_{[x]:\overline{n}|} \approx \frac{_m P_{[x]:\overline{n}|}}{1 - \frac{m'-1}{2m'} \cdot d - \frac{1}{2} \cdot {}_m P_{[x]:\overline{n}|}}$$

Note that, except for the term $\dfrac{m'-1}{2m'} \cdot d$ in the denominator, the approximation of $_m P^{(m')}_{[x]:\overline{n}|}$ does not depend on the mode of premium payments. In practice, this term is often omitted so that the reserve factor can be applied to the entire group of policies, regardless of mode of premium payment.

Fully continuous factors (and discounted continuous factors) already make allowance for nondeduction of premiums and refund of premium at death, so that it is not necessary to establish these additional liabilities if continuous factors are used.

The following table illustrates which of the miscellaneous liabilities discussed above are needed for a traditional product with both nondeduction of deferred fractional premium at death and a refund of premium feature, under various assumptions as to the primary reserve basis.

Comparison of Whole Life Net Premiums Terminal Reserves for Primary Reserve Bases

Type	Net Premium	Terminal Reserve	Mean Reserve
Curtate	$P_x = \dfrac{A_x}{\ddot{a}_x}$	$_tV_x = A_{x+t} - P_x \cdot \ddot{a}_{x+t}$	$\dfrac{1}{2}\left(_{t-1}V_x + {_tV_x} + P_x\right)$
Fully Continuous	$\bar{P}(\bar{A}_x) = \dfrac{\bar{A}_x}{\bar{a}_x}$	$_t\bar{V}(\bar{A}_x) = \bar{A}_{x+t} - \bar{P}(\bar{A}_x)\cdot\bar{a}_{x+t}$	$\dfrac{1}{2}\left[_{t-1}\bar{V}(\bar{A}_x) + {_t\bar{V}(\bar{A}_x)}\right]$
Discounted Continuous	$\bar{P}(\bar{A}_x)$ used in calculating terminal reserves $\bar{a}_{\overline{1}|} \cdot \bar{P}(\bar{A}_x)$ used in calculating mean reserves	$_t\bar{V}(\bar{A}_x) = \bar{A}_{x+t} - \bar{P}(\bar{A}_x)\cdot\bar{a}_{x+t}$	$\dfrac{1}{2}\left[_{t-1}\bar{V}(\bar{A}_x) + {_t\bar{V}(\bar{A}_x)} + \bar{a}_{\overline{1}|}\cdot\bar{P}(\bar{A}_x)\right]$
Semi-continuous	$P(\bar{A}_x) = \dfrac{\bar{A}_x}{\ddot{a}_x}$	$_tV(\bar{A}_x) = \bar{A}_{x+t} - P(\bar{A}_x)\cdot\ddot{a}_{x+t}$	$\dfrac{1}{2}\left[_{t-1}V(\bar{A}_x) + {_tV(\bar{A}_x)} + P(\bar{A}_x)\right]$

Note: Arguably, mean reserves are not applicable in the fully continuous case.

Necessary Miscellaneous Liabilities Under Primary Reserve Bases

Type	Refund Reserve	Nondeduction Reserve	Deferred Premiums		Unearned Premiums	
			If Mean	If Mid-Terminal	If Mean	If Mid-Terminal
Curtate	Yes	Yes	Yes	Yes	No	Yes
Fully Continuous	No	No	N/A	No	N/A	Yes
Discounted Continuous	No	No	Yes	No	No	N/A
Semi-continuous	Yes	Yes	Yes	No	No	Yes

5.5 EXERCISES

5.5.1 Key Terms

Valuation methodology
Commissioners Reserve Valuation Method (CRVM)
premium payment period
policy year
expense allowance
full preliminary term reserve method
interpolated mean reserve
terminal reserve
mean reserves
unearned premium
immediate payment of claims
fully continuous reserves
discounted continuous premiums

net level premium (NLP)
issue date
policy duration (or duration)
modified reserve
unamortized expense allowance
deferred premiums
mean reserve factor
initial reserve
mid-terminal reserves
interpolated terminal reserve
semicontinuous reserves
discounted continuous reserves
nondeduction reserve

5.5.2 Questions

a. Write the terminal reserve formula for modified reserves using the formulas for the net level premium reserve and the unamortized expense allowance.

b. For an m payment, n year endowment, when are the terminal reserves under the CRVM method less than the terminal reserves under the net level premium reserve method and when are they equal?

c. For an m payment, n year endowment, when are the terminal reserves under the CRVM method greater than the terminal reserves under the full preliminary term reserve method and when are they equal?

d. Show that the terminal reserve under the full preliminary term reserve method at the end of the first year is zero.

e. Show that the net liability is the same for mid-terminal and mean reserves when policies are issued uniformly throughout the year.

f. Derive the successive reserve formula appearing in the Excel workbook Chapter 5.xls.

5.5.3 Problems

a. Using the Excel workbook, Chapter 5.xls and the following parameters:

Parameters	
Issue Date	7/1/2005
Maturity Date	9/1/2040
Valuation Date................................	12/31/2006
Issue Age.......................................	65
Gender	Male ▼
Gross Premium	10,000
Premium Payment Mode......................	35 years
Premium Payment Period....	Monthly ▼
Paid-to-Date	1/1/2008
Face Amount...................................	100,000
Endowment Amount	100,000
Statutory Valuation Standard:	
Mortality Table...........................	1980 CSO ▼
Interest Rate	4.00%
Method	NLP ▼
Function	Curtate ▼
Age Rule	ANB ▼
Smoking Class	Nonsmoker ▼
Select Period..............................	Aggregate ▼
Deferred Premium Method	Before Codification ▼

Show how the values in the Summary work were determined:

Parameters	
Premium Payment Period..	34
Benefit Period	34
Policy Duration	1
Net Level Premium	5,227.59
Expense Allowance	0
Net Premium – alpha	5,227.59
Net Premium – beta..	5,227.59
Terminal Reserve – Prior Duration	3,395.44
Terminal Reserve – Current Duration	6,786.75
Mean Reserve	7,704.89
Mid-terminal Reserve..	5,091.10
Advance (Uncollected) Premium	10,000.00
Deferred Premium	5,000.00
Unearned Premium	0

b. What changed after codification?

c. Why is there no unearned premium?

6 ✧ Whole Life

6.1 Introduction

Prior to the introduction of universal life in the early 1980's, individual life insurance sales generally were participating whole life contracts sold by mutual life insurance companies through a career agency system. Accordingly, many of the principles discussed in these earlier chapters were developed to reflect the features of these types of contracts.

The primary purpose of this chapter is to apply the principles discussed in Chapters 2, 4 and 5 to whole life contracts. In addition, policyholder dividend liability, deficiency reserves, and excess cash surrender value reserves will also be discussed.

6.2 Product Classification

For whole life, limited payment life and endowment contracts, the contract terms are fixed and guaranteed. This means:

- premiums must be paid when due for a specified number of years or to a specified age;
- death benefits are guaranteed at issue and do not change unless the policy has a cost-of-living adjustment rider,[1] or is participating and the policyholder dividend[2] is used to purchase additional insurance; and
- nonforfeiture benefits are guaranteed at issue and do not change unless the policy is participating and the policyholder dividend is used to either purchase additional insurance or deposited in an accumulation account.

As was noted earlier, whole life contracts, limited payment contracts and endowment contracts will collectively be referred to as whole life contracts.

6.3 Example

Associated with this chapter is an Excel workbook, Chapter 6.xls. The worksheets will feature the same illustrative policy used in Chapter 5. Similar to Chapter 5.xls, this information is captured in the first worksheet, called "Parameters," in Chapter 6.xls:

---

[1] A cost-of-living adjustment rider increases the death benefit of the policy based on the increase in the consumer price index.

[2] The policyholder dividend that is paid on the policy anniversary can be: (1) paid in cash, (2) applied against the next year's premium; (3) left to accumulate with the company in an accumulation account; (4) used to purchase paid-up insurance; or (5) used to purchase term insurance.

Parameters	
Issue Date	9/1/2000
Maturity Date...	9/1/2015
Valuation Date	12/31/2005
Issue Age	50
Gender	Male ▼
Gross Premium	10,000
Premium Payment Period	10 years
Premium Payment Mode	Quarterly ▼
Paid-to-Date..	12/1/2006
Face Amount..	100,000
Endowment Amount......................................	100,000
Statutory Valuation Standard:	
Mortality Table.....................................	1980 CSO ▼
Interest Rate...	5.00%
Method	CRVM ▼
Function...	Curtate ▼
Age Rule...	ANB ▼
Smoking Class.......................................	Nonsmoker ▼
Select Period..	Aggregate ▼
Deferred Premium Method....................	Before Codification ▼

6.4 STATUTORY ANNUAL STATEMENT

Using the illustrative policy, this section will show how the accounting entries are recorded in the following financial statements discussed in Chapter 2:

(1)   The liability and surplus sections of the Balance Sheet

(2)   Capital and Surplus Account

(3)   Cash Flow Statement

(4)   Analysis of Operations by Lines of Business

(5)   Analysis of Increase in Reserves During the Year

(6)   Exhibit 1 – Part 1 – Premiums and Annuity Considerations

(7)   Exhibit 5 – Aggregate Reserve For Life Policies and Contracts

It will be helpful if the worksheets from Chapter 5.xls with the same illustrative policy are readily available as a reference.

6.4.1 EXHIBIT 5

A natural place to begin is with Exhibit 5 which shows the aggregate reserve for life contracts by valuation standard (i.e., reserve methodology and assumptions) and the total reserve:

Exhibit 5 Aggregate Reserve for Life Policies	
Valuation Standard	**Ordinary**
Section A: Life Insurance: 1980 CSO 5.00% CRVM Curtate	40,619

For the illustrative policy, this information came from the above "Parameters" worksheets and the highlighted information in the "Summary" worksheet:

Summary	
Premium Payment Period	10
Benefit Period	15
Policy Duration	5
Net Level Premium	6,379.48
Expense Allowance	2,191.71
Net Premium – Alpha	4,465.17
Net Premium – Beta	6,656.88
Terminal Reserve – Prior Duration	33,195.15
Terminal Reserve – Current Duration	41,386.26
Mean Reserve	40,619.14
Mid-terminal Reserve	37,290.70
Advance (Uncollected) Premium	7,500.00
Deferred Premium	5,000.00
Unearned Premium	1,666.67
Print	

6.4.2 EXHIBIT 1

The following is the renewal section of Exhibit 1 which shows how the premium for this policy was converted from a cash basis to an accrual basis:

	Ordinary		
	3 **Life** **Insurance**	**4** **Individual** **Annuities**	**5** **Supplementary** **Contracts**

Exhibit 1 – Part 1

Premiums and Annuity Considerations for
Life and Accident and Health Policies and Contracts

	3 **Life** **Insurance**	**4** **Individual** **Annuities**	**5** **Supplementary** **Contracts**
RENEWAL			
Uncollected	0		
Deferred and accrued			
Direct	5,000		
Reinsurance assumed			
Reinsurance ceded			
Net	5,000		
Advance	7,500		
Collected during year:			
Direct	17,500		
Reinsurance assumed			
Reinsurance ceded			
Net	17,500		
Prior year (uncollected + deferred and accrued − advance)	5,000		
Renewal premiums and considerations:			
Direct	10,000		
Reinsurance assumed			
Reinsurance ceded			
Net	10,000		
TOTAL			
Total premiums and considerations:			
Direct	10,000		
Reinsurance assumed			
Reinsurance ceded			
Net	10,000		

Since the premium payment mode is quarterly, a quarterly premium of $2,500 is due on March 1, 2006 and June 1, 2006. These are the only premium payments that are due before the next policy anniversary, which is September 1, 2006. Therefore, the deferred premium is $5,000. The paid-to-date in the "Parameters" worksheet indicates that the policy is paid to December 1, 2006 which means that these three quarterly premiums have been paid before they were due. As a result, there is a $7,500 advance premium associated with this policy.

Using this information, the collected premium was determined as follows:

February 1, 2005	$2,500
June 1, 2005	2,500
September 1, 2005	2,500
December 1, 2005	2,500
Advance premium	7,500
Collected premium	$17,500

The collected premium is on a cash basis. It is converted to an accrual basis as follows:

	Collected premium	$17,500
+	Deferred (current period)	5,000
−	Advance (current period)	7,500
−	Deferred-Advance (prior period)	5,000
	Direct Premium	$10,000

The above methods of calculating advance premium and deferred premium were used prior to codification. After codification, advance premium and deferred premium were re-defined. Only paid premiums covering the period after the next anniversary are included in advance premium. Deferred premium is calculated as before, but then reduced by any paid premiums covering periods from the valuation date until the paid-to-date or next anniversary date, if earlier. For example, the "Parameters" worksheet specified the following deferred method (see highlighted area):

Parameters	
Issue Date	9/1/2000
Maturity Date	9/1/2015
Valuation Date	12/31/2005
Issue Age	50
Gender	Male ▼
Gross Premium	10,000
Premium Payment Period	10 years
Premium Payment Mode	Quarterly ▼
Paid-to-Date	12/1/2006
Face Amount	100,000
Endowment Amount	100,000
Statutory Valuation Standard:	
Mortality Table	1980 CSO ▼
Interest Rate	5.00%
Method	CRVM ▼
Function	Curtate ▼
Age Rule	ANB ▼
Smoking Class	Nonsmoker ▼
Select Period	Aggregate ▼
Deferred Premium Method	After Codification ▼

Calculate

Based on this specification, the advance premium and deferred premium would appear as follows in the Summary worksheet:

Summary	
Premium Payment Period	10
Benefit Period..	15
Policy Duration..	5
Net Level Premium...	6,379.48
Expense Allowance	2,191.71
Net Premium – Alpha..	4,465.17
Net Premium – Beta	6,656.88
Terminal Reserve – Prior Duration.............................	33,195.15
Terminal Reserve – Current Duration	41,386.26
Mean Reserve	40,619.14
Mid-terminal Reserve	37,290.70
Advance (Uncollected) Premium................................	2,500.00
Deferred Premium	0.00
Unearned Premium...	1,666.67

The remainder of this chapter will use the method prior to codification.

6.4.3 Analysis of Increase in Reserves During the Year

The following Analysis of Increase in Reserves During the Year[3] shows how the reserve increased from $32,630 at the end of the previous year to $40,619:

Analysis of Increase in Reserves During the Year				
		Ordinary		
		3 Life Insurance	4 Individual Annuities	5 Supplementary Contracts
	Reserves December 31, prior year	32,630		
+	Tabular net premiums of considerations	6,657		
+	Tabular interest	1,798		
−	Tabular cost	746		
−	Reserves released by death	(279)		
−	Reserves released by other terminations (net)	0		
+	Other changes	0		
=	Reserve December 31, current year	40,619		

Notice that the $40,619 "foots" to the total in Exhibit 5. The information for this exhibit came from the highlighted information in the following successive statutory reserve worksheet, "SSR", in the Chapter 5.xls workbook:

---

[3] Tabular is a term that was developed prior to the extensive use of computers and reflects that these values were literally from a table of monetary values published by the Society of Actuaries.

				Successive Statutory Reserves			
(1)	(2)	(3)	(4)	(5)	(6)	(7)	(8)
x	t	$V(t)$ +	$P(t)$ +	$I(t)$ −	$B^d(t)$ +	$V^d(t)$ =	$V(t+1)$
50	0	0	4,465	223	491	21	4,218
51	1	4,218	6,657	544	535	59	10,942
52	2	10,942	6,657	880	586	105	17,999
53	3	17,999	6,657	1,233	643	163	25,409
54	4	25,409	6,657	1,603	709	235	33,195
55	5	33,195	6,657	1,993	782	324	41,386
56	6	41,386	6,657	2,402	863	432	50,014
57	7	50,014	6,657	2,834	949	561	59,116
58	8	59,116	6,657	3,289	1,042	716	68,736
59	9	68,736	6,657	3,770	1,147	905	78,921
60	10	78,921	0	3,946	1,264	1,045	82,648
61	11	82,648	0	4,132	1,394	1,207	86,593
62	12	86,593	0	4,330	1,542	1,400	90,781
63	13	90,781	0	4,539	1,711	1,630	95,238
64	14	95,238	0	4,762	1,902	1,902	100,000

For example, tabular interest was determined as follows:

$$
\begin{array}{ll}
\text{Duration 4} & 1,603 \\
\text{Duration 5} & +1,993 \\
\hline
& 3,596/2 = 1,798
\end{array}
$$

6.4.4 ANALYSIS OF OPERATIONS BY LINES OF BUSINESS

The above supporting exhibits would be used to complete the following sections of the Analysis of Operations by Lines of Business:

Analysis of Operations by Lines of Business	Ordinary
	3 Life Insurance
Revenue	
Premiums and annuity considerations	10,000
Net investment income	
Amortization of interest maintenance reserve	
Separate account net gain, excluding unrealized gains and losses	
Other income	
Total **Revenue**	10,000
Costs	
Death benefits	
Matured endowments	
Annuity benefits	
Disability benefits and benefits under accident and health contracts	
Surrender benefits and withdrawals for life contracts	
Interest on deposit-type contracts	
Payments on supplementary contracts with life contingencies	
Increase in aggregate reserves for life and accident and health contracts	7,989
Subtotal, **Benefit Costs**	7,989
Commissions on premiums, annuity considerations and deposit-type contracts	
General insurance expenses	
Insurance taxes, licenses and fees, excluding federal income taxes	
Increase in loading on deferred and uncollected premiums	0
Net transfers to (or from) separate accounts	
Other Costs	
Total **Costs**	7,989
Net gain from operations before dividends and FIT[1]	2,011
Dividends to policyholders	
Net gain from operations after dividends and before FIT	2,011
Federal income taxes, excluding taxes on capital gains	
Net gain from operations after dividends and FIT and before realized capital gains	2,011

[1]Dividends means dividends to policyholders and FIT means federal income taxes

6.4.5 CASH FLOW STATEMENT

Exhibit 1 would be used to complete the following sections of the Cash Flow Statement:

Cash Flow		
	1 **Current Year**	**2** **Prior Year**
Cash from Operations		
Premium collected net of reinsurance	17,500	10,000
Net investment income		
Miscellaneous income		
Sub-total		
Net transfers to (or from) separate accounts		
Commissions, expenses and other deductions		
Dividend to policyholders		
Federal income taxes		
Sub-total		
Net cash from Operations	17,500	10,000
Cash from Investments		
Proceeds from investments sold, matured of repaid		
Cost of investments acquired (long-term only)		
Net increase in (or decrease) in policy loans and premium notes		
Net Cash from Investments		
Cash from Financing and Miscellaneous Sources		
Net Cash from Financing and Miscellaneous Sources		
RECONCILIATION OF CASH AND SHORT-TERM INVESTMENTS		
Net change in cash and short-term investments	17,500	10,000
Cash and short-term investments:		
Beginning of year	10,000	0
End of period	27,500	10,000

To complete this statement, it was assumed that the collected premium was held in a cash account. If it was used to purchase a bond, the line item "Cost of investments acquired (long-term only)" would be –$17,500 and the line item "net change in cash and short-term investments" would be $0.

6.4.6 CAPITAL AND SURPLUS ACCOUNT

Net income from Summary of Operations (which in this example is the same as the Analysis of Operations by Lines of Business) would be used to complete the following sections of the Capital and Surplus Account:

Capital and Surplus Account		
	1 **Current Year**	**2** **Prior Year**
Capital and Surplus, December 31, prior year	2,402	0
Net Income	2,011	2,402
Change in unrealized gains		
Change in reserve in account of change in valuation basis		
Dividends to stockholders		
Other changes		
Capital and Surplus, December 31, current year	4,413	2,402

6.4.7 LIABILITY AND SURPLUS SECTIONS OF THE BALANCE SHEET

Exhibit 1, Exhibit 5 and the Capital and Surplus Account would be used to complete the following sections of the Balance Sheet:

Liabilities, Surplus and Other Funds		
	1 Current Year	2 Prior Year
Liabilities		
Aggregate reserve for life contracts	40,619	32,630
Aggregate reserve for accident and health contracts		
Liability for deposit-type contracts		
Contract claims:		
Life		
Accident and health		
Policyholders' dividend due and unpaid		
Provision for policyholders' dividends payable in the following year		
Premium and considerations received in advance	7,500	0
Contract liabilities not included elsewhere		
Other liabilities (excluding separate accounts)		
Separate accounts liabilities		
Total **Liabilities**	48,119	32,630
Surplus	4,413	2,402
Total Liabilities and Surplus	52,532	35,032

6.5 POLICYHOLDER DIVIDENDS

If a life insurance company has in force participating policies, the Board of Directors usually declares prior to the end of the current fiscal year, that a policyholder dividend will be paid on the policy anniversary in the following fiscal year. Accordingly, the life insurance company has made a relatively firm commitment to make a payment to the policyholder, except in the rare circumstance that the Board subsequently votes to reverse this payment. Accordingly, a liability must be established.

The liability section of the Balance Sheet has a line item titled "Provision for Policyholders' Dividends Payable in the Following Year." This is the liability for the policyholder dividend that will be paid on the anniversary in the next fiscal year. For example, if the illustrative policy was participating and the Board voted to pay a policyholder dividend calculated to be $5,000 on September 1, 2006, then a policyholder dividend liability of $5,000 would be established for this policy[4].

---

[4] If the payment of this dividend by the life insurance company is contingent on the payment by the policyholder of the premium that is due on September 1, 2006, then some life insurance companies hold a slightly lower amount to reflect that not all policyholders will make this premium payment.

6.6 EXHIBIT 5G

Section G – Miscellaneous Reserves of Exhibit 5 shows miscellaneous policy reserves for the current reporting period that are not shown in the other sections of this exhibit:

Exhibit 5	
Aggregate Reserve for Life Policies	
1	4 Ordinary
Section G: Miscellaneous Reserves:	
For excess of valuation net premium over corresponding gross premium on respective policies, computed according to standard of valuation required for this state	
For surrender values in excess of reserves otherwise required and carried in this schedule	
For options not matured	
For immediate payment of claims	

In most circumstances, the two largest miscellaneous policy reserves for whole life policies are deficiency reserves and the portion of the cash surrender value in excess of the other policy reserves.

6.6.1 DEFICIENCY RESERVES

The basic prospective reserve definition is the present value of future benefits less the present value of future net premiums. However, what if gross premiums are less than the valuation net premiums? Is it prudent to subtract the present value of future net premiums when the policyholder will be remitting less than the annual net premium to the insurance company?

Deficiency reserves are reserves which may be required in addition to basic policy reserves when the gross premium[5] is below a certain level as described below. Before the 1976 changes, the Standard Valuation Law required deficiency reserves if the gross premium for a policy were less than the valuation net premium actually used.

Deficiency reserves were subject to criticism for several reasons:

(1) Suppose that a company voluntarily strengthens reserves by reducing the valuation interest rate from 3.5% to 3%, and suppose the gross premiums for a policy are greater than the net premiums at 3.5%, but less than at 3%. Reserve strengthening would cause the basic policy reserve to increase. Yet as a result of lowering the valuation rate, deficiency reserves would be required as well.

(2) Although reserve strengthening occurs rarely in practice, this example illustrates that the prior law sometimes required companies with conservative reserve bases to hold deficiency reserves even though they would not have been necessary if a more liberal basis had been adopted.

(3) Deficiency reserves have not been allowed as a tax reserve in the U.S since the early 1980's.

---

[5] Some whole life contracts have a current premium and a guaranteed premium. The current premium is the premium billed the policyholder by the life insurance company. It can be increased by the life insurance company under provisions specified in the contract. However, the current premium can not exceed the guaranteed premium specified in the contract. Deficiency reserves are determined using the guaranteed premium.

The 1976 amendments to the Standard Valuation Law removed any explicit reference to deficiency reserves. Instead, basic policy reserves are required to be increased under certain circumstances. Under the 1976 amendments, if the gross premium for a policy is less than the valuation net premium calculated using the valuation method actually used, but using the minimum standards of mortality and interest, then the required total reserve is the greater of (a) or (b), defined as

(a) the reserve calculated according to the method, mortality table, and interest rate actually used for the policy, and

(b) the reserve calculated by the method actually used for the policy, but using the minimum valuation standards of mortality and interest, and replacing the valuation net premium by the actual gross premium in each year that the actual gross premium is less than the valuation net premium.

Although the Standard Valuation Law now makes no explicit reference to deficiency reserves, the excess of reserves described in (b) over those described in (a) is often referred to as a deficiency reserve.

The important changes resulting from the new definition are that (1) regardless of the basis of mortality and interest actually used in the basic reserves, the test for premium deficiency is now performed against a net premium calculated using the minimum allowable standards for mortality and interest, and (2) where the test reveals any deficiencies, the policy gets credit for the excess of the actual basic reserve over the reserve calculated using the minimum basis of mortality and interest, and this credit is used to offset any deficiency reserves which would otherwise be required. These changes generally eliminate many of the inequities which occur when a company strengthens reserves, and when two companies use different reserving bases for essentially similar policies. Note, however, that both the test for premium deficiency and the calculation of adjusted reserves utilize the actual valuation method used by the company. In particular, if a company were to strengthen reserves by switching from Commissioners' Reserve Valuation Method to some other basis, the new definition might not offer complete relief from deficiency reserves.

The additional reserve required under the new definition can be defined by the following terminal reserve formula for an m-payment, n-year endowment:

$$ {}^{m}_{t}V^{Def}_{[x]:\overline{n}|} = \text{Max}\left(0, {}^{m}_{t}V'_{[x]:\overline{n}|} - {}^{m}_{t}V_{[x]:\overline{n}|}\right) $$

where

$\quad {}^{m}_{t}V^{Def}_{[x]:\overline{n}|} \quad = \quad$ deficiency reserve at duration t;

$\quad {}^{m}_{t}V'_{[x]:\overline{n}|} \quad = \quad$ the reserve at duration t determined using the minimum allowable standards for mortality and interest; and

$\quad {}^{m}_{t}V_{[x]:\overline{n}|} \quad = \quad$ the basic policy reserve at duration t.

Deficiency reserves do not follow the usual pattern of premium paying life reserves in that they generally begin at their maximum value at issue and decrease with time. The initial deficiency reserve may be much greater than the initial premium for a given policy. For example, if the gross premium for the illustrative policy was $5,000 instead of $10,000, then the policy would require deficiency reserves that would gradually decrease to zero by the end of the premium payment period shown in the following chart:

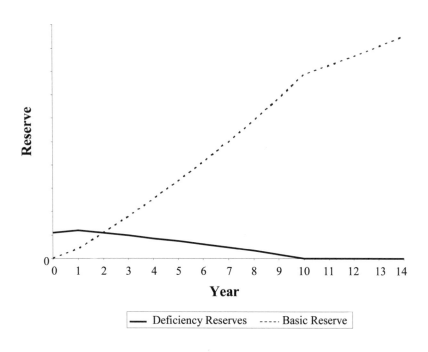

Figure 6.1

Because of the resulting surplus strain, actuaries try to design products which either do not require or which minimize deficiency reserves.

The gross premium used in the calculation of deficiency reserves under the 1976 amendments to the Standard Valuation Law is the total annualized gross premium for the base policy, including modal[6] loading and policy fee. Although premiums for benefits and riders are not allowed to be used in calculation of deficiencies for the base policy, sufficiency in one benefit is allowed to offset deficiencies in another benefit, including the base policy. For example, deficiencies in a whole life policy may be reduced by any sufficiency in a term rider.

Because of these complications, the most common means of calculating these reserves is by the seriatim[7] method, with either the minimum required net premium, or the amount of deficiency maintained in the valuation record. The inclusion of policy fees in most policies makes it impossible to use factor type approaches without having to make critical assumptions as to the average policy size. The potential significant size of deficiency reserves, and the fact that they frequently start out at their maximum value combine to cause most companies to calculate these reserves on a fairly exact basis rather than relying on crude approximations.

---

[6] "Modal" indicates the frequency of premium payment is more often than once per year (e.g. monthly, quarterly or semi-annually)

[7] "Seriatim" means on a policy by policy basis.

As discussed above, the 1976 amendments require companies to recalculate the basic policy reserves for policies with deficient premiums, using the gross premium in lieu of the valuation net premium under the policy. Because this could involve fairly complicated reserve calculations based upon first principles, many companies continue to calculate additional required reserves using the old technique, although substituting the minimum basis of mortality and interest. As discussed above, this produces the exact answer in the typical case where the policy is reserved at the minimum basis of mortality and interest. Using this method, the mid-year deficiency reserve for an n-pay-life policy is

$$\left({}_m P_{[x]:\overline{n}|} - GP_{[x]} \right) \cdot \left[\frac{a_{[x]+t-1:\overline{m-t-1}|} - \ddot{a}_{[x]+t:\overline{m-t}|}}{2} \right] \approx \left({}_m P_{[x]:\overline{n}|} - GP_{[x]} \right) \cdot \left[\frac{\ddot{a}_{[x]+t:\overline{m-t}|}}{1+\frac{i}{2}} \right]$$

where

$$GP_{[x]} = \text{gross premium; and}$$

$$ {}_m P_{[x]:\overline{n}|} = \text{net premium.}$$

In practice, the actual formula used may be much more complicated than that given above, although the basic principle will be the same. Common complications include the utilization of modified reserve methods which grade from one basis to another, producing varying net premiums, and the existence of additional benefits with sufficiencies which may be used to offset the deficiencies of the base policy.

6.6.2 EXCESS CASH SURRENDER VALUE

Another common miscellaneous reserve appearing in Exhibit 5G is an excess cash surrender value reserve. This is an additional reserve that is held when the cash surrender value exceeds the total policy reserve. The total policy reserve used in this comparison would be the basic reserve, deficiency reserve and rider reserves. The formula for this reserve is:

$$ {}_t^m V_{[x]:\overline{n}|}^{XCV} = \max \left[0, {}_t^m CV_{[x]:\overline{n}|} - \left({}_t^m V_{[x]:\overline{n}|} + {}_t^m V_{[x]:\overline{n}|}^{Def} + \text{other rider reserves} \right) \right]$$

where

$$ {}_t^m V_{[x]:\overline{n}|}^{XCV} = \text{excess cash surrender value reserve at duration } t; \text{ and}$$

$$ {}_t^m CV_{[x]:\overline{n}|} = \text{cash surrender value at duration } t.$$

6.7 EXERCISES

6.7.1 Questions

a. With regards to product classification, what does the phrase "the contract terms are fixed and guaranteed" mean?

b. Explain why the m payment, n year endowment in section 6.3 would not have any deficiency reserves.

c. What is the lowest gross premium for the m payment, n year endowment in section 6.3 for which there would be no deficiency reserves?

d. Calculate the deficiency reserve on the valuation date if the gross premium for the m payment, n year endowment in section 6.3 was $4,000.

6.7.2 Problems

a. Using only the Excel workbook, Chapter 5.xls and the following parameters:

Parameters	
Issue Date	7/1/2005
Maturity Date	9/1/2040
Valuation Date	12/31/2006
Issue Age	65
Gender	Male
Gross Premium	10,000
Premium Payment Period	35 years
Premium Payment Mode	Monthly
Paid-to-Date	1/1/2008
Face Amount	100,000
Endowment Amount	100,000
Statutory Valuation Standard:	
Mortality Table	1980 CSO
Interest Rate	4.00%
Method	NLP
Function	Curtate
Age Rule	ANB
Smoking Class	Nonsmoker
Select Period	Aggregate
Deferred Premium Method	Before Codification

Complete the Analysis of Increase in Reserves During the Year assuming the policy is in force on the valuation date.

b. Complete the Analysis of Increase in Reserves During the Year assuming the insured died on the valuation date.

c. Complete the Analysis of Increase in Reserves During the Year assuming the policy surrendered on the valuation date.

7 ✧ TERM LIFE INSURANCE

7.1 INTRODUCTION

In the 1970's, term life insurance started to become a popular alternative to participating whole life. Today, most life insurance sold in the United States is term insurance. The following table[1] shows that in 2004 approximately 71.8% of face amount issued was term life insurance with 87.5% of that amount being level term.

	Face Amount		Policies Issued	
Plan Type	Amount (in millions)	Percent of Total	Number (in thousands)	Percent of Total
Term Insurance				
Level	1,165,857	62.8	5,076	41.4
Decreasing	36,842	2.0	144	1.2
Other	130,449	7.0	---	---
Total Term	1,333,148	71.8	5,220	42.6
Permanent Insurance	524,742	28.2	7,039	57.4
Total	1,857,890	100.0	12,259	100.0

Individual Life Insurance Purchases by Plan Type, 2004

This chapter will discuss how policy reserves for the most common forms of term life insurance are determined in a statutory valuation. Most of this discussion will be based on the Valuation of Life Insurance Policies Model Regulation (sometimes referred to as Guideline XXX). This model regulation was adopted by the National Association of Insurance Commissioners to address issues with regards to the application of the Standard Valuation Law to level premium term life insurance and universal life with secondary guarantees.

7.2 PRODUCT CLASSIFICATION

The most common forms of term life insurance issued by life insurance companies fall into four broad categories:

- yearly renewable and convertible term;
- n-year renewable and convertible term;
- n-year level premium term; and
- n-year decreasing term.

---

[1] 2006 *Life Insurers Fact Book*, Table 7.2 [7].

The primary emphasis of all these forms of term insurance is death protection at a low net cost. Accordingly, these forms do not generally have a cash surrender value[2].

7.2.1 Yearly Renewable and Convertible Term

Yearly renewable and convertible term has a level death benefit to a certain expiry age, at which the policy expires (i.e., coverage ends) without value. The two most common expiry ages are age 70 and age 100. The premium is paid over the entire benefit period and increases on each policy anniversary to reflect higher mortality.

The term "convertible" means that these policies give the policyholder the right to convert the term life insurance policy to a permanent life insurance policy (e.g., whole life insurance) without evidence of insurability.

7.2.2 N-Year Renewable and Convertible Term

Similar to yearly renewable and convertible term, n-year renewable and convertible term has a level death benefit to a certain expiry age (e.g., age 70 or age 100), at which the policy expires without value. The premium is paid over the entire benefit period. But instead of increasing every policy year, the premium increases every n years. For example, a five-year renewable and convertible term policy has a level premium for the first five policy years. In the sixth policy year the premium increases and remains level until the eleventh policy year when the premium increases again. This pattern continues to the expiry age of the policy.

N-year renewable and convertible term also gives the policyholder the right to convert the term life insurance policy to a permanent life insurance policy without evidence of insurability. This conversion privilege typically expires at age 70 or age 75.

7.2.3 N-Year Level Premium Term

A very popular product introduced in the 1990's is n-year level premium term. This type of term life insurance combines some of the features of yearly renewable and convertible term with some of the features of n-year renewable and convertible term. In particular, n-year level premium term has a level death benefit to a certain expiry age, after which the policy expires without value. The premium is paid over the entire benefit period, but like n-year renewable and convertible term the premium remains level for the first n policy years. Thereafter, the premium increases every policy year in a way similar to a yearly renewable and convertible term.

N-year level premium term also gives the policyholder the right to convert the term life insurance policy to a permanent life insurance policy without evidence of insurability.

7.2.4 N-Year Decreasing Term

N-year decreasing term provides death protection for n-years, after which the policy expires without value. However, the death benefit decreases over this n-year benefit period. Often these types of term policies are purchased to pay the outstanding loan balance on a mortgage if the insured should die while the policy is in force. Accordingly, the decreases in the death benefit are coordinated with the amortization schedule of the mortgage.

The premium is usually level, but typically ends two years prior to the end of the benefit period since the death benefit is low in the final two years.

---

[2] For certain forms of term life insurance, particularly 30-year level premium term, the term policy may have a modest cash surrender value at the older ages in order to comply with the Standard Nonforfeiture Law. This may have an effect on the statutory reserve reported in Section G of Exhibit 5.

7.2.5 GRADED PREMIUM WHOLE LIFE

Technically speaking, a graded premium whole life policy is a whole life policy that provides level death protection for the life of the insured with premiums that increase annually for the first n-policy years (e.g., 20 policy years) and are a level amount thereafter. The premiums in the first several years are usually very low and are comparable to yearly renewable term. The yearly rate at which the premium increases usually results in no cash surrender values until the end of the increase period. Accordingly, these types of policies have many of the characteristics of term life insurance. Many of the concepts discussed in this chapter apply to graded premium whole life.

7.3 VALUATION OF LIFE INSURANCE POLICIES MODEL REGULATION

Consider a 10-year level term policy with a 20 year benefit period issued to a 50 year old male nonsmoker with a $1,000,000 face amount and premiums as shown in the following table:

10 Year Level Term			
(1) Age	(2) Duration	(3) Face Amount	(4) Premium
50	0	1,000,000	5,000
51	1	1,000,000	5,000
52	2	1,000,000	5,000
53	3	1,000,000	5,000
54	4	1,000,000	5,000
55	5	1,000,000	5,000
56	6	1,000,000	5,000
57	7	1,000,000	5,000
58	8	1,000,000	5,000
59	9	1,000,000	5,000
60	10	1,000,000	7,580
61	11	1,000,000	9,060
62	12	1,000,000	10,790
63	13	1,000,000	12,830
64	14	1,000,000	15,220
65	15	1,000,000	16,900
66	16	1,000,000	19,890
67	17	1,000,000	23,270
68	18	1,000,000	27,080
69	19	1,000,000	29,810

The following policy reserves would result from the Commissioners' Reserve Valuation Method[3], as discussed in Chapter 5:

---

[3] The statutory assumptions are 1980 CSO nonsmoker with select factors and a 5% interest rate.

				Successive Statutory Reserves			
(1)	(2)	(3)	(4)	(5)	(6)	(7)	(8)
x	t	$V(t)$ +	$P(t)$ +	$I(t)$ −	$B^d(t)$ +	$V^d(t)$ =	$V(t+1)$
50	0	0	3,534	411	3,732	0	0
51	1	0	5,997	534	4,066	9	2,240
52	2	2,240	5,997	648	4,688	19	3,979
53	3	3,979	5,997	736	5,401	28	5,101
54	4	5,101	5,997	795	5,956	34	5,731
55	5	5,731	5,997	828	6,569	38	5,783
56	6	5,783	5,997	834	7,249	37	5,157
57	7	5,157	5,997	805	8,067	30	3,675
58	8	3,675	5,997	734	8,857	12	1,310
59	9	1,310	5,997	620	9,750	(20)	(2,098)
60	10	(2,098)	9,091	602	12,640	(68)	(5,365)
61	11	(5,365)	10,866	523	13,940	(115)	(8,279)
62	12	(8,279)	12,941	473	15,420	(165)	(10,690)
63	13	(10,690)	15,388	462	17,110	(212)	(12,390)
64	14	(12,390)	18,254	502	19,020	(249)	(13,112)
65	15	(13,112)	20,269	543	21,130	(294)	(13,909)
66	16	(13,909)	23,855	652	23,400	(310)	(13,267)
67	17	(13,267)	27,909	846	25,860	(278)	(10,764)
68	18	(10,764)	32,478	1,148	28,500	(167)	(5,867)
69	19	(5,867)	35,753	1,494	31,380	0	0

Notice how the terminal reserve turns negative in the tenth policy year. By the fifteenth policy year, the terminal reserve is –$13,908.56. Thereafter, the reserve gradually becomes less negative until the final policy year, when it is zero.

These negative reserves are caused by the slope of the gross premium schedule. In the final policy years, the premium is significantly higher than in the earlier years. Accordingly, these higher premiums in the later policy years are being relied upon to provide for the cost of insurance in the early policy years. This becomes evident when the above reserves are compared to the reserves for a 10-year level premium term life policy that expires at the end of 10 years and has the same $5,000 level annual premium:

				Successive Statutory Reserves			
(1)	(2)	(3)	(4)	(5)	(6)	(7)	(8)
x	t	$V(t)$ +	$P(t)$ +	$I(t)$ −	$B^d(t)$ +	$V^d(t)$ =	$V(t+1)$
50	0	0	3,554	406	3,732	0	0
51	1	0	6,171	517	4,066	10	2,423
52	2	2,423	6,171	616	4,688	20	4,356
53	3	4,356	6,171	690	5,401	31	5,683
54	4	5,683	6,171	733	5,956	39	6,529
55	5	6,529	6,171	750	6,569	45	6,811
56	6	6,811	6,171	737	7,249	47	6,428
57	7	6,428	6,171	690	8,067	42	5,204
58	8	5,204	6,171	600	8,857	28	3,114
59	9	3,115	6,171	464	9,750	0	0

Until the mid 1970's, it was common practice in the life insurance industry to consider renewable term policies as a series of separate policies for purposes of calculating deficiency reserves. Most companies only held reserves for the deficiencies during the current period of level premiums. According to this view, deficiency reserves would never be required for a yearly renewable and convertible term policy. As a practical matter, this practice did not threaten company solvency, as term rates were, for the most part, in excess of net valuation premiums.

Then in the late 1970's and early 1980's, yearly renewable and convertible term premium rates fell as new product types and nonsmoker discounts were introduced. State regulators became concerned that premium rates below the valuation net premium level were being guaranteed without a corresponding deficiency reserve. Several states introduced requirements that renewable term products be viewed as ongoing policies for purposes of deficiency reserve calculations.

Since that time, two ways of looking at valuation premiums for renewable term policies have developed:

(1)   The **unitary method** considers the entire stream of future gross premiums and develops a set of valuation net premiums which are proportional. This method follows from a literal reading of the Standard Valuation Law, which requires that the valuation net premiums for a policy be proportional to the gross premiums.

(2)   The **term method** looks separately at the gross premiums for each renewal period and develops separate, independent sets of valuation net premiums within each period.

Although the unitary method may appear to be more in line with the Standard Valuation Law, it quickly fell into disfavor with regulators. Because this method considers the entire stream of gross premiums, regardless of how low the premiums are in the early durations, it is always possible to avoid deficiency reserves by setting the gross premiums at the extreme older attained ages high enough to offset any deficiencies at the younger ages. In 1984 the NAIC adopted Actuarial Guideline IV, which was applicable to term policies without cash values, valued using the 1958 CSO table. For applicable policies, Actuarial Guideline IV required that term method reserves be established for the current period of level premiums, and that additional reserves be established if future guaranteed premiums were less than valuation net premiums, calculated according to a special basis specified in the Guideline.

In 1995 the NAIC adopted the Valuation of Life Insurance Policies Model Regulation, which clarifies both basic and deficiency reserve treatment for all policies with nonlevel premiums or benefits. This model regulation was controversial and took several years to develop. Its primary purpose was to address issues, like the one just discussed, that had arisen with regards to the application of the Standard Valuation Law to certain types of life insurance plans, primarily term life insurance and universal life with secondary guarantees.

The Valuation of Life Insurance Policies Model Regulation refined the definition of the Commissioners Reserve Valuation Method for policies falling within the scope of this regulation. To mitigate its impact and to reflect advances in the underwriting process since the 1980 CSO Mortality Table was adopted, this model regulation also adopted a new set of select factors and rules for how these factors could be used.

The remainder of this chapter will discuss how statutory policy reserves would be determined for an n-year level term policy in accordance with the Valuation of Life Insurance Policies Model Regulation. This determination is rather complex so it will be broken down into five steps:

> *Step 1*: Determination of Contract Segments;
>
> *Step 2*: Calculation of Segmented Net Premiums;
>
> *Step 3*: Calculation of Segmented Reserves;
>
> *Step 4*: Calculation of Unitary Reserves; and
>
> *Step 5*: Calculation of Basic Reserves

7.3.1 CONTRACT SEGMENTATION METHOD

The Valuation of Life Insurance Policies Model Regulation (previously known as Actuarial Guideline XXX and Model Regulation 830) defines the **contract segmentation method** as "the method of dividing the period from issue to mandatory expiration of a policy into successive segments, with the length of each segment being defined as the period from the end of the prior segment (from policy inception, for the first segment) to the end of the latest policy year"[4] for which the yearly rate of increase of the gross premium is less than the yearly rate of increase of the valuation mortality rate. Algebraically, the length of each segment is defined as the maximum value of t for which

$$r^P_{[x]+k_i+t} < r^q_{[x]+k_i+t} \quad \text{and} \quad r^P_{[x]+k_i+t+1} \ge r^q_{[x]+k_i+t+1}$$

where

k_i = the number of policy years from the issue date to the beginning of the ith segment (where $k_1 = 0$);

$r^P_{[x]+k_i+t}$ = premium ratio;

$$= \begin{cases} \dfrac{GP_{[x]+k_i+t}}{GP_{[x]+k_i+t-1}} & \text{if } GP_{[x]+k_i+t} \ne 0 \text{ and } GP_{[x]+k_i+t-1} \ne 0 \\ 1,000 & \text{if } GP_{[x]+k_i+t} = 0 \text{ and } GP_{[x]+k_i+t-1} \ne 0 \\ 0 & \text{if } GP_{[x]+k_i+t} = 0 \text{ and } GP_{[x]+k_i+t-1} = 0 \end{cases};$$

$GP_{[x]+k_i+t}$ = guaranteed gross premium per unit of insurance for policy year $k_i + t$, excluding policy fees[5];

$r^q_{[x]+k_i+t}$ = mortality ratio[6];

$$= Max\left[1, \frac{q_{[x]+k_i+t}}{q_{[x]+k_i+t-1}}\right];$$

$q_{[x]+k_y+t}$ = valuation mortality rate for deficiency reserves excluding X-factors (which are discussed later) for policy year $k_i + t$.

---

[4] See [4], Paragraph B of Section 4 of "Valuation of Life Insurance Policies Model Regulation."

[5] The policy fee is excluded only if it is a level amount during the premium payment period

[6] This ratio may be increased or decreased by one percent in any policy year, but it can not be less than one.

As stated in the model regulation the purpose of the one percent tolerance in the $r^q_{[x]+k_i+t}$ "is to prevent irrational segment lengths due to such things as premium rounding. For example, consider a plan in which gross premiums are designed at some point to be a ratio times the underlying ultimate mortality rates, where the ratio varies by issue age. The resulting segments may be greater than one year, because the guaranteed gross premiums are not expressed in fractional cents. The tolerance factor allows the creation of one year segments for a plan in which premiums parallel the underlying valuation mortality table."[7]

Continuing with the example introduced at the beginning of this section, the following contract segments[8] would result:

Segment Information								
(1)	(2)	(3)	(4)	(5)	(6)	(7)	(8)	(9)
x	t	$GPM(t)$	$1000 \cdot q(t)$	$r^P(t)$	$r^q(t)$	i	k_i	n_i
50	0	5.00	3.73	1.000	1.000	1	0	10
51	1	5.00	4.07	1.000	1.080	1	0	10
52	2	5.00	4.69	1.000	1.143	1	0	10
53	3	5.00	5.40	1.000	1.142	1	0	10
54	4	5.00	5.96	1.000	1.093	1	0	10
55	5	5.00	6.57	1.000	1.093	1	0	10
56	6	5.00	7.25	1.000	1.094	1	0	10
57	7	5.00	8.07	1.000	1.103	1	0	10
58	8	5.00	8.86	1.000	1.088	1	0	10
59	9	5.00	9.75	1.000	1.091	1	0	10
60	10	7.58	12.64	1.516	1.286	2	10	1
61	11	9.06	13.94	1.195	1.093	3	11	1
62	12	10.79	15.42	1.191	1.096	4	12	1
63	13	12.83	17.11	1.189	1.100	5	13	1
64	14	15.22	19.02	1.186	1.102	6	14	1
65	15	16.90	21.13	1.110	1.101	7	15	1
66	16	19.89	23.40	1.177	1.097	8	16	1
67	17	23.27	25.86	1.170	1.095	9	17	1
68	18	27.08	28.50	1.164	1.092	10	18	1
69	19	29.81	31.38	1.101	1.091	11	19	1

Notice how the policy was segmented into a 10-year level premium term policy with a 10 year benefit period and a yearly renewable term policy, thereafter.

7.3.2 SEGMENTED NET PREMIUMS

The Valuation of Life Insurance Policies Model Regulation requires the determination of **segmented net premiums.** In particular, the model regulation specifies that "the net premiums within each segment are a uniform percentage of the respective guaranteed gross premiums within the segment"; and they are

---

[7] See [4], Paragraph B of Section 4 of "Valuation of Life Insurance Policies Model Regulation."

[8] In this exhibit, n_i = number of policy years in the ith segment.

determined such that, at the beginning of the segment, the present value of the net premiums within the segment equals:

(a) The present value of the death benefits within the segment, plus

(b) The present value of any unusual guaranteed cash value at the end of the segment, less

(c) Any unusual guaranteed cash value occurring at the start of the segment.

The determination of segmented net premiums is complicated by any **unusual guaranteed cash values**. A policy is considered to have an unusual pattern of guaranteed cash surrender values if any future guaranteed cash surrender value exceeds the prior year's guaranteed cash surrender value by more than the sum of:

(a) One hundred ten percent of the scheduled gross premium for that year;

(b) One hundred ten percent of one year's accrued interest on the sum of the prior year's guaranteed cash surrender value and the scheduled gross premium using the nonforfeiture interest rate used for calculating policy guaranteed cash surrender values; and

(c) Five percent of the first policy year surrender charge, if any.

These definitions lead to the following equation:

$$AB^1_{[x]+k_i:\overline{n_i}} + v^{n_i} \cdot {}_{n_i}p_{[x]+k_i} \cdot BW^u_{[x]+k_i+n_i} - BW^u_{[x]+k_i} = {}_{m_i}PB_{[x]+k_i:\overline{n_i}} \cdot \ddot{a}_{[x]+k_i:\overline{m_i}}$$

where

$$v = \text{discount factor;}$$
$$= \frac{1}{1+i};$$

$$n_i = \text{the length of the } i^{th} \text{ segment;}$$
$$= \begin{cases} k_1 & \text{if } i = 1 \\ k_i - k_{i-1} & \text{if } i > 1 \end{cases}$$

$AB^1_{[x]+k_i:\overline{n_i}}$ = present value of future death benefits within the ith segment at the beginning of the ith segment (i.e., duration k_i);

$BW^u_{[x]+k_i+n_i}$ = unusual guaranteed cash value at the end of the ith segment;

$BW^u_{[x]+k_i}$ = unusual guaranteed cash value at the beginning of the ith segment;

${}_{m_i}PB_{[x]+k_i:\overline{n_i}}$ = net premium in the first policy year of the ith segment; and

$\ddot{a}_{[x]+k_i:\overline{m_i}}$ = present value of annuity due within the ith segment at the beginning of the ith segment.

Using the valuation mortality table and interest rate, the present value of future death benefits as of duration $k_i + t$ is defined by the following formula:

$$AB^1_{[x]+k_i+t:\overline{n_i-t}|} = \sum_{s=0}^{n_i-t-1} v^{s+1} \cdot {}_sP_{[x]+k_i+t} \cdot q_{[x]+k_i+t+s} \cdot BD_{[x]+k_i+t+s}$$

where

v = discount factor;

= $\dfrac{1}{1+i}$;

${}_sP_{[x]+k_i+t}$ = probability that the insured who survived to duration $k_i + t$ will survive to duration $k_i + t + s$;

= $\displaystyle\prod_{r=0}^{s-1}(1 - q_{[x]+k_i+t+r})$;

$q_{[x]+k_i+t+s}$ = valuation mortality rate for attained age $x + k_i + t + s$;

$BD_{[x]+k_i+t+s}$ = death benefit amount[9] between durations $k_i + t + s$ and $k_i + t + s + 1$ and assumed to be paid at duration $k_i + t + s + 1$.

In order for the net premiums to be a constant percentage of the gross premiums, the pattern of gross premiums is reflected in the formula for the present value of an annuity as follows:

$$\ddot{a}_{[x]+k_i+t:\overline{m_i-t}|} = \sum_{s=0}^{m_i-t-1} v^s \cdot {}_sP_{[x]+k_i+t} \cdot r^{GP}_{[x]+k_i+t+s} \qquad \text{if} \qquad m_i \neq 0$$

where

m_i = length of the premium payment period within the ith segment;

= $\begin{cases} k_{i+1} - k_i & \text{if } m > k_{i+1} \\ m - k_i & \text{if } k_i < m < k_{i+1} \\ 0 & \text{if } k_i \geq m \end{cases}$

$r^{GP}_{[x]+k_i+t+s}$ = gross premium ratio;

= $\dfrac{GP_{[x]+k_i+t+s}}{GP_{[x]+k_i}}$; and

$GP_{[x]+k_i+t+s}$ = annual gross premium[10] due at duration $k_i + t + s$.

---

[9] This is the death benefit for the primary or base coverage of the policy. In most circumstances, it will be the face amount of the policy.

[10] This is the annual premium payable at the beginning of the policy year for the primary coverage of the policy. As noted above, it excludes the policy fee, if it is a level amount.

In the first segment, the segment reserve is determined using the Commissioners Reserve Valuation Method as discussed in Chapter 5. Accordingly, the net premiums in the first segment are determined using the following formula:

$$
_{m_1}P_{[x]+t:\overline{n_1}|} = \begin{cases} _{m_1}PB_{[x]:\overline{n_1}|} + {}_{m_1}PE_{[x]:\overline{n_1}|} - {}_{m_1}EA_{[x]}^{CRVM} & \text{if} \quad t=0 \\ r_{[x]+t}^{GP} \cdot \left({}_{m_1}PB_{[x]:\overline{n_1}|} + {}_{m_1}PE_{[x]:\overline{n_1}|} \right) & \text{if} \quad 0 < t \le m_1 \end{cases}
$$

where

$$
_{m_1}P_{[x]+t:\overline{n_1}|} = \text{net premium at duration } t;
$$

$$
_{m_1}PB_{[x]:\overline{n_1}|} = \frac{AB_{[x]:\overline{n_1}|}^1 + v^{n_1} \cdot {}_{n_1}p_{[x]} \cdot BW_{[x]+n_1}^u}{\ddot{a}_{[x]:\overline{m_1}|}}
$$

and

$$
_{m_1}PE_{[x]:\overline{n_1}|} = \frac{{}_{m_1}EA_{[x]}^{CRVM}}{\ddot{a}_{[x]:\overline{m_1}|}}
$$

For the other segments, the net premium at duration $k_i + t$ is determined using the following formula:

$$
_{m_i}PB_{[x]+k_i+t:\overline{n_i}|} = \begin{cases} \dfrac{AB_{[x]+k_i:\overline{n_i}|}^1 + v^{n_i} \cdot {}_{n_i}p_{[x]+k_i} \cdot BW_{[x]+k_i+n_i}^u - BW_{[x]+k_i}^u}{\ddot{a}_{[x]+k_i:\overline{m_i}|}} & \text{if} \quad m_i \ne 0 \quad \text{and} \quad t=0 \\ r_{[x]+k_i+t}^{GP} \cdot {}_{m_i}PB_{[x]+k_i:\overline{n_i}|} & \text{if} \quad m_i \ne 0 \quad \text{and} \quad 0 < t \le m_i \\ 0 & \text{if} \quad m_i = 0 \quad \text{and} \quad m_i = 0 \end{cases}
$$

where ${}_{m_i}PB_{[x]+k_i+t:\overline{n_i}|}$ = net level premium at duration $k_i + t$.

7.3.3 SEGMENTED RESERVES

The Valuation of Life Insurance Policies Model Regulation defines the ***segmented reserves*** as "reserves, calculated using segments produced by the contract segmentation method, equal to the present value of all future guaranteed benefits less the present value of all future net premiums to the mandatory expiration of a policy."[11] This definition leads to the following formulas. In the first segment, the segmented reserve is determined as follows:

$$
_t^{m_1}V_{[x]:\overline{n_1}|} = AB_{[x]+t:\overline{n_1-t}|}^1 + v^{n_1-t} \cdot {}_{n_1-t}p_{[x]+t} \cdot BW_{[x]+n_1}^u - {}_{m_1}P_{[x]:\overline{n_1}|} \cdot \ddot{a}_{[x]+t:\overline{m_1-t}|}
$$

where $_t^{m_1}V_{[x]:\overline{n_1}|}$ = segment reserve for the first segment at duration t.

---

[11] See [4], Paragraph G(1) of Section 4 of "Valuation of Life Insurance Policies Model Regulation."

For the other segments, the segmented reserve is determined using the following formula:

$$ {}^{m_i}_t V_{[x]+k_i:\overline{n_i}|} = AB^1_{[x]+k_i+t:\overline{n_i-t}|} + v^{n_i-t} \cdot {}_{n_i-t}P_{[x]+k_i} \cdot BW^u_{[x]+k_i+n_i} - BW^u_{[x]+k_i} - {}_{m_i}PB_{[x]+k_i:\overline{n_i}|} \cdot \ddot{a}_{[x]+k_i-t:\overline{m_i-t}|} $$

where ${}^{m_i}_t V_{[x]+k_i:\overline{n_i}|}$ = segment reserve for the first segment at duration $k_i + t$.

Continuing with the above example, the following segment reserves would result:

				**Segment Reserves**				
(1)	(2)	(3)	(4)	(5)		(6)	(7)	(8)
x	i	k_i	t	$AB(k_i+t)$	$-$	$P(k_i)$ $\cdot$	$\ddot{a}(k_i+t)$ $=$	$V(k_i+t)$
50	1	0	0	46,378		3,554	7.93990	0
51	1	0	1	45,134		6,171	7.31419	0
52	1	0	2	43,502		6,171	6.65697	2,423
53	1	0	3	41,182		6,171	5.96779	4,356
54	1	0	4	38,045		6,171	5.24451	5,683
55	1	0	5	34,195		6,171	4.48343	6,529
56	1	0	6	29,530		6,171	3.68179	6,811
57	1	0	7	23,931		6,171	2.83644	6,428
58	1	0	8	17,200		6,171	1.94395	5,204
59	1	0	9	9,285		6,171	1.00000	3,114
60	2	10	0	12,038		12,038	1.00000	0
61	3	11	0	13,276		13,276	1.00000	0
62	4	12	0	14,686		14,686	1.00000	0
63	5	13	0	16,295		16,295	1.00000	0
64	6	14	0	18,114		18,114	1.00000	0
65	7	15	0	20,124		20,124	1.00000	0
66	8	16	0	22,286		22,286	1.00000	0
67	9	17	0	24,629		24,629	1.00000	0
68	10	18	0	27,143		27,143	1.00000	0
69	11	19	0	29,886		29,886	1.00000	0

Notice how the reserves for the first segment are the same as the reserves for the ten-year level premium term policy with a ten year benefit period discussed at the beginning of this section.

7.3.4 UNITARY RESERVES

The Valuation of Life Insurance Policies Model Regulation defines the **unitary reserves** to be "the present value of all future guaranteed benefits less the present value of all future modified net premiums, where:

(a)   Guaranteed benefits and modified net premiums are considered to the mandatory expiration of the policy; and

(b)   Modified net premiums are a uniform percentage of the respective guaranteed gross premiums, where the uniform percentage is such that, at issue, the present value of the net premiums equals the present value of all death benefits and pure endowments, plus the excess of Item (i) over Item (ii), as follows:

(i) A net level annual premium equal to the present value, at the date of issue, of the benefits provided for after the first policy year, divided by the present value, at the date of issue, of an annuity of one per year payable on the first and each subsequent anniversary of the policy on which a premium falls due. However, the net level annual premium shall not exceed the net level annual premium on the nineteen-year premium whole life plan of insurance of the same renewal year equivalent level amount at an age one year higher than the age at issue of the policy.

(ii) A net one year term premium for the benefits provided for in the first policy year.[12]

This is the definition of the Commissioners Reserve Valuation Method discussed in Chapter 5 for an n-year, m-pay endowment policy and leads to the following unitary reserves:

							Unitary Reserves			
(1) (2)		(3)	(4)	(5)	(6)	(7)	(8)	(9)	(10)	(11)
x t		$AB(t)$	$- PB(0)$.	$\ddot{a}(t)$ =	$VB(t)$	$PE(0)$.	$\ddot{a}(t)$	$= VE(t)$	$P(t) = PB(t) - PE(t)$	$V(t) = VB(t) - VE(t)$
50	0	128,121	5,885	21.77246	0	112	21.77246	2,443	3,554	0
51	1	131,286	5,885	21.89278	2.456	112	21.89278	2,456	5,997	0
52	2	134,330	5,885	22.02698	4,711	112	22.02698	2,471	5,997	2,240
53	3	137,001	5,885	22.18232	6,468	112	22.18232	2,489	5,997	3,979
54	4	139,202	5,885	22.36222	7,610	112	22.36222	2,509	5,997	5,101
55	5	141,046	5,885	22.56472	8,263	112	22.56472	2,532	5,997	5,731
56	6	142,465	5,885	22.79267	8,341	112	22.79267	2,557	5,997	5,783
57	7	143,379	5,885	23.04940	7,743	112	23.04940	2,586	5,997	3,157
58	8	143,640	5,885	23.34014	6,294	112	23.34014	2,619	5,997	1,675
59	9	143,234	5,885	23.66676	3,965	112	23.66676	2,655	5,997	1,310
60	10	142,031	8,921	23.03443	599	170	24.03443	2,697	9,091	(2,098)
61	11	138,239	10,663	23.94704	(2,678)	203	23.94704	2,687	10,866	(5,365)
62	12	133,066	12,699	23.57036	(5,635)	242	23.57036	2,645	12,941	(8,279)
63	13	126,246	15,100	22.83510	(8,128)	288	22.83510	2,562	15,388	(10,690)
64	14	117,458	17,913	21.65303	(9,960)	342	21.65303	2,429	18,254	(12,390)
65	15	106,334	19,890	19.91833	(10,877)	379	19.91833	2,235	20,269	(13,112)
66	16	92,474	23,409	17.74010	(11,918)	446	17.74010	1,990	23,855	(13,909)
67	17	75,464	27,387	14.79644	(11,606)	522	14.79644	1,660	27,909	(13,267)
68	18	54,794	31,871	10.93227	(9,537)	608	10.93227	1,227	32,478	(10,764)
69	19	29,886	35,084	5.96200	(5,198)	669	5.96200	669	35,753	(5,867)
70	20	0								

7.3.5 BASIC RESERVES

The minimum reserve for a policy falling within the scope of the Valuation of Life Insurance Policies Model Regulation is the **basic reserve**. The basic reserve is the greater of the segmented reserve and the unitary reserve using the same valuation mortality table and select factors.

---

[12] See [4] Paragraph J(1) of Section 4 of "Valuation of Life Insurance Policies Model Regulation."

At the option of the insurer, the segmented net premiums and reserves can be determined using either of the following:

(1) Treat the unitary reserve, if greater than zero, applicable at the end of each segment as a pure endowment and subtract the unitary reserve, if greater than zero, applicable at the beginning of each segment from the present value of guaranteed life insurance and endowment benefits for each segment.

(2) Treat the guaranteed cash surrender value, if greater than zero, applicable at the end of each segment as a pure endowment; and subtract the guaranteed cash surrender value, if greater than zero, applicable at the beginning of each segment from the present value of guaranteed life insurance and endowment benefits for each segment.

The purpose of these optional adjustments is to avoid an unusually large increase in the minimum reserve at the start of a new segment.

The basic reserve for the sample policy used as an example in this section is as follows:

Basic Reserves				
(1)	(2)	(3)	(4)	(5)
x	t	${}^{Segment}V(t)$	${}^{Unitary}V(t)$	${}^{Basic}V(t) = Max\left[{}^{Segment}V(t),\ {}^{Unitary}V(t)\right]$
50	0	0	0	0
51	1	0	0	0
52	2	2,423	2,240	2,423
53	3	4,356	3,979	4,356
54	4	5,683	5,101	5,683
55	5	6,529	5,731	6,529
56	6	6,811	5,783	6,811
57	7	6,428	5,157	6,428
58	8	5,204	3,675	5,204
59	9	3,114	1,310	3,114
60	10	0	(2,098)	0
61	11	0	(5,365)	0
62	12	0	(8,279)	0
63	13	0	(10,690)	0
64	14	0	(12,390)	0
65	15	0	(13,112)	0
66	16	0	(13,909)	0
67	17	0	(13,267)	0
68	18	0	(10,764)	0
69	19	0	(5,867)	0
70	20	0		0

7.3.6 MINIMUM VALUE

The basic reserve may not be less than the tabular cost (i.e., one-year cost of insurance) for the balance of the policy year, if mean reserves are used in the preparation of the statutory annual statement. If mid-terminal reserves are used, then the basic reserve cannot be less than the tabular cost for the balance of the current model period (i.e., the period between the valuation date and next premium due date) or the paid-to-date, if later. In the above example, the mean reserve would be one-half the tabular cost starting in duration 10 since the basic terminal reserve is zero for durations 10 through 20.

7.3.7 DEFICIENCY RESERVES

A deficiency reserve must be established if the gross premium is less than the net premium. For purposes of determining whether a deficiency reserve must be established, the life insurance company can elect to recalculate the net premium using select mortality factors. If the life insurance company elects to use select factors for this test, the select factors may be:

(a)   the ten-year select mortality factors adopted with the 1980 amendments to the Standard Valuation Law; or

(b)   the twenty-year select mortality factors in the appendix of the Valuation of Life Insurance Policies Model Regulation[13].

In addition, the life insurance company may use X percent of the twenty-year select mortality factors in the appendix of the Valuation of Life Insurance Policies Model Regulation for the first segment. X is based on the life insurance company's experience subject to certain criteria specified in the Valuation of Life Insurance Policies Model Regulation.

The resulting net premium is the net premium for the segmented reserve when the segmented reserve exceeds the unitary reserve. Otherwise, it is the net premium for the unitary reserve.

If a deficiency reserve must be established, it is the excess of (a) or (b), where

(a)   is the basic reserve calculated using the gross premium instead of the net premium when the gross premium is less than the net premium[14]; and

(b)   is the basic reserve.

7.3.8 EXEMPTIONS

The Valuation of Life Insurance Policies Model Regulation has exemptions for certain types of policies to reflect that prior valuation methods were already adequate and sufficient. Two of these exceptions are for attained age[15] yearly renewable term and n-year renewal term.

Most life insurance companies would calculate the mean reserve for yearly renewable term as one-half the cost of insurance. These life insurance companies would also calculate a deficiency reserve as the present value from the valuation date to the expiry date of the excess, if any, of the cost of insurance over the corresponding gross premium. At the option of the life insurance company, they may continue to use these methods. A similar exemption exists for n-year renewable term.

---

[13] The select period is 25 years when using the 2001 CSO Mortality Table.

[14] This calculation is done using the select factors, if any, chosen by the life insurance company in the comparison of gross premiums to the net premiums.

[15] Attained age means the gross premium schedule is based on the attained age of the insured and does not have a select period.

7.1   EXERCISES

7.4.1   Key Terms

renewable and convertible term   level premium term
decreasing term   graded premium whole life
unitary method   term method
contract segment method

7.4.2   Questions

a.   Why was the Valuation of Life Insurance Policies Model Regulation adopted by the NAIC?

b.   Briefly describe the major steps to calculate policy reserves for an n-year level term plan under the Valuation of Life Insurance Policies Model Regulation.

c.   What is the contract segment method?

d.   How are the lengths of the segments determined under the contract segment method?

e.   What is the formula for the segments' net premiums and reserves under the contract segment method?

f.   What is the unitary reserve method? This method is the same as what other method?

Problems

a. Consider a level term policy issued to a 40 year old male nonsmoker with the following gross premiums:

Level Term			
(1)	(2)	(3)	(4)
Age	Duration	Fact Amount	Premium
40	0	1,000,000	3,000
41	1	1,000,000	3,000
42	2	1,000,000	3,000
43	3	1,000,000	3,000
44	4	1,000,000	3,000
45	5	1,000,000	4,000
46	6	1,000,000	4,000
47	7	1,000,000	4,000
48	8	1,000,000	4,000
49	9	1,000,000	4,000
50	10	1,000,000	6,000
51	11	1,000,000	6,000
52	12	1,000,000	6,000
53	13	1,000,000	6,000
54	14	1,000,000	6,000
55	15	1,000,000	6,000
56	16	1,000,000	6,000
57	17	1,000,000	6,000
58	18	1,000,000	6,000
59	19	1,000,000	6,000

(1) Calculate the number of segments under the contract segment method.

(2) Determine the length of each segment.

b. Using only the Excel workbook, Chapter 7.xls and the same assumptions for the 10-year level term policy introduced in Section 7.3, determine the statutory reserves for this policy.

Note: the variable, $GPM(t)$, in the "Segments" worksheet will need to be changed to reflect the above gross premium pattern.

8 ✧ Universal Life Insurance

8.1 Introduction

Whole life policies provide a guaranteed set of future cash values and death benefits for a specified premium. In other words, the terms are fixed and guaranteed[1] and statutory valuations have a long established history using prospective methods. Even participating products are easily valued using traditional valuation techniques since dividends are typically paid in cash, used to buy additional term coverage, used to buy paid-up additions, or used to pay premiums. With any of these options, dividends do not affect the basic coverage guaranteed by the terms of the contract.

Universal life policies develop cash surrender values that are based on a retrospective accumulation of premiums (which may be flexible) minus expense charges and cost of insurance charges, at a rate of interest declared by the company or based upon some index. In addition, the pattern of future death benefits may not be known. These features are not compatible with the valuation procedures used for whole life policies.

This chapter will discuss how policy reserves for the most common forms of universal life insurance are determined in a statutory valuation. Most of this discussion will be based on the Universal Life Insurance Model Regulation. This model regulation was adopted by the National Association of Insurance Commissioners to supplement existing insurance regulations with regards to such issues as valuation, nonforfeiture and cost disclosure.

8.2 Product Classification

Universal life insurance contracts have "terms that are not fixed and guaranteed," which means one or more of the following conditions exist:

- the amount and timing of premium payments may be varied by the policyholder within certain limits specified in the contract; or
- expense charges and cost of insurance charges are not guaranteed, except that they will not exceed certain rates specified in the contract; or
- benefits are not guaranteed at issue and will vary based on the amount and timing of premium payments, charges actually assessed, investment performance and other items.

Universal life contracts have a current set of expense charge rates, cost of insurance rates, and credited interest rates which are used to determine the actual expense charges, cost of insurance charges and benefits for each individual contract. The life insurance company can change these rates based on their expectation of future expenses, investment performance, mortality, persistency and other factors. However, the expense charge rates and cost of insurance rates cannot be increased above a set of guaranteed rates specified in the

---

[1] See Chapter 6 for a discussion of the phrase "fixed and guaranteed."

contract. In addition, the current credited interest rate cannot be decreased below a guaranteed rate specified in the contract.

8.2.1 FUND VALUE

Universal life insurance contracts typically have a "fund[2]." Premiums less expense charges are credited to this fund, along with periodic interest credits, and expense charges and cost of insurance charges are regularly deducted. The cash value, which is the amount available to the policyholder upon voluntary termination of the contract, may be equal to the fund, or it may be equal to the fund less a surrender charge[3].

The following table of policy values[4,5] illustrates the determination of the fund value and death benefit on a "current basis[6]" for a sample policy.

				Current Policy Values				
(1)	(2)	(3)	(4)	(5)	(6)	(7)	(8)	(9)
x	t	$^{C}FV(t)$	$+$ $^{C}GP(t)$	$-$ $^{C}EC(t)$	$-$ $^{C}TC(t)$	$+$ $^{C}IC(t)$	$=$ $^{C}FV(t+1)$	$^{C}BD(t)$
50	0	0	1,750	138	271	94	1,435	100,000
51	1	1,435	1,750	138	291	193	2,949	100,000
52	2	2,949	1,750	138	314	297	4,546	100,000
53	3	4,546	1,750	138	338	407	6,227	100,000
54	4	6,227	1,750	138	366	523	7,997	100,000
55	5	7,997	1,750	138	395	645	9,859	100,000
56	6	9,859	1,750	138	427	773	11,818	100,000
57	7	11,818	1,750	138	458	908	13,881	100,000
58	8	13,881	1,750	138	491	1,050	16,053	100,000
59	9	16,053	1,750	138	525	1,200	18,340	100,000
⋮	⋮	⋮	⋮	⋮	⋮	⋮	⋮	⋮
98	48	402,150	1,750	138	0	28,263	432,026	432.026

This worksheet centers around the following successive fund value formula:

$$_{t+1}FV_{[x]} = {}_{t}FV_{[x]} + GP_{[x]+t} - EC_{[x]+t} - TC_{[x]+t} + IC_{[x]+t}$$

---

[2] The term **fund value** will refer to the value of this fund and *cash surrender value* or *cash value* will be the fund value less any surrender penalties. Fund value is often referred to as account value or account balance.

[3] Surrender charge and surrender penalty will be used interchangeably. It is the charge assessed against the fund value for termination of the contract during the surrender charge period. This charge is not assessed on the death of the insured and usually expires before maturity.

[4] The superscript '*C*' will be used to denote that these policy values were calculated on a current basis. A superscript of '*G*' will denote that the policy values were calculated on a guaranteed basis.

[5] This workbook calculates values on an annual basis. In practice, most life insurance companies do these calculations on a monthly basis.

[6] **Current basis** will mean that the policy values were calculated using current expense charge, cost of insurance charge and credited interest rates. **Guaranteed basis** will mean that the policy values were calculated using guaranteed expense charge, cost of insurance charge and credited interest rates.

where

$$[x] = \text{issue age;}$$
$$x = \text{attained age}$$
$$_{t+1}FV_{[x]} = \text{fund value at duration } t+1;$$
$$_{t}FV_{[x]} = \text{fund value at duration } t;$$
$$GP_{[x]+t} = \text{gross premium collected at duration } t;$$
$$EC_{[x]+t} = \text{expense charge deducted at duration } t;$$
$$TC_{[x]+t} = \text{cost of insurance (or term charge) deducted at duration } t; \text{ and}$$
$$IC_{[x]+t} = \text{credited interest earned between } t \text{ and } t+1 \text{ and paid at duration } t+1.$$

Also, please note that in the above table the variable BD denotes death benefit.

This successive formula is similar to the successive reserve formula discussed in Chapter 2.

8.2.2 PREMIUMS

Universal life insurance contracts are classified as either flexible premium universal life or fixed premium universal life. A *flexible premium universal life* contract is defined as "a universal life insurance policy which permits the policyowner to vary, independently of each other, the amount or timing of one or more premium payments or the amount of insurance.[7]" *Fixed premium universal life* is a universal life insurance contract that does not satisfy this definition. In other words, the policyowner must pay a specified premium when due.

8.2.3 DEATH BENEFIT OPTIONS

Most universal life insurance contracts provide at least two *death benefit options* – a "level" death benefit or a "level" net amount at risk. The death benefit under the "level" death benefit option is the face amount unless the policy is "in the corridor" as explained below. This death benefit option is often called "Option 1" or "Option A." The death benefit under the "level" net amount at risk option is the face amount plus the fund value. This death benefit option is often called "Option 2" or "Option B."

To qualify as life insurance under the Internal Revenue Code and receive favorable tax treatment, the relationship of the death benefit to the fund value must satisfy either the guideline level premium test or the cash value accumulation test as defined in Section 7702 of the Internal Revenue Code. Most universal life contracts use the guideline level premium test.

Under the guideline level premium test, the death benefit must equal or exceed a certain multiple of the fund value. The percentages vary based on the attained age of the insured and these percentages are often called *corridor factors*. The following are the corridor factors for a policy issued in 1984 or later:

---

[7] See [4], Section 3, "Universal Life Insurance Model Regulation."

Corridor Factors					
Age	Factor	Age	Factor	Age	Factor
40 or younger	2.50				
41	2.43	61	1.28	81	1.05
42	2.36	62	1.26	82	1.05
43	2.29	63	1.24	83	1.05
44	2.22	64	1.24	84	1.05
45	2.15	65	1.20	85	1.05
46	2.09	66	1.19	86	1.05
47	2.03	67	1.18	87	1.05
48	1.97	68	1.17	88	1.05
49	1.91	69	1.16	89	1.05
50	1.85	70	1.15	90	1.05
51	1.78	71	1.13	91	1.04
52	1.71	72	1.11	92	1.03
53	1.64	73	1.09	93	1.02
54	1.57	74	1.07	94	1.01
55	1.50	75	1.05	95 & older	1.00
56	1.46	76	1.05		
57	1.42	77	1.05		
58	1.38	78	1.05		
59	1.34	79	105		
60	1.30	80	1.05		

The corridor factors can have a significant effect on the policy reserve under a statutory valuation.

8.3 UNIVERSAL LIFE INSURANCE MODEL REGULATION

Flexible premium products introduce special valuation problems using traditional methods in that some assumption as to future premiums is required. The typical "present value of future benefits less the present value of future net premiums" formula is challenging to apply to flexible premium universal life policies since neither "future premiums" nor "future benefits" are known for any particular policy.

Many of the early companies which sold universal life policies held the cash surrender value as a reserve and used the following rationale for doing so:

(1)   The cash value formula was the monthly equivalent of a retrospective reserve formula.

(2)   The product was sold as permanent coverage. Policyholders could, of course, develop many different benefit patterns depending on their level of contributions.

(3)   First year expense or surrender charges were typically less than the Commissioners Reserve Valuation Method (CRVM) expense allowance for permanent plans. Hence, the retrospective reserve could be argued to use less of an expense allowance than permitted under the Commissioners Reserve Valuation Method.

Other early entrants to the universal life market argued that, at any point in time, the product could be thought of as a paid-up policy, since no future premiums were required. On this basis, for front-loaded[8] products, the cash value was argued to be a proper reserve for future guaranteed benefits if policy guarantees of mortality and interest were identical to the valuation basis.

However, as products were developed which incorporated back-end loads[9] assessed only on surrender, it became a matter of some controversy as to whether the fund value, the cash value (net of surrender charges), or some intermediate value would be the appropriate reserve.

In December of 1983, the National Association of Insurance Commissioners adopted the Universal Life Insurance Model Regulation that sets forth minimum reserve standards for universal life policies. These standards represent an effort to fit universal life into traditional valuation methodologies. An assumption was made regarding future premium payments and a factor was developed to adjust for actual policy performance.

The minimum reserve standards specified in this regulation are rather involved. When the regulation was first adopted, it provided a challenge for many life insurance companies to implement in their existing valuation processes.

The following is a summary of the steps needed to be performed to determine the statutory reserve for a flexible premium universal life policy under this regulation:

(1)   A Guaranteed Maturity Premium is calculated using policy guarantees (i.e., guaranteed expense charges, cost of insurance charges, credited interest rates, etc.). The Guaranteed Maturity Premium is the level gross premium that provides for an endowment for the face amount at the latest permissible maturity date under the contract.

(2)   A set of Guaranteed Maturity Funds is calculated. Guaranteed Maturity Funds (GMFs) are the projected fund values calculated as of the issue date using policy guarantees and assuming that Guaranteed Maturity Premiums are paid.

(3)   The actual or current fund value at the valuation date must be known.

(4)   The policy fund is projected forward from the valuation date, on a guaranteed basis, using the larger of the current fund or the Guaranteed Maturity Fund at each future valuation date, and assuming that Guaranteed Maturity Premiums are paid. This projection produces a set of "guaranteed death benefits" and a "guaranteed endowment benefit" for valuation purposes.

(5)   A net level premium is calculated based on the plan of insurance produced at issue on a guaranteed basis assuming Guaranteed Maturity Premiums are paid.

(6)   The present value of future guaranteed benefits as of the valuation date is calculated. The guaranteed benefits are the set of "guaranteed death benefits" and "guaranteed endowment benefit" calculated in the fourth step.

(7)   The ratio, r-ratio, of the current fund value to the Guaranteed Maturity Fund at the valuation date is calculated. The r-ratio is never allowed to exceed 1.

(8)   A net level reserve is calculated as r-ratio times the difference between the present value of guaranteed benefits and the present value of net level premiums.

---

[8] A front-end load refers to expense charges that are assessed either against the premium at time of payment or against the fund value in the first policy year.

[9] A back-end load refers to charges that are assessed at time of surrender.

(9) The Commissioners Reserve Valuation Method reserve is calculated as the difference between the net level reserve determined in step eight, and *r*-ratio times the unamortized Commissioners Reserve Valuation Method expense allowance for the plan of insurance generated at issue on a guaranteed basis and assuming Guaranteed Maturity Premiums are paid.

In essence, the model regulation assumes that at issue, all universal life policies are permanent plans. The *r*-ratio is meant to measure the extent to which the policy is "on track" as a permanent plan. The remainder of this section will provide a detailed description of each of these steps.

8.1.1 EXAMPLE

Associated with this chapter is an Excel workbook, Chapter 8.xls. This workbook will be used to illustrate the determination of the statutory reserve for a flexible premium universal life policy. The policy used for illustration purposes will be a universal life policy issued to a 50 year old male on September 1, 2000. The policy will mature at age 99 or September 1, 2049 for the value of the fund at that time. This information is captured in the first worksheet, "Parameters", of this workbook:

Parameters	
Issue Date	9/1/2000
Maturity Date	9/1/2049
Valuation Date	12/31/2005
Issue Age	50
Gender	Male ▼
Gross Premium	1,750 ⇐ If 0, premium will be calculated
Premium Payment Mode	49 years
Premium Payment Period	Annual ▼
Face Amount	100,000
Death Benefit Option	Face Amount ▼
Fund Value	0
Statutory Valuation Standard:	
Mortality Table	1980 CSO ▼
Interest Rate	4.50%
Method	CRVM ▼
Function	Curtate ▼
Age Rule	ANB ▼
Smoking Class	Nonsmoker ▼
Select Period	Aggregate ▼

UNIVERSAL LIFE INSURANCE ❖ 125

8.3.2 GUARANTEED MATURITY VALUES

The **Guaranteed Maturity Premium** is the level gross premium, paid on the issue date and periodically thereafter during the premium payment period, that provides for an endowment for the face amount at the latest permissible maturity date under the contract. As its name implies, the Guaranteed Maturity Premium is calculated as of the issue date using policy guarantees as to expense charges, cost of insurance charges and interest credits.

Guaranteed Maturity Fund at any duration is the "amount which, together with future guaranteed maturity premiums, will mature the policy based on all policy guarantees at issue."[10] The Guaranteed Maturity Fund is used to determine a scale of future benefits which, in turn, is used to determine the net level premium. If there are no structural changes to the policy (e.g., face amount changes), then the Guaranteed Maturity Premium and Guaranteed Maturity Fund Values are fixed at issue. If there are structural changes to the policy (e.g., face amount changes), then the Guaranteed Maturity Premium and Guaranteed Maturity Fund Values are recalculated reflecting the changes.

The worksheet "GMPV" shows how Guaranteed Maturity Premiums, $^{GM}GP_{[x]+t}$, and Guaranteed Maturity Fund Values, $^{GM}_{t}FV_{[x]}$, were determined as of the issue date of the illustrative policy[11]:

Guaranteed Maturity Policy Values								
(1)	(2)	(3)	(4)	(5)	(6)	(7)	(8)	(9)
x	t	$^{GM}FV(t)$ +	$^{GM}GP(t)$ −	$^{GM}EC(t)$ −	$^{GM}TC(t)$ +	$^{GM}IC(t)$ =	$^{GM}FV(t+1)$	$^{GM}BD(t)$
50	0	0	2,347	167	461	77	1,796	100,000
51	1	1,796	2,347	167	493	157	3,639	100,000
52	2	3,639	2,347	167	530	238	5,527	100,000
53	3	5,527	2,347	167	569	321	7,458	100,000
54	4	7,458	2,347	167	614	406	9,430	100,000
55	5	9,430	2,347	167	663	493	11,439	100,000
56	6	11,439	2,347	167	714	581	13,485	100,000
57	7	13,485	2,347	167	767	670	15,568	100,000
58	8	15,568	2,347	167	821	762	17,689	100,000
59	9	17,689	2,347	167	880	855	19,844	100,000
⋮	⋮	⋮	⋮	⋮	⋮	⋮	⋮	⋮
98	48	93,514	2,347	167	0	4,306	100,000	100,000

Guaranteed Maturity Values will refer to the set of policy values calculated as of the issue date. The Guaranteed Maturity Values for this illustrative policy define a plan of insurance that is essentially an *n*-pay, *n*-year endowment where *n* equals 49.

8.3.3 CURRENT VALUES

To determine the policy reserve, the actual or current fund value at the valuation date must be known. For illustration purposes, the values in the worksheet "CPV" will be used for this purpose:

---

[10] See [4], Paragraph B of Section 5 of the "Universal Life Insurance Model Regulation."

[11] The superscript "GM" denotes Guaranteed Maturity.

				Current Policy Values				
(1)	(2)	(3)	(4)	(5)	(6)	(7)	(8)	(9)
x	t	$^{C}FV(t)$ +	$^{C}GP(t)$ −	$^{C}EC(t)$ −	$^{C}TC(t)$ +	$^{C}IC(t)$ =	$^{C}FV(t+1)$	$^{C}BD(t)$
50	0	0	1,750	138	271	94	1,435	100,000
51	1	1,435	1,750	138	291	193	2,949	100,000
52	2	2,949	1,750	138	314	297	4,546	100,000
53	3	4,546	1,750	138	338	407	6,227	100,000
54	4	6,227	1,750	138	366	523	7,997	100,000
55	5	7,997	1,750	138	395	645	9,859	100,000
56	6	9,859	1,750	138	427	773	11,818	100,000
57	7	11,818	1,750	138	458	908	13,881	100,000
58	8	13,881	1,750	138	491	1,050	16,053	100,000
59	9	16,053	1,750	138	525	1,200	18,340	100,000
⋮	⋮	⋮	⋮	⋮	⋮	⋮	⋮	⋮
98	48	402,150	1,750	138	0	28,263	432,026	432,026

Current values will be used to refer to the policy values calculated on a current basis reflecting actual experience up to the valuation date.

To illustrate this concept, the values in the "CPV" worksheet and the "GMPV" worksheet were based on the policy values assumptions appearing in the worksheet "PVA":

				Policy Value Assumptions					
(1)	(2)	(3)	(4)	(5)	(6)	(7)	(8)	(9)	(10)
x	t	$RGP(t)$	$ECGP(t)$	$ECP(t)$	$^{G}TCM(t)$	$^{G}ic(t)$	$^{C}TCM(t)$	$^{C}ic(t)$	$RBD(t)$
50	0	1.00	.0500	50.00	4.91	.0450	2.95	.0700	1.85
51	1	1.00	.0500	50.00	5.35	.0450	3.21	.0700	1.78
52	2	1.00	.0500	50.00	5.86	.0450	3.52	.0700	1.71
53	3	1.00	.0500	50.00	6.43	.0450	3.86	.0700	1.64
54	4	1.00	.0500	50.00	7.09	.0450	4.25	.0700	1.57
55	5	1.00	.0500	50.00	7.82	.0450	4.69	.0700	1.50
56	6	1.00	.0500	50.00	8.63	.0450	5.18	.0700	1.46
57	7	1.00	.0500	50.00	9.49	.0450	5.69	.0700	1.42
58	8	1.00	.0500	50.00	10.42	.0450	6.25	.0700	1.38
59	9	1.00	.0500	50.00	11.47	.0450	6.88	.0700	1.34
⋮	⋮	⋮	⋮	⋮	⋮	⋮	⋮	⋮	⋮
98	48	1.00	.0500	50.00	657.98	.0450	394.79	.0700	1.00

In this workbook, the variable *RGP* is the premium payment ratio and indicates what portion of the billed premium is actually paid.

8.3.4 GUARANTEED VALUES

The policy fund is projected forward from the valuation date, on a guaranteed basis, using the larger of the actual fund or the Guaranteed Maturity Fund, and assuming that Guaranteed Maturity Premiums are paid. This projection produces a set of *guaranteed values*.

The worksheet "GPV" shows how the guaranteed values were determined as of the valuation date:

Guaranteed Policy Values								
(1) (2)		(3)	(4)	(5)	(6)	(7)	(8)	(9)
x $\quad t$		$^{G}FV(t)$ +	$^{G}GP(t)$ −	$^{G}EC(t)$ −	$^{G}TC(t)$ +	$^{G}IC(t)$ =	$^{G}FV(t+1)$	$^{G}BD(t)$
55	5	9,430	2,347	167	663	493	11,439	100,000
56	6	11,439	2,347	167	714	581	13,485	100,000
57	7	13,485	2,347	167	767	670	15,568	100,000
58	8	15,568	2,347	167	821	762	17,689	100,000
59	9	17,689	2,347	167	880	855	19,844	100,000
60	10	19,844	2,347	167	943	949	22,029	100,000
61	11	22,029	2,347	167	1,011	1,044	24,242	100,000
62	12	24,242	2,347	167	1,085	1,140	26,477	100,000
63	13	26,477	2,347	167	1,167	1,237	28,727	100,000
64	14	28,727	2,347	167	1,256	1,334	30,985	100,000
⋮	⋮	⋮	⋮	⋮	⋮	⋮	⋮	⋮
98	48	93,514	2,347	167	0	4,306	100,000	100,000

For this illustration, the Guaranteed Maturity Fund and current fund value at the end of the fifth policy year ($t = 5$) are:

$$\text{Guaranteed Maturity Fund Value at } t = 5 \qquad \$9,430$$
$$\text{Current Fund Value at } t = 5 \qquad 7,997$$

Since the Guaranteed Maturity Fund is larger than the current fund value, the guaranteed values are calculated using the Guaranteed Maturity Fund. Notice the resulting values are the same as the values in the worksheet "GMPV"[12].

By the end of the fourteenth policy year, the current fund value is projected to exceed the Guaranteed Maturity Fund for the first time:

$$\text{Guaranteed Maturity Fund Value at } t = 14 \qquad \$28,727$$
$$\text{Current Fund Value at } t = 14 \qquad 28,765$$

So if the valuation date was December 31, 2014 instead, the following guaranteed values would result:

---

[12] If the life insurance company guarantees the current cost of insurance rate or current credited interest rate to the next policy anniversary, then the guaranteed fund value would be calculated using the current cost of insurance rate or current credited interest rate until the next policy anniversary.

				Guaranteed Policy Values				
(1)	(2)	(3)	(4)	(5)	(6)	(7)	(8)	(9)
x	t	$^{G}FV(t)$ +	$^{G}GP(t)$ −	$^{G}EC(t)$ −	$^{G}TC(t)$ +	$^{G}IC(t)$ =	$^{G}FV(t+1)$	$^{G}BD(t)$
64	14	28,765	2,347	167	1,255	1,336	31,026	100,000
65	15	31,026	2,347	167	1,349	1,434	33,290	100,000
66	16	33,290	2,347	167	1,443	1,531	35,558	100,000
67	17	35,558	2,347	167	1,539	1,629	37,828	100,000
68	18	37,828	2,347	167	1,634	1,727	40,101	100,000
69	19	40,101	2,347	167	1,730	1,825	42,375	100,000
70	20	42,375	2,347	167	1,834	1,922	44,643	100,000
71	21	44,643	2,347	167	1,979	2,018	46,862	100,000
72	22	46,862	2,347	167	2,074	2,114	49,082	100,000
73	23	49,082	2,347	167	2,213	2,207	51,256	100,000
⋮	⋮	⋮	⋮	⋮	⋮	⋮	⋮	⋮
98	48	112,007	2,347	167	0	5,138	119,325	119,325

Notice the resulting values are no longer the same as the values in the worksheet "GMPV." In fact, the maturity value is now $119,325. This will have a direct effect on the policy reserve.

8.3.5 NET LEVEL PREMIUM RESERVES

Net level premiums are calculated based on the plan of insurance produced at issue on a guaranteed basis assuming Guaranteed Maturity Premiums are paid. In other words, it is based on the Guaranteed Maturity Values and utilizes the same formulas that were discussed in Chapter 5:

$$_{m}PB_{[x]:\overline{n}|} = \frac{AB_{[x]:\overline{n}|}}{\ddot{a}_{[x]:\overline{m}|}}$$

and

$$AB_{[x]:\overline{n}|} = \sum_{s=0}^{n-1} v^{t+1} \cdot {}_{t}p_{[x]} \cdot q_{[x]+t} \cdot BD_{[x]+t} + v^{n} \cdot {}_{n}p_{[x]} \cdot BM_{[x]+n}$$

where

$_{m}PB_{[x]:\overline{n}|}$ = net level premium;

$AB_{[x]:\overline{n}|}$ = present value of future benefits;

$BD_{[x]+t}$ = death benefit amount between durations t and t+1 and assumed to be paid at duration t+1;

    = $^{GM}BD_{[x]+t}$;

    = Guaranteed Maturity Death Benefit; and

$BM_{[x]+n}$ = maturity benefit amount paid on the maturity date;

    = $^{GM}_{n}FV_{[x]}$; and

    = Guaranteed Maturity Fund Value at maturity.

To calculate the net level premium reserve, the present value of future guaranteed benefits as of the valuation date must be determined. The guaranteed benefits are the set of "guaranteed death benefits" and the "guaranteed endowment benefit" starting on the valuation date resulting from the projection of the larger of the current fund or the Guaranteed Maturity Fund. In other words, it is based on the Guaranteed Values. This definition leads to a refinement of the formula that was discussed in Chapter 5:

$$AB_{[x]+[t]:\overline{n-t}|} = \sum_{s=0}^{n-t-1} v^{s+1} \cdot {}_sP_{[x]+t} \cdot q_{[x]+t+s} \cdot BD_{[x]+[t]+s} + v^{n-t} \cdot {}_{n-t}P_{[x]+t} \cdot BM_{[x]+n}$$

where

$[t]$ = denotes the "state" of the policy on the valuation date.

For example, on December 31, 2005 the guaranteed death benefits and guaranteed maturity benefit were $100,000. On December 31, 2014, the guaranteed maturity benefit increased from $100,000 to $119,325 because the current fund value was larger than the guaranteed maturity fund value. In other words, the following relationship is not always true:

$$AB_{[x]+[t-1]+1:\overline{n-t}|} = AB_{[x]+[t]:\overline{n-t}|}$$

In fact, for the illustrative policy,

$$AB_{[x]+[t-s]+s:\overline{n-t}|} = AB_{[x]+[t]:\overline{n-t}|} \quad \text{if} \quad 0 \le t \le 13$$

and

$$AB_{[x]+[t-s]+s:\overline{n-t}|} < AB_{[x]+[t]:\overline{n-t}|} \quad \text{if} \quad 13 < t$$

where

$AB_{[x]+[t-s]+s:\overline{n-t}|}$ = present value at duration t of future benefits on the valuation date associated with $[t-s]$; and

$AB_{[x]+[t]:\overline{n-t}|}$ = present value at duration t of future benefits on the valuation date associated with $[t]$.

This relationship is the result of the following relationship between Guaranteed Maturity Fund Values and current fund values:

$$_{[t]}^{C}FV_{[x]} < {}_{t}^{GM}FV_{[x]} \quad \text{if} \quad 0 \le t \le 13$$

and

$$_{[t]}^{C}FV_{[x]} > {}_{t}^{GM}FV_{[x]} \quad \text{if} \quad 13 < t$$

Finally, the net level premium reserve is calculated using the following formula:

$$_{[t]}^{m}VB_{[x]:\overline{n}|} = r_{[x]+[t]}^{FV} \cdot \left[AB_{[x]+[t]:\overline{n-t}|} - {}_mPB_{[x]:\overline{n}|} \cdot \ddot{a}_{[x]+t:\overline{m-t}|} \right]$$

where

$_{[t]}^{m}VB_{[x]:\overline{n}|}$ = net level premium reserve at duration t on the valuation date;

$$r^{FV}_{[x]+[t]} = \text{"r-ratio" at duration } t \text{ on the valuation date;}$$

$$= \text{smaller of } \begin{cases} \dfrac{^{C}_{t}FV_{[x]}}{^{GM}_{t}FV_{[x]}} \\ 1 \end{cases}$$

The net level premium reserve for the illustrative policy is as follows:

				Net Level Premium Reserve			
(1)	(2)	(3)	(4)	(5)	(6)	(7)
x	t	$RFV(t+1)$ ·	$[AB(t)$ −	$PB(0)$ ·	$\ddot{a}(t)]$ =	$VB(t)$
50	0	0.80	33,607	2,180	15.42	0
51	1	0.81	34,799	2,180	15.14	1,456
52	2	0.82	36,023	2,180	14.86	2,993
53	3	0.84	37,276	2,180	14.57	4,615
54	4	0.85	38,559	2,180	14.27	6,325
55	5	0.86	39,868	2,180	13.96	8,127
56	6	0.88	41,202	2,180	13.65	10,025
57	7	0.89	42,560	2,180	13.34	12,023
58	8	0.91	43,943	2,180	13.02	14,128
59	9	0.92	45,351	2,180	12.69	16,349
60	10	0.94	46,782	2,180	12.36	18,690
61	11	0.96	48,233	2,180	12.02	21,159
62	12	0.98	49,702	2,180	11.68	23,763
63	13	1.00	51,186	2,180	11.34	26,477
64	14	1.00	52,718	2,180	10.99	28,765
65	15	1.00	54,873	2,180	10.64	31,679

8.3.6 COMMISSIONERS MINIMUM VALUATION RESERVE

The Commissioners Reserve Valuation Method reserve is calculated as the difference between the net level reserve and, the "r-ratio" times the unamortized Commissioners Reserve Valuation Method expense allowance. Similar to the net level premium, this expense allowance is determined for the plan of insurance generated at issue on a guaranteed basis and assuming Guaranteed Maturity Premiums are paid. In other words, it is based on the Guaranteed Maturity Values and utilizes the same formulas that were discussed in Chapter 5:

$$_{m}EA^{CRVM}_{[x]:\overline{n}|} = \begin{cases} _{m}EA^{FPT}_{[x]:\overline{n}|} & \text{if } _{m}EA^{FPT}_{[x]} < _{20}EA^{FPT}_{[x]:\overline{n}|} \\ _{20}EA^{FPT}_{[x]:\overline{n}|} & \text{if } _{m}EA^{FPT}_{[x]} \geq _{20}EA^{FPT}_{[x]:\overline{n}|} \end{cases}$$

The unamortized Commissioners Reserve Valuation Method expense allowance is calculated using the following formula:

$$^{m}_{[t]}VE_{[x]:\overline{n}|} = r^{FV}_{[x]+[t]} \cdot _{m}PE_{[x]:\overline{n}|} \cdot \ddot{a}_{[x]+t:\overline{m-t}|}.$$

The worksheet "SR" shows the calculation of the Commissioners Reserve Valuation Method reserves for the illustrative policy[13]:

										$P(t) =$	$V(t) =$
(1)	(2)	(3)	(4)	(5)	(6)	(7)	(8)	(9)	(10)	(11)	(12)
x	t	$AB(t)$	$- PB(0) \cdot$	$\ddot{a}(t)$	$= VB(t)$	$PE(0) \cdot$	$\ddot{a}(t)$	$= VE(t)$	$RFV(t+1)$	$RFV(t+1)$ $\cdot[PB(t)$ $-PE(t)]$	$RFV(t+1)$ $\cdot[VB(t)$ $-VE(t)]$
50	0	33,607	2,180	15.41791	0	119	15.41791	1,828	0.79916	375	0
51	1	34,799	2,180	15.14106	1,796	119	15.14106	1,796	0.81052	1,863	0
52	2	36,023	2,180	14.85689	3,639	119	14.85689	1,762	0.82246	1,890	1,521
53	3	37,276	2,180	14.56581	5,527	119	14.56581	1,727	0.83496	1,919	3,125
54	4	38,559	2,180	14.26801	7,458	119	14.26801	1,692	0.84810	1,949	4,814
55	5	39,868	2,180	13.96408	9,430	119	13.96408	1,656	0.86190	1,981	6,593
56	6	41,202	2,180	13.65424	11,439	119	13.65424	1,619	0.87640	2,014	8,464
57	7	42,560	2,180	13.33879	13,485	119	13.33879	1,582	0.89159	2,049	10,432
58	8	43,943	2,180	13.01757	15,568	119	13.01757	1,544	0.90749	2,086	12,504
59	9	45,351	2,180	12.69060	17,689	119	12.69060	1,505	0.92422	2,124	14,687
⋮	⋮	⋮	⋮	⋮	⋮	⋮	⋮	⋮	⋮	⋮	⋮
98	48	404,330	2,180	1.00000	402,150	119	1.0000	119	1.00000	2,298	402,032
99	49	422,525									

Note that the above formulas define terminal reserves for the policy. Appropriate adjustments would have to be made in order to calculate mean reserves.

8.3.7 SUCCESSIVE RESERVES

The r-ratio and the projection of the larger of the current fund value or Guaranteed Maturity Fund Value necessitate modifications of the successive reserve formula for a whole life policy discussed in Chapter 6 as follows:

$$_{[t]+1}^{m}V_{[x]:\overline{n}|} = {}_{[t-1]+1}^{m}V_{[x]:\overline{n}|} + {}_{m}P_{[x]+[t]:\overline{n}|} + I_{[x]+[t]} - B_{[x]+[t]}^{d} + {}_{[t]}^{m}V_{[x]}^{d} - \Delta{}_{[t]}^{m}V_{[x]}$$

where

$$_{[t]+1}^{m}V_{[x]:\overline{n}|} = \text{reserve at duration } t+1 \text{ as of the valuation date associated with } [t];$$

$$_{[t-1]+1}^{m}V_{[x]:\overline{n}|} = \text{reserve at duration } t \text{ as of the valuation date associated with } [t-1];$$

$$_{m}P_{[x]+[t]:\overline{n}|} = \text{net premium at duration } t;$$

$$= r_{[x]+[t]}^{FV} \cdot \left[{}_{m}PB_{[x]+t:\overline{n}|} + {}_{m}PE_{[x]+t:\overline{n}|} \right]$$

$$I_{[x]+[t]} = \text{tabular interest between } t \text{ and } t+1;$$

$$= \left[{}_{[t]}^{m}V_{[x]:\overline{n}|} + {}_{m}P_{[x]+[t]:\overline{n}|} \right] \cdot i_{t}$$

$$B_{[x]+[t]}^{d} = \text{tabular death benefits between } t \text{ and } t+1;$$

$$= {}^{G}BD_{[x]+[t]} \cdot q_{[x]+t}$$

---

[13] In this worksheet, the net level premium reserve and unamortized expense allowance have not been multiplied by the r-ratio.

$$_{[t]+1}^{m}V_{[x]}^{d} = \text{reserves released on death between } t \text{ and } t+1;$$

$$= {}_{[t]+1}^{m}V_{[x]:\overline{n}|} \cdot q_{[x]+t}$$

$\Delta_{[t]}^{m}V_{[x]} = $ change in reserve due to changes in guaranteed values between the valuation date associated with $[t]$ and the valuation date associated with $[t-1]$

$$= {}_{[t-1]+1}^{m}V_{[x]:\overline{n}|} \cdot \left[\frac{r_{[x]+[t]}^{FV}}{r_{[x]+[t-1]+1}^{FV}} - 1 \right] + \left[AB_{[x]+[t]:\overline{n-t}|} - AB_{[x]+[t-1]+1:\overline{n-t}|} \right]$$

The workbook "SSR" shows the calculation of the successive Commissioners Reserve Valuation Method reserves for the illustrative policy:

		Successive Statutory Reserves						
(1)	(2)	(3)	(4)	(5)	(6)	(7)	(8)	(9)
x	t	$V(t)$	$+ P(t)$	$+ I(t)$	$- B^d(t)$	$+ V^d(t)$	$+\Delta V(t)$	$= V(t+1)$
50	0	0	375	17	392	0	0	0
51	1	0	1,863	84	434	8	0	1,521
52	2	1,521	1,890	155	482	18	22	3,125
53	3	3,125	1,919	229	537	31	47	4,814
54	4	4,814	1,949	308	601	47	76	6,593
55	5	6,593	1,981	391	674	66	107	8,464
56	6	8,464	2,014	478	756	90	142	10,432
57	7	10,432	2,049	570	846	119	181	12,504
58	8	12,504	2,086	667	946	153	223	14,687
59	9	14,687	2,124	769	1,060	195	271	16,985
⋮	⋮	⋮	⋮	⋮	⋮	⋮	⋮	⋮
98	48	402,032	2,298	18,195	278,013	278,013	0	422,525

The formula $\Delta_{[t]}^{m}V_{[x]}$ is a direct result of the r-ratio and the projection of the larger of the current fund value or Guaranteed Maturity Fund Value. For the illustrative policy, the r-ratio increases for the first thirteen policy years, and as a result, the reserve is adjusted upward as a result of this increase by the following adjustment:

$$_{[t-1]+1}^{m}V_{[x]:\overline{n}|} \cdot \left[\frac{r_{[x]+[t]}^{FV}}{r_{[x]+[t-1]+1}^{FV}} - 1 \right]$$

Starting in the fourteenth policy year and thereafter, guaranteed values increase and the reserve is adjusted upward by the change in the present value of the guaranteed benefits:

$$\left[AB_{[x]+[t]:\overline{n-t}|} - AB_{[x]+[t-1]+1:\overline{n-t}|} \right]$$

The worksheet "Delta V" shows a further analysis of this term of the successive reserve formula for the illustrative policy:

				Analysis of $\Delta V(t)$					
(1)	(2)	(3)	(4)	(5)	(6)	(7)	(8)	(9)	(10)
x	t	$RFV(t)$	$\frac{RFV(t+1)}{RFV(t)}-1$ $\cdot$	$V(t)$	$(3)\cdot(4)$	$AB(t+1)$ $-$	$AB(t)+1$ $=$	$\Delta AB(t)$	$\frac{(6)+(9)}{\Delta V(t)}$
50	0	1.00000							
50	1	0.79916	(0.20084)	0	0	34,799	34,799	0	0
51	2	0.81052	0.01423	0	0	36,023	36,023	0	0
52	3	0.82246	0.01473	1,521	22.40	37,276	37,276	0	22.40
53	4	0.83496	0.01520	3,125	47.48	38,559	38,559	0	47.48
54	5	0.84810	0.01574	4,814	75.79	39,868	39,868	0	75.49
55	6	0.86190	0.01627	6,593	107.29	41,202	41,202	0	107.29
56	7	0.87640	0.01682	8,464	142.36	42,560	42,560	0	142.36
57	8	0.89159	0.01733	10,432	180.74	43,943	43,943	0	180.74
58	9	0.90749	0.01784	12,504	223.08	45,351	45,351	0	223.08
⋮	⋮	⋮	⋮	⋮	⋮	⋮	⋮	⋮	⋮
97	48	1.00000	0.00000	374,051	0	404,330	395,527	8,803.26	8,803.26
98	49	1.00000	0.00000	402,032	0	422,525	422,525	0	0

8.3.8 ALTERNATIVE MINIMUM RESERVES

Alternative minimum reserves may be required for flexible premium universal life plans if the Guaranteed Maturity Premium is less than the valuation net premium for the plan of insurance produced at issue, on a guaranteed basis, assuming that Guaranteed Maturity Premiums are paid.

If the Guaranteed Maturity Premium is less than the valuation net premium calculated using minimum standards of mortality and interest, then the reserve held shall be the larger of (a) or (b), defined below:

(a) is the reserve calculated according to the reserve method, mortality basis, and valuation interest rate actually used for the policy, and

(b) is the reserve calculated by the reserve method actually used for the policy but using the minimum standards of mortality and interest allowable for deficiency reserves and replacing the valuation net premium by the Guaranteed Maturity Premium.

Following the Universal Life Insurance Model Regulation precisely, one discovers that, unlike for traditional insurance plans, the expense deferral portion of the valuation net premium has been dealt with separately by referring to an unamortized expense allowance and a net level premium separately. Thus, the "valuation net premium" referred to above is not explicitly defined in the Universal Life Insurance Model Regulation.

It is the interpretation of most companies that a valuation net premium should be determined for the purpose of calculating alternative minimum reserves as

$$ {}_m P_{[x]:\overline{n|}} = {}_m PB_{[x]:\overline{n|}} + {}_m PE_{[x]:\overline{n|}} $$

Product features that can lead to alternative minimum reserves include the following:

(1) No-load products[14] can develop alternative minimum reserves if the guaranteed mortality charges and interest rates are very similar to the valuation basis.

(2) Guaranteed cost of insurance rates that are lower than valuation mortality can lead to alternative minimum reserves, especially if the guaranteed interest rate equals the valuation interest rate and the level of front-end loads is fairly low.

(3) Guaranteed interest rates in excess of the valuation rate can lead to alternative minimum reserves, especially if the guaranteed cost of insurance rates equal the valuation mortality and the level of loads is fairly low.

(4) Any product feature that tends to lower the Guaranteed Maturity Premium creates the potential for alternative minimum reserves. In other words, any guarantee that is more liberal than the corresponding valuation assumption creates this potential.

8.3.9 FIXED PREMIUM UNIVERSAL LIFE

Many companies offer products whose cash values are calculated using universal life accumulation procedures, but which lack complete flexibility in premium payments. Some of these products also offer the policyholder a "secondary guarantee[15]." Secondary guarantees are discussed in detail later in this chapter.

When these products were first sold, the typical reserving practice was to hold the higher of (a) or (b) as a statutory reserve, where:

(a) is a traditionally calculated Commissioners Reserve Valuation Method reserve for the plan of insurance provided by the secondary guarantee, and

(b) is the actual cash value.

This sort of product fits traditional statutory valuation rules and procedures far better than flexible premium universal life. At any point in time, the present value of future benefits can be determined and future premium payments are fixed (although they may be waived through a "vanishing premium[16]" provision).

This product falls under a similar set of valuation rules set out in the Universal Life Insurance Model Regulation. The key differences in the valuation procedure for fixed premium policies are as follows:

(1) The Guaranteed Maturity Premium is equal to the gross premium.

(2) The expense allowance and the rate of amortization are determined by the plan of insurance guaranteed at issue.

(3) The r-ratio always equals one.

Given these parameters, the procedure to calculate Commissioners Reserve Valuation Method reserves can be simplified for fixed premium products as follows:

(1) Project future benefits on a guaranteed basis, taking secondary guarantees into account where necessary.

(2) Value the benefits described above using valuation mortality and interest.

---

[14] A no-load product is a product that has no front-end loads and no surrender charges.

[15] "Primary guarantees" are the guaranteed expense charge rates, cost of insurance rates and credited interest rates specified in the contract.

[16] "Vanishing premium" is when the fund value has sufficient "excess funds" to pay the premium when due. The "excess funds" usually are due to interest being credited more favorably than the guaranteed rate or lower charges being deducted than the guaranteed rates.

(3)   Subtract the present value of future Commissioners Reserve Valuation Method net premiums for the plan of insurance guaranteed at issue.

The need to project future benefits based on the actual policy fund value causes these reserves to be cumbersome to calculate. However, a plan of insurance may be constructed such that a projection is not required to ensure that the reserves meet minimum standards.

8.4 SECONDARY GUARANTEES

Both fixed and flexible premium Universal Life policies may contain secondary guarantees. A *secondary guarantee* provides the policyholder a guaranteed set of cash values, death benefits and/or maturity benefits that will be provided regardless of the performance of the fund. Examples include:

- A fixed premium universal life whose premium is at a level which would not carry the policy to maturity on a guaranteed basis, but nonetheless provides that, as long as the policyholder keeps paying the level premium, the policy will stay inforce regardless of the performance of the fund (even though the policy generally lapses if the fund goes to zero).
- A flexible premium universal life insurance policy which normally lapses when the fund minus the surrender charge is zero, but which provides that, if the policyholder pays a stated minimum premium each of the first ten years, the policy will not lapse during the ten year period, even if the fund minus the surrender charge is negative.

Secondary guarantees fall within the scope of the Valuation of Life Insurance Policies Model Regulation discussed in Chapter 7. This regulation (previously know as Actuarial Guideline XXX and Model Regulation 830) imposes minimum reserve requirements on universal life policies that contain secondary guarantees which cause the policy to remain inforce over a period exceeding 5 years, subject only to the payment of specified premiums. In particular, the regulation requires that reserves for a policy with such a secondary guarantee are at least equal to minimum reserves for the form implied by the secondary guarantee.

8.4.1 ACTUARIAL GUIDELINE XXXVIII

The purpose of Actuarial Guideline XXXVIII is to provide guidance on the application of the Valuation of Life Insurance Policies Model Regulation to certain product designs. This guideline contains two examples (Example 7 and Example 8 as defined in the regulation) that explain how the basic reserve and deficiency reserve should be determined for universal life insurance policies that contain the type of secondary guarantees discussed in these examples.

8.4.1.1 Example 7

Example 7 describes a universal life policy that has a "premium catch-up provision." This provision provides that the policy will remain in force as long as a stated minimum premium ("stipulated premium") is paid each year. If the policyholder paid less than this stipulated premium in any policy year, then the policyholder has the right to make up past premium deficiencies ("catch-up") to maintain the secondary guarantee[17].

 The basic reserve and deficiency reserve discussed in Chapter 7 are determined as if the minimum premium requirement has been satisfied, even if the policyholder has not paid the minimum premium amount in each year and has not "caught-up". However, the basic reserve is adjusted to reflect the "catch-up amount," if any. Specifically, the basic reserve is reduced by multiplying (A) by (B), where:

---

[17] Without this "catch-up" provision, the secondary guarantee expires as soon as the policyholder pays less than the minimum premium amount.

(A) is the "catch-up amount", if any, as of the valuation date; and

(B) is the ratio of (1) divided (2), where

    (1) is the basic reserve without any adjustment; and

    (2) is the sum of the basic reserve and deficiency reserve without any adjustment

Similarly, the deficiency reserve is reduced by multiplying (A) by (B), where:

(A) is the "catch-up amount", if any, as of the valuation date; and

(B) is the ratio of (1) divided (2), where

    (1) is the deficiency reserve without any adjustment; and

    (2) is the sum of the basic reserve and deficiency reserve without any adjustment

8.5 OFF-ANNIVERSARY RESERVES AND OTHER MINIMUM RESERVE REQUIREMENTS

The Universal Life Insurance Model Regulation defines terminal reserves but is silent on how to calculate off-anniversary reserves. As a consequence, many reasonable methods have been developed and are in current use. The main issues in calculating off-anniversary reserves include the following:

(1)   How to calculate r-ratio; should r-ratio be calculated as of the valuation date, or as of either the prior or next policy anniversary?

(2)   How to calculate the Guaranteed Maturity Fund on the valuation date in the event r-ratio is calculated as of the valuation date.

(3)   Whether to calculate the reserve factors from first principles as of the valuation date, or, alternatively, to calculate a mean, mid-terminal, or interpolated reserve.

Although it may not be unreasonable to calculate off-anniversary reserves using an r-ratio calculated as of either the prior or next policy anniversary, it is generally considered to be more accurate to calculate an r-ratio as of the valuation date. This raises the question of how to calculate the Guaranteed Maturity Fund as of the valuation date, and specifically whether to use annual Guaranteed Maturity Premiums or Guaranteed Maturity Premiums consistent with the policy's planned premium mode. It is important that the choice be consistent with the reserve method used. For example, if the Guaranteed Maturity Fund is calculated assuming annual Guaranteed Maturity Premiums and mean reserve factors are used, no deferred premiums are required for the policy. If, on the other hand, the Guaranteed Maturity Fund is calculated using Guaranteed Maturity Premiums based on the planned premium mode for the policy and mean reserve factors are used, then net deferred premiums are required for monthly mode policies. These net deferred premiums should be multiplied by r-ratio.

Whether net deferred premiums or unearned premiums are required is based on the assumption inherent in the Guaranteed Maturity Fund, not on the actual policy mode. Thus, if the Guaranteed Maturity Fund is based on monthly Guaranteed Maturity Premiums and mean reserves are used, net deferred premiums are required. Similarly, if the Guaranteed Maturity Fund is calculated assuming annual Guaranteed Maturity Premiums and mid-terminal reserves are held, unearned premiums must be held.

One advantage of calculating reserve factors from first principles as of the date of valuation is that it is possible to avoid net deferred and unearned premiums.

8.5.1 One-half Cost of Insurance Minimum Reserve

If the current fund value is very low, or in some cases zero, the "r-ratio" can result in a reserve that is less than the expected mortality. Accordingly, the policy reserve is equal to the cost of insurance (i.e., $c_{[x]+t}$).

Since most universal life reserves are calculated on a monthly basis, the cost of insurance is calculated on a monthly basis.

8.5.2 Excess Cash Surrender Value

As was discussed in Chapter 5, a common miscellaneous reserve appearing in Exhibit 5G is an excess cash surrender value reserve. This is an additional reserve that is held when the cash surrender value exceeds the total policy reserve. The total policy reserve used in this comparison would be the basic reserve, deficiency reserve and rider reserves. The formula for this reserve is:

$$ {}_t^m V_{[x]:\overline{n|}}^{XCV} = \text{Max}\left[0, {}_t^m CV_{[x]:\overline{n|}} - \left({}_t^m V_{[x]:\overline{n|}} + {}_t^m V_{[x]:\overline{n|}}^{Def} + other\ rider\ reserves \right) \right] $$

where

$$ {}_t^m V_{[x]:\overline{n|}}^{XCV} = \text{excess cash surrender value reserve at duration } t;\ \text{and} $$

$$ {}_t^m CV_{[x]:\overline{n|}} = \text{cash surrender value reserve at duration } t. $$

8.6 Guaranteed Maturity Premium Method

Some actuaries feel that the Commissioners Reserve Valuation Method for universal life is unnecessarily complex and that alternative methods should be investigated. In addition, there is concern that in certain situations, the reserve may be inadequate. From time to time, the National Association of Insurance Commissioners Actuarial Task Force has exposed different proposals for changing the model regulation, but none of the proposals has been adopted. To some degree, the industry has opposed simplification of the model regulation, since, for existing business, tax reserves for universal life are defined in terms of the existing Universal Life Insurance Model regulation. Therefore, some companies felt that for tax reporting purposes they would be forced to calculate universal life reserves using two different methodologies indefinitely into the future.

One method which has received extensive consideration is called the guaranteed maturity premium method. This method produces results that are consistent with the existing model regulation. Under the Guaranteed Maturity Premium method, the company would still have to calculate guaranteed maturity premiums and guaranteed maturity funds. However, projections as of the valuation date of future guaranteed benefits would be unnecessary. Under the Guaranteed Maturity Premium method, the r-ratio and traditional Commissioners Reserve Valuation Method reserves would be used to calculate the Universal Life CRVM reserve. The "traditional Commissioners Reserve Valuation Method reserves" would be those based on a permanent life insurance plan with a maturity at the latest possible maturity date under the universal life plan:

$$ {}_t^m V_{[x]:\overline{n|}}^{GMP\ Method} = \begin{cases} r_{[x]+t}^{FV} \cdot {}_t^m V_{[x]:\overline{n|}}^{CRVM} & \text{if} \quad {}_t^C FV_{[x]} < {}_t^{GM} FV_{[x]} \\ {}_t^m V_{[x]:\overline{n|}}^{CRVM} + {}_t^C FV_{[x]} - {}_t^{GM} FV_{[x]} & \text{if} \quad {}_t^C FV_{[x]} \geq {}_t^{GM} FV_{[x]} \end{cases} $$

where

$${}_{t}^{m}V_{[x]:\overline{n}|}^{CRVM}$$ = the traditional Commissioners Reserve Valuation Method reserve for an *m*-pay, *n*-year endowment.

For policies where the *r*-ratio factor is less than 1, this method often produces values that will duplicate the model regulation[18]. For policies where the account value is larger than the Guaranteed Maturity Fund Value, the Guaranteed Maturity Premium method was felt to be a reasonable approximation for most products.

8.7 THE CALIFORNIA UNIVERSAL LIFE REGULATION

In 1991 the California Department of Insurance issued a regulation on universal life reserves for policies issued after December 31, 1991. It is similar to the National Association of Insurance Commissioners Universal Life Insurance Model Regulation, except that the valuation interest rate may not exceed the credited rate guaranteed in the contract. This causes minimum reserves to be higher than otherwise, since it had been common for companies to guarantee a credited rate such as 4% and to use a valuation rate such as 5.5%.

The California regulation allows companies, at their option, to alternatively hold a reserve equal to the mean of the cash value and the fund value. This method is defined in the regulation as the California Method. Note that the California Method may produce reserves greater or less than the model regulation reserves, depending upon the relationship of the fund to the GMF and the contract design. For example, reserves under the California Method would always equal the cash value for a front-end loaded Universal Life plan, and might well be below those required by the model regulation. In 1994 New York adopted Regulation 147, which permits the California method as an elective alternative basis for Universal Life reserves only for policies issued before January 1, 2000.

As discussed in Chapter 1, since the 1992 valuation actuary opinion under the new Standard Valuation Law requires that reserves be "at least as great as the minimum aggregate amounts required by the state in which this statement is filed," companies filing a California statement will need to take account of this regulation, even if California is not their state of domicile. Also note that since tax reserves are required to be based on the National Association of Insurance Commissioners' Universal Life Insurance Model Regulation, companies opting for the simpler California Method will still be required to calculate Model Regulation reserves for their tax return.

8.8 MINIMUM VERSUS ADEQUATE RESERVES

Use of the cash value as the reserve for flexible premium universal life contracts can result in deferring losses to later years. The Commissioners Reserve Valuation Method for universal life as defined by the National Association of Insurance Commissioners, while offering some improvement, may be considered inadequate in some cases, particularly for back-loaded products.

For many universal life products with surrender charges, cash values become larger than Commissioners Reserve Valuation Method reserves once the surrender charges begin to grade off. If the Universal Life Insurance Model Regulation reserves are used with no modification, renewal losses may occur when the

---

[18] If the life insurance company provides guarantees that are more liberal than the reserve assumptions (such as guaranteeing the current cost of insurance rate or current credited interest rate beyond the valuation date), then this method might understate the reserve.

increase in cash value is not supportable by the gross premium. An example of the statutory profit pattern of one such product is given in the following table.

Example		
Year	Statutory Book Profit	Present Value of Future Profits
0		63
1	(299)	370
2	553	(130)
3	(23)	(124)
4	(51)	(91)
5	(60)	(44)
6	(101)	51

As we can see from the column labeled "Present Value of Future Profits," at some durations, the reserve together with future anticipated gross premiums and investment earnings may not be sufficient to provide for expenses and anticipated policyholder benefits. In this scenario, the statutory profits recognized in year two are so large that renewal losses occur as the surrender charge grades off. The plan is profitable at issue, but the statutory reserving basis used recognizes earnings too early. Although this example may not be typical of results obtained by the Universal Life Insurance Model Regulation, it illustrates problems that can arise with any product (including traditional life products) whose cash values exceed the reserves.

If a cash surrender value pattern such as this example were to occur in a traditional life insurance policy, the policy would fall under the unusual cash surrender value provision of the Valuation of Life Insurance Policies Model Regulation, which was discussed in Chapter 7. However, the unusual cash surrender value provision is in a section of the Valuation of Life Insurance Policies Model Regulation which does not apply to universal life insurance.

8.2   Exercises

8.9.1   Key Terms

fund value   current basis
guaranteed basis   flexible premium
fixed premium   death benefit options
corridor factors   guaranteed maturity premium
guaranteed maturity fund   guaranteed maturity values
current values   guaranteed values
alternate minimum reserves   secondary guarantees

8.9.2   Questions

a.   With regards to product classification, what does the phrase "terms are not fixed and guaranteed" mean?

b.   How can the successive fund value formula be used to develop analytical ratios that can be used to monitor the valuation process on a regular basis? What else can these ratios be used for?

c.   What is the purpose of the corridor factors? How do they affect reserves?

d.   Summarize the steps that need to be performed to determine the reserves for a flexible premium universal life policy. How do they differ from a fixed premium universal life policy?

8.9.3 Problems

a. Using the following graph form the excel workbook, Chapter 8.xls:

Fund Value Comparison

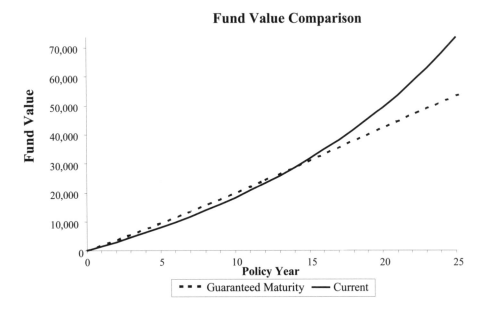

explain the effect on the successive reserves.

b. Explain how lowering the gross premium effects the reserve.

c. Explain how raising the gross premium effects the reserve.

d. Compare the reserves of a universal life product with high front loads and low back-end loads with a universal life product with low front-end loads and high back-end loads.

9 ✧ VARIABLE LIFE INSURANCE

9.1 INTRODUCTION

Surprisingly, life insurance companies began marketing variable life insurance before the first life insurance company began marketing universal life insurance. However, only a small number of life insurance companies initially offered these types of products.

After universal life insurance sales began to increase in the 1980's, a large number of life insurance companies began offering a new type of variable life insurance. These products have design features similar to universal life insurance and therefore, are called variable universal life.

As noted in Actuarial Guideline XXXVII, life insurance companies have not applied uniform reserve standards to determine policy reserves for variable life insurance products. Although the Variable Life Insurance Model Regulation defines the reserve methodology for variable life products, there are two versions (1983 Version and 1989 Version) of this regulation. Many states have not adopted either version. Accordingly, life insurance companies use one or more of the following to determine policy reserves for variable life products:

- Standard Valuation Law
- Variable Life Insurance Model Regulation (1983 Version)
- Variable Life Insurance Model Regulation (1989 Version)
- Universal Life Insurance Model Regulation.

This chapter will discuss how policy reserves for the most common forms of variable life insurance are determined in a statutory valuation. Since the reserve methodology depends upon product type, the discussion considers the major categories of products separately.

9.2 PRODUCT CLASSIFICATION

A *variable life insurance* policy gives the policyholder the choice to invest policy premiums in a variety of separate accounts[1]. Unlike universal life insurance, the fund value varies in accordance with the investment performance of the separate accounts selected by the policyholder, and therefore, the contractholder bears most of the investment risk[2]. Since the investment performance is not guaranteed, the fund might not be able to support the death benefit due to poor investment performance. Accordingly, many life insurance companies offer designs that provide a minimum death benefit guarantee. This feature promises a death benefit (usually

---

[1] A separate account is similar to a mutual fund.

[2] Most life insurance companies offer a general account option. This portion of the fund value has similar guarantees as universal life (i.e., a minimum guaranteed credited interest rate).

the initial face amount) will be paid on the death of the insured regardless of the performance of the separate accounts.

Variable life insurance is often classified into two major product categories: fixed premium variable life insurance and flexible premium variable universal life insurance. Within each of these categories, a distinction is sometimes made between annual premium and single premium product designs.

9.2.1 FIXED PREMIUM VARIABLE LIFE INSURANCE

Fixed premium variable life insurance requires periodic premiums which are fixed by the insurer. Typically, fixed premium variable life products are front-end loaded. The death benefit is adjusted to reflect investment performance in one of two ways, commonly referred to as the New York Life design and the Equitable design.

Under the New York Life design the death benefit at any point in time is the original face amount times the ratio of the actual cash value to a hypothetical tabular cash value which has been calculated using an assumed interest rate (AIR). Additionally, the policy has a guaranteed minimum death benefit (GMDB) equal to the initial face amount.

Associated with this Chapter is an Excel Workbook "Chapter 9.xls." This workbook demonstrates how policy values are calculated under the New York Life design. For example, the worksheet "Parameters" shows a variable life policy issued to a 50 year old male with an assumed interest rate of 5% and a $100,000 face amount.

Parameters	
Plan Design...	New York Life ▼
Assume interest rate.....................................	5.00%
Actual investment return..............................	6.00%
Issue Date	9/1/2000
Maturity Date...	9/1/2049
Issue Age	50
Gender	Male ▼
Gross Premium	0
Premium Payment Period	49 years
Face Amount	100,000
Guaranteed Minimum Death Benefit..........	100,000

This illustration will assume that the separate accounts selected earned a level 6% over the projection period.

The worksheet "CPV" illustrates the determination of the current policy values based on the values in the "Parameters" worksheet, the "PVA" worksheet and "APV" worksheet:

						Current Policy Values			
(1)	(2)	(3)	(4)	(5)	(6)	(7)	(8)	(9)	(10)
x	t	$^C FV(t)$ +	$^C GP(t)$ −	$^C EC(t)$ −	$^C TC(t)$ +	$^C IC(t)$ =	$^C FV(t+1)$	$^C BD(t)$	$^{GM} BD(t)$
50	1	0	2,469	173	622	100	1,774	100,000	100,000
51	2	1,774	2,469	173	673	204	3,600	101,320	100,000
52	3	3,600	2,469	173	722	310	5,484	101,572	100,000
53	4	5,484	2,469	173	777	420	7,423	101,967	100,000
54	5	7,423	2,469	173	839	533	9,413	102,390	100,000
55	6	9,413	2,469	173	903	648	11,454	102,826	100,000
56	7	11,454	2,469	173	970	767	13,546	103,273	100,000
57	8	13,546	2,469	173	1,037	888	15,692	103,727	100,000
58	9	15,692	2,469	173	1,106	1,013	17,894	104,188	100,000
59	10	17,894	2,469	173	1,177	1,141	20,152	104,656	100,000
⋮	⋮	⋮	⋮	⋮	⋮	⋮	⋮	⋮	⋮
98	48	119,662	2,469	173	(956)	7,375	130,289	130,289	100,000

The variable $^C BD(t)$ is the current death benefit and was determined using the following formula:

$$^C BD(t) = FA0 \cdot \frac{^C FV(t)}{^A FV(t)}$$

where

$$FA0 = \text{initial face amount;}$$
$$^C FV(t) = \text{current fund value at duration } t; \text{ and}$$
$$^A FV(t) = \text{assumed fund value at duration } t.$$

Under the Equitable Design, any net investment earnings over the assumed interest rate are used to purchase variable paid-up additions at net single premium rates using the assumed interest rate; if net investment earnings are less than the assumed interest rate, paid-up additions are canceled (effectively "negative" paid-up additions are purchased). A guaranteed minimum death benefit is provided in that if the paid-up additions are negative in total, this negative amount is carried forward notionally (and is used to offset future positive paid-up additions), but it does not affect the actual death benefit currently in place.

The worksheet "CPV" also illustrates the determination of the current policy values under the Equitable Design:

					Current Policy Values				
(1)	(2)	(3)	(4)	(5)	(6)	(7)	(8)	(9)	(10)
x	t	$^CFV(t)$ +	$^CGP(t)$ −	$^CEC(t)$ −	$^CTC(t)$ +	$^CIC(t)$ =	$^CFV(t+1)$	$^CBD(t)$	$^{GM}BD(t)$
50	0	0	2,469	173	622	100	1,774	100,000	100,000
51	1	1,774	2,469	173	664	204	3,609	100,067	100,000
52	2	3,609	2,469	173	711	312	5,505	100,182	100,000
53	3	5,505	2,469	173	763	422	7,460	100,344	100,000
54	4	7,460	2,469	173	821	536	9,470	100,551	100,000
55	5	9,470	2,469	173	882	653	11,536	100,803	100,000
56	6	11,536	2,469	173	945	773	13,659	101,096	100,000
57	7	13,659	2,469	173	1,008	897	15,843	101,431	100,000
58	8	15,843	2,469	173	1,073	1,024	18,089	101,806	100,000
59	9	18,089	2,469	173	1,140	1,155	20,399	102,220	100,000
⋮	⋮	⋮	⋮	⋮	⋮	⋮	⋮	⋮	⋮
98	48	138,919	2,469	173	(2,609)	8,629	152,453	152,453	100,000

Under the Equitable Design, the variable $^CBD(t)$ was determined using the following formula:

$$^CBD(t) = FA0 + \frac{^CFV(t) - {^AFV(t)}}{AB(t)}$$

where

$$
\begin{aligned}
FA0 &= \quad \text{initial face amount;} \\
{^CFV(t)} &= \quad \text{current fund value at duration } t; \\
{^AFV(t)} &= \quad \text{assumed fund value at duration } t; \text{ and} \\
AB(t) &= \quad \text{net single premium at duration } t
\end{aligned}
$$

The net single premiums were calculated using the following formula from Chapter 5 utilizing the assumed interest rate and guaranteed cost of insurance charges.

$$AB_{[x]+t:\overline{n-t}|} = \sum_{s=0}^{n-t-1} v^{s+1} \cdot {_sp_{[x]+t}} \cdot q_{[x]+t+s} \cdot BD_{[x]+t+s} + v^{n-t} \cdot {_{n-t}p_{[x]+t}} \cdot BM_{[x]+n}$$

Fixed premium variable life insurance sales have declined significantly, and now represent a small portion of the variable life insurance market.

9.2.2 FLEXIBLE PREMIUM VARIABLE UNIVERSAL LIFE INSURANCE

Flexible premium variable universal life (VUL) insurance is similar to flexible premium universal life insurance in that it has a fund. Premiums less loads are credited to this fund, and expense charges and cost of insurance charges are regularly deducted. The cash value, which is the amount available to the policyholder upon termination of the contract, may be equal to the fund, or it may be equal to the fund less a surrender charge.

Within certain limits, the policyowner has a choice regarding the amount and timing of premium payments. Like universal life, variable universal life insurance policies provide at least two death benefit options – a "level" death benefit or a "level" net amount at risk. In addition, to qualify as life insurance under the Internal Revenue Code and receive favorable tax treatment, the relationship of the death benefit to the cash value must satisfy either the guideline premium test or the cash value accumulation test as defined in Section 7702 of the Internal Revenue Code and described in Chapter 8. Most universal life contracts use the guideline premium test.

In short, the only significant difference between flexible premium variable universal life products and flexible premium universal life is that the fund value of a variable universal life policy is invested in and varies with the performance of the separate account, and the policyholder therefore bears most of the investment risk.

Variable universal life has become quite popular, and now accounts for virtually all variable life insurance sales in the United States.

9.2.3 SINGLE PREMIUM VARIABLE LIFE INSURANCE

There are two basic types of "single premium" variable life: Flexible Single Premium and Fixed Single Premium.

Flexible single premium variable life is marketed as a single premium product. However, the contract gives the policyholder the right to make future premium payments, and typically is identical mechanically to a flexible premium variable universal life policy.

Fixed single premium variable life does not allow payment of premiums after the initial single premium. These contracts generally provide a guaranteed minimum death benefit, with the gross premium calculated based on an assumed interest rate. Fixed single premium contracts may be of the Equitable design, the New York Life design, or may use a universal life design to generate cash values.

Since the introduction of tax law changes in 1988, the popularity of both types of single premium variable life has declined dramatically.

9.3 VALUATION OF VARIABLE LIFE INSURANCE

Problems arise in applying traditional reserve methodology to variable life insurance policies. The Commissioners Reserve Valuation Method defines minimum reserves prospectively, based on future policy guarantees. However, variable products do not have future investment guarantees.

The National Association of Insurance Commissioners Variable Life Insurance Model Regulation states as follows:

"Reserve liabilities for variable life insurance policies shall be established under the Standard Valuation Law in accordance with actuarial procedures that recognize the variable nature of the benefits provided and any mortality guarantees."

Initially, actuaries grappled with how to interpret the phrase "in accordance with actuarial procedures that recognize the variable nature" of the product. Earlier product designs lend themselves to reasonable interpretations of traditional reserve methodology. More recent product designs are subject to multiple interpretations.

9.3.1 FIXED PREMIUM VARIABLE LIFE INSURANCE

Ignoring the guaranteed minimum death benefit, reserves per $1,000 of current death benefit under the New York Life design are identical to those of an m-pay, n-year endowment policy with the same current death benefit, issue age, and duration. For example, the net level premium reserve would be determined using the formula in Chapter 5 with the face amount equal to the current face amount:

$$ {}^{m}_{t}VB_{[x]:\overline{n}|} = AB_{[x]+t:\overline{n-t}|} - {}_{m}PB_{[x]:\overline{n}|} \cdot \ddot{a}_{[x]+t:\overline{m-t}|} $$

Reserves for the basic policy under the Equitable design are equal to tabular reserves calculated for an m-pay, n-year endowment policy of the same face amount, issue age, and duration. Reserves for the paid-up additions (if positive) are equal to those for similar traditional paid-up additions:

$$ FA0 \cdot \left[AB_{[x]+t:\overline{n-t}|} - {}_{m}PB_{[x]:\overline{n}|} \cdot \ddot{a}_{[x]+t:\overline{m-t}|} \right] + \left[{}^{C}FA - FA0 \right] \cdot AB_{[x]+t:\overline{n-t}|} $$

where

$$ FA0 = \text{initial face amount; and} $$
$$ {}^{C}FA = \text{current face amount.} $$

In both cases, additional reserves must be held for the minimum death benefit guarantee.

9.3.2 FLEXIBLE PREMIUM VARIABLE UNIVERSAL LIFE INSURANCE

The Universal Life Insurance Model Regulation specifically exempts variable products. At any rate, application of the reserve definition in the Universal Life Insurance Model Regulation to variable universal life insurance without modification would be inappropriate, as this model uses a prospective technique based on a projection of future guaranteed benefits. In the absence of industry standards, it is the responsibility of the valuation actuary to ensure that the method used is appropriate for the particular product being valued.

For fully front-end loaded variable universal life products, it was generally felt (prior to the 1989 Amendments to the Variable Life Model Regulation) that the policy's cash value represents a sufficient reserve in the absence of future mortality guarantees more liberal than the valuation basis. In the case where the first year expense charges exceed renewal expense charges by more than the first year expense allowance under the Commissioners Reserve Valuation Method, or in the presence of a minimum death benefit provision that exists in order to comply with the definition of life insurance, the appropriateness of the cash value (net of surrender charges) as a reserve is subject to question.

Today, the policy reserve is typically determined in accordance with the Universal Life Model Regulation, with one of the following interest rates used to calculate projected future benefits:

(1)   For contracts with a fixed-account option, the long-term guaranteed rate in the fixed account;

(2)   The valuation rate, less some or all of the contractual asset-based charges[3];

(3)   4% interest; or

(4)   The rate credited to policy loans.

An additional reserve must be held for the minimum death benefit guarantee. This reserve is discussed later in this chapter.

---

[3] Asset-based charges are charges that are assessed on the fund value as a reduction to the investment earnings, including the mortality and expense risk charge, investment management charges and other charges based on assets.

9.3.3 SEPARATE ACCOUNT RESERVE

Both the Securities and Exchange Commission and the Variable Life Insurance Model Regulation require that assets in the separate account be at least equal to the fund value. Without this requirement, a significant mismatch between assets and liabilities would exist.

To illustrate this mismatch, consider a variable life insurance policy with a fund value of $10,000 and a surrender charge of $1,000. Suppose further that the policy reserve is $9,000, the cash value. If only the statutory reserve was held in the separate account, the balance sheet for the separate account would be as follows:

Separate Account (Policy Reserve = $9,000)			
Invested Assets	$9,000	Separate Account Liabilities	$9,000
Other Assets	0	Surplus	0
Total Assets	$9,000	Total Liabilities & Surplus	$9,000

The balance sheet for the general account would be as follows:

General Account			
Separate Account Assets	$ 9,000	Separate Account Liabilities	$ 9,000
Other Assets	1,000	Surplus	1,000
Total Assets	$10,000	Total Liabilities & Surplus	$10,000

If the surrender charge reduces to zero next year and the return on the separate account assets was zero, the policy reserve[4] would increase to $10,000 and the life insurance company would transfer $1,000 from the general account to the separate account to fund the amortization of the $1,000 surrender charge.

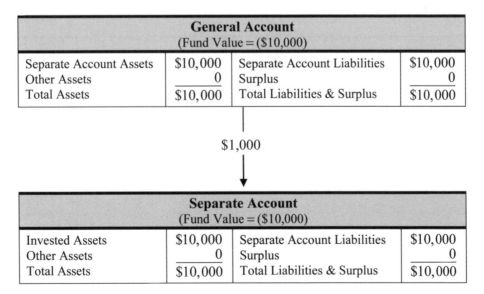

General Account (Fund Value = ($10,000)			
Separate Account Assets	$10,000	Separate Account Liabilities	$10,000
Other Assets	0	Surplus	0
Total Assets	$10,000	Total Liabilities & Surplus	$10,000

$1,000

Separate Account (Fund Value = ($10,000)			
Invested Assets	$10,000	Separate Account Liabilities	$10,000
Other Assets	0	Surplus	0
Total Assets	$10,000	Total Liabilities & Surplus	$10,000

If the separate accounts double over the next year, the life insurance company would be required to fund $2,000, as the $1,000 excess of the fund value over the policy reserve will have doubled:

---

[4] Ignoring cost of insurance charges and expense charges , the fund value and cash value would be $10,000.

General Account			
(Fund Value = ($20,000)			
Separate Account Assets	$20,000	Separate Account Liabilities	$20,000
Other Assets	0	Surplus	(1,000)
Total Assets	$20,000	Total Liabilities & Surplus	$19,000

$2,000

Separate Account			
(Fund Value = ($20,000)			
Invested Assets	$20,000	Separate Account Liabilities	$20,000
Other Assets	0	Surplus	0
Total Assets	$20,000	Total Liabilities & Surplus	$20,000

However, if the $1,000 excess of fund value over reserve had been in the separate account, it too would have doubled, and the life insurance company would only have to transfer $1,000 to the separate account. Therefore, the proper accounting is to hold the entire fund value in the separate account as follows:

Separate Account			
(Fund Value = ($10,000)			
Invested Assets	$10,000	Separate Account Liabilities	$ 9,000
Other Assets	0	Surplus	1,000
Total Assets	$10,000	Total Liabilities & Surplus	$10,000

The general account would appear as follows:

General Account			
Separate Account Assets	$10,000	Separate Account Liabilities	$ 9,000
Amount Due from Separate Account	0	Surplus	1,000
Total Assets	$10,000	Total Liabilities & Surplus	$10,000

9.4 MINIMUM DEATH BENEFIT GUARANTEE (MDBG) RESERVE

Actuarial Guideline XXXVII's primary focus is "to clarify the appropriate projection assumptions and methodologies used to determine statutory reserve liabilities for Guaranteed Minimum Death Benefits (GMDBs) offered with variable life insurance products."[5] This guideline defines a Guaranteed Minimum Death Benefit as "any guarantee which provides death benefit protection which would not otherwise be provided in the absence of such a guaranteed benefit or provision."[6] An additional reserve is required for variable life insurance policies that provide a minimum death benefit guarantee.

---

[5] See [4], Actuarial Guideline XXXVII.
[6] Ibid.

In the commentary to the Variable Life Insurance Model Regulation, the subcommittee who drafted this regulation concluded that "the acceptable MDBG reserve system should have the following characteristics:

(1)   The MDBG reserve should be held in the general account of the company so that it will be backed by the general assets of the company, most of which are debt obligations valued at amortized cost and, therefore, are of a fixed dollar nature. It would not be proper to hold the MDBG reserve in the separate account since the reserve would not be supported by fixed dollar assets but by assets that are moving in the opposite direction from the risk, i.e., value moving downward while the risk increases and vice versa.

(2)   The MDBG reserve should be adequate to cover, under all but the most extreme circumstances, the MDBG death claims for the next year, so that the regulatory authorities can be assured the company will not run into financial trouble from this source before the next annual statement is filed.

(3)   The MDBG reserve should react slowly but steadily to an extended period of poor investment experience of the separate account.

(4)   The MDBG reserve should not overreact and cause unnecessary fluctuations in surplus by increasing too rapidly in a sharp market downswing. Also, the reserve should not decrease too rapidly in a sharp market upswing after a period of poor market experience."[7]

This guideline maintains these four principles. In addition, it recognizes the following principles:

(1)   Determine the guaranteed death benefits which are not valued in the basic policy reserves.

(2)   Establish a reserve for these benefits over the period of time in which revenue is collected to pay for such benefits; however, no greater than the period of time these guaranteed benefits are provided.

(3)   Collected revenue should not be deminimus in order to reduce the reserve.

(4)   The reserve established is in addition to basic reserves.

The MDGB reserve is the larger of (A) and (B), where:

A.   is the accumulation of amounts allocated by the life insurance company to the minimum guaranteed death benefit reserve, less actual minimum guaranteed death benefit claims paid[8]; and

B.   is the larger of (1) and (2), where:

   (1) is a one-year term reserve to assure coverage of next year's claims; and

   (2) is a reserve designed to protect against an extended period of poor investment experience of the separate account.

The accumulated amounts in Part A depend upon the design characteristics of the variable life insurance policy, the life insurance company's judgment of the risk it has assumed, and its assessment of the possible impact on its surplus of future changes in Part B. It is more of a principles-based reserve rather than a reserve based on a specified formula.

The Part B reserves are based on a specified methodology and assumptions. Part B(1) is called the ***One-Year Term (OYT) Method*** and Part B(2) is called the ***Attained Age Level Reserve (AALR) Method***. Valuation interest and mortality rates used in computing both the one-year term reserve and attained age level reserve

---

See [4], Actuarial Guideline XXXVII.

[8] Part A only applies to fixed premium variable life products that following the 1983 Version of Variable Life Insurance Model Regulation.

need not be the same as those used for the basic reserves, but must conform to the permissible standards for the valuation of life insurance products.

9.4.1 ONE-YEAR TERM METHOD

The one-year term method requires that the reserve be sufficient to cover all claims in the following year if there is an immediate one-third drop in the value of the separate account assets. The one-year term reserve is equal to the term cost, if any, of the excess of the guaranteed minimum death benefit over the otherwise payable death benefit, covering a period of one full year from the valuation date, assuming an immediate one-third depreciation in the current value of the assets in the separate accounts, followed by an investment return equal to the assumed investment rate. Algebraically,

$$v \cdot q_{[x]+t} \cdot \left[\,^{GM}BD_{[x]+t} - BD_{[x]+t} \right]$$

where

$$^{GM}BD_{[x]+t} \; = \; \text{guaranteed minimum death benefit at duration } t; \text{ and}$$

$$BD_{[x]+t} \; = \; \text{death benefit at duration t assuming an immediate one-third depreciation.}$$

9.4.2 ATTAINED AGE LEVEL RESERVE METHOD

The attained age level method produces a gradual increase in the reserve if this is necessary to cover minimum guaranteed death benefit claims arising from an extended period of poor investment performance. The technique used is to fund the cost of future minimum guaranteed death benefit claims by level payments over the future premium paying period of the contract.

The attained age level reserve is equal to the "residue" of the prior year's attained age level reserve for the contract, increased or decreased by the current "payment" as described below. Neither the attained age level reserve nor the residue for any policy can be less than zero.

The "residue" equals the prior year's attained age level reserve for the contract, increased at the valuation interest rate, and decreased for tabular valuation mortality based on the excess, if any, of the guaranteed minimum death benefit over the death benefit which otherwise would have been in effect during the preceding year. The result is then divided by the tabular probability of survival. The initial residue is zero.

Algebraically:

$$^{MDBG}_{[t]+1}V_{[x]:\overline{n}|} = \frac{{}^{MDBG}_{[t-1]+1}V_{[x]:\overline{n}|} \cdot (1+i) - \left[\,^{GM}BD_{[x]+[t]} - {}^{C}BD_{[x]+[t]} \right] \cdot q_{[x]+t}}{1 - q_{[x]+t}} + {}^{MDBG}_{m}P_{[x]+[t]:\overline{n}|}$$

The "payment" is recomputed annually, and is the level annual premium, positive or negative, equal to

$$^{MDBG}_{m}P_{[x]+[t]:\overline{n}|} = \frac{\left[\,^{MDBG}AB_{[x]+[t]:\overline{n}|} - {}^{MDBG}_{[t-1]+1}V_{[x]:\overline{n}|} \right]}{\ddot{a}_{[x]+[t]:\overline{m-t}|}}$$

where

$${}^{MDBG}AB_{[x]+[t]:\overline{n}|}$$ = present value of the excess of the guaranteed minimum death benefit over the death benefit payable in absence of the guaranteed minimum death benefit; and

$$m$$ = the number of future years for which charges for this risk will be collected under the contract (typically the remaining premium paying period).

An attained age level reserve does not have to be established for a variable universal life policy to provide for any period during which there would be a death benefit in absence of this guarantee, since this benefit would be reflected in the basic reserve.[9] This is an important distinction. If the fund value is projected to go negative after ten years, the attained age level reserve builds up over the first ten years even though there is no excess benefit during the time period.

9.4.3 PROJECTION ASSUMPTIONS

Actuarial Guideline XXXVII specifies the following assumptions to be used in the projection of policy values:

(1) Cost of insurance rates are equal to the minimum valuation mortality.

(2) The MDBG is assumed to be in effect for the maximum period of the MDBG. All minimum requirements necessary to maintain the MDBG in force subsequent to the valuation date are assumed to be met at the latest point in time sufficient to maintain the MDBG through its maximum period. Contingent requirements, if any, necessary to reinstate or catch-up as of the valuation date are assumed to occur on the valuation date. If the MDBG would continue in effect subsequent to the valuation date with no additional actions required, contingent requirements are assumed not to resume until the latest point in time which would prevent the termination of the MDBG.

(3) The general account policy values and separate account policy values are projected at the valuation interest rate. The assumed investment rate, if any, is used when determining the OYT reserve.

(4) The guaranteed period covered is determined assuming all contingent requirements are met.

(5) Policy options and benefits are assumed to continue unchanged as of the valuation date. Examples include fixed and variable account allocation and the death benefit option.

(6) The projection of policy values is made for the entire guarantee period, regardless of whether projected policy values are positive or negative at any point in the projection. Any negative policy value would be set to zero.

---

[9] An attained age level reserve would result only if the fund value turns negative during the guaranteed period because the minimum premium requirements plus interest credits are not enough to pay for the cost of insurance charges.

10 ✧ Deferred Annuities

10.1 INTRODUCTION

Proper statutory reserve methodology for deferred annuities was not clearly defined prior to the 1976 amendments to the Standard Valuation Law. Historically, annuities had been a relatively unimportant part of the life insurance industry, primarily used to provide a guaranteed income stream after retirement. However, with the dramatic increase in interest rates in the 1970's, more and more companies began to sell single and flexible premium deferred annuities designed to serve primarily as cash accumulation vehicles. Today, annuities are an important part of the life insurance industry.

With the increase in annuity reserves in the 1970's, the National Association of Insurance Commissioners felt it necessary to formalize the basis of minimum reserves for such policies. As a result, the Commissioners Annuity Reserve Valuation Method (CARVM) was developed.

After adoption of the CARVM as the standard annuity reserve valuation method, many life insurance companies were slow to implement this method, at least partly due to its perceived complexity. Instead, many companies continued to hold more conservative reserves (e.g., the fund value) which were easier to calculate. However, with the adoption of the CARVM as the required methodology for calculation of Federally Prescribed Tax Reserves (FPTR's) and with the increasing complex plan designs, companies have been forced to implement this reserve methodology.

This chapter will discuss the CARVM and some problems that may arise in applying it to common annuity designs. The primary focus in this chapter will be on deferred annuities, and Chapter 11 will focus on immediate annuities.

10.2 PRODUCT CLASSIFICATION

An ***annuity contract*** is an insurance contract that guarantees to pay a series of annuity payments that begin either immediately or at some future date. Contracts with payments beginning immediately are called ***immediate annuities*** and contracts with payments beginning at some future date are called ***deferred annuities***[1].The period of time between the issue date and the commencement of a series of payments is called the ***accumulation period***, and the period of time during which annuity payments are made is called the ***payout period***[2].

Similar to a universal life contract, a deferred annuity has a fund[3]. Premiums[4] less expense charges are credited to this fund, along with periodic investment credits, and expense charges and insurance charges are

---

[1] Actuarial Guideline IX-B defines "an immediate annuity as an annuity wherein the first payment begins in thirteen months or less after issue and a deferred annuity as an annuity wherein the first payment begins after thirteen months."

[2] Accordingly, a deferred annuity is often called an accumulation annuity and an immediate annuity is often called a payout annuity.

[3] The term *fund value* will refer to the value of this fund and *cash surrender value* or *cash value* will be the fund value less any surrender penalties. Fund value is often referred to as account value or account balance.

[4] The premium paid by the contractholder is also called a ***consideration***.

regularly deducted. Premium payments can be made in a lump sum amount (*single premium deferred annuity*), or periodically (*flexible or fixed premium*[5] *deferred annuity*). At the end of the accumulation period, the policyholder may elect to receive a lump sum distribution or may elect to receive periodic payments for life, for a specific period, or some combination thereof. Most deferred annuities offer a cash surrender value which is the fund value less a surrender charge[6].

A *fixed deferred annuity* is an annuity that has a minimum guaranteed interest rate that will be credited to the fund. Typically, the assets supporting this annuity are invested in the life insurance company's general account and the fund value does not fluctuate with the fair value of these assets. In other words, the life insurance company "bears most of the investment risk" and the contractholder is able to surrender the contract at "book value."

A *variable deferred annuity* gives the contractholder the choice to invest in a variety of separate accounts[7]. Unlike a fixed annuity, the fund value varies in accordance with the investment performance of the separate accounts selected by the contractholder, and therefore, the contractholder "bears most of the investment risk." A minimum death benefit is often guaranteed during the accumulation period and these contracts are, therefore, classified as life contracts.

A *modified guaranteed annuity* is a fixed deferred annuity with *a market value adjustment (MVA)*. The market value adjustment modifies the fund value upon surrender relative to an index to reflect the market value of the assets held in support of the annuity. This adjustment passes the interest rate risk, but not the default risk, to the contractholder.

An *equity indexed annuity* is a fixed deferred annuity with a credited interest rate that is X% of the increase in a specified equity market index over a specified period (e.g., 60% of the increase in the S&P 500 index over the five year period). These contracts also guarantee to credit a minimum rate (such as 3%) on net deposits (e.g. 90% of the gross considerations). For example, an equity index annuity might specify that the fund value at the end of five years will be the larger of (A) or (B), where

> (A) is 60% of the increase in the S&P 500 index over the five year period; and

> (B) is 90% of gross considerations accumulated at a 3% interest credited rate.

The 60% in the above example is called the *participation rate*.

10.2.1 INSURANCE FEATURES

All insurance contracts provide some form of insurance protection (e.g., death, disability, health or longevity). Many insurance contracts (but not all) also provide some form of savings or investment feature. For example, one-year renewable and convertible term only provides a death benefit, whereas whole life provides both a death benefit and a cash value or withdrawal benefit. However, the primary emphasis of term and whole life is the death benefit. With a deferred annuity, the primary emphasis is on savings—the death benefit is a relatively minor feature. In other words, insurance products fall on a continuum with regard to the emphasis on insurance protection and savings or investment.

---

[5] Similar to fixed premium universal life insurance, a fixed premium deferred annuity requires that a premium be paid on the due date.

[6] Surrender charge and surrender penalty will be used interchangeably. It is the charge assessed against the fund value for termination of the contract during the surrender charge period. This charge is usually not assessed on the death of the insured and usually expires before maturity.

[7] A separate account is similar to a mutual fund in that it has defined investment objectives.

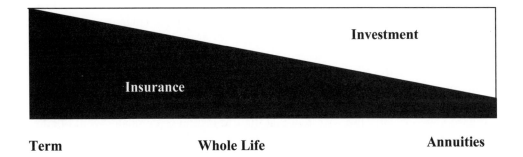

The insurance features of a deferred annuity, primarily variable annuities, can be divided into two broad categories:

- Living benefits
- Death benefits

These classifications are based on the status of the contractholder.

Living benefits include those insurance features that can be exercised by the contractholder while he or she is still alive. This category includes:

- Annuitization (or payout annuity) options
  - Annuity certain,
  - Life contingent annuity,
  - n-year certain and life thereafter;
- Guaranteed minimum accumulation benefits (GMAB),
- Guaranteed minimum income benefits (GMIB),
- Guaranteed minimum withdrawal benefits (GMWB),
- Guaranteed payout annuity floor (GPAF), and
- Tax equalization benefit.

A brief description of each is provided in the Appendix.

Death benefits include those insurance features that provide some form of death protection upon the death of the contractholder. This category includes:

- Return-of-premium
- Reset
- Roll-up
- Ratchet (or Step-up)
- Earnings enhancement
- Combination of one or more of the above (e.g., ratchet with earnings enhancement)

These features are called minimum death benefit guarantees and a brief description of each is also provided in the Appendix.

10.2.2 Other Product Features

In addition to living benefits and death benefits, there are a variety of other product features. Some of the more common features are:

Nursing Home Waiver Rider

A nursing home waiver rider waives the surrender charges if the annuitant enters a nursing home.

Bailout Provision

This feature provides that, if the nonguaranteed current credited interest rate falls more than a specified amount below the initial guaranteed credited interest rate or a specified index, then all or part of the surrender charge will be waived for a limited time period. These provisions were designed to allay the fears of prospective purchasers who might otherwise feel that the life insurance company would be tempted to lower the attractive initial guaranteed credited interest rate after their money had been locked into a contract with significant surrender charges.

Market Value Adjustments

Market value adjustments (MVA's) attempt to modify the cash surrender value to take into account the change in the supporting assets backing the contract due to changes in interest rates during the time since the premium was originally deposited with the company. Thus, if the annuity was originally purchased with interest rates at the 8% level and two years later interest rates had risen to 10%, the market value adjustment would lower the cash value of the contract in order to account for the decrease in the fair value of the assets purchased by the life insurance company to back the annuity. Market value adjustments are expressed in formula form rather than referring specifically to the assets supporting the annuity. Factors in the formula may include the original interest rate credited, the rate credited at the time of surrender, and the rate credited on newly issued policies. Generally market value adjustments serve to decrease or increase the cash value, but some companies have market value adjustments which adjust in a downward direction only. Some life insurance companies register these products with the Securities and Exchange Commission since the adjustment might invade principal.

Free Partial Withdrawals

Free partial withdrawals (FPW's) gives the contractholder the right to withdraw a portion a of the fund value annually without incurring the surrender charge (e.g., 10% of the fund value). Sometimes this right is restricted to a period, such as 30 days, after each anniversary date.

Annuity Purchase Rates

In order to encourage annuitization, a number of companies provide incentives in the form of purchase rate enhancements. Three types of enhancements are common:

> (1) Purchase Rates More Favorable than Guarantees. In practice, companies generally use current annuity purchase rates which are more liberal than those guaranteed in the contract, since annuitants would otherwise withdraw their fund value at time of annuitization and purchase an immediate annuity with another life insurance company.

> (2) Waiver of Surrender Charge. Companies commonly waive the surrender charge in the event of annuitization.

> (3) Two Tiered Interest Credits. Some companies have developed contracts which effectively accumulate two separate funds: one which is used to determine nonforfeiture values and death benefits, and another which is used to calculate the amount applied toward annuitization and, possibly, the death benefit. Typically, the funds differ in that the second is credited interest at a rate which is a specified amount (such as 1%) higher than that used for the first fund.

Interest Index

Some contracts guarantee to credit a minimum rate (such as 3%), but also guarantee that the rate credited will not be less than a specified market interest rate index.

Equity Index

Some contracts guarantee to credit a minimum rate (such as 3%), but also guarantee that the rate credited will not be less than X% of the increase in a specified equity market index over a specific time period (e.g., 60% of the increase in the S&P 500 index over a five year period).

Although these are some of the more common features, there are other product features marketed by life insurance companies that are not listed above.

10.3 COMMISSIONERS ANNUITY RESERVE VALUATION METHOD

The 1976 amendments to the Standard Valuation Law define the *Commissioners Annuity Reserve Valuation Method* (CARVM) in the following paragraph:

"Reserves according to the commissioners annuity reserve method for benefits under annuity or pure endowment contracts, excluding any disability and accidental death benefits in such contracts, shall be the greatest of the respective excesses of the present values, at the date of valuation, of the future guaranteed benefits, including guaranteed nonforfeiture benefits, provided for by such contracts at the end of each respective contract year, over the present value, at the date of valuation, of any future valuation considerations derived from future gross considerations, required by the terms of such contract, that become payable prior to the end of such respective contract year. The future guaranteed benefits shall be determined by using the mortality table, if any, and the interest rate, or rates, specified in such contracts for determining guaranteed benefits. The valuation considerations are the portions of the respective gross considerations applied under the terms of such contracts to determine nonforfeiture values."[8]

The Commissioners Annuity Reserve Valuation Method is the minimum standard for individual annuities, and also for group annuities, unless they are issued to a qualified pension plan or to an Individual Retirement Account.

10.3.1 BASIC APPLICATION OF COMMISSIONERS ANNUITY RESERVE VALUATION METHOD

The determination of the policy reserve under the CARVM involves several steps. First, the fund value is projected forward on a guaranteed basis. These projected fund values are used to determine the future guaranteed benefits. These guaranteed benefits include all of the benefit streams guaranteed under the contract, including annuity benefits, death benefits, and nonforfeiture benefits. Second, for each future guaranteed benefit, it is then necessary to calculate the present value of that benefit, as of the date of valuation, less the present value of future "valuation considerations"[9] which are required to be paid under the contract, with all present values taken at the valuation basis for mortality and interest. Finally, the CARVM reserve is the greatest of the net present values which have been so calculated. The CARVM can thus be considered a "worst case" valuation method, in that the reserve for a particular contract is calculated taking into account the scenario which maximizes the liability.

10.3.2 SIMPLE EXAMPLE[10]

To illustrate determination of the policy reserve under the CARVM, assume a contractholder deposits $10,000 into an annuity contract that guarantees a credited interest rate of 6% for five years, at which time the

---

[8] See [4], Paragraph B of Secton 5 of Standard Valuation Law.

[9] Ibid.

[10] This example will ignore partial withdrawals, death benefits and annuitization benefits.

contracts matures for the accumulated value. During this five year period there is a surrender penalty of 4% in the first year grading linearly to 0% by the end of the five year period. Finally, assume that the statutory valuation interest rate is 5%. The following summarizes these assumptions:

Assumptions	
Premium	10,000
Credited interest rate	6.00%
Guaranteed Period..	5 years
Surrender Penalty:	
First year	4.00%
Second year	3.00%
Third year	2.00%
Fourth year	1.00%
Fifth year	0.00%
Statutory Interest Rate..	5.00%

The first step is to project the cash surrender value using the 6% guaranteed credited rate and the surrender penalty specified in the above table as follows:

Projected Cash Surrender Values					
	Assumed Surrender Values				
Contract Year	1	2	3	4	5
1	10,176				
2	10,176	10,899			
3	10,176	10,899	11,672		
4	10,176	10,899	11,672	12,499	
5	10,176	10,899	11,672	12,499	13,382

The next step is to discount the cash surrender value using the 5% statutory interest rate back to the valuation date which will be assumed to be the issue date:

Present Value of Cash Surrender Values						
		Assumed Surrender Period				
Contract Year	Present Values @ 5%	1	2	3	4	5
1	9,691	10,176				
2	9,886		10,899			
3	10,083			11,672		
4	10,283				12,499	
5	10,485					13,382

The Commissioners Annuity Reserve Valuation reserve is $10,485, which is the maximum present value.

There are several interesting points about these mechanics. First, the CARVM requires explicit recognition of future nonforfeiture values in the future benefit component of the reserve calculation. This is unlike the reserve methodologies discussed in Chapters 4-9, where only death benefits and endowment payments are explicitly taken into account. Second, in order to calculate the CARVM reserve in the general case for a particular annuity contract, it is necessary to determine every possible future death benefit, nonforfeiture value, and annuity payment under the contract at the end of each contract year, and then to calculate the present value of each of these benefits. A typical annuity contract may have at least half a dozen annuity options, and there may be dozens of anniversaries where annuitization is possible. Accordingly, extensive analysis may be necessary to calculate the CARVM reserve for a single contract.

10.3.3 VALUATION ASSUMPTIONS

Actuaries sometimes confuse the accumulation rate of interest (i.e., credited interest rate) and the valuation basis of interest and mortality under CARVM. To use CARVM, two separate procedures are performed. In the first phase, it is necessary to calculate future guaranteed benefits. This may involve accumulating the fund, and it may involve applying the fund value at various times to purchase annuity benefits using guaranteed annuity purchase rates. When accumulating in this manner, guaranteed fund values are used (including any guarantees, such as excess interest, declared since issue), and when applying the fund to determine annuity benefits, the guaranteed annuity purchase rates in the contract are utilized. The second phase of CARVM involves discounting the benefits derived in the first phase. The valuation rate of interest and, where appropriate, the valuation basis of mortality is used in this discounting. The valuation interest rate will vary depending on the type of benefit being discounted. It is important to realize that the accumulation basis and the valuation basis are completely separate, but both are always used in the CARVM calculations.

10.4 BENEFIT STREAMS

At the end of each contract year, the following are some of the events that might occur:

- The contractholder may make a partial withdrawal;
- The contractholder may make a full withdrawal by surrendering the contract;
- The contractholder may annuitize the contract;
- The annuitant may become disabled and receive benefits under a disability rider;
- The annuitant may enter a nursing home and receive benefits under a nursing home rider; or
- The annuitant may die.

Actuarial Guideline XXXIII classifies these benefits into two categories – Non-elective benefits and elective benefits. *Non-elective benefits* are "benefits that are payable … after the occurrence of a contingent or scheduled event independent of a contract owner's election of an option specified in the contract..."[11] This would include death benefits, disability benefits and nursing home benefits. *Elective benefits* are benefit options that may be elected by the contract holder in accordance with the terms of the contract. This would include partial withdrawals, full withdrawals and annuitization.

10.4.1 INTEGRATED BENEFIT STREAMS

An *integrated benefit stream* is a series of possible benefit payments. For example, the contractholder might make a free partial withdrawal of $1,000 at the end of the second, third and fourth contract year and then make a full withdrawal of $60,000 at the end of the fifth contract year. In addition, the possibility that the annuitant might die and a death benefit becomes payable also must be considered. This would lead to the following integrated benefit stream:

---

[11] See [4], Paragraph 1 of Definition of Actuarial Guideline XXXIII.

Year	Withdrawals +	Expected Death Benefits Payments =	Benefit Stream
1	0	100	100
2	1,000	200	1,200
3	1,000	300	1,300
4	1,000	400	1,400
5	60,000	500	60,500

The benefit stream would be discounted using interest and survival.

Benefit streams will be classified into three categories:

(1)   Integrated benefit streams ending in full withdrawal;
(2)   Integrated benefit streams ending in annuitization; and
(3)   Integrated benefit streams ending via other elective benefits.

A *cash value benefit stream* is a series of partial withdrawals that terminate in a full withdrawal. An *annuitization benefit stream* is a series of partial or full withdrawals that terminate in a full annuitization. Finally, *other elective benefits streams* are series of possible other guaranteed elective benefits, if any, available under the contract.

10.4.2 INCIDENCE RATES

An *incident rate* is the probability that an elective or non-elective event will occur in a particular contract year that will lead to a benefit payment by the life insurance company.

For all mortality based benefits under the contract (e.g., death benefits and annuitization benefits), the incident rate will be based on the annuity mortality table permitted under the Standard Valuation Law. In addition, this table will be used to discount the other types of benefit payments for survivorship.

For elective benefits, all possible elective benefit incidence rates between 0% and 100% must be considered to determine the "greatest present value." However, as noted in Actuarial Guideline XXXIII, "In practice, such a greatest present value will typically occur assuming an incidence rate of either 0% or 100%."[12]

10.5 DETERMINATION OF VALUATION INTEREST RATES

As was discussed in Chapter 4, the 1980 amendments to the Standard Valuation Law introduced a multitude of annuity valuation interest rate categories. This multitude results from the determination of valuation interest rates being based on the following parameters:

(a)   the method of valuation (issue year versus change in fund);
(b)   whether or not the contract permits cash settlement options;
(c)   whether interest is guaranteed on premiums received twelve months following the issue date (or the valuation date for the change in fund method);
(d)   the interest guarantee period; and
(e)   plan type.

---

[12] See [4], paragraph 2 of Definitions.

Actuarial Guideline XXXIII states that parameters (a), (b), and (c) should be determined at the contract level and parameters (d) and (e) should be determined at the benefit level.

10.5.1 INTEREST GUARANTEE PERIOD

Actuarial Guideline XXXIII specifies the determination of guarantee duration for the different benefits.

For portions of the integrated benefit stream attributable to partial and full withdrawals, the guarantee duration is the number of years that the guaranteed credited interest rate exceeds the valuation interest rate for life insurance policies with guarantee duration in excess of twenty years. For example, if the interest guarantee is 7.5% for the first five contract years and 3% thereafter and the valuation interest rate for life insurance policies is 4.5%, then the guarantee duration is five years.

For portions of the integrated benefit stream attributable to annuitization, the guarantee duration is the number of years from the issue date to the date that annuitization is assumed to occur. This implies different guarantee durations, and thus different valuation interest rates are used in valuing the annuitization benefits that may be elected at different dates.

For portions of the integrated benefit stream attributable to non-elective benefits, the guarantee duration is the number of years from the issue date to the date that the first non-elective benefit may first be paid. This requires that an integrated benefit stream be split into an elective portion and a non-elective portion in order to discount the benefit payments at the appropriate interest rate. For example, consider the above cash value stream:

Year	Withdrawals	+	Expected Death Benefits Payments	=	Benefit Stream
1	0		100		100
2	1,000		200		1,200
3	1,000		300		1,300
4	1,000		400		1,400
5	60,000		500		60,500

The withdrawals may have a valuation interest rate of 4% and the death benefit may have a valuation interest rate of 5%. The 4% would be used to discount the withdrawal benefits and the 5% would be used to discount the death benefits.

10.5.2 PLAN TYPE

Actuarial Guideline XXXIII specifies that different benefits under a deferred annuity may be valued assuming different plan types. For example, when calculating the greatest present value of the cash withdrawal benefits available under a contract that does not have a market value adjustment, the cash value benefit streams should generally be valued using interest rates applicable under Plan Type C.

On the other hand, when valuing the greatest present value of the annuitization benefits available under the contract, Plan Type A interest rates are generally used, since the underlying assumption is that no cash surrender values will be exercised if the annuity benefits are elected. Similarly, for non-elective benefits, Plan Type A interest rates are generally used.

10.6 EXAMPLES

Associated with this chapter is an Excel workbook, Chapter 10-DFA.xls. This workbook will be used to illustrate the determination of the policy reserve under the CARVM for a fixed deferred annuity plan design.

10.6.1 SINGLE PREMIUM DEFERRED ANNUITY

The first example will be a single premium annuity contract. This contract will have the following product features:

Expense charges:	$50 policy fee deducted from the fund at the beginning of each year	

Guaranteed Credited Interest:

Policy Year	Interest Rate
1	7.0%
2	7.0
3	7.0
4	7.0
5	7.0
6 and later	3.0

Surrender Charge:

Policy Year	Percent of Fund
1	7%
2	6
3	5
4	4
5	3
6	2
7	1
8 and later	0

Free Partial withdrawals: 10% of fund value, after first contract year

Death Benefit: Fund value

Annuitization Options: Life only annuity with the income benefit determined using the fund value and the guaranteed purchase rates. The guaranteed purchase rates are determined using the valuation mortality table and an interest rate at time of election of 7% in the first contract year and 3%, thereafter.

Most of these plan design features are specified in the worksheet, "CVA":

Contract Value Assumptions									
(1)	(2)	(3)	(4)	(5)	(6)	(7)	(8)	(9)	(10)
x	(t)	$RGP(t)$	$ECGP(t)$	$ECP(t)$	$^{G}ic_{(t)}$	$SCFV(t)$	$RFPW(t)$	$a'(t+1)$	$bPWB(t)$
60	0	1.00	0.0000	50.00	0.0700	0.0700	0.0000	10.09072	End
61	1	0.00	0.0000	50.00	0.0700	0.0600	0.1000	14.40613	End
62	2	0.00	0.0000	50.00	0.0700	0.0500	0.1000	13.98426	End
63	3	0.00	0.0000	50.00	0.0700	0.0400	0.1000	13.55854	End
64	4	0.00	0.0000	50.00	0.0700	0.0300	0.1000	13.13011	End
65	5	0.00	0.0000	50.00	0.0300	0.0200	0.1000	12.70008	End
66	6	0.00	0.0000	50.00	0.0300	0.0100	0.1000	12.26949	End
67	7	0.00	0.0000	50.00	0.0300	0.0000	0.1000	11.83937	End
68	8	0.00	0.0000	50.00	0.0300	0.0000	0.1000	11.41067	End
69	9	0.00	0.0000	50.00	0.0300	0.0000	0.1000	10.98424	End

Following is the definition of the variables used in this worksheet:

$RGP(t)$ = proportion of gross premium shown in the "Parameters" worksheet paid at duration t;

$ECGP(t)$ = expense charge rate that is multiplied times the gross premium paid at time t to determine portion of expense charge that is deducted from the gross premium at time of payment;

$ECP(t)$ = expense charge that is deducted from the fund at time t;

$^{G}ic_{t}$ = guaranteed credited interest rate between t and $t+1$;

$SCFV(t)$ = surrender charge rate that is multiplied times the fund value between t and $t+1$ to determine surrender penalty for cash withdrawals between t and $t+1$; and

$RFPW(t)$ = free partial withdrawal rate that is multiplied times the fund value between t and $t+1$ to determine amount of fund value that may be withdrawn between t and $t+1$ without a surrender penalty[13];

$a'(t+1)$ = annuity purchase rate used to determine annuity income benefit $BI_{[x]+t+1}$ for the annuity elected between t and $t+1$ (all elections are assumed to occur at duration $t+1$)

$$= \sum_{s=0}^{w-x-t-1} \left(1+ic_{t}^{a}\right)^{-s-1} \cdot {}_{s+1}p_{[x]+t+1}^{a};$$

ic_{t}^{a} = annuitization interest rate from the worksheet "Parameters"; and

$bPWB(t)$ = indicates whether partial withdrawals occur at the beginning or end of the contract year.

This example will assume that the illustrative contract was issued to a 60 year old male on July 1, 2000. He is both the owner and annuitant. The single premium paid on the issue date was $50,000.

The first worksheet, "Parameters," specifies information about the contract, certain plan design features and

---

[13] If $RPW(t)$ exceeds this rate, then a surrender charge is accessed on the excess amount and added to the expense charge.

the valuation standard:

Parameters	
Issue Date	7/1/2000
Maturity Date..	7/1/2030
Valuation Date...	7/1/2000
Issue Age	60
Gender	Male ▼
Gross Premium	50,000
Premium Payment Period	1 year
Fund Value	50,000
Cash Value..	46,500
Death Benefit Option..	Fund Value ▼
Annuitization Option	Fund Value ▼
Initial Guaranteed Credited Interest	
– Initial Rate	7.00%
– Ultimate Rate..	3.00%
– Initial Period...	5 years
Annuitization interest rate	
– Initial Rate ....7.00%← used to determine purchase rates	
– Ultimate Rate................................	3.00%
– Initial Period................................	1 year
Statutory Valuation Standard:	
Mortality Table – Death Benefits	1983 IAM ▼
– Annuitization Benefits	1983 IAM ▼
Interest Rate – Death Benefits.................................	7.00%
– Cash Withdrawals.............................	5.50%
Method..	Issue Year ▼
Function..	Curtate ▼
Age Rule...	ANB ▼

| Calculate |

As was noted earlier, the valuation interest rate used in valuing the annuitization benefits, i_t^a, depends on the type of annuity elected and when it is elected. The worksheet "SVIRAB" shows the valuation interest rates for a life annuity that varies by issue year and guarantee duration:

Statutory Valuation Interest Rates for Annuitization Benefits				
Plan Type: A				
Issue	Guarantee Duration				
Year	0	1 - 5	6 - 10	11 - 20	21 or longer
1981	0.1150	0.1150	0.1100	0.1000	0.0775
1982	0.1325	0.1325	0.1250	0.1125	0.0875
1983	0.1125	0.1125	0.1075	0.0975	0.0775
1984	0.1125	0.1125	0.1075	0.0975	0.0750
1985	0.1100	0.1100	0.1050	0.0950	0.0750
1986	0.0925	0.0925	0.0875	0.0800	0.0650
1987	0.0800	0.0800	0.0775	0.0725	0.0600
1988	0.0875	0.0875	0.0850	0.0775	0.0625
1989	0.0875	0.0875	0.0825	0.0750	0.0625
1990	0.0825	0.0825	0.0800	0.0725	0.0600
1991	0.0825	0.0825	0.0800	0.0725	0.0600
1992	0.0775	0.0775	0.0750	0.0675	0.0575
1993	0.0700	0.0700	0.0675	0.0625	0.0525
1994	0.0650	0.0650	0.0650	0.0600	0.0500
1995	0.0725	0.0725	0.0700	0.0650	0.0550
1996	0.0675	0.0675	0.0650	0.0600	0.0500
1997	0.0675	0.0675	0.0650	0.0600	0.0525
1998	0.0625	0.0625	0.0600	0.0575	0.0475
1999	0.0625	0.0625	0.0600	0.0550	0.0475
2000	0.0700	0.0700	0.0675	0.0625	0.0525
2001	0.0675	0.0675	0.0650	0.0600	0.0500
2002	0.0650	0.0650	0.0625	0.0600	0.0500
2003	0.0600	0.0600	0.0575	0.0550	0.0475
2004	0.0550	0.0550	0.0550	0.0500	0.0450
2005	0.0525	0.0525	0.0500	0.0475	0.0425

Since this contract was issued in the year 2000 and the valuation date is July 1, 2000, the highlighted row shows the valuation interest rates that apply to this illustrative contract for the annuitization benefit streams. For example, in the 10th contract year, the valuation interest rate used for the present value of annuitization benefits is 6.75%.

Using the information in the "Parameters" and "CVA" worksheets, the worksheet "CV" illustrates the determination of the fund value, cash value, death benefit and annuitization income benefit on a "guaranteed basis[14]."

---

[14] *Guaranteed basis* means that the contract values were calculated using guaranteed expense charges and credited interest rates.

					Contract Values						
(1)	(2)	(3)	(4)	(5)	(6)	(7)	(8)	(9)	(10)	(11)	(12)
x	t	$FV(t)$	$+ GP(t)$	$- EC(t)$	$+ IC(t)$	$- PW(t)$	$= FV(t+1)$	$- SC(t+1)$	$= CV(t+1)$	$DB(t)$	$BI(t)$
60	0	0	50,000	50	3,497	0	53,447	3,741	49,705	53,447	5,297
61	1	53,447	0	50	3,738	0	57,134	3,085	54,049	57,134	3,966
62	2	57,134	0	50	3,996	0	61,080	2,749	58,332	61,080	4,368
63	3	61,080	0	50	4,272	0	65,302	2,351	62,951	65,302	4,816
64	4	65,302	0	50	4,568	0	69,820	1,885	67,935	69,820	5,318
65	5	69,820	0	50	2,093	7,186	64,677	1,294	63,383	64,677	5,093
66	6	64,677	0	50	1,939	6,657	59,909	599	59,310	59,909	4,883
67	7	59,909	0	50	1,796	6,165	55,489	0	55,489	55,489	4,687
68	8	55,489	0	50	1,663	5,710	51,392	0	51,392	51,392	4,504
69	9	51,392	0	50	1,540	5,288	47,594	0	47,594	47,594	4,333

This worksheet centers around the following successive fund value formula:

$$_{t+1}FV_{[x]} = {}_tFV_{[x]} + GP_{[x]+t} - EC_{[x]+t} + IC_{[x]+t} - PW_{[x]+t}$$

where

$$_{t+1}FV_{[x]} = \text{fund value at duration } t+1;$$
$$_tFV_{[x]} = \text{fund value at duration } t;$$
$$GP_{[x]+t} = \text{gross premium collected at duration } t;$$
$$EC_{[x]+t} = \text{expense charge deducted at duration } t;$$
$$IC_{[x]+t} = \text{interest earned between } t \text{ and } t+1 \text{ and credited at duration } t+1; \text{ and}$$
$$PW_{[x]+t} = \text{partial withdrawal between } t \text{ and } t+1 \text{ and assumed to occur at duration } t \text{ or } t+1, \text{ depending on the value of } bPWB(t).$$

The variable $BI(t+1)$ is the income from an annuity purchased at duration $t+1$ using either the fund value or cash value at duration $t+1$ and is determined using the following formula:

$$BI(t+1) = \begin{cases} FV(t+1)/a'(t+1) & \text{if } \text{fund value is used on annuitization} \\ CV(t+1)/a'(t+1) & \text{if } \text{cash value is used on annuitization} \end{cases}$$

10.6.2 BENEFIT STREAMS

The worksheets "PW" and "FW" illustrate the determination of withdrawal benefits that will be used to determine the benefit streams. The worksheet "PW" shows the partial withdrawals for each benefit stream:

						Partial Withdrawal Benefits					
$x+t$	t	$BPW(0\|t)$	$BPW(1\|t)$	$BPW(2\|t)$	$BPW(3\|t)$	$BPW(4\|t)$	$BPW(5\|t)$	$BPW(6\|t)$	$BPW(7\|t)$	$BPW(8\|t)$	$BPW(9\|t)$
60	0	0									
61	1	0	0								
62	2	0	0	0							
63	3	0	0	0	0						
64	4	0	0	0	0	0					
65	5	0	0	0	0	0	7,186				
66	6	0	0	0	0	0	7,186	6,657			
67	7	0	0	0	0	0	7,186	6,657	6,165		
68	8	0	0	0	0	0	7,186	6,657	6,165	5,710	
69	9	0	0	0	0	0	7,186	6,657	6,165	5,710	5,288
⋮	⋮	⋮	⋮	⋮	⋮	⋮	⋮	⋮	⋮	⋮	⋮
89	29	0	0	0	0	0	7,186	6,657	6,165	5,710	5,288

In this worksheet, each row represents a benefit stream that starts at the contract year following the valuation date and ends at duration $t+1$. The values are from the "CV" worksheet. The variable $BPW(s\,|\,t)$ is the partial withdrawal between duration s and $s+1$ for a benefit stream that terminates at duration $t+1$. These withdrawals are assumed to occur at exactly duration $s+1$ and are defined as follows:

$$BPW(s\,|\,t) = PW(s)$$

where

$PW(s) = $ partial withdrawal between t and $t+1$ and assumed to occur at duration t or $t+1$, depending on the value of $bPWB(t)$.

Similarly, the worksheet "FW" shows the full withdrawals that will be used to determine the cash value benefit streams.

						Full Withdrawals					
$x+t$	t	$BFW(0\|t)$	$BFW(1\|t)$	$BFW(2\|t)$	$BFW(3\|t)$	$BFW(4\|t)$	$BFW(5\|t)$	$BFW(6\|t)$	$BFW(7\|t)$	$BFW(8\|t)$	$BFW(9\|t)$
60	0	49,705									
61	1	0	54,049								
62	2	0	0	58,332							
63	3	0	0	0	62,951						
64	4	0	0	0	0	67,935					
65	5	0	0	0	0	0	63,383				
66	6	0	0	0	0	0	0	59,310			
67	7	0	0	0	0	0	0	0	55,489		
68	8	0	0	0	0	0	0	0	0	51,392	
69	9	0	0	0	0	0	0	0	0	0	47,594

The values are from the "CV" worksheet. The variable $BFW(s\,|\,t)$ is the amount of full withdrawal between duration s and $s+1$ for a benefit stream that terminates at duration $t+1$. These withdrawals are assumed to occur at exactly duration $t+1$ and are defined as follows:

$$BFW(s \mid t) = \begin{cases} 0 & \text{if} \quad s < t \\ CV(s+1) & \text{if} \quad s = t \end{cases}$$

where

$$CV(s+1) \;=\; \text{cash surrender value at duration } s+1.$$

The worksheet "AB" illustrates the determination of annuitization benefits that will be used to determine the annuitization benefit streams:

						Annuitization Benefits					
$x+t$	t	$BA(0 \mid t)$	$BA(1 \mid t)$	$BA(2 \mid t)$	$BA(3 \mid t)$	$BA(4 \mid t)$	$BA(5 \mid t)$	$BA(6 \mid t)$	$BA(7 \mid t)$	$BA(8 \mid t)$	$BA(9 \mid t)$
60	0	53,447									
61	1	0	39,243								
62	2	0	0	42,331							
63	3	0	0	0	45,666						
64	4	0	0	0	0	49,267					
65	5	0	0	0	0	0	46,051				
66	6	0	0	0	0	0	0	43,850			
67	7	0	0	0	0	0	0	0	40,962		
68	8	0	0	0	0	0	0	0	0	36,260	
69	9	0	0	0	0	0	0	0	0	0	35,733

The variable $BA(s \mid t)$ is the present value at duration $t+1$ of the annuity elected between duration s and $s+1$ for a benefit stream that terminates at duration $t+1$. These elections are assumed to occur at exactly duration $t+1$ and are defined as follows:

$$BA(s \mid t) = \begin{cases} 0 & \text{if} \quad s < t \\ BI(s+1) \cdot a_{[x]+s+1} & \text{if} \quad s = t \end{cases}$$

where $BI(s+1) \;=\;$ income benefit at duration $s+1$.

The worksheet "DB" illustrates the determination of death benefits that will be integrated into the cash value benefit streams and annuitization benefit streams:

						Death Benefits					
$x+t$	t	$BD(0\|t)$	$BD(1\|t)$	$BD(2\|t)$	$BD(3\|t)$	$BD(4\|t)$	$BD(5\|t)$	$BD(6\|t)$	$BD(7\|t)$	$BD(8\|t)$	$BD(9\|t)$
60	0	53,447									
61	1	53,447	57,134								
62	2	53,447	57,134	61,080							
63	3	53,447	57,134	61,080	65,302						
64	4	53,447	57,134	61,080	65,302	69,820					
65	5	53,447	57,134	61,080	65,302	69,820	64,677				
66	6	53,447	57,134	61,080	65,302	69,820	64,677	59,909			
67	7	53,447	57,134	61,080	65,302	69,820	64,677	59,909	55,489		
68	8	53,447	57,134	61,080	65,302	69,820	64,677	59,909	55,489	51,392	
69	9	53,447	57,134	61,080	65,302	69,820	64,677	59,909	55,489	51,392	47,594

In this worksheet, each row represents the death benefit that would be paid if the annuitant dies. The values are from the "CV" worksheet. The variable $BD(s\,|\,t)$ is the death benefit at duration $s+1$ and defined as follows:

$$BD(s\,|\,t) \;=\; DB(s+1)$$

where $DB(s+1)$ = death benefit at duration $s+1$.

10.6.3 PRESENT VALUE OF THE BENEFIT STREAMS

In order to determine the integrated benefit stream with the "greatest present value," the present value of the benefit streams must be determined as of the valuation date using the valuation interest rate and mortality table. The present value of an integrated benefit stream ending in full withdrawal is the sum of (a) and (b), where:

(a)   is the present value of withdrawal benefits using the valuation interest rate for cash surrender values and survival factor; and

(b)   is the present value of death benefits using the valuation interest rate and mortality rates for death benefits.

In particular, the present value of the partial withdrawals is determined using the following formula[15]:

$$ABPW(d\,|\,t) = \begin{cases} \left(\dfrac{1}{1+i_t^w}\right)^{na} \cdot \left(1 - \dfrac{na}{12}\cdot q_{[x]+d}\right) \cdot \displaystyle\sum_{s=d}^{t}\left(\dfrac{1}{1+i_s^w}\right)^{s} \cdot {}_{s-d}P_{[x]+d} \cdot BPW(s\,|\,t) & \text{if } bPWB(t) = \text{beginning} \\[2em] \left(\dfrac{1}{1+i_t^w}\right)^{na} \cdot \left(1 - \dfrac{na}{12}\cdot q_{[x]+d}\right) \cdot \displaystyle\sum_{s=d}^{t}\left(\dfrac{1}{1+i_s^w}\right)^{s+1} \cdot {}_{s-d}P_{[x]+d} \cdot BPW(s\,|\,t) & \text{if } bPWB(t) = \text{end} \end{cases}$$

where

na = number of months from the valuation date to next contract anniversary;

d = number of years from the issue date to valuation date, rounded down to the nearest whole year; and

$ABPW(d\,|\,t)$ = present value of the partial withdrawals in the benefit stream that ends at duration $t+1$.

The worksheet "PVPW" illustrates the determination of the present value of partial withdrawals that will be used to determine the "greatest present value":

---

[15] The present value is first discounted to the contract anniversary following the valuation date, and then discounted from that anniversary to the valuation date.

Present Value of Partial Withdrawals

x+t	t	ABPW(0|t) =	nap·vna·	[PVBPW(0|t)	+ PVBPW(1|t)	+ PVBPW(2|t)	+ PVBPW(3|t)	+ PVBPW(4|t)	+ PVBPW(5|t)	+ PVBPW(6|t)	+ PVBPW(7|t)	+ PVBPW(8|t)	+ PVBPW(9|t)]
60	0	0	1.0000	0									
61	1	0	1.0000	0	0								
62	2	0	1.0000	0	0	0							
63	3	0	1.0000	0	0	0	0						
64	4	0	1.0000	0	0	0	0	0					
65	5	4,960	1.0000	0	0	0	0	0	4,960				
66	6	9,258	1.0000	0	0	0	0	0	4,960	4,299			
67	7	12,978	1.0000	0	0	0	0	0	4,960	4,299	3,720		
68	8	16,193	1.0000	0	0	0	0	0	4,960	4,299	3,720	3,215	
69	9	18,966	1.0000	0	0	0	0	0	4,960	4,299	3,720	3,215	2,773

Next, the present value of the full withdrawals is determined using the following formula:

$$ABFW(d\,|\,t) = \left(\frac{1}{1+i_t^w}\right)^{na} \cdot \left(1 - \frac{na}{12}\cdot q_{[x]+d}\right)\cdot \sum_{s=d}^{t}\left(\frac{1}{1+i_s^w}\right)^{s+1} \cdot {}_{s-d+1}p_{[x]+d}\cdot BFW(s\,|\,t),$$

where $ABFW(d\,|\,t)$ = present value of the full withdrawals for the benefit stream that ends at duration $t+1$.

The worksheet "PVFW" illustrates the determination of the present value of full withdrawals that will be used to determine the "greatest present value" of the cash value stream:

Present Value of Full Withdrawals

x+t	t	ABFW(0|t) = nap·vna·		[PVFW(0|t)	+ PVFW(1|t)	+ PVFW(2|t)	+ PVFW(3|t)	+ PVFW(4|t)	+ PVFW(5|t)	+ PVFW(6|t)	+ PVFW(7|t)	+ PVFW(8|t)	+ PVFW(9|t)]
60	0	46,721	1.0000	46,721									
61	1	47,723	1.0000	0	47,723								
62	2	48,344	1.0000	0	0	48,344							
63	3	48,927	1.0000	0	0	0	48,927						
64	4	49,464	1.0000	0	0	0	0	49,464					
65	5	43,182	1.0000	0	0	0	0	0	43,182				
66	6	37,756	1.0000	0	0	0	0	0	0	37,756			
67	7	32,956	1.0000	0	0	0	0	0	0	0	32,956		
68	8	28,428	1.0000	0	0	0	0	0	0	0	0	28,428	
69	9	24,473	1.0000	0	0	0	0	0	0	0	0	0	24,473

The present value of the death benefits stream is determined using the following formula:

$$ABD(d \mid t) = \left(\frac{1}{1+i_t^{.d}}\right)^{na} \left[\frac{na}{12} \cdot q_{[x]+d} \cdot BD(d \mid t) + \left(1 - \frac{na}{12} \cdot q_{[x]+d}\right) \cdot \sum_{s=d+1}^{t} \left(\frac{1}{1+i_s^{.d}}\right)^{s} \cdot {}_{s-d}p_{[x]+d} \cdot q_{[x]+s} \cdot BD(s \mid t) \right]$$

where

$ABD(d \mid t)$ = present value of the death benefits for benefit stream that ends at duration $t+1$.

The worksheet "PVDB" illustrates the determination of the present value of death benefit streams:

Present Value of Death Benefits

$x+t$	t	$ABD(0\mid t)$	= $PVBD(0\mid t)$	+ $nap \cdot vna \cdot$ [$PVBD(1\mid t)$	+ $PVBD(2\mid t)$	+ $PVBD(3\mid t)$	+ $PVBD(4\mid t)$	+ $PVBD(5\mid t)$	+ $PVBD(6\mid t)$	+ $PVBD(7\mid t)$	+ $PVBD(8\mid t)$	+ $PVBD(9\mid t)$]
60	0	416	416	1.0000								
61	1	861	416	1.0000	445							
62	2	1,338	416	1.0000	445	477						
63	3	1,854	416	1.0000	445	477	515					
64	4	2,413	416	1.0000	445	477	515	559				
65	5	2,940	416	1.0000	445	477	515	559	527			
66	6	3,437	416	1.0000	445	477	515	559	527	498		
67	7	3,907	416	1.0000	445	477	515	559	527	498	470	
68	8	4,351	416	1.0000	445	477	515	559	527	498	470	444
69	9	4,769	416	1.0000	445	477	515	559	527	498	470	444	418

Similarly, the present value of an integrated benefit stream ending in full annuitization is the sum of (a), (b) and (c), where:

(a) is the present value of partial withdrawals using the valuation interest rate for cash surrender value benefits and survival factor;

(b) is the present value of annuitization benefits using the valuation interest rate for annuitization benefits and survival factor; and

(c) is the present value of death benefits using the valuation interest rate and mortality rates for death benefits.

The present value of the annuitization benefits stream is determined using the following formula:

$$ABA(d\,|\,t) = \left(\frac{1}{1+i_t^a}\right)^{na} \cdot \left(1 - \frac{na}{12}\cdot q_{[x]+d}\right) \cdot \sum_{s=d}^{t}\left(\frac{1}{1+i_s^a}\right)^{s+1} \cdot {}_{s-d+1}p_{[x]+d}\cdot BA(s\,|\,t)$$

where

$ABA(d\,|\,t)$ = present value of the annuitization benefits for the benefit stream that ends at duration $t+1$.

The worksheet "PVAB" illustrates the determination of the present value of annuitization benefit streams:

Present Value of Annuitization Benefits

$x+t$	t	$ABA(0\|t)$	$= nap \cdot vna \cdot [PVBA(0\|t) + PVBA(1\|t) + PVBA(2\|t) + PVBA(3\|t) + PVBA(4\|t) + PVBA(5\|t) + PVBA(6\|t) + PVBA(7\|t) + PVBA(8\|t) + PVBA(9\|t)]$										
60	0	49,534	1.0000	49,534									
61	1	33,685	1.0000	0	33,685								
62	2	33,628	1.0000	0	0	33,628							
63	3	33,544	1.0000	0	0	0	33,544						
64	4	33,427	1.0000	0	0	0	0	33,427					
65	5	28,825	1.0000	0	0	0	0	0	28,825				
66	6	25,705	1.0000	0	0	0	0	0	0	25,705			
67	7	22,140	1.0000	0	0	0	0	0	0	0	22,140		
68	8	19,035	1.0000	0	0	0	0	0	0	0	0	19,035	
69	9	16,332	1.0000	0	0	0	0	0	0	0	0	0	16,332

10.6.4 GREATEST PRESENT VALUE

The worksheet "PVBS" shows the present value of the cash value benefit streams and annuitization benefit streams:

		Present Value of Benefit Streams								
		Cash Value Benefit Streams				**Annuitization Benefit Streams**				
$x+t$	t	$ABCVS(0\|t)$ =	$ABPW(0\|t)$ +	$ABFW(0\|t)$ +	$ABD(0\|t)$	$ABAS(0\|t)$ =	$ABPW(0\|t)$ +	$ABA(0\|t)$ +	$ABD(0\|t)$
60	0	47,138	0	46,721	416	49,950	0	49,534	416
61	1	48,584	0	47,723	861	34,546	0	33,685	861
62	2	49,682	0	48,344	1,338	34,967	0	33,628	1,338
63	3	50,781	0	48,927	1,854	35,398	0	33,544	1,854
64	4	51,876	0	49,464	2,413	35,840	0	33,427	2,413
65	5	51,081	4,960	43,182	2,940	36,725	4,960	28,825	2,940
66	6	50,452	9,258	37,756	3,437	38,401	9,258	25,705	3,437
67	7	49,842	12,978	32,956	3,907	39,026	12,978	22,140	3,907
68	8	48,972	16,193	28,428	4,351	39,579	16,193	19,035	4,351
69	9	48,208	18,966	24,473	4,769	40,068	18,966	16,332	4,769

In this illustration, the greatest present value is the cash value benefit stream at time 4. This occurs at the end of the initial guarantee credited interest rate period and is due to the relationship between the valuation interest rates, credited interest rate, interest rate used to determine annuitization benefits and surrender charges. In particular, a detailed analysis will reveal the following:

(1) The maximum value of the cash value benefit streams occurs right after the initial guaranteed credited interest rate period ends, even though there is a 2% surrender charge. This is because in the 6th contract year the fund value is accumulated at 3.0% and the discount rate is 5.5%, a difference that is more than the 2% surrender charge in the 6th contract year;

(2) The maximum value of the annuitization benefit streams occurs in the first contract year. This is because the interest rate used in the determination of the purchase rates decreases from 7.0% in the first contract year to 3% in renewal contract years, the valuation interest rates for annuitization exceed 3% and there are no surrender charges on annuitization.

   In other words, the present value of the annuity elected at the time of annuitization is less than the fund value at the time of annuitization (i.e., $BI(t+1) \cdot a(t+1) < FV(t+1)$) because the present value of the annuity purchase rates are greater than the present value of the annuity (i.e., $a'(t+1) > a(t+1)$); and

(3) The maximum value was achieved by assuming no partial withdrawals in the first five years[16]. This is because the 5.5% valuation interest rate used to discount cash withdrawals is less than the 7.0% credited interest in the first five years.

The worksheet "Summary" shows the determination of the policy reserve. The basic reserve is the larger of (a) and (b), where:

---

[16] To assume no partial withdrawals between t and $t+1$, set $RPW(t) = 0$ in the "SRA" worksheet.

(a)   is the greatest present value of cash value benefit streams; and

(b)   is the greatest present value of annuitization benefit streams.

Since in this illustration the greatest present value of cash value streams is larger, the basic reserve is $51,876.49.

Summary	
Policy Duration	0.0 years
Cash Value Stream:	
Maximum duration	4
Present value of partial withdrawals	0.00
Present value of full withdrawals..	49,463.78
Present value of death benefits...	2,412.72
Greatest present value of cash value stream	51,876.49
Annuitization Stream:	
Maximum duration	0
Present value of partial withdrawals	0.00
Present value of annuitization benefits	49,533.52
Present value of death benefits...	416.48
Greatest present value of annuitization stream	49,950.00
Basic reserve..	51,876.49
Cash value..	46,500.00
Cash value in excess of basic reserve	0.00
Total reserve	51,876.49

Finally, the cash value on the valuation date is $46,500.00. Since it is less than the basic reserve, the total policy reserve is $51,876.49. If the cash value exceeded the basic reserve, the excess would be recorded in Exhibit 5, Section G and the total reserve would be the cash value.

10.6.5 CALENDAR YEAR VALUATIONS

When calculating the reserve on an off-anniversary date, the fund balance as of the valuation date is accumulated using the guaranteed credited interest rate to the next contract anniversary.[17] Also, as before, the fund balance is accumulated to the end of each future policy year in order to determine benefits as of the end of each contract year. A common mistake is to calculate the benefits at the end of future calendar years rather than contract years. Once the benefit streams have been determined as of the next contract anniversary, they are discounted to the valuation date using the appropriate valuation interest rate for that stream. The reserve is the benefit stream leading to the "greatest present value." This reserve is compared to the cash surrender value and the larger of the two is the total reserve.

To illustration these points, assume the valuation date is December 31, 2000 and the fund value and cash value are as follows:

---

[17] Many companies guarantee current interest rates on a policy year basis. In such a case, current rates which are guaranteed for remaining fractional policy years are taken into account.

Parameters	
Issue Date	7/1/2000
Maturity Date..	7/1/2030
Valuation Date...	12/31/2000
Issue Age	60
Gender	Male ▼
Gross Premium	50,000
Premium Payment Mode	1 year
Fund Value..	51,720
Cash Value..	48,100
Death Benefit Option	Fund Value ▼
Annuitization Option	Fund Value ▼
Initial Guaranteed Credited Interest	
– Initial Rate..	7.00%
– Ultimate Rate	3.00%
– Initial Period..	5 years
Annuitization Interest Rate Factor	
– Initial Rate................... 7.00% ← used to determine life purchase rates	
– Ultimate Rate	3.00%
– Initial Period...	1 year
Statutory Valuation Standard:	
Mortality Table – Death Benefits..............................	1983 IAM ▼
– Annuitization Benefits	1983 IAM ▼
Interest Rate – Death Benefits.................................	7.00%
– Cash Withdrawals	5.50%
Method..	Issue Year ▼
Function	Curtate ▼
Age Rule	ANB ▼

[Calculate]

The fund value is projected to the next contract anniversary using the 7% guaranteed credited interest rate:

Contract Values											
(1)	(2)	(3)	(4)	(5)	(6)	(7)	(8)	(9)	(10)	(11)	(12)
x	t	$FV(t)$	$+ GP(t)$	$- EC(t)$	$+ IC(t)$	$- PW(t)$	$= FV(t+1)$	$- SC(t+1)$	$= CV(t+1)$	$DB(t+1)$	$BI(t+1)$
60	0.5	51,720	0	0	1,780	0	53,500	3,745	49,755	53,500	5,302
61	1.0	53,500	0	50	3,741	0	57,191	3,088	54,103	57,191	3,970
62	2.0	57,191	0	50	4,000	0	61,141	2,751	58,390	61,141	4,372
63	3.0	61,141	0	50	4,276	0	65,367	2,353	63,014	65,367	4,821
64	4.0	65,367	0	50	4,572	0	69,890	1,887	68,002	69,890	5,323
65	5.0	69,890	0	50	2,095	7,193	64,741	1,295	63,446	64,741	5,098
66	6.0	64,741	0	50	1,941	6,663	59,969	600	59,369	59,969	4,888
67	7.0	59,969	0	50	1,798	6,172	55,545	0	55,545	55,545	4,692
68	8.0	55,545	0	50	1,665	5,716	51,444	0	51,444	51,444	4,508
69	9.0	51,444	0	50	1,542	5,294	47,642	0	47,642	47,642	4,337

Note: The first row of values brings the contract values from the valuation date to the next anniversary date.

The benefit streams are then discounted backed to the valuation dates using the valuation interest rate for that stream. For example, partial withdrawals and full withdrawals would be discounted back using the 5.5% valuation interest rate for cash withdrawals. The present value of partial withdrawals would be:

Present Value of Partial Withdrawals

$$ABPW(0|t) = nap \cdot vna\,[PVBPW(0|t) + PVBPW(1|t) + PVBPW(2|t) + PVBPW(3|t) + PVBPW(4|t) + PVBPW(5|t) + PVBPW(6|t) + PVBPW(7|t) + PVBPW(8|t) + PVBPW(9|t)]$$

x+t	t	ABPW(0|t)	nap·vna	PVBPW(0|t)	PVBPW(1|t)	PVBPW(2|t)	PVBPW(3|t)	PVBPW(4|t)	PVBPW(5|t)	PVBPW(6|t)	PVBPW(7|t)	PVBPW(8|t)	PVBPW(9|t)
60	0	0	.96953	0									
61	1	0	.96953	0	0								
62	2	0	.96953	0	0	0							
63	3	0	.96953	0	0	0	0						
64	4	0	.96953	0	0	0	0	0					
65	5	5,121	.96953	0	0	0	0	0	5,282				
66	6	9,559	.96953	0	0	0	0	0	5,282	4,578			
67	7	13,400	.96953	0	0	0	0	0	5,282	4,578	3,962		
68	8	16,719	.96953	0	0	0	0	0	5,282	4,578	3,962	3,423	
69	9	19,582	.96953	0	0	0	0	0	5,282	4,578	3,962	3,423	2,953

The present value of full withdrawals would be:

Present Value of Full Withdrawal

$$ABFW(0|t) = nap \cdot vna\,[PVFW(0|t) + PVFW(1|t) + PVFW(2|t) + PVFW(3|t) + PVFW(4|t) + PVFW(5|t) + PVFW(6|t) + PVFW(7|t) + PVFW(8|t) + PVFW(9|t)]$$

x+t	t	ABFW(0|t)	nap·vna	PVFW(0|t)	PVFW(1|t)	PVFW(2|t)	PVFW(3|t)	PVFW(4|t)	PVFW(5|t)	PVFW(6|t)	PVFW(7|t)	PVFW(8|t)	PVFW(9|t)
60	0	48,238	.96953	49,755									
61	1	49,273	.96953	0	50,822								
62	2	49,914	.96953	0	0	51,483							
63	3	50,516	.96953	0	0	0	52,104						
64	4	51,070	.96953	0	0	0	0	52,675					
65	5	44,584	.96953	0	0	0	0	0	45,986				
66	6	38,983	.96953	0	0	0	0	0	0	40,208			
67	7	34,027	.96953	0	0	0	0	0	0	0	35,096		
68	8	29,351	.96953	0	0	0	0	0	0	0	0	30,274	
69	9	25,268	.96953	0	0	0	0	0	0	0	0	0	26,062

Similarly, the present value of annuitization benefits would be determined using the valuation rates for annuitization benefits:

Present Value of Annuitization Benefits

x+t	t	ABA(0|t) = nap · vna ·		[PVBA(0|t) +	PVBA(1|t) +	PVBA(2|t) +	PVBA(3|t) +	PVBA(4|t) +	PVBA(5|t) +	PVBA(6|t) +	PVBA(7|t) +	PVBA(8|t) +	PVBA(9|t)]
60	0	51,504	.97068	53,500									
61	1	35,026	.96271	0	36,382								
62	2	34,966	.96271	0	0	36,321							
63	3	34,879	.96271	0	0	0	36,230						
64	4	34,757	.96271	0	0	0	0	36,103					
65	5	29,972	.96271	0	0	0	0	0	31,133				
66	6	26,697	.96271	0	0	0	0	0	0	27,699			
67	7	22,995	.96383	0	0	0	0	0	0	0	23,857		
68	8	19,770	.96383	0	0	0	0	0	0	0	0	20,512	
69	9	16,963	.96383	0	0	0	0	0	0	0	0	0	17,599

Finally, the present value of death benefits would be determined using the valuation rate for death benefits:

Present Value of Death Benefits

x+t	t	ABD(0|t) = PVBD(0|t) + nap · vna		[PVBD(1|t) +	PVBD(2|t) +	PVBD(3|t) +	PVBD(4|t) +	PVBD(5|t) +	PVBD(6|t) +	PVBD(7|t) +	PVBD(8|t) +	PVBD(9|t)]
60	0	216	216	.96271								
61	1	678	216	.96271	480							
62	2	1,174	216	.96271	480	515						
63	3	1,710	216	.96271	480	515	557					
64	4	2,291	216	.96271	480	515	557	604				
65	5	2,839	216	.96271	480	515	557	604	569			
66	6	3,357	216	.96271	480	515	557	604	569	537		
67	7	3,845	216	.96271	480	515	557	604	569	537	508	
68	8	4,307	216	.96271	480	515	557	604	569	537	508	479
69	9	4,742	216	.96271	480	515	557	604	569	537	508	479	452

10.7 CONTINUOUS CARVM

A common question concerns the typical situation where the annuity contract has a surrender charge expressed as a percentage of the fund, where the percentage grades off at the beginning of each policy year. As an example, consider a contract with a 5% initial surrender charge which grades off 1% for each full policy year. Assume that the projected guaranteed fund balance at the end of the second policy year is $10,000, producing a cash surrender value of $9,600. If one more day is projected, to the beginning of the third year, the cash value jumps to $9,700 (plus whatever additional interest may have accrued overnight). In this case, projecting to the beginning of each policy year would produce a larger present value than discounting to the end.

However, the CARVM requires calculating present values based on benefits as of the end of each policy year. The language specifically states end of year values should be used, and examples found in the National Association of Insurance Commissioners Proceedings use end of year methodology, even though beginning of the year methodology would have produced larger reserves for the policies shown in these examples. Thus it is clear that drafters of CARVM intended for end of year values to be used, even though they realized (as evidenced by the example in the Proceedings) that typical single premium deferred annuity designs would produce larger reserves if beginning of the year values had been used.

New York is the only state where a literal interpretation of CARVM is that reserves be calculated using the maximum present values of benefits on any day (i.e., not just end of year benefits). It should be noted that New York law does not define CARVM using the model language, which is quoted at the beginning of this chapter. Rather, New York law is silent on CARVM methodology, and states, "the Superintendent shall, by regulation, issue guidelines for the application of the reserve valuation method to annuity contracts."[18] New York regulations then define CARVM as follows:

> "(ii) The minimum reserve for contracts with unconditional surrender charges or with conditional surrender charges not considered to be meaningful shall be the greater of (1) the contract cash surrender value and (2) the greatest of the respective excesses of the present values, at the date of valuation, of the future cash surrender values provided for by the contract on any day of each respective contract year, over the present value, at the date of valuation, of any future valuation net considerations derived from future gross considerations, required by the terms of the contract that become payable prior to such day of such respective contract year."[19]

So, New York's requirement to use all cash values, rather than only end of year values, is consistent with New York law, which differs significantly from other states on this point.

A number of other state insurance departments have expressed a preference for the continuous CARVM methodology used in New York. Some state regulators prefer the continuous approach for all annuities, while others only prefer the technique for certain types of annuities, such as those where the policyholder can withdraw funds without incurring a surrender penalty for a limited window period after the policy anniversary. Actuarial Guideline XXXIII, which was intended to address several technical CARVM issues, has ambiguous wording relative to the continuous CARVM issue. According to one of the drafters of the Guideline, the language is intentionally ambiguous on this point to allow for varying viewpoints. Unless otherwise specified, the remaining examples in this text use standard CARVM methodology as specified in the National Association of Insurance Commissioners model.

---

[18] See [22], Section 4217(6)(D)
[19] See [22], Section 95.11(C)(5)(ii)

10.8 HANDLING CERTAIN COMMON PRODUCT FEATURES

In practice, a number of common product features can create complications in calculating the CARVM reserve for single premium deferred annuities. Some of these are discussed below.

10.8.1 NURSING HOME WAIVER

Some life insurance companies offer a nursing home waiver, where the surrender charges are waived if the annuitant enters a nursing home. Similar to death benefits, Actuarial Guideline 33 classifies nursing home benefits as a Non-elective Benefit. As such, nursing home incidence rates are applied to the full nursing home benefits (e.g., fund value) paid upon incidence. This becomes another benefit stream that is included in the integrated cash value and annuitization streams. Also, the persistency factor used in discounting the benefits streams should reflect both mortality and nursing home incidence rates.

10.8.2 BAILOUT PROVISIONS

If a bailout provision is in effect at the date of valuation, so that the surrender charge is not then currently in effect, this "phantom" surrender charge should not be considered when comparing the current cash value to the basic reserve. Often this will result in a policy reserve equal to the current fund value in such a situation. However, the appropriateness of taking future surrender charges into account when calculating basic reserve for contracts with bailout provisions is not at first clear if the bailout provision is inoperable at the time of the valuation.

In 1985 the National Association of Insurance Commissioners adopted Actuarial Guideline XIII which states that the value of future guaranteed benefits under CARVM may not be reduced by contingent surrender charges which may not be available upon cash surrender. This guideline clears up the situation with respect to bailout provisions by making most such future contingent surrender charges inappropriate for use in calculating the basic reserve.

New York Regulation 126 requires that the reserve for contracts with contingent surrender charges be the greater of (a) the fund at date of valuation without deduction of any surrender charge, and (b) the basic reserve calculated by ignoring surrender charges when determining future cash values.

10.8.3 PURCHASE RATES MORE FAVORABLE THAN GUARANTEES

In practice, companies generally use current annuity purchase rates which are more liberal than those guaranteed in the contract, since annuitants would otherwise withdraw their fund balances at time of annuitization and purchase immediate annuities on the open market. This practice can produce large discontinuities in the policy reserve at the annuitization date. Actuarial Guideline XXXIII deals with the situation where the contract guarantees that the company will offer, at the time of annuitization, the rates offered to new purchasers of immediate annuities. For such contracts, the basic reserve shall be no less than 93% of the amount used to purchase annuitization benefits at time of valuation.

10.8.4 MARKET VALUE ADJUSTMENTS

Two issues arise with regards to market value annuities: (1) whether the market value adjustment should be recognized, if operable, when calculating the cash value at the date of valuation, and (2) to what extent possible future market value adjustments should be taken into account when calculating future benefit streams.

In the absence of guidance to the contrary, assuming the underlying assets are held in the insurer's general account and not in a separate account, the market value adjustment should be excluded from all calculations, both at the date of valuation and when calculating future benefit streams. This is because the assets held in support of the policy reserve are not revalued under statutory accounting principles, and it would be inconsistent to adjust the policy reserve to take into account interest rate changes without also adjusting the assets.

The National Association of Insurance Commissioners Modified Guaranteed Annuity Model Regulation requires that the assets held in support of market value annuities be held in a separate account. This model gives broad guidance as to reserve requirements, with minimum reserves equal to the cash surrender value including the effect of the market value adjustment. This model regulation applies in those states that have adopted it.

10.8.5 TWO TIERED INTEREST CREDITS

As noted earlier, some companies have developed contracts which effectively accumulate two separate funds: one which is used to determine cash surrender values and death benefits, and another which is used to calculate the amount applied toward annuitization and, possibly, the death benefit. Typically, the funds differ in that the second is credited interest at a rate which is a specified amount (such as 1%) higher than that used for the first fund.

To value these contracts, the first fund is used to determine the greatest present value of cash surrender values. Then, the second fund is used to calculate fund balances which are applied to purchase annuities at guaranteed purchase rates. These annuity benefits are then discounted to the date of annuitization using the valuation rate of interest and mortality, and then discounted to the date of valuation. The CARVM reserve is the greatest present value produced by these two sets of calculations. CARVM calculations may be greatly complicated since the annuity benefits must be taken into account.

10.9 CHANGE-IN-FUND VALUATION BASIS

The Standard Valuation Law allows the use of either an issue year basis or a change-in-fund basis for calculating the policy reserve under CARVM. While these are technically not differences in CARVM, they affect the calculation of reserves under CARVM. Furthermore, different interest rates are appropriate depending upon which basis is used.

Under an issue year basis, the valuation interest rate is determined as of the issue date of the contract, and those rates are used for discounting all of the guaranteed future benefits under the contract and remains constant throughout the life of the contract.

Under a change-in-fund basis, the future benefits are discounted using different interest rates depending upon when the increase in the fund value occurred which generated the specific benefits.

The advantage to the life insurance company of using a change-in-fund basis is that the initial maximum valuation rates are usually greater than when an issue year method is used; however, if interest rates were to fall subsequent to the issue date, it is possible that the maximum rates applicable to increases in the fund value could be less than if an issue year method had been used.

Change-in-fund basis valuation methodology is not defined precisely under CARVM, and different companies compute the reserves under this method using different methodologies. One reasonable method is to calculate CARVM reserves in the calendar year of issue using the change-in-fund valuation interest rate appropriate for that calendar year. In the next calendar year, the policy reserve would be calculated using the valuation interest rate for the calendar year of issue to discount benefits attributable to all fund balances up to those in effect at the end of the first calendar year, and using the change-in-fund basis valuation interest rate for the second calendar year for any benefits attributable to funds in excess of this amount. Similarly, in subsequent years, any benefits due to the increase in the fund value would be valued using the then appropriate change-in-fund valuation rates. Net decreases in the aggregate balances would be treated on a Last-In-First-Out (LIFO) basis. Note that the benefits are discounted separately. Thus, when calculating the second year reserve, the first year fund may produce a maximum present value when projected to the third year, and the second year change in fund may produce a maximum present value when projected to the seventh year. In such a case, these two present values of benefits in different years are added together to arrive at the policy reserve. As can be seen, while it is possible for the change-in-fund method to produce a lower reserve, it considerably complicates the calculations.

10.10 FIXED PREMIUM DEFERRED ANNUITIES

The preceding principles also apply to annual premium annuities. The only difference is that the present value of appropriate future "valuation considerations" is subtracted from the present value of each of the future benefits, and these differences are compared to determine the basic reserve. Valuation considerations are defined to be the "portions of the respective gross considerations applied" under the contract.

10.11 FLEXIBLE PREMIUM DEFERRED ANNUITIES

The CARVM requires that future valuation considerations "required by the terms of such contract" be taken into account. Because flexible premium deferred annuities do not generally require future premium payments, they are reserved assuming at the time of valuation that no future premiums are paid.

10.12 VARIABLE ANNUITIES

With a variable annuity, the contractholder may have chosen several different investment options. Some of these investment options may have a guaranteed credited interest rate and others will vary in accordance with the investment performance of the separate accounts selected. For example, the contractholder may have selected the following investments:

Fund File					
Policy Number	Fund ID	Fund Type	Interest Rate	Guarantee Date	Balance
A123456789	F05	Fixed	5.00%	7/1/2010	15,000
A123456789	V01	Equity			60,000
A123456789	V02	Bond			20,000
A123456789	V03	Money Market			10,000

The determination of the policy reserve for this variable annuity contract under the CARVM requires that the fund value be segmented into four sub funds. A fixed sub fund would be created for the fixed investment option that has a guaranteed credited interest rate of 5% until July 1, 2010. Three variable sub funds would be created for the remaining investment options. Specially, Actuarial Guidelines XXXIV, which will be discussed in the following section, requires that the separate account funds be classified into five asset classes[20]:

---

[20] Appendix III of Actuarial Guidelines XXXIV [4] contains a description of these asset classes.

- Equity class
- Bond class
- Balanced class
- Money market class
- Specialty class

When projecting the fund value in order to determine future contract values, the fixed sub fund would use the 5% guaranteed credited interest rate until July 1, 2010 and the minimum guaranteed credited interest rate would be used thereafter. For the variable sub funds, there is no minimum guaranteed credited interest rate. Accordingly, one reasonable approach is to project these sub funds using a "credited interest rate" equal to the valuation interest rate less asset-based charges[21].

Finally, most variable annuities have minimum guaranteed death benefits and guaranteed living benefits. Actuarial Guidelines XXXIV and XXXIX provide guidance on the determination of the reserve for these benefits.

10.13 ACTUARIAL GUIDELINE XXXIV

The cost of minimum guaranteed death benefits cannot be determined using a deterministic[22] model. In fact, using a deterministic model based on historical assumptions would dramatically underestimate the potential cost of this benefit. For example, if the fund value was projected from the issue date to the maturity date assuming a level 8% return, then the death benefit (i.e., the fund value) would exceed the minimum guaranteed death benefit and the contract would never be "in the money."[23] At a minimum, a range of scenarios must be analyzed to determine the potential cost of this benefit.

Actuarial Guideline XXXIV specifies that the reserve for variable annuity contracts with a minimum guaranteed death benefit is determined "by assuming an immediate drop in the values of the assets supporting the variable annuity contract, followed by a subsequent recovery at a net assumed return until the maturity of the contract. The projection should reflect the contractual definition of the MGDB and any contractual limitations, such as provisions that terminate the MGDB at a given age and those that restrict the MGDB to a given multiple of contract contributions. The immediate drops and assumed returns used in the projection vary by five asset classes in order to reflect the risk/return differentials inherent in each class."[24]

Actuarial Guideline XXXIV also specifies that the mortality rates from the 1994 Variable Annuity Minimum Guaranteed Death Benefit Table (1994 VA MGDB Table) be applied to the minimum guaranteed death benefit resulting from the immediate drop and recovery.

The following summaries the steps to determine the statutory reserve under this guideline for a variable annuity contract with minimum guaranteed death benefits:

---

[21] Asset-based charges typically refer to mortality and expense charges (M&E charges) and investment management charges.

[22] **Deterministic** means using the expected value or average value of a random variable. For example, the yearly return on equities is a random variable that averaged approximately 11% from 1926 to 2004. A deterministic method uses this average value of 11% to estimate future yearly returns. A stochastic method recognizes that the yearly return during this time period varied significantly from one year to the next, and that it will continue to do so in the future. Accordingly, an assumption is made about the underlying probability distribution of this random variable and a range of values are generated in accordance with this distribution for each year in the future.

[23] "**In the money**" is used to describe a contract where the death benefit exceeds the fund value due to the minimum guaranteed death benefit.

[24] See [4].

(1)   The fund value, minimum guaranteed death benefit and other contract information must be determined as of the valuation date.

(2)   The fund value is projected forward from the valuation date, ignoring any minimum death benefit guarantees, assuming a "credited interest rate" equal to the valuation interest rate less appropriate asset based charges (e.g., mortality and expense charges and investment management fees)[25].

(3)   From this projection, a set of benefit streams is determined.

(4)   Next, the fund value is projected forward from the valuation date, including any minimum death benefit guarantees, using the fund value on the valuation date and assuming that the fund value drops immediately in value and then recovers over the projection period.

(5)   From this second projection, a stream of minimum guaranteed death benefits and a stream of net amount at risks are determined.

(6)   An **Integrated Reserve** is determined using all contract benefits, including minimum guaranteed death benefits.

(7)   A **Separate Account Reserve** is determined ignoring minimum death benefit guarantees.

(8)   Finally, a reserve for minimum death benefit guarantees is determined as the Integrated Reserve less the Separate Account Reserve. This reserve is held in the general account of the life insurance company and cannot be less than zero.

The reminder of this section will illustrate the detailed procedures encompassed in each of these steps.

10.13.1 EXAMPLE

Associated with this chapter is an Excel workbook, Chapter 10-DVA.xls. This workbook will be used to illustrate the determination of the policy reserve under the CARVM for a deferred variable annuity with a guaranteed minimum death benefit. This contract will have the following product design features:

Expense charges:	$50 policy fee deducted from the fund at the beginning of each year
Asset-based charges:	1.25% mortality and expense charges plus 0.25% investment management fees

Surrender Charge:

Policy Year	Percent of Fund
1	7%
2	6
3	5
4	4
5	3
6	2
7	1
8 and later	0

Free Partial withdrawals:	10% of fund value, after first contract year
Death Benefit:	One-Year Ratchet, but not less than the fund value on the date of death
Annuitization Options:	Life only annuity with the income benefit determined using the fund value and the guaranteed purchase rates. The guaranteed purchase rates are determined using the valuation mortality table and an interest rate at time of election of 7% in the first contract year and 3%, thereafter.

---

[25] The portion of the fund value invested in fixed accounts is projected using the guaranteed credited interest rates for these fixed accounts.

Similar to the workbook Chapter 10-DFA.xls, most of these plan design features are specified in the worksheet, "CVA":

(1)	(2)	(3)	(4)	(5)	(6)	(7)	(8)	(9)	(10)	(11)
						Contract Value Assumptions				
x	t	$RGP(t)$	$ECGP(t)$	$ECFV(t)$	$ECP(t)$	$^A ic(t)$	$SCFV(t)$	$RFPW(t)$	$a'(t{+}1)$	$bPWB(t)$
60	0	1.00	0.0000	0.0150	50.00	0.2000	0.0700	0.0000	10.30809	End
61	1	0.00	0.0000	0.0150	50.00	(0.1500)	0.0600	0.1000	14.40613	End
62	2	0.00	0.0000	0.0150	50.00	(0.0500)	0.0500	0.1000	13.98426	End
63	3	0.00	0.0000	0.0150	50.00	0.0400	0.0400	0.1000	13.55854	End
64	4	0.00	0.0000	0.0150	50.00	0.0800	0.0300	0.1000	13.13011	End
65	5	0.00	0.0000	0.0150	50.00	0.0400	0.0200	0.1000	12.70008	End
66	6	0.00	0.0000	0.0150	50.00	0.0400	0.0100	0.1000	12.26949	End
67	7	0.00	0.0000	0.0150	50.00	0.0400	0.0000	0.1000	11.83937	End
68	8	0.00	0.0000	0.0150	50.00	0.0400	0.0000	0.1000	11.41067	End
69	9	0.00	0.0000	0.0150	50.00	0.0400	0.0000	0.1000	10.98424	End

The definitions of the variables used in this worksheet are the same as the variables in the workbook Chapter 10-DFA.xls, except:

EC_t^{FV} = asset based charges between t and $t{+}1$ that are subtracted from the assumed gross return to determine the assumed net return;

$^A ic_t$ = assumed net return after deduction of asset based charges between t and $1; t{+}1$;

$$= \begin{cases} i_t^{Historical} & \text{before valuation date} \\ i_t^w - EC_t^{FV} & \text{after valuation date} \end{cases}$$

$i_t^{Historical}$ = historical gross returns between t and $t{+}1$.

The assumed gross returns from the issue date to the valuation date are specified in the worksheet, "Historical Returns" as follows:

(1)	(2)	(3)
	Historical Gross Returns	
x	t	$i^{Historical}(t)$
60	0	21.50%
61	1	−13.50%
62	2	−3.50%
63	3	5.50%
64	4	9.50%
65	5	9.50%
66	6	9.50%
67	7	9.50%
68	8	9.50%
69	9	9.50%

This example will assume that the illustrative contract was issued to a 60 year old male on July 1, 2000. He is both the owner and annuitant. The single premium paid on the issue date was $50,000. The first worksheet, "Parameters," specifies information about the contract, certain plan design features and the valuation standard:

Parameters	
Issue Date	7/1/2000
Maturity Date	7/1/2030
Valuation Date	12/31/2005
Issue Age	60
Gender	Male ▼
Gross Premium	50,000
Premium Payment Mode	1 year
Death Benefit Option	One Year Rachet ▼
Roll-up Rate .... 5.00%←	ignored, if death benefit option is not roll-up
Annuitization Option	Fund Value ▼
Annuitization interest rate	
– Initial Rate .... 6.75%←	used to determine life purchase rates
– Ultimate Rate	3.00%
– Initial Period	1 year
Distribution of Fund Value by Asset Class:	
Equity Class	60.00%
Bond Class	20.00%
Balanced Class	10.00%
Money Market Class	5.00%
Specialty Class	5.00%
Total Fund Value	100.00%
Statutory Valuation Standard:	
Mortality Table – Death Benefits	1983 IAM ▼
– Annuitization Benefits	1983 IAM ▼
– MGDB Benefits	1994 VA MGDB ▼
Interest Rate – Death Benefits	7.00%
– Cash Withdrawals	5.50%
Method	Issue Year ▼
Function...	Curtate ▼
Age Rule	ANB ▼

10.13.2 PROJECTED UNREDUCED ACCOUNT VALUES

After all the information about the contract has been specified, the next step is to project the fund value from the valuation date to the maturity date[26] assuming a "credited interest rate" equal to the valuation interest rate less appropriate asset based charges (e.g., mortality and expense charges and investment management fees). This projection ignores any minimum guaranteed death benefits. These projected fund values are referred to as **Projected Unreduced Account Values** and appear in the worksheet "CV" as follows:

						Unreduced Contract Values						
(1)	(2)	(3)	(4)	(5)	(6)	(7)	(8)	(9)	(10)	(11)	(12)	
x	t	$FV(t)$ +	$GP(t)$ −	$EC(t)$ +	$IC(t)$ −	$PW(t)$ =	$FV(t+1)$ −	$SC(t+1)$ =	$CV(t+1)$	$DB(t)$	$BI(t+1)$	
60	0	0	50,000	50	9,900	0	59,940	4,196	55,744	59,940	5,815	
61	1	59,940	0	50	(8,984)	5,091	45,816	2,749	43,067	45,816	3,180	
62	2	45,816	0	50	(2,288)	4,348	39,130	1,956	37,173	39,130	2,798	
63	3	39,130	0	50	1,563	4,064	36,579	1,463	35,116	36,579	2,698	
64	4	36,579	0	50	2,922	3,945	35,506	1,065	34,441	35,506	2,704	
65	5	35,506	0	50	1,418	3,687	33,187	664	32,523	33,187	2,613	
66	6	33,187	0	50	1,325	3,446	31,016	310	30,706	31,016	2,528	
67	7	31,016	0	50	1,239	3,220	28,984	0	28,984	28,984	2,448	
68	8	28,984	0	50	1,157	3,009	27,082	0	27,082	27,082	2,373	
69	9	27,082	0	50	1,081	2,811	25,302	0	25,302	25,302	2,304	

All the values in this worksheet, including the Projected Unreduced Account Values, will be collectively referred to as unreduced contract values.

10.13.3 BASE BENEFIT STREAMS

The projected unreduced contract values are used to determine a set of benefit streams which are referred to as **Base Benefit Streams**. The two primary base benefit streams are the cash value benefit stream and the annuitization benefit stream.

The worksheet "PW" shows the partial withdrawals that will be integrated into the basic benefit streams:

					Partial Withdrawal Benefits						
$x+t$	t	$BPW(5\|t)$	$BPW(6\|t)$	$BPW(7\|t)$	$BPW(8\|t)$	$BPW(9\|t)$	$BPW(10\|t)$	$BPW(11\|t)$	$BPW(12\|t)$	$BPW(13\|t)$	$BPW(14\|t)$
65	5	3,687									
66	6	3,687	3,446								
67	7	3,687	3,446	3,220							
68	8	3,687	3,446	3,220	3,009						
69	9	3,687	3,446	3,220	3,009	2,811					
70	10	3,687	3,446	3,220	3,009	2,811	2,626				
71	11	3,687	3,446	3,220	3,009	2,811	2,626	2,453			
72	12	3,687	3,446	3,220	3,009	2,811	2,626	2,453	2,291		
73	13	3,687	3,446	3,220	3,009	2,811	2,626	2,453	2,291	2,139	
74	14	3,687	3,446	3,220	3,009	2,811	2,626	2,453	2,291	2,139	1,997

---

[26] Guideline XXXIV refers to this period as the Calculation Period.

Similarly, the worksheet "FW" shows the full withdrawals for the cash value basic benefit stream:

		Full Withdrawals									
$x+t$	t	$BFW(5\|t)$	$BFW(6\|t)$	$BFW(7\|t)$	$BFW(8\|t)$	$BFW(9\|t)$	$BFW(10\|t)$	$BFW(11\|t)$	$BFW(12\|t)$	$BFW(13\|t)$	$BFW(14\|t)$
65	5	32,523									
66	6	0	30,706								
67	7	0	0	28,984							
68	8	0	0	0	27,082						
69	9	0	0	0	0	25,302					
70	10	0	0	0	0	0	23,636				
71	11	0	0	0	0	0	0	22,077			
72	12	0	0	0	0	0	0	0	20,617		
73	13	0	0	0	0	0	0	0	0	19,251	
74	14	0	0	0	0	0	0	0	0	0	17,972

The worksheet "AB" shows annuitization benefits for the annuitization basic benefit streams:

		Annuitization Benefits									
$x+t$	t	$BA(5\|t)$	$BA(6\|t)$	$BA(7\|t)$	$BA(8\|t)$	$BA(9\|t)$	$BA(10\|t)$	$BA(11\|t)$	$BA(12\|t)$	$BA(13\|t)$	$BA(14\|t)$
65	5	27,157									
66	6	0	26,048								
67	7	0	0	24,462							
68	8	0	0	0	22,970						
69	9	0	0	0	0	21,565					
70	10	0	0	0	0	0	20,243				
71	11	0	0	0	0	0	0	19,342			
72	12	0	0	0	0	0	0	0	18,139		
73	13	0	0	0	0	0	0	0	0	17,007	
74	14	0	0	0	0	0	0	0	0	0	15,942

Finally, the worksheet "DB" shows the death benefits that will be integrated into the cash value basic benefit streams and annuitization basic benefit streams:

		Death Benefits									
$x+t$	t	$BD(5\|t)$	$BD(6\|t)$	$BD(7\|t)$	$BD(8\|t)$	$BD(9\|t)$	$BD(10\|t)$	$BD(11\|t)$	$BD(12\|t)$	$BD(13\|t)$	$BD(14\|t)$
65	5	33,187									
66	6	33,187	31,016								
67	7	33,187	31,016	28,984							
68	8	33,187	31,016	28,984	27,082						
69	9	33,187	31,016	28,984	27,082	25,302					
70	10	33,187	31,016	28,984	27,082	25,302	23,636				
71	11	33,187	31,016	28,984	27,082	25,302	23,636	22,077			
72	12	33,187	31,016	28,984	27,082	25,302	23,636	22,077	20,617		
73	13	33,187	31,016	28,984	27,082	25,302	23,636	22,077	20,617	19,251	
74	14	33,187	31,016	28,984	27,082	25,302	23,636	22,077	20,617	19,251	17,972

Since the unreduced contract values ignore the minimum guaranteed death benefit, the death benefit is the fund value.

10.13.4 PROJECTED REDUCED ACCOUNT VALUES

After basic benefit streams have been determined, the next step is to project the fund value over the same projection period and assuming that the fund value drops immediately in value and then recovers over the projection period. The immediate drop and recovery rates vary by asset class and appear in the worksheet, "Drop & Recovery Rates" as follows[27]:

Immediate Drop Percentages and Gross Assumed Returns		
Asset Class	**Immediate Drop**	**Gross Assumed Return**
Equity Class	14.000%	14.000%
Bond Class	6.500%	9.500%
Balanced Class	9.000%	11.500%
Money Market Class	2.500%	6.500%
Specialty Class	9.000%	9.500%
Weighted Average	11.175%	12.250%

The weighted averages in this worksheet were determined using the distribution of fund value by asset class from the "Parameters" worksheet. In particular, the weighted gross assumed return was determined using the following formula:

$$i^{Gross\ Assumed\ Return} = \sum_{j=1}^{5} r_j^{FV} \cdot i_j^{Gross\ Assumed\ Return}$$

where

$$
\begin{aligned}
i^{Gross\ Assumed\ Return} &= \text{weighted average gross assumed return (i.e., recovery rate);} \\
r_i^{FV} &= \text{proportion of fund value in } j^{th} \text{ asset class (from "Parameters" worksheet); and} \\
i_j &= \text{gross assumed return (or recovery) rate for } j^{th} \text{ asset class.}
\end{aligned}
$$

A similar formula was used to determine the weighted average immediate drop.[28]

The worksheet "CVA-Reduced" is the same as the worksheet "CVA", except the assumed return is the weighted average gross assumed return from the Drop & Recovery worksheet less asset-based charges:

---

[27] Appendix I of Actuarial Guidelines XXXIV [4] specifies the drop and recovery rates for each asset classes.

[28] To simplify this illustration, the weighted average gross return and immediate drop will be used. This approach may or may not be sufficiently accurate in practice.

					Reduced Contract Value Assumptions					
(1)	(2)	(3)	(4)	(5)	(6)	(7)	(8)	(9)	(10)	(11)
x	t	$RGP(t)$	$ECGP(t)$	$ECFV(t)$	$ECP(t)$	$^A ic(t)$	$SCFV(t)$	$RFPW(t)$	$a'(t+1)$	$bPWB(t)$
60	0	1.00	0.0000	0.0150	50.00	0.000	0.0700	0.0000	10.30809	End
61	1	0.00	0.0000	0.0150	50.00	(0.1500)	0.0600	0.1000	14.40613	End
62	2	0.00	0.0000	0.0150	50.00	(0.0500)	0.0500	0.1000	13.98426	End
63	3	0.00	0.0000	0.0150	50.00	0.0400	0.0400	0.1000	13.55854	End
64	4	0.00	0.0000	0.0150	50.00	0.0800	0.0300	0.1000	13.13011	End
65	5	0.00	0.0000	0.0150	50.00	0.1075	0.0200	0.1000	12.70008	End
66	6	0.00	0.0000	0.0150	50.00	0.1075	0.0100	0.1000	12.26949	End
67	7	0.00	0.0000	0.0150	50.00	0.1075	0.0000	0.1000	11.83937	End
68	8	0.00	0.0000	0.0150	50.00	0.1075	0.0000	0.1000	11.41067	End
69	9	0.00	0.0000	0.0150	50.00	0.1075	0.0000	0.1000	10.98424	End

The formula for the assumed net return in the above worksheet is as follows:

$$^A ic_t = \text{assumed net return after deduction of asset based charges between } t \text{ and } t+1;$$

$$= \begin{cases} i_t^{Historical} - EC_t^{FV} & \text{before valuation date} \\ i^{Gross\ Assumed\ Return} - EC_t^{FV} & \text{after valuation date} \end{cases}$$

This projection includes any minimum guaranteed death benefits and the projected fund values are referred to as **Projected Reduced Account Values** and appear in the worksheet "CV-Reduced" as follows:

												Reduced Contract Values											
(1)	(2)	(3)	(4)	(5)	(6)	(7)	(8)	(9)	(10)	(11)	(12)
x	t	$FV(t)$ +	$(GP(t)$ −	$EC(t)$ +	$IC(t)$ −	$PW(t)$ =	$FV(t+1)$ −	$SC(t+1)$ =	$CV(t+1)$	$DB(t+1)$	$BI(t+1)$
60	0	0	50,000	50	9,990	0	59,940	4,196	55,774	59,940	5,815
61	1	59,940	0	50	(8,984)	5,091	45,816	2,749	43,067	54,849	3,180
62	2	45,816	0	50	(2,288)	4,348	39,130	1,956	37,173	50,502	2,798
63	3	39,130	0	50	1,563	4,064	36,579	1,463	35,116	46,437	2,698
64	4	36,579	0	50	2,922	3,945	35,506	1,065	34,441	42,492	2,704
65	5	31,538	0	50	3,385	3,487	31,386	628	30,758	38,805	2,471
66	6	31,386	0	50	3,369	3,470	31,234	312	30,922	35,359	2,546
67	7	31,234	0	50	3,352	3,454	31,083	0	31,083	32,138	2,625
68	8	31,083	0	50	3,336	3,437	30,932	0	30,932	30,932	2,711
69	9	30,932	0	50	3,320	3,420	30,781	0	30,781	30,781	2,802

10.13.5 PROJECTED NET AMOUNT AT RISK

This projection produces an array of minimum guaranteed death benefits. From this array, net amounts at risk are calculated. The net amount at risk is determined as the minimum guaranteed death benefit less the reduced account value. The worksheet "MGDB-Reduced" shows the determination of minimum guaranteed death benefits and the net amounts at risk:

	**Reduced Minimum Guaranteed Death Benefit**
(1)	(2)	(3)	(4)	(5)	(6)	(7)	(8)	(9)	(10)	(11)	(12)
x	t	$GP(t)$	$PW(t)$	$SumGP(t{+}1)$	$SumPW(t{+}1)$	$AccGP(t{+}1)$	$AccPW(t{+}1)$	$FV(t{+}1)$	$DBMin(t{+}1)$	$BD(t{+}1)$	$NAR(t{+}1)$
60	0	50,000	0	50,000	0	52,500	0	59,940	50,000	59,940	0
61	1	0	5,091	50,000	5,091	55,125	5,345	45,816	54,849	54,849	9,034
62	2	0	4,348	50,000	9,438	57,881	10,178	39,130	50,502	50,502	11,372
63	3	0	4,064	50,000	13,503	60,775	14,954	36,579	46,437	46,437	9,859
64	4	0	3,945	50,000	17,448	63,814	19,844	31,538	42,492	42,492	6,986
65	5	0	3,487	50,000	20,935	67,005	24,498	31,386	38,805	38,805	7,419
66	6	0	3,470	50,000	24,406	70,355	29,367	31,234	35,359	35,359	4,125
67	7	0	3,454	50,000	28,859	73,873	34,461	31,083	32,138	32,138	1,056
68	8	0	3,437	50,000	31,296	77,566	39,793	30,932	29,129	30,932	0
69	9	0	3,420	50,000	34,716	81,445	45,374	30,781	28,120	30,781	0

'
The worksheet "NAR" shows the net amount at risk that will be integrated into the cash value basic benefit streams and annuitization basic benefit streams to determine the contract reserve:

	**Net Amounts at Risk**
$x{+}t$	t	$NAR(5|t)$	$NAR(6|t)$	$NAR(7|t)$	$NAR(8|t)$	$NAR(9|t)$	$NAR(10|t)$	$NAR(11|t)$	$NAR(12|t)$	$NAR(13|t)$	$NAR(14|t)$
65	5	7,419									
66	6	7,419	4,125								
67	7	7,419	4,125	1,056							
68	8	7,419	4,125	1,056	0						
69	9	7,419	4,125	1,056	0	0					
70	10	7,419	4,125	1,056	0	0	0				
71	11	7,419	4,125	1,056	0	0	0	0			
72	12	7,419	4,125	1,056	0	0	0	0	0		
73	13	7,419	4,125	1,056	0	0	0	0	0	0	
74	14	7,419	4,125	1,056	0	0	0	0	0	0	0

10.13.6 INTEGRATED RESERVE

The ***Integrated Reserve*** is the CARVM reserve determined using all contract benefits, including the minimum death benefit guarantees. In other words, it is the greatest present value of "future Integrated Benefit Streams available under the terms of the contract."

The Integrated Reserve is determined using the same procedures that were utilized for the deferred fixed annuity discussed earlier except one additional procedure is added to integrate the net amount at risk. The worksheet "PVPW" shows the present value of partial withdrawals:

Present Value of Partial Withdrawals

$x+t$	t	$ABPW(5|t) =$	$nap \cdot vma \cdot$	$[PVBPW(5|t) +$	$[PVBPW(6|t) +$	$[PVBPW(7|t) +$	$PVBPW(8|t) +$	$PVBPW(9|t) +$	$PVBPW(10|t) +$	$PVBPW(11|t) +$	$PVBPW(12|t) +$	$PVBPW(13|t) +$	$PVBPW(14|t)$
65	5	3,567	.96733	3,687									
66	6	6,727	.96733	3,687	3,267								
67	7	9,486	.96733	3,687	3,267	2,852							
68	8	11,891	.96733	3,687	3,267	2,852	2,487						
69	9	13,984	.96733	3,687	3,267	2,852	2,487	2,164					
70	10	15,802	.96733	3,687	3,267	2,852	2,487	2,164	1,879				
71	11	17,376	.96733	3,687	3,267	2,852	2,487	2,164	1,879	1,628			
72	12	18,737	.96733	3,687	3,267	2,852	2,487	2,164	1,879	1,628	1,407		
73	13	19,910	.96733	3,687	3,267	2,852	2,487	2,164	1,879	1,628	1,407	1,213	
74	14	20,918	.96733	3,687	3,267	2,852	2,487	2,164	1,879	1,628	1,407	1,213	1,042

Similarly, the worksheet "PVFW" shows the present value of full withdrawals:

Present Value of Full Withdrawals

$x+t$	t	$ABFW(5|t) =$	$nap \cdot vma \cdot$	$[PVFW(5|t) +$	$[PVFW(6|t) +$	$[PVFW(7|t) +$	$PVFW(8|t) +$	$PVFW(9|t) +$	$PVFW(10|t) +$	$PVFW(11|t) +$	$PVFW(12|t) +$	$PVFW(13|t) +$	$PVFW(14|t)$
65	5	31,460	.96733	32,523									
66	6	27,754	.96733	0	28,692								
67	7	24,442	.96733	0	0	25,268							
68	8	21,271	.96733	0	0	0	21,989						
69	9	18,473	.96733	0	0	0	0	19,097					
70	10	16,008	.96733	0	0	0	0	0	16,548				
71	11	13,837	.96733	0	0	0	0	0	0	14,304			
72	12	11,928	.96733	0	0	0	0	0	0	0	12,331		
73	13	10,253	.96733	0	0	0	0	0	0	0	0	10,599	
74	14	8,784	.96733	0	0	0	0	0	0	0	0	0	9,081

The worksheet "PVAB" shows the present value of annuitization benefits:

Present Value of Annuitization Benefits

$x+t$	t	$ABA(5|t)$	$= nap \cdot vna +$	$PVBA(5|t)$ +	$[PVBA(6|t)$ +	$PVBA(7|t)$ +	$PVBA(8|t)$ +	$PVBA(9|t)$ +	$PVBA(10|t)$ +	$PVBA(11|t)$ +	$PVBA(12|t)$ +	$PVBA(13|t)$ +	$PVBA(14|t)$
65	5	26,301	.97311	27,157									
66	6	23,713	.96848	0	24,456								
67	7	20,876	.96963	0	0	21,529							
68	8	18,343	.96963	0	0	0	18,918						
69	9	16,085	.96963	0	0	0	0	16,589					
70	10	14,072	.96963	0	0	0	0	0	14,513				
71	11	12,698	.96963	0	0	0	0	0	0	13,080			
72	12	11,071	.96963	0	0	0	0	0	0	0	11,404		
73	13	9,624	.97079	0	0	0	0	0	0	0	0	9,914	
74	14	8,339	.97079	0	0	0	0	0	0	0	0	0	8,589

The worksheet "PVDB" shows the present value of death benefits. These death benefits are equal to the unreduced fund values.

Present Value of Death Benefits

$x+t$	t	$ABD(5|t)$	$=$	$PVBD(5|t)$ +	$nap \cdot vna$	$[PVBD(6|t)$ +	$PVBD(7|t)$ +	$PVBD(8|t)$ +	$PVBD(9|t)$ +	$PVBD(10|t)$ +	$PVBD(11|t)$ +	$PVBD(12|t)$ +	$PVBD(13|t)$ +	$PVBD(14|t)$
65	5	206		206	.96052									
66	6	601		206	.96052	412								
67	7	978		206	.96052	412	392							
68	8	1,337		206	.96052	412	392	374						
69	9	1,678		206	.96052	412	392	374	355					
70	10	2,002		206	.96052	412	392	374	355	337				
71	11	2,307		206	.96052	412	392	374	355	337	318			
72	12	2,595		206	.96052	412	392	374	355	337	318	300		
73	13	2,865		206	.96052	412	392	374	355	337	318	300	281	
74	14	3,117		206	.96052	412	392	374	355	337	318	300	281	263

Finally, the present value of the net amount at risk stream is determined using the following formula:

$$ABNAR(d\mid t) = \left(\frac{1}{1+i_t^d}\right)^{na}\left[\frac{na}{12}\cdot q_{[x]+t}^{MGDB}\cdot NAR(d\mid t) + \left(1-\frac{na}{12}\cdot q_{[x]+d}\right)\cdot\sum_{s=d+1}^{t}\left(\frac{1}{1+i_s^d}\right)^s\cdot {}_{s-d}p_{[x]+d}+q_{[x]+s}^{MGDB}\cdot NAR(s\mid t)\right]$$

where

$ABNAR(d\mid t)$ = present value of the net amount for benefit streams that end at duration $t+1$;

$q_{[x]+s}^{MGDB}$ = mortality rates from the 1994 Variable Annuity Minimum Guaranteed Death Benefit Table (1994 VA MGDB Table) between $x+t$ and $x+t+1$.

Note ${}_{s-d}p_{[x]+d}$ is determined using the valuation mortality, which in this illustration is 1983 Individual Annuity Mortality Table.

The worksheet "PVNAR" shows the present value of the net amounts at risk:

Present Value of Net Amounts at Risk

$x+t$	t	$ABNAR(5\mid t) =$	$[PVNAR(5\mid t)$	$+\ nap\cdot vna\cdot$	$[PVNAR(6\mid t)+PVNAR(7\mid t)+PVNAR(8\mid t)+PVNAR(9\mid t)+PVNAR(10\mid t)+PVNAR(11\mid t)+PVNAR(12\mid t)+PVNAR(13\mid t)+PVNAR(14\mid t)]$								
65	5	62	62	.96052	74								
66	6	133	62	.96052	74								
67	7	151	62	.96052	74	19							
68	8	151	62	.96052	74	19	0						
69	9	151	62	.96052	74	19	0	0					
70	10	151	62	.96052	74	19	0	0	0				
71	11	151	62	.96052	74	19	0	0	0	0			
72	12	151	62	.96052	74	19	0	0	0	0	0		
73	13	151	62	.96052	74	19	0	0	0	0	0	0	
74	14	151	62	.96052	74	19	0	0	0	0	0	0	0

The worksheet "PVBS" shows the present value of the cash value benefit streams and annuitization benefit streams:

Present Value of Benefit Streams

$x+t$	t	Cash Value Benefit Streams						Annuitization Benefit Streams					
		$ABCVS(5\mid t)$	=	$ABPW(5\mid t)$	+ $ABFW(5\mid t)$	+ $ABD(5\mid t)$	+ $ABNAR(5\mid t)$	$ABAS(5\mid t)$	=	$ABPW(5\mid t)$	+ $ABA(5\mid t)$	+ $ABD(5\mid t)$	+ $ABNAR(5\mid t)$
66	6	35,215		6,727	27,754	601	133	31,174		6,727	23,713	601	133
67	7	35,058		9,486	24,442	978	151	31,491		9,486	20,876	978	151
68	8	34,650		11,891	21,271	1,337	151	31,723		11,891	18,343	1,337	151
69	9	34,287		13,984	18,473	1,678	151	31,898		13,984	16,085	1,678	151
70	10	33,962		15,802	16,008	2,002	151	32,027		15,802	14,072	2,002	151
71	11	33,672		17,376	13,837	2,307	151	32,533		17,376	12,698	2,307	151
72	12	33,412		18,737	11,928	2,595	151	32,555		18,737	11,071	2,595	151
73	13	33,179		19,910	10,253	2,865	151	32,551		19,910	9,624	2,865	151
74	14	32,971		20,918	8,784	3,117	151	32,526		20,918	8,339	3,117	151

The worksheet "Summary" shows the determination of the Integrated Reserve. The Integrated Reserve is the larger of (a) and (b), where:

(a) is the greatest present value of cash value benefit stream; and

(b) is the greatest present value of annuitization benefit stream.

Since in this illustration the greatest present value of cash value stream is larger, the basic reserve is $35,295.16.

Summary	
Policy Duration	5.50 years
Number of Months to Next Anniversary	6
Cash Value Stream:	
Maximum duration	5
Present value of partial withdrawals	3,566.94
Present value of full withdrawals	31,460.42
Present value of death benefits	206.15
Present value of net amount at risk	61.65
Greatest present value of cash value stream	35,295.16
Annuitization Stream:	
Maximum duration	12
Present value of partial withdrawals	18,737.23
Present value of annuitization benefits	11,071.28
Present value of death benefits	2,595.23
Present value of net amount at risk	151.39
Greatest present value of Annuitization stream	32,555.14
Basic reserve	35,295.16
Cash value	33,771.90
Cash value in excess of basic reserve	0.00
Total reserve	35,295.16

10.13.7 SEPARATE ACCOUNT RESERVE

The *Separate Account Reserve* is the reserve that would be held ignoring the minimum guaranteed death benefits. The Separate Account Reserve would be the basic reserve less the present value of the net amount at risk:

Basic reserve	$35,295.16
Present value of net amount at risk	−61.65
Separate Account Reserve	$35,233.51

Finally, a reserve for minimum death benefit guarantees is determined as the Integrated Reserve less the Separate Account Reserve. This reserve is held in the general account of the life insurance company and can not be less than zero.

Integrated Reserve	$ 35,295.16
Separate Account Reserve	−35,233.51
General Account Reserve	$ 61.65

See Chapter 9, Section 9.3.3 regarding the discussion about separate account assets and fund value.

10.14 ACTUARIAL GUIDELINE XXXIX

Actuarial Guideline XXXIX specifies that the reserve for variable annuity contracts with guaranteed living benefits is the sum of (1) and (2), where:

(1) equals the aggregate reserves for the variable annuity contracts ignoring both the future revenues and benefits from the guaranteed living benefits; and

(2) equals the guaranteed living benefits reserve, determined as the sum of the aggregate guaranteed living benefits charges from the date of issue to the valuation date for contracts still eligible for the guaranteed living benefits.

For the purpose of determining future revenues and benefits for guaranteed living benefits, a charge should be imputed in the event that there are no explicit guaranteed living benefits charges. Actuarial Guideline XXXIX also requires that "the appointed actuary must perform a standalone asset adequacy analysis of the VAGLB reserve. If such analysis reveals a reserve shortfall, VAGLB reserves must be increased."[29]

---

[29] See [4] Actuarial Guideline XXXIX.

10.15 EXERCISES

10.15.1 Key Terms

annuity contract
deferred annuities
payout period
flexible or fixed premium deferred annuity
variable deferred annuity
Commissioners Annuity Reserve Valuation Method
benefit streams
elective benefits
cash value benefit stream
incident rate
issue year method

integrated reserve
immediate annuities
accumulation period
single premium deferred annuity
fixed deferred annuity
non-elective benefits
integrated benefit stream
annuitization benefit stream
greatest present value
change-in-fund method
separate account reserve

10.15.2 Questions

a. What is the distinguishing characteristic of annuity contracts?

b. What is a fixed deferred annuity?

c. What is a variable deferred annuity?

d. What is the primary emphasis of a deferred annuity?

e. What are some of the primary insurance features of a deferred annuity?

f. Give a brief description of the Commissioners Annuity Reserve Valuation Method.

g. What is the difference between the accumulation rate of interest (i.e., credited interest rate) and the valuation interest rate?

h. Define non-elective benefits.

i. Give examples of elective benefits.

j. Define elective benefits.

k. Give examples of elective benefits.

l. Define cash value benefit stream.

m. Define annuitization benefit stream.

n. Define greatest present value.

o. What are the advantages of the change-in-fund method? What are its disadvantages?

p. Summarize the major steps taken to determine the statutory reserve for a variable annuity contract with minimum death benefit guarantees under Actuarial Guidelines XXXIV.

q. What is the difference between the integrated reserve and the separate account reserve?

r. Why is it important that the assets held in the separate account be equal to the portion of the fund value invested in the separate account, as opposed to the cash surrender value?

10.15.3 Problems

a. Using the Excel workbook Chapter 10-DFA.xls and the following deferred annuity plan issued to a 60 year old male on July 1, 2000:

Expense charges: $50 policy fee deducted from the fund at the beginning of each year

Guaranteed Credited Interest:	Policy Year	Interest Rate
	1	5.0%
	2	5.0
	3	5.0
	4	5.0
	5	5.0
	6 and later	3.0

Surrender Charge:Policy Year	Percent of Fund
1	7%
2	6
3	5
4	4
5	3
6	2
7	1
8 and later	0

Free Partial withdrawals: 10% of fund value, after first contract year

Death Benefit: Fund value

Annuitization Options: Life only annuity with the income benefit determined using the fund value and the guaranteed purchase rates. The guaranteed purchase rates are determined using the valuation mortality table and an interest rate at time of election of 7% in the first five contract years and 3%, thereafter.

(1) Determine the CRVM reserve on December 31, 2000 using the issue year method, curtate functions and the 1983 IAM Table on an ANB basis.

(2) What benefit stream leads to the greatest present value? Why?

(3) What changes when the function is changed from curtate to continuous? Why?

11 ✧ IMMEDIATE ANNUITIES

11.1 INTRODUCTION

Consider a 65 year old male who is retired and has $100,000 to invest. He needs the earnings from this investment to supplement his retirement income. One option he is considering is to buy an investment grade bond that will mature in twenty years and has a 6% coupon rate. Another option he is also considering is to purchase an immediate life annuity from a life insurance company that guarantees to pay $7,500 every year as long as he lives.

He views that the advantages of the life annuity are:

- the annual payment is $1,500 or 25% higher;
- the payments are guaranteed as long as he is alive; and
- the annuity has investment characteristics that are different than the other investments he owns (i.e., it will help him diversify his investments).

In contrast, he views the disadvantages of the life annuity are:

- it is not liquid (i.e., he can not reliably sell this investment in the open market and it does not have a cash surrender value);
- when he dies it has no value (i.e., he is not able to transfer any wealth to his heirs through this type of investment); and
- the $7,500 annual payment is not adjusted for inflation, so it will gradually become less valuable.

Immediate annuities are expected to become a major source of new revenue for the life insurance industry over the next several years. Today, these types of products do not present any major problems under statutory accounting principles, but as life insurance companies design product features that address some of the disadvantages noted above, this may change.

The primary focus of this chapter is immediate annuities and the determination of contract reserves under a statutory valuation.

11.2 PRODUCT CLASSIFICATION

An *immediate annuity* is an insurance contract that provides for benefit payments at regular intervals for a specified period. Since the valuation interest rate allowed for immediate annuities is generally greater than that allowed for deferred annuities, the National Association of Insurance Commissioners adopted Actuarial Guidelines IX and IX-B, which define an immediate annuity as one where:

(a)   the first payment is due not more than thirteen months from the annuity issue date,

(b)   succeeding payments are due at least annually for at least 5 years, and

(c)   the underlying pattern of payments due in any contract year are not greater than 115% of those in the prior contract year.

The contractholder may elect to receive periodic payments for life, for a specific period, or some combination thereof. In addition, the contract may specify one annuitant or more than one annuitant.

Finally, an immediate annuity contract may provide a death benefit. The following is a description of the more common types of immediate annuities[1].

A *life annuity* is an immediate annuity with the payments contingent on the life of one or more annuitants. In contrast, a *certain annuity* is an immediate annuity with payments made over a specified period without regard to the life of the annuitant(s).

A *life annuity with a period certain* works essentially the same way as that life annuity in that the annuitant receives periodic payments for as long as the annuitant lives. However, if the annuitant dies before the end of the specified "certain" period, payments are continued to a beneficiary until the specified number of "certain" payments (i.e., .the specified period in the contract) is completed.

A *refund annuity* is similar to the life annuity with a period certain in which the annuitant receives periodic payments for as long as the annuitant lives. There are two variants of this type of annuity. Under the cash refund annuity, a lump-sum payment is made at the death of the annuitant. The payment is equal to the excess, if any, of the purchase price of the annuity over the sum of the annuity payments made up to date of death. The installment refund annuity provides that annuity payments are to continue to a beneficiary after the death of the annuitant until the sum of all payments made equals the purchase price.

A *joint and survivorship annuity* provides for the continuation of payments after the death of one of the annuitants during the lifetime of the surviving annuitant.

11.2.1 Fixed versus Variable Immediate Annuities

A *fixed immediate annuity* guarantees the periodic payments. Typically, the assets supporting this annuity are invested in the life insurance company's general account and the payments do not fluctuate with the fair value of these assets. In other words, the life insurance company "bears most of the investment risk" and the contractholder receives a "fixed payment[2]."

A *variable immediate annuity* gives the contractholder the choice to invest in a variety of separate accounts. Unlike a fixed immediate annuity, the payments vary in accordance with the investment performance of the separate accounts selected by the contractholder, and therefore, the contractholder "bears most of the investment risk." When a variable immediate annuity is purchased, the contractholder or the company chooses an *assumed investment rate (AIR)*. This rate is used to increase or decrease the periodic payment on the contract anniversary using the following formula:

$$BI_{[x]+t+1} \;=\; BI_{[x]+t} \cdot \frac{1 + i_t^{actual}}{1 + i^{AIR}}$$

---

[1] These descriptions appear in SSAP No. 50 [18].

[2] Some contracts have a cost-of-living rider or stipulate that the payments will increase at a specified rate. Otherwise, the payments are fixed.

where

$$BI_{[x]+t} \quad = \quad \text{income benefit between durations t and t+1;}$$

$$i_t^{actual} \quad = \quad \text{actual return of the separate account between durations t and t+1; and}$$

$$i^{AIR} \quad = \quad \text{assumed investment rate;}$$

Some contracts guarantee that the payment will not decrease below a minimum amount.

11.2.2 SUPPLEMENTARY CONTRACTS

A *supplementary contract* is a contract that is issued when the policyholder elects a settlement option ("annuitizes") within a life insurance or an annuity contract. A *supplementary contract with life contingencies* is an immediate annuity with the payments contingent on the life of one or more annuitants. This differs from a *supplementary contract without life contingencies* under which the payments are made over a specified period without regard to the life of the annuitant(s).

11.2.3 STRUCTURED SETTLEMENTS

Structured settlements are immediate annuities with "customized" payment patterns, which may include lump-sum payments. Structured settlements are often issued in conjunction with personal injury settlements, and so may be priced assuming substandard mortality. Guidelines IX-A and IX-B address special valuation considerations involving structured settlements, including the use of substandard mortality, and acceptable methods for valuing lump sum and increasing payments.

11.3 VALUATION OF IMMEDIATE ANNUITIES

Immediate annuities generally present no particular problems under the CARVM. In the case of immediate annuities without cash surrender values, the contract reserve is equal to the present value of the annuity benefits, which is the same as the method prior to the adoption of CARVM. If an immediate annuity has cash surrender values, it is possible that the present value of one of the cash values could exceed the present value of the annuity benefits. The reserves for cash surrender values are determined separately using the methods described in Chapter 10.

In the case of a deferred annuity which annuitizes, or a settlement option arising from a life insurance or an annuity contract, most companies value the "new" immediate annuity at the valuation rate in effect at the date of annuitization. Guideline IX-B allows this practice, as well as the practice of using the rate in effect at the original issue date, but requires consistency from year to year in the method used.

11.3.1 VALUATION ASSUMPTIONS

Mortality has improved approximately 2% each year for the past twenty-five years. In order to produce conservative reserves, minimum standards of valuation mortality for immediate annuities have a projection scale that is used to reflect future mortality improvement. For a long period of time, most life insurance companies used the 1983 Immediate Annuity Mortality Tables with Projection Scale G to calculate statutory reserves for immediate annuities. The mortality rates used in this chapter were determined using the following formula:

$$q_{[x]+t}^{Projected} \quad = \quad q_{[x]+t}^{Unprojected} \cdot A_{[x]+t}^{i^d}$$

where

$$[x] \ = \ \text{issue age;}$$

$$t \ = \ \text{duration;}$$

$$q_{[x]+t}^{Unprojected} \ = \ \text{valuation mortality rate between } t \text{ and } t+1 \text{ without improvement;}$$

$$q_{[x]+t}^{Projected} \ = \ \text{valuation mortality rate between } t \text{ and } t+1 \text{ with improvement;}$$

$$A_{[x]+t}^{i^d} \ = \ \text{cumulative improvement factor;}$$

$$= \ \prod_{s=0}^{t}\left(1 - i_{[x]+s}^{q}\right)$$

$$i_{[x]+s}^{q} \ = \ \text{annual improvement factor between } t \text{ and } t+1.$$

Most states require that a sex distinct mortality table be used as the minimum standard even if the immediate annuity was issued on a unisex basis.

11.3.2 Valuation Methodology

The contract reserve for an immediate annuity without cash surrender values is the present value of the annuity benefits using the appropriate valuation mortality table and interest rate. This present value of future benefits as of duration t is defined by the following formula:

$$_t V_{[x]:\overline{n}|} = \begin{cases} a_{\overline{nCP-t}|} + {}_{nCP-t|}a_{x+t} & \text{if} \quad t < nCP \\ a_{x+t} & \text{if} \quad t \geq nCP \end{cases}$$

$$= \begin{cases} \displaystyle\sum_{s=0}^{nCP-t-1} v^{s+1} \cdot BI_{[x]+t+s} + \sum_{s=nCP}^{n-t-1} v^{s+1} \cdot {}_{s+1}P_{[x]+t} \cdot BI_{[x]+t+s} & \text{if} \quad t < nCP \\ \displaystyle\sum_{s=0}^{n-t-1} v^{s+1} \cdot {}_{s}P_{[x]+t} \cdot BI_{[x]+t+s} & \text{if} \quad t \geq nCP \end{cases}$$

where

$$n \ = \ \text{number of years from the issue date to the end of the benefit period;}$$

$$nCP \ = \ \text{number of years from the issue date to the end of the certain period;}$$

$$v \ = \ \text{discount factor;}$$

$$= \ \frac{1}{1+i};$$

$$i \ = \ \text{valuation interest rate;}$$

$$_s P_{[x]+t} \ = \ \text{probability that the annuitant who survived to duration } t \text{ will survive to duration } t+s;$$

$$= \ \prod_{r=0}^{s-1}(1 - q_{[x]+t+r});$$

$$q_{[x]+t+r} \ = \ \text{valuation mortality rate for attained age } x+t+r;$$

$$BI_{[x]+t} \ = \ \text{income benefit between durations } t \text{ and } t+1 \text{ and assumed to be paid at duration } t+1;$$

11.3.3 EXAMPLE

Similar to previous chapters, associated with this chapter is an Excel workbook, Chapter 11.xls. This workbook will be used to demonstrate some of the concepts discussed in this chapter. The contract used for illustration purposes will be a 10 year certain and life annuity with a benefit payment of $10,000, payable at the end of each contract year. The annuitant is a 65 year old male. This information is captured in the first workbook, called "Parameters," in this workbook:

Parameters	
Issue Date	1/1/2000
Valuation Date	12/31/2000
Issue Age	65
Gender	Male ▼
Annual Income	10,000
Periods:	
Certain Period	10 years
Benefit Period	100 years
Statutory Valuation Standard:	
Mortality Table	1983 IAM ▼
Projection Scale	None ▼
Interest Rate	5.00%
Function	Curtate ▼
Age Rule	ANB ▼

The worksheet "SRA" shows the statutory reserve assumptions used in the calculation of the contract reserve:

Statutory Reserve Assumptions							
(1)	(2)	(3)	(4)	(5)	(6)	(7)	(8)
x	t	$i(t)$	$i^q(t)$	$q^d(t)$ ·	$AIQ(t)$ =	$q(t)$	$p(t)$
65	0	.0500	.0000	.01285	1.00000	.01285	1.00000
66	1	.0500	.0000	.01420	1.00000	.01420	.98715
67	2	.0500	.0000	.01572	1.00000	.01572	.97313
68	3	.0500	.0000	.01741	1.00000	.01741	.95784
69	4	.0500	.0000	.01930	1.00000	.01930	.94116
70	5	.0500	.0000	.02137	1.00000	.02137	.92300
71	6	.0500	.0000	.02365	1.00000	.02365	.90327
72	7	.0500	.0000	.02613	1.00000	.02613	.88191
73	8	.0500	.0000	.02884	1.00000	.02884	.85887
74	9	.0500	.0000	.03179	1.00000	.03179	.83410

Using these assumptions, the worksheet "PV" shows the calculation of the present value of future benefits as of the issue date:

Present Values									
(1)	(2)	(3)	(4)	(5)	(6)	(7)	(8)	(9)	(10)
x	t	$v(t+1)$ $\cdot$	$p(t+1)$ $\cdot$	$CRA(t)$ $\cdot$	$BI(t)$ $=$	$PVBI(t)$	$a_{\overline{n-t}}$	$+{}_{n-t\vert}a_{x+t}$ $=$	$a(t)$
65	0	0.95238	1.00000	1.00000	10,000	9,524	77,217	38,548	115,765
66	1	0.90703	1.00000	1.00000	10,000	9,070	71,078	41,002	112,081
67	2	0.86384	1.00000	1.00000	10,000	8,638	64,632	43,673	108,305
68	3	0.82270	1.00000	1.00000	10,000	8,227	57,864	46,589	104,452
69	4	0.78353	1.00000	1.00000	10,000	7,835	50,757	49,785	100,542
70	5	0.74622	1.00000	1.00000	10,000	7,462	43,295	53,303	96,597
71	6	0.71068	1.00000	1.00000	10,000	7,107	35,460	57,190	92,650
72	7	0.67684	1.00000	1.00000	10,000	6,768	27,232	61,504	88,736
73	8	0.64461	1.00000	1.00000	10,000	6,446	18,594	66,312	84,906
74	9	0.61391	1.00000	1.00000	10,000	6,139	9,524	71,695	81,219
75	10	0.58468	0.77928	1.00000	10,000	4,556	0	77,752	77,752
76	11	0.55684	0.74918	1.00000	10,000	4,172	0	74,604	74,604
77	12	0.53032	0.71727	1.00000	10,000	3,804	0	71,482	71,482
78	13	0.50507	0.68359	1.00000	10,000	3,453	0	68,395	68,395
79	14	0.48102	0.64821	1.00000	10,000	3,118	0	65,353	65,353

Finally, the worksheet "SSR" shows the calculation of the contract reserve for all durations:

Successive Statutory Reserves							
(1)	(2)	(3)	(4)	(5)	(6)	(7)	(8)
x	t	$V(t)$ $+$	$NP(t)$ $+$	$I(t)$ $-$	$BI(t)$ $+$	$VD(t)$ $=$	$V(t+1)$
65	0	0	115,765	5,788	10,000	527	112,081
66	1	112,081	0	5,604	10,000	620	108,305
67	2	108,305	0	5,415	10,000	732	104,452
68	3	104,452	0	5,223	10,000	867	100,542
69	4	100,542	0	5,027	10,000	1,029	96,579
70	5	96,579	0	4,830	10,000	1,222	92,650
71	6	92,650	0	4,632	10,000	1,454	88,736
72	7	88,736	0	4,437	10,000	1,733	84,906
73	8	84,906	0	4,245	10,000	2,067	81,219
74	9	81,219	0	4.061	10,000	2,472	77,752
75	10	77,752	0	3,888	10,000	2,965	74,604
76	11	74,604	0	3,730	10,000	3,148	71,482
77	12	71,482	0	3,574	10,000	3,339	68,395
78	13	68,395	0	3,420	10,000	3,538	65,353
79	14	65,353	0	3,268	10,000	3,745	62,365

This workbook centers around the following formula:

$$
{}_{t+1}V_{[x]:\overline{n}} = \begin{cases} {}_{t}V_{[x]:\overline{n}} \cdot (1+i) - BI_{[x]+t} + q_{[x]+t} \cdot {}_{nCP-t-1\vert}a_{x+t-1} & \text{if } t < nCP \\ \dfrac{{}_{t}V_{[x]:\overline{n}} \cdot (1+i)}{1 - q_{[x]+t}} - BI_{[x]+t} & \text{if } t \geq nCP \end{cases}
$$

11.4 EXERCISES

11.4.1 Key Terms

immediate annuity   life annuity
certain annuity   assumed interest rate
supplementary contracts   structured settlements

11.4.2   Questions

a. What is the distinguishing characteristic of immediate annuities?

b. What are the major differences between deferred annuities and immediate annuities?

c. What are the major differences between whole life and immediate annuities?

d. What are the unique risks of selling immediate annuities?

e. How do you think the market will evolve to address the disadvantages discussed in Section 11.1? What effect do you think this will have on the methodology for determining reserves?

12 ✧ Miscellaneous Reserves

12.1 Introduction

This chapter deals with the calculation of reserves which are held in addition to the basic policy reserves. Some of these reserves are held for supplemental benefits which are sold with, or as an inherent part of, the basic life insurance policy. Others are additional liabilities associated with the basic policy benefits, which may be required due to the product design or the type of basic policy reserve used by the company. Also discussed in this chapter are basic reserve considerations for last-to-die policies.

Many miscellaneous reserves tend to be quite small in relation to the reserves for the basic policy benefits. Several of these miscellaneous reserves are not only relatively insignificant, but are also quite complicated to calculate on an exact basis, and hence, in practice, tend to be calculated using considerably less precise techniques than for the basic policy benefit reserves. Sometimes single average ages are used, and a single set of reserve factors may be used for a wide range of policy forms which would theoretically require calculation of separate factors. It is generally felt that the use of gross approximations is acceptable for many of these reserves; however, the valuation actuary, as always, has the responsibility for certifying that the reserves in total make good and sufficient provision for the unmatured policy obligations, and should be able to prove to his or her own satisfaction that the use of such approximations will not cause the reported reserve to be significantly less than the exact reserve. Furthermore, given that life insurance companies in the United States must use Federally Prescribed Tax Reserves to determine taxable income, the valuation actuary must also be prepared to show that such approximations do not significantly overstate reserve liabilities, resulting in lower taxable income. This is not to imply that the use of approximations is unacceptable for these reserves. However, the valuation actuary must review the approximations from time to time to be satisfied as to their continued acceptability.

There are several methods used in practice to calculate reserves for many of these benefits, with the method chosen dependent upon each company's available data. The methods illustrated in the following pages are not necessarily more acceptable or more accurate than other methods which are in common use.

12.2 Accidental Death Benefit

Reserves for Accidental Death Benefit (ADB) are usually calculated using the accidental death tables mentioned in the Standard Valuation Law (the 1959 ADB Table for 1966 and later issues) along with permissible levels of general mortality and interest determined by the basic policy type. The Canadian valuation laws are silent as to the valuation bases for accidental death benefit, as they are silent for life benefits, and it is the actuary's responsibility that the method and assumptions are appropriate.

In practice, in both countries the method used to calculate accidental death benefit reserves is normally similar to the method used to calculate basic policy reserves. A company could use either a mean or mid-terminal approach for these extra reserves.

The terminal reserve for an *m*-pay, *n*-year benefit would be:

$$_t^m V_{x:\overline{n}|}^{ADB} = A_{x+t:\overline{n-t}|}^{ADB} - _m P_{x:\overline{n}|}^{ADB} \cdot \ddot{a}_{x+t:\overline{m-t}|}$$

where

n = number of years from the issue date to the end of the benefit period for accidental death benefit coverage[1];

m = number of years from the issue date to the end of the premium payment period for accidental death benefit coverage[2];

$_t^m V_{x:\overline{n}|}^{ADB}$ = the accidental death benefit reserve at duration *t*;

$A_{x+t:\overline{n-t}|}^{ADB}$ = present value of future accidental death benefits at duration *t*;

$_m P_{x:\overline{n}|}^{ADB}$ = net premium for accidental death in the first policy year; and

$\ddot{a}_{[x]+t:\overline{m-t}|}$ = present value of annuity due at duration *t*.

Using the valuation mortality table and interest rate, the present value of future accidental death benefits as of duration *t* is defined by the following formula:

$$A_{x+t:\overline{n-t}|}^{ADB} = \sum_{s=0}^{n-t-1} v^{s+1} \cdot {_s}p_{[x]+t} \cdot q_{[x]+t+s}^{ADB} \cdot B_{x+t+s}^{ADB}$$

where

v = discount factor;

= $\dfrac{1}{1+i}$;

$_s p_{[x]+t}$ = probability that the insured who survived to duration *t* will survive to duration *t+s*;

= $\displaystyle\prod_{r=0}^{s-1}(1 - q_{[x]+t+r})$;

$q_{[x]+t+r}$ = valuation mortality rate for all causes of death for attained age *x+t+r*;

$q_{[x]+t+s}^{ADB}$ = valuation mortality rate for accidental death for attained age *x+t+s*; and

B_{x+t}^{ADB} = accidental death benefit amount[3] between durations *t* and *t+1* and assumed to be paid at duration *t+1*.

Similar to the basic policy reserve, the net premiums are a constant percentage of the gross premiums and not necessarily a level amount. In order for the net premiums to be a constant percentage of the gross premiums, the pattern of gross premiums is reflected in the formula for the present value of an annuity as follows:

---

[1] In most circumstances, coverage for accidental death ends at age 65, 70 or 75.

[2] In most circumstances, the premium payment period is the earlier of the base policy premium payment period or when the coverage for accidental death ends.

[3] This is the additional death benefit for the amount payable, as defined in the policy rider, when the covered insured dies by accidental means. In most circumstances, it will be equal to the face amount of the policy, hence, the commonly used term "double indemnity."

$$\ddot{a}_{[x]+t:\overline{m-t}|} = \sum_{s=0}^{m-t-1} v^s \cdot {}_s p_{[x]+t} \cdot r^{GP^{ADB}}_{x+t+s}$$

where

$$r^{GP^{ADB}}_{x+t+s} \quad = \quad \text{gross premium ratio;}$$

$$= \quad \frac{GP^{ABD}_{x+t+s}}{GP^{ABD}_x} \text{ ; and}$$

$$GP^{ABD}_{x+t+s} \quad = \quad \text{annual gross premium for accidental death due at duration } t+s.$$

Finally, the net premium at duration t is determined using the following formula:

$$_m P^{ADB}_{x+t:\overline{n}|} = \begin{cases} \dfrac{A^{ADB}_{x:\overline{m}|}}{\ddot{a}_{x:\overline{m}|}} & \text{if } t=0 \\[2ex] r^{GP^{ADB}}_{x+t} \cdot {}_m P^{ADB}_{x:\overline{n}|} & \text{if } 0 < t \le m \end{cases}$$

where $_m P^{ADB}_{x+t:\overline{n}|}$ = net premium for accidental death at duration t.

Many approximations are in use for accidental death benefit reserves. Some companies develop factors based on age grouping, and it is not uncommon to group plans, even when the premium payment periods are not identical.

Many home service companies market life policies with accidental death benefit (and other benefits) as an inherent part of the policy, without a separately identifiable gross premium for the benefit. The calculation of accidental death benefit reserves (or reserves for any other inherent benefit) is particularly complicated when the gross premiums for the policy extend beyond the accidental death benefit benefit period.

Calculating accidental death benefit reserves assuming payment of net premiums beyond the benefit period is awkward and presents practical difficulties. However, if a portion of the gross premiums is assumed to pay for the accidental death benefit only during the life of that benefit, the remaining gross premium, which pays for the basic policy benefit, is an increasing amount, which means that the reserves for the base policy should be based on an increasing premium. It is probably safe to say that few companies, if any, are recalculating base policy reserves in this theoretically justifiable way. It is the responsibility of the valuation actuary to assure that the actual method used is reasonable, and methods which assume payment of the accidental death benefit net premium beyond the benefit period should be avoided, if practical to do so.

The accidental death benefit is commonly available on many universal life insurance policies, sometimes with a scale of accidental death benefit cost of insurance charges based on issue age, and sometimes with a set based on attained age. In the case of charges based on issue age, reserve considerations would be identical to those for the same benefit on a traditional whole life product. In the case of a scale which varies by attained age, reserve considerations are much the same as for a yearly renewable term policy. In this latter case, if the slope of the accidental death benefit cost of insurance charges bears a reasonable resemblance to the accidental death benefit valuation table, and if those charges generally exceed net premiums based on that table, a reasonable and commonly used approximation is to hold the unearned portion, or one-half of the most recent month's charges for the benefit. Alternatively, monthly net accidental death benefit premiums could be calculated and used to determine the reserve.

12.3 DISABILITY WAIVER OF PREMIUM BENEFITS

The Standard Valuation Law requires this benefit to be valued using the tables of Period 2 disablement rates of the 1952 Disability Study of the Society of Actuaries. For active lives, this table is combined with a mortality table and interest rate permitted for calculating the basic policy reserves.

12.3.1 ACTIVE LIFE RESERVES

A question which needs to be addressed in both premium and reserve calculations for disability waiver benefits is what premium is to be waived on a disability claim. Should it be the gross premium or the net premium for the basic policy benefits? Should it include the disability premium? What about other benefits, such as accidental death benefit?

Most companies continue to pay commissions and policyholder dividends whether or not premiums are being waived. In this case, the disability reserve should be set up to provide for waiver of the gross, rather than the net premium under the policy.

In practice, most companies also waive the disability premium, as well as the premium for other benefits such as accidental death benefit. Active life reserves may be calculated assuming that only the basic premium is waived. Then, the ratio of the average premium for accidental death benefit to the average base policy premium, and the percentage of policies having accidental death benefit, may be applied to the disability reserve to approximate the reserve required to waive the premium for the accidental death benefit premium.

Practical considerations in calculating active life disability waiver of premium reserves are similar to those for accidental death benefit. As with accidental death benefit, many approximations are used in practice, and companies tend to use plan grouping rather than calculating exact waiver of premium factors for each plan of insurance. Also as with accidental death benefit, waiver of premium is found as an inherent benefit on many home service policies, and once again the actuary should avoid, if practical, net premiums for such a benefit which are assumed to extend beyond the benefit period. Finally, the reserves should reflect the premiums. For a yearly renewable term policy, the benefit is an increasing amount.

Waiver of premium is another common benefit offered on many Universal Life policies. Two types of waiver of premium are generally available:

(1)   Waiver of the Cost of Insurance waives the total cost of insurance and expense charges for the basic policy, and usually for all riders as well.

(2)   Waiver of Planned Premium waives a specified premium amount on a monthly basis.

The primary difference is that Waiver of the Cost of Insurance stops deductions from the fund, and Waiver of Planned Premium actually increments the fund by a fixed amount on a monthly basis. It is possible, if unlikely, that this specified amount could be less than the monthly deductions for a particular policy. To avoid this situation, a number of companies have developed riders which waive the greater of the two amounts.

If the Waiver of Planned Premium rates are on an issue age basis, reserve calculations are the same as those for a traditional whole life policy. If the Waiver of Cost of Insurance rates are on an attained age basis, reserve calculations[4] are similar to those for a similar yearly renewable term policy, although much more complicated theoretically, since the future premiums to be waived are not known. If the rates for either type of waiver are on an attained age basis, if the slope of the rates is similar to the slope of the disability table used

---

[4] The guaranteed cost of insurance rates are used in these calculations.

for valuation, and if the rates per $100 waived are not less than the corresponding valuation table rates, it is reasonable to hold the unearned portion, or one-half, of the most recent month's charge for the benefit. Alternatively, net valuation premiums can be calculated in this latter case.

12.3.2 DISABLED LIFE RESERVES

Reserves for disabled lives consist of liabilities for four types of claim status:

(1)   Approved claims

(2)   In course of settlement (pending approval)

(3)   Resisted

(4)   Incurred but unreported

The last three are considered policy claim liabilities. Liabilities for claims in course of settlement and for resisted claims are determined based upon actual data as of the valuation dates. Liabilities for claims incurred but unreported are generally based on factors derived from prior years' experience. Factors are developed which may be applied to claims approved during the year, outstanding disability benefits, or some other known item.

Valuation factors for approved claims usually consist of disabled life annuities based on the tables mentioned in the Standard Valuation Law (or the Canadian actuary's best judgment) together with an appropriate valuation interest rate. Approved claims are then valued by applying these factors to the amount being waived[5]. The expression for mean reserves for the waiver of $1 per year, as specified in the Society's 1952 Disability Study, is

$$\ddot{a}_{[x+0.5]+t-0.5:\overline{n-0.5|}}$$

where

x =   the insurance age attained on the policy anniversary before disability;

t =   the number of years the insured has been disabled; and

n =   the number of years from the time the insured became disabled to the end of the benefit period.

Since the valuation depends on age at disability, duration since disability, and number of years to run, and since there are relatively few claims compared to the active life in force, a seriatim valuation is normally used.

For universal life and variable life policies, disabled life reserves are usually calculated from first principles. The formula above is not appropriate for nonlevel benefits. However, it is important in this case to use a benefit stream consistent with that used in the calculation of the base policy reserve.

12.4 PAYOR BENEFITS

The typical payor benefit waives premiums to a child's age 21 or 25 upon the death or disability of the parent. The theoretical reserve for payor benefits is complicated as there are two lives involved, and, in the case of the disability payor benefit, both death and disability must be considered. This coverage is essentially decreasing term, and small or negative reserves are to be expected, so approximations are normally used.

---

[5] For waiver of cost of insurance rates, the guaranteed costs of insurance rates are used.

Usually the mortality of the child is ignored when determining the reserves. As the terminal reserves for juvenile active payor benefits are often negative, many companies hold one-half of the gross annual premiums as an approximate unearned premium reserve.

The reserve after the death of the payor is an annuity for the number of future premiums payable under the terms of the benefit. This is usually approximated by using an annuity-certain and ignoring the mortality of the child. The result held upon the disability of the payor would be the regular disabled life waiver reserve for the remaining period during which premiums can be waived. Again, the mortality of the child is often ignored when calculating these reserves.

12.5 SURRENDER VALUES IN EXCESS OF RESERVES

In the event that the surrender value on any policy or contract in the United States exceeds the reserve otherwise required or held, then an additional reserve equal in amount to such excess must be established in Exhibit 5G of the annual statement. The additional reserve, if any, should be determined on a policy-by-policy basis, as opposed to a determination in the aggregate on all policies and contracts combined. In other words, there should be no offsetting of policies and contracts with reserves greater than surrender values against those with reserves less than surrender values in arriving at the additional reserves. This interpretation appears to be commonly accepted within the industry.

12.6 LAST-TO-DIE POLICIES

A *last-to-die, or last-survivor, policy* pays a death benefit at the later death of two (or more) insureds. Last-to-die policies are of two types:

(1)   Traditional policies either pay an extra, reduced, death benefit, or become paid-up at the first death. After the first death, the cash values for these policies are calculated using single life values for the remaining life.

(2)   Frasier-type policies have no change in status at the first death. Cash values are calculated independently of whether a death has occurred.

Reserves for last-to-die policies vary according to the policy type.

12.6.1 RESERVES FOR TRADITIONAL POLICIES

For traditional policies, the reserve before the first death should take into account any benefits upon the first death, and should also take into account that both insureds are alive at the time of valuation. For a traditional policy which becomes paid up at the first death of (x) and (y), the terminal reserve at t is

$$ {}^m_t V_{\overline{xy:n}} \;=\; A_{\overline{x+t:y+t:n-t}} \;-\; {}_m P_{\overline{xy:n}} \cdot \ddot{a}_{\overline{x+t:y+t:m-t}} $$

After the first death, the reserve is based on functions of the remaining life. Assuming the prior death of (y), the terminal reserve would be

$$ {}^m_t V_{\overline{x:n}} \;=\; \begin{cases} A_{\overline{x:n-t}} & \text{if} \quad \text{paid-up on first death} \\[2mm] A_{\overline{x:n-t}} - {}_m P_{\overline{x:n}} \cdot \ddot{a}_{\overline{x+t:m-t}} & \text{if} \quad \text{not paid-up on first death} \end{cases} $$

12.6.2 RESERVES FOR FRASIER-TYPE POLICIES

For a Frasier-type policy, the reserve is independent of the first death status. Special functions must be calculated based on

$$_t P_{\overline{xy}} = {}_t P_{[x]} + {}_t P_{[y]} - {}_t P_{xy}$$

and

$$q_{\overline{xy}+t} = 1 - \frac{{}_{t+1} P_{\overline{xy}}}{{}_t P_{\overline{xy}}}$$

For a Frasier[6] policy, the terminal reserve at duration t using the special functions is

$$_t^m V_{\overline{xy}:\overline{n|}} = A_{\overline{x+t:y+t:\overline{n-t|}}} - {}_m P_{\overline{xy}:\overline{n|}} \cdot \ddot{a}_{\overline{x+t:y+t:\overline{m-t|}}}$$

where

$$A_{\overline{x+t:y+t:\overline{n-t|}}} = \sum_{s=0}^{n-t} v^{s+1} \cdot {}_t P_{\overline{xy}} \cdot q_{\overline{xy}+t} \cdot BD_t$$

and

$$\ddot{a}_{\overline{x+t:y+t:\overline{n-t|}}} = \sum_{s=0}^{n-t} v^s \cdot {}_t P_{\overline{xy}} \cdot r_t^{GP}$$

The resulting reserve is independent of whether one of either (x) or (y) has died. All that is known is that they were both alive at policy issue, and at least one is now alive.

Another issue with last-to-die (as well as first-to-die) policies of either type is the use of a joint equal age calculation. In order to simplify calculations (and allow the use of factor tables), a joint equal age table is often used to find an age z, such that $A_{\overline{x+t:y+t:\overline{n-t|}}}$ may be replaced by $A_{\overline{z:\overline{n-t|}}}$ in the above calculations.

Actuarial Guideline XX gives acceptable joint equal age rules for valuation of first-to-die products based on the 1980 CSO Table. Many companies use these rules for last-to-die policies, although the theoretical joint equal age treatment would be different for last-to-die policies, and many other rules are also in common use.

---

[6] "Frasier" refers to a method discussed in an article published by William M. Frasier [13]. It treats the two insureds as one unit. The unit is "alive" if at least one insured is alive.

13 ✧ CASH FLOW TESTING

13.1 INTRODUCTION

The earlier chapters in this book discussed the assumptions, methodologies and procedures that are required as part of a statutory valuation. These discussions covered an important aspect of an actuary's work because the actuary is required to certify that the policy reserves prepared in accordance with statutory accounting principles meet minimum legal requirements. Once these minimum requirements have been satisfied, an important question remains to be answered: Do the reserves make "good and sufficient"[1] provision for the liabilities undertaken by the company?" In other words, are reserves and related liabilities adequate under ***moderately adverse*** conditions?[2]

Minimum valuation standards are generally intended to be conservative but this is not always the case. This can occur for a variety of reasons such as unexpected results from product features, different marketing techniques or underlying experience evolving differently than expected. For example, consider the reserves for a single premium immediate annuity. The Standard Valuation Law specifies a maximum rate of interest that can be used in valuing these liabilities. For a given year's issues this interest rate is level for the term of the contract[3]. For example, the valuation interest rate for a single premium immediate annuity issued in 1982 was as high as 13.25%. Rates available on investments made during that period were well in excess of 13.25%. However, it is difficult to invest for the full benefit period associated with immediate annuities. Even if the company does invest fairly long, issuers of bonds may elect to call them if interest rates change. As a result, money might have to be reinvested at rates well below 13.25%.

In practice any number of events might occur that would make the statutory minimum reserves prescribed by law insufficient. The Standard Valuation Law cannot contemplate all of these items. Therefore, actuarial judgment and testing is required to ensure that reserves not only meet legal requirements but that the assets supporting the reserves are sufficient to cover outstanding liabilities.

Not too many years ago, a discussion of the good and sufficient provision would have emphasized gross premium valuations. A gross premium valuation involves the calculation of reserves, reflecting best estimate assumptions and including all policyholder benefits and expenses. This sort of approach was suggested to cover the following situations:

(1)   The statutory valuation methodology was deficient because it did not consider withdrawals or expenses;

(2)   The experience mortality was actually higher than mortality contemplated by the statutory valuation standard; or

(3)   Reserve strengthening was needed due to investment yields not supporting the valuation interest rate.

---

[1] In the 1970's a valuation task of the Society of Actuaries introduced the phrase "good and sufficient" without giving it a precise definition. This phrase has recently been replaced by "moderately adverse conditions." See Item 3.4.2 of Actuarial Standard of Practice No. 22 (ASOP No. 22) [2].

[2] Generally, "moderately adverse" means that reserves are adequate 85% of the time or cover 65% Conditional Tail Expectation (CTE). This concept is discussed in Chapter 16.

[3] Unless the life insurance company strengthens reserves by lowering the valuation interest rate.

Today this discussion has led to what has been termed the *valuation actuary concept* and *principle-based reserves*. The valuation actuary must consider whether or not reserves make good and sufficient provision for future obligations not only under expected experience but under a number of different scenarios that might be plausible.

The valuation actuary concept has led to the analysis of many different items that might affect the adequacy of reserves, including but not limited to the following:

(1) Cash flow testing that includes the interaction between assets and liabilities under a number of different scenarios;

(2) Determination of the cost of embedded options;

(3) Evaluation of the impact of mortality deterioration due to selective cancellation by the policyholder on certain types of term products; or

(4) Estimation of the impact of epidemics such as AIDS and SARS on the adequacy of the company's reserves.

An area currently receiving considerable attention is asset adequacy analysis. Cash flow testing is one of the primary procedures used in an asset adequacy analysis. This chapter is devoted to this topic.

13.2 CASH FLOW TESTING

Actuarial Standard of Practice No. 7 (ASOP No. 7), *Analysis of Life, Health, or Property/Casualty Insurer Cash Flows,* is an important standard of practice with regards to cash flow testing. Its primary purpose is to provide guidance to actuaries who are performing a cash flow analysis. An actuary who is performing a cash flow analysis should be familiar with this standard.

13.2.1 DEFINITION

The definition section of Actuarial Standard of Practice No. 7 defines *cash flow analysis* as "any evaluation of the risks associated with the timing or amount of cash flows."[4] In general terms, a cash flow analysis provides insight to such questions as:

(1) What cash obligations (e.g., expenses, claims, taxes) will the life insurance company have in the future?

(2) When will these obligations occur?

(3) What will be the amount of these obligations?

(4) Is there a sufficient amount of assets set aside to provide for these obligations?

(5) Are they the right types of assets (for example, will the life insurance company be able to sell the assets without incurring a loss when the investment proceeds are needed to pay for an obligation)?

(6) Analysis must also include documentation of findings and recommendations.

Actuarial Standard of Practice No. 7 also defines *cash flow testing* as "a form of cash flow analysis involving the projection and comparison of the timing and amount of cash flows resulting from economic and other

---

[4] See Section 2.5 of Actuarial Standard of Practice No.7, [1].

assumptions."[5] In other words, cash flow testing addresses the above questions under a range of scenarios to develop an understanding of the underlying risks and to assess their impact on the capital and surplus of the life insurance company.

13.2.2 SCOPE

An actuary must have an understanding of the life insurance company's insurance products, its investments, financial reporting and financial modeling to perform this type of analysis. This is because the actuary must consider:

(1)　the type of liabilities included in the analysis;

(2)　the type of assets supporting these liabilities;

(3)　the various risks associated with the liabilities and assets and the severity of these risks;

(4)　the options embedded in the assets and liabilities and the likelihood that these options will be exercised at a time that may result in a financial loss;

(5)　the interrelationship between assumptions (e.g., between lapse rates and mortality rates, or between lapse rates and the difference between credited interest rates and competitor rates);

(6)　financial reporting requirements; and

(7)　company policy with regards to:

   (a)　non-guaranteed elements or dividends in different economic environments;

   (b)　use of financial derivatives; and

   (c)　investment policies, guidelines and restrictions.

Cash flow testing is often complex, requiring the skills of several individuals who collectively have extensive training and knowledge in investments, financial reporting and financial modeling. It also requires someone with strong management skills that has the knowledge and authority to identify and plan the tasks, to assign and coordinate the resources, and to motivate and communicate with a wide variety of individuals.

13.3 CASH FLOW TESTING PROCESS

The most common approaches[6] to cash flow testing can be grouped into the following activities:

(1)　Identification of the assets and liabilities included in the cash flow analysis;

(2)　Selection and validation of models for asset and liabilities cash flows;

(3)　Selection of appropriate scenarios;

(4)　Projection of the selected asset and liabilities cash flows under each scenario; and

(5)　Development of conclusions based on analysis of the cash flow projections.

Similar to the valuation process, cash flow testing utilizes a significant amount of data and resources. The following diagram is a flow chart of a typical cash flow testing system.

---

[5] See Section 2.6 of Actuarial Standard of Practice No. 7, [1].

[6] See Appendix 1, Current Practices of Actuarial Standard of Practice No. 7, [1].

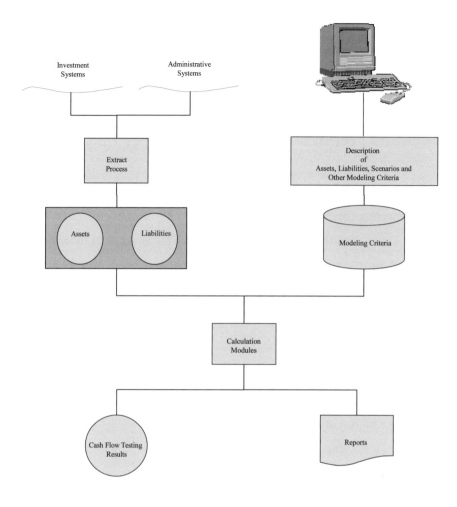

This flow chart divides a cash flow testing system into five major parts:

(1)   Extract process;
(2)   Description of assets, liabilities, scenarios and other criteria;
(3)   Calculation modules;
(4)   Cash flow testing results; and
(5)   Reports.

The next several sections provide a brief description of these parts.

13.3.1 EXTRACT FILES

The primary purpose of the extract process is to retrieve information from investment systems and the policy administrative systems that is needed during the cash flow testing process. This information is stored in computer files or databases. Typically, there are two types of files created during this process: *asset files* and *liability files*.

Asset files contain information about the assets currently held in support of the existing liabilities. For example, if bonds are held in support of the liabilities, these files would contain the type of bonds, the par value, the coupon rate, the call provisions and the maturity date and other critical information. The following is the type of information that is stored for each bond in an asset file:

Asset File	
Asset Number	B123456789
Cusip	17303MGW3
Asset Type	Bond
Industry	Financial
Moody's Rating	Aa2
S&P Rating	A+
SVO Classification	2
Issue Date	7/1/2000
Maturity Date	7/1/2009
Coupon Type	Fixed
Coupon Rate	7.00%
Frequency of Coupon Payments	Semiannually
Callable	Yes
First Call Date	7/1/2004
Call Premium	1.00%
Par Value	100,000
Market Value	105,000
Book Value	100,000

Liability files contain information about the current liabilities. The most important liability files are the policy extract files. The policy extracts contain information about insureds such as gender, issue age and smoking habit[7]. They also identify the plan of insurance and the amount of insurance coverage.

The following is the type of information that is stored for each policy in a policy extract:

Policy Extract	
Policy Number	P001
Plan Code	UL2000
Policy Status	Active
Underwriting Criteria	Medical
Extract Date	12/31/2005
Issue Date	7/1/2000
Maturity Date	7/1/2040
Issue Age	60
Gender	Male
Smoking Criteria	Nonsmoker
Gross Premium	35,000
Premium Payment Period	40 years
Face Amount	1,000,000
Fund Value	100,000
Cash Value	90,000
Statutory Reserve	95,000

In most circumstances, policy extract files will contain a large amount of data. As was noted earlier, it is not uncommon for a policy extract to have several million records, with each record in the policy extract having

---

[7] Often the policy extract file is produced from the seriatim files used to determine formula reserves under a statutory valuation, as discussed in Chapter 3.

25 or more fields. To reduce the size of these files, most life insurance companies group similar policies into representative cells. The rules used to group these files must be chosen carefully in order to accurately model the risks. A cash flow analysis using grouped files should lead to the same conclusions and discussions as a cash flow analysis using detailed files. In other words, the differences between a cash flow analysis using grouped files and a cash flow analysis using detailed files should be immaterial[8].

For example, the policy extract file might contain the following policies:

Policy Extract File					
Policy No.	**P001**	**P002**	**P003**	**P004**	**P005**
Plan ID	VUL2000	VUL2000	VUL2000	VUL2000	VUL2000
Underwriting Criteria	Medical	Paramedical	Nonmedical	Medical	Medical
Issue Date	7/1/2000	7/1/2000	10/1/2000	7/1/2000	4/1/2000
Issue Age	60	62	60	64	61
Gender	Male	Male	Male	Male	Male
Smoking Criteria	Nonsmoker	Nonsmoker	Nonsmoker	Nonsmoker	Nonsmoker
Gross Premium	35,000	9,000	3,750	40,000	20,000
Face Amount	1,000,000	250,000	100,000	1,000,000	500,000
Fund Value	100,000	25,000	10,000	100,000	50,000
Cash Value	90,000	22,500	9,000	90,000	45,000
Statutory Reserve	95,000	23,750	9,500	95,000	47,500

The grouping rules might be:

Plan Groups:	One group for each Plan ID
Underwriting Groups:	Guaranteed Issue, Simplified Issue or Fully Underwritten[9]
Issue Date Groups:	One group for each Issue Year
Issue Age Groups:	0-9, 10-19, 20-29, 30-34, 35-39, 40-44, 45-49, 50-54, 55-59, 60-64, 65-69, 70-74, 75-79 or 80 & older
Gender:	Male or Female
Smoking Criteria:	Nonsmoker, smoker or unknown

These grouping rules would lead to the following representative model cell[10]:

---

[8] Materiality addresses the question "Is this item large enough for users of the information to be influenced by it?" It is important that the actuary discuss materiality with those who make accounting decisions which typically is the accounting department. See Section VI in the Preamble of the NAIC *Accounting Practices and Procedures Manual* [18] for a more through discussion of materiality.

[9] Fully underwritten would include nonmedical, paramedical and medical.

[10] A model cell is a representative policy of all the policies in the policy extract that have been "grouped" together.

Model Cell	
Cell Number	VUL2000-F-2000-60:64-M-NS
Plan Code	VUL2000
Underwriting Criteria	Full
Extract Date	12/31/2005
Issue Year	2000
Average number of years to maturity	38
Issue Age	62
Gender	Male
Smoking Criteria	Nonsmoker
Average Gross Premium.................................	21,150
Average Premium Payment Period..................	38 Years
Average Face Amount	570,000
Average Fund Value.......................................	57,000
Average Cash Value	51,200
Average Statutory Reserve	54,150
Number of Policies in Cell	5

13.3.2 DESCRIPTION FILES

In order to project the cash flows for each asset in the asset files and each model cell in the liability files, the information about the assets and liabilities must be specified. In addition, the valuation method, assumptions and scenarios must also be specified. The primary purpose of this part of the cash flow testing process is to gather this information and store it in a database. The following list is the type of information that is needed:

- Valuation basis
- Premium rates
- Cash value scales
- Reserve factors
- Dividend scales
- Expense charges
- Cost of insurance charges
- Surrender charges
- Liability assumptions (e.g., expenses, morality, lapses, etc.)
- Asset assumptions (e.g., yield curves, defaults rates, reinvestment rates, etc.)
- Scenarios

This information will depend on the type of assets and liabilities being tested.

13.3.3 CALCULATION MODULES

The calculation modules perform three major functions. First, these modules project the asset and liability cash flows into the future for each scenario specified. Second, they store the result of these projections and other information in a results file. Third, they produce various reports.

When projecting the asset cash flows for a given scenario, the characteristics of the assets of the life insurance company must be considered. As discussed in Actuarial Standard of Practice No. 7, the "characteristics of an asset affect the timing and amounts of its cash flows. The cash flows of some assets are relatively immune to external factors and can be predicted on the basis of asset structure alone (for example, high-quality noncallable bonds). The cash flows of other assets (for example, callable bonds, mortgage-backed securities, common stocks, derivative contracts, or premium receivables) are more sensitive to external events, and their analysis should be based on a combination of their structure and external factors. The actuary should consider the following issues in making cash flow projections:

(a)   the sensitivity to economic factors, such as interest rates, equity, or other market returns, and inflation rates on the insurer's asset cash flows;

(b)   any limitations on the ability to use asset cash flows to support policy or other liability cash flows, such as when a block of assets is specifically held in support of a particular block of business by contract or regulation;

(c)   the impact on cash flow associated with asset quality as it relates to the risk of a delay in asset cash flows being collected, asset default, or other financial nonperformance;

(d)   the associated costs of maintaining the assets or of converting the assets into cash when necessary;

(e)   the historical experience of similar assets, to the extent such experience is credible and relevant to the projection of future asset cash flows; and

(f)   other known factors that are likely to have a material effect on asset cash flows, particularly those factors that are likely to have an effect on asset risk or investment rate-of-return risk.[11]"

Equally important is the investment strategy of the life insurance company. Actuarial Standard of Practice No. 7 lists the following items that an actuary should consider[12]:

(a)   the insurer's strategy regarding the sale of assets prior to maturity;

(b)   asset segmentation in support of the insurer's policy cash flows;

(c)   the insurer's strategy regarding the sale of assets with a declining market value;

(d)   the insurer's strategy for the investment of future positive or negative cash flows;

(e)   to the extent the insurer's investment strategy contemplates borrowing to cover negative cash flows, whether the funds borrowed pursuant to the strategy are reasonable in relation to the insurer's existing indebtedness, borrowing capacity, and cost of borrowing funds;

(f)   the insurer's use of derivative contracts, including strategies to mitigate asset, policy, or other liability cash flow risk;

(g)   to the extent the insurer's investment strategy contemplates capital contributions from a parent or other source, whether the capital contributions can be sustained and are appropriate for the type of analysis;

(h)   the costs or gains due to asset, policy, or other liability cash flows denominated in foreign currencies; and

(i)   any other known factors that are likely to have a material effect on investment strategy or the insurer's ability to execute its investment strategy.

Similarly, when projecting the liability cash flows for a given scenario, the characteristics of the liabilities of the life insurance company must be considered. As discussed in Actuarial Standard of Practice No. 7, the "characteristics of a policy affect the timing and amounts of its cash flows. The actuary should consider the following factors in projecting policy cash flows:

---

[11] See Section 3.4.1, <u>Asset Characteristics</u> of Actuarial Standard of Practice No. 7, [1].

[12] See Section 3.4.2, <u>Asset Characteristics</u> of Actuarial Standard of Practice No. 7, [1].

(a) the risk of insolvency or other nonperformance by providers of services, including reinsurers and other counter-parties;

(b) the associated costs of maintaining, collecting, or paying out the policy cash flows;

(c) the historical experience of similar policy cash flows, to the extent such experience is credible and relevant to the projection of future cash flows;

(d) the effect of external factors such as interest rates, equity or other market returns, unemployment rates, and inflation rates on the insurer's policy cash flows;

(e) the ability of the policyholder or other party to exercise options under the policy that have an effect on policy cash flows (for example, put options subject to a predefined event occurring, or allowing the transfer of funds between contracts or funding vehicles);

(f) the effect of changes in premium (for example, rate increases) or changes in other policy charges (for example, cost of insurance charges in universal life contracts); and

(g) other known factors that are likely to have a material effect on policy cash flows, including off-balance sheet items."[13]

Finally, the "actuary should consider management policy concerning the settlement or payment of liabilities, and the effect that this management policy may be reasonably expected to have on the projection of policy cash flows. Considerations that might affect the projection include claim settlement and benefit payment practices, expense control strategies, company philosophy relative to the determination of policyholder dividends, and charges or benefits that vary at the discretion of the company, as well as significant relationships between management policy and the scenarios analyzed."[14]

13.3.4 MODEL VALIDATION

The model should be tested and validated to determine that:

(1) The liabilities and assets have been properly grouped into represented cells;

(2) The data in the extract files and plan description files is accurate and is being accessed correctly by the calculation routines;

(3) The formulas in the calculation routines have been programmed correctly; and

(4) The model can replicate past performance.

With regards to this last point, a scenario should be run with assumptions that closely match recent past experience. Certain key financial results produced by the model for this scenario should be compared to actual financial results. For example, assume paid death claims in 2000 for a particular product line was $10,000,000. What did the model produce using the most recent mortality study? For certain balance sheet items, the difference between actual results and modeled results should be less than 1%. For income statement items, the difference should be less than 10%. If the model results are outside these ranges, the data, assumptions and formulas should be examined closely to determine the cause of this inaccuracy, and the model should then be corrected accordingly.

Model validation can be a time consuming, tedious and, at times, frustrating activity. However, it is the only way to determine the reliability of the modeling process. If it cannot accurately reproduce recent historical experience, then it is unlikely that it can relied upon to assess future risks.

---

[13] See Section 3.5.1, <u>Policy Cash Flow Characteristics</u> of Actuarial Standard of Practice No. 7, [1].

[14] See Section 3.5.2, <u>Management Policy</u> of Actuarial Standard of Practice No. 7, [1].

13.3.5 MODEL REPORTS

A critical part of the cash flow testing process is the generation of reports:

(1) To demonstrate that the data in the extract files and plan description files is accurate and is being accessed correctly;

(2) To demonstrate that the formulas in the calculation routines have been programmed correctly;

(3) To determine that all the liabilities and assets have been processed correctly;

(4) To validate the model; and

(5) To document the results of the cash flow analysis.

The following diagram is a high level flow chart of types of reports a cash flow testing system should produce:

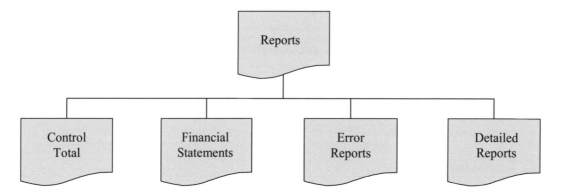

A control report contains critical date, time and other information to help determine if the appropriate assets and liabilities files have been accessed and processed correctly for each scenario. Financial reports would include a projection of the balance sheet, income statement and other financial statements for each scenario. Not only are these reports needed for the cash flow analysis, but they are necessary for model validation. An error report lists the errors encountered during the cash flow testing process. This list would contain a brief description or error code indicating the type of problem encountered. Finally, detailed reports would provide enough information to show exactly how the cash flows for the assets and liabilities for a particular scenario were calculated. This is particularly important in order to determine that the formulas in the calculations modules have been programmed correctly and the files are being accessed correctly.

13.4 SCENARIOS

To perform cash flow testing, the actuary must first choose a set of future economic scenarios under which the asset and liability cash flows will be calculated. There are several methods currently in use for selecting a set of scenarios. These methods fall into two broad categories:

- *Deterministic*; and
- *Stochastic*.

13.4.1 Deterministic

Under this approach, scenarios are selected by choosing future scenarios that are of particular interest to the tester. This is the approach followed in both the regulations supporting the 1990 Standard Valuation Law, and in New York Regulation 126. The advantage of this approach is that the cash flow tester generally has more comfort with looking at results on a scenario-by-scenario basis, since he or she has constructed the scenarios. Scenarios constructed under this method tend to be easy to describe and can be generally categorized as "rapidly increasing," "down and up," "wave," and so forth. Some disadvantages of this approach are:

(a)   It is very cumbersome to generate a large number of handpicked scenarios;

(b)   Choosing handpicked scenarios can also lead to disagreement over the probability of a given scenario;

(c)   In certain instances (reserve testing is probably one) a large set of scenarios may be necessary to generate statistical credibility; and

(d)   If the starting yield curve is too low, it may understate the cost of certain embedded options and overstate others (the opposite is true, if the starting yield curve is too high).

Finally, deterministic scenarios tend, in practice, to produce more favorable results than would be expected statistically.

13.4.2 STOCHASTIC

A stochastic approach recognizes that the assumptions are random variables. Accordingly, for certain key assumptions (e.g., interest rates and equity returns), an assumption is made about the underlying probability distribution of these random variables and a range of values is generated in accordance with this distribution for each year in the future. Some advantages of this approach are:

(a)   It tests a large number of possibilities;

(b)   Outliers can provide significant insight; and

(c)   It gives a much better perspective on the range of possible outcomes.

Some disadvantages of this approach are:

(a)   It is difficult to test that the formulas are working correctly;

(b)   It can become a very complex and timing consuming exercise;

(c)   It generates a large amount of data to analyze;

(d)   It is sometimes difficult to summarize;

(e)   It is difficult to decide which simulations are realistic and which are not; and

(f)   It is difficult to establish reliable correlation among all the variables.

13.4.3 INTEREST RATE MODELS

Excluding variable products, most of the invested assets held in the general account of a life insurance company in support of the liabilities are bonds and, to a lesser extent, mortgages. Accordingly, the choice of an interest model is critical. The following are some of the characteristics of a good interest model:

(1)   The current spot rate curve can be reproduced;

(2)   Projected rates tend to revert to their long-term averages (i.e., mean-reverting);

(3)   Projected rates are consistent with historical information and judgments about the future;

(4)   Rates at different maturities are positively correlated, with higher correlation for maturities that are closer together than those that are further apart;

(5)   Rates are not negative; and

(6)   The rates are arbitrage-free[15].

---

[15] An investor can not enter into two or more financial transactions simultaneously to create a risk-free profit.

It is very difficult to build a model that satisfies all these conditions[16].

13.4.4 INVESTMENT STRATEGY

In performing cash flow testing, the actuary and investment officer must work together to develop an investment strategy. The life insurance company usually establishes an investment strategy for a particular product within the context of investment limitations approved by the Board of Directors. For example, a life insurance company may have the following investment limitations for bonds:

Investment Limitations as a Percentage of Total Assets	
Bond Limitations by Issue:	
AAA	1.00%
AA	0.80%
A	0.60%
BBB	0.40%
BB	0.20%
B	0.10%
Foreign Bond Limitations:	
AAA	5.00%
AA	4.00%
A	3.00%
BBB	2.00%
BB	1.00%
B	0.50%
Overall Bond Rating	A or higher
Bond Limitations by Industry	10% limit in any one industry
Effective duration	Less than 1 year difference between duration of assets and liabilities

Also, it is suggested that increasing the domestic bond percentages since it is more probable that a company will invest more of its assets in domestic bonds than foreign bonds as presented in this example.

These limitations will have a direct impact on the investment strategy. Thus the actuary and the investment officer must work closely together to define how positive cash flows will be invested in the future. This is generally done either by specifying a portion of cash flows to be invested in each type of security or by maintaining a balance of each type of security in the total portfolio. As a simple example, a company might decide to invest 50% of each positive cash flow in ten-year BBB bonds and 50% in ten-year Treasuries. The second approach would be to maintain 50% of the total portfolio in each of these two securities and solve for the percentage of each cash flow that must be invested in each in order to maintain this balance. Obviously, real-life reinvestment strategies are more complicated.

The reinvestment strategy may also define situations under which it is anticipated that this strategy will change. Key examples of points in time that changes in reinvestment strategies might be projected to occur include inversions of yield curves, increases or decreases in interest rates above specified levels, or changes in overall asset durations.

In setting up the parameters for a cash flow study, a decision must also be made with regard to negative cash flows. If negative cash flows occur in the projection, they may be modeled by selling assets, by buying

---

[16] The paper by Kevin C. Ahlgrim, et al. [3] discusses how well some of the popular models currently satisfy these conditions.

negative assets (this is used to simulate borrowing between lines of business, and has an impact similar to selling assets), or borrowing at a short-term rate.

13.4.5 POLICYHOLDER BEHAVIOR

Although difficult to predict, anticipating how policyholders will behave under various scenarios will affect the results of a cash flow analysis. The following are some other items that the actuary should consider when doing a cash flow analysis:

(1)   How should lapses be modeled?

(2)   How should mortality be modeled?

(3)   How should changes in the tax law be handled?

(4)   How should embedded options be valued?

(5)   How should additional deposits be modeled?

(6)   How should partial deposits be modeled?

(7)   How should switches between fixed and variable accounts be modeled?

For example, when performing a cash flow analysis of variable annuity contracts with minimum guaranteed death benefits, the lapse rate should be a function of how much the contract is "in the money." In particular, the lapse rate for a contract that is significantly "in the money" should be lower than an otherwise identical contract that is significantly "out of the money." Similarly, when performing a cash flow analysis for universal life policies, the mortality rates should reflect some antiselection due to excess lapses. Conversely, mortality might be more favorable due to lower lapses. Finally, the utilization of certain embedded options might be very difficult to value. For example, the cost of dollar-for-dollar partial withdrawals under early variable annuity minimum guaranteed death benefit designs can be very large. The only way to handle this cost is to monitor experience very closely and adjust the cash flow analysis accordingly.

Recognition should be given to the notion that policyholders do not always behave in a financially rational manner (i.e., they do not always choose an option that maximizes personal wealth). Consideration should be given to such questions as:

(1)   Why was the product purchased?

(2)   How was the product marketed?

(3)   Who is the financial decision maker?

(4)   How sophisticated is the financial decision maker?

(5)   How long has the policy been inforce?

Many of the functional relationships in cash flow testing key off of the relationship between credited interest rates, market rates, and lapse rates. The competitor rate or market rate describes what is available to a policyholder who surrenders his policy and buys a comparable new policy. This market rate can be defined in terms of credited interest rates on a universal life policy or single premium deferred annuity policy, or dividend rates on a participating whole life policy.

The market rate is used to make an assessment of how competitive the policy is in a future scenario relative to the other options available to the policyholder. Obviously the company cannot perform a competitive survey of financial products available in the future. As a simplifying assumption, the competitor rate often is defined as a single interest rate. When defining the competitor rate, it is important to consider the life insurance company's competitive profile and the characteristics of the policy from a sales perspective (for example, how important the interest rate is). If the sales channel requires a credited rate in the top 10% of competitors to meet competitive objectives, this should be reflected in the choice of a definition of competitor rate.

Market rate assumptions will also depend on the type of product being studied. Often market rate assumptions are based on some function of a current interest rate and a moving average of an interest rate. The moving average is generally meant to reflect the impact of competitors who use portfolio rate crediting strategies, as well as a tendency for some companies to lag the market.

Generally, the life insurance company should experience excess lapse rates[17] when its credited rate lags the market. However, other factors that might dampen these excess lapses include surrender penalties, market value adjustments, underwriting, taxes and general inertia of the policyholder.

13.4.6 NONGUARANTEED ELEMENTS PRACTICES

For some contracts this is as simple as determining the interest rate crediting strategy. For others, however, there is not a specific interest rate credited, but rather interest rates influence dividends or other non-guaranteed elements. In any event, the actuary must make some assumption regarding the impact of future economic environments on the benefits passed on to policyholders.

For example, a universal life product that credits a company-declared rate might use one of the following strategies:

(1)   Credit the earned rate less an investment margin.

(2)   Credit some function of the market rate.

(3)   Use a hybrid approach.

Other strategies might include multipliers rather than constant investment margins that would increase or decrease the investment margin as interest rates go up or down or as time passes.

13.4.7 LAPSE RATES

The actuary must come up with a best estimate of future lapse rates and some forecast for how lapses may depart from this best estimate if the economic environment changes. There is little published industry experience with regard to the interaction between lapse rates and credited rates on life insurance and annuities. There is some indication during the mid to late 1970s that as investment returns on alternate investments became very attractive, companies experienced higher than expected withdrawals of their cash values and extensive use of the policy loan provision. The lapse assumption is based upon the common sense argument that as policyholders' other options become more and more attractive they will be more likely to surrender their policies.

Items to consider in developing a lapse function include the following:

(1)   The presence and level of any surrender charges. Many lapse rate functions take into account the level of surrender charge relative to policyholder account values.

(2)   The marketing techniques and loyalty of the field force.

(3)   The prominence of the interest rate in the marketing and maintenance of the policy. Arguments have been put forth that participating business may be less sensitive to excess lapses since the credited interest rate often is not obvious to the policyholder.

---

[17] "Excess lapse rate" means lapses in excess of the expected or baseline lapse rate.

(4)   Duration from issue.

(5)   Type of products sold. Products that are primarily investment products such as single premium deferred annuities might be more subject to excess lapsation than more protection-oriented products.

(6)   Other guarantees available under the contract (e.g., a variable annuity contract with a minimum guaranteed death benefit that is "in the money" will most likely have a lower propensity to lapse than an otherwise identical contract that is "out of the money.")

In practice, when performing cash flow testing the actuary must develop estimates of the amount of excess lapsation expected at various differentials between crediting rates and market rates, and adjust these for the expected impact of surrender charges. The parameters of the excess lapse formula would then be set to produce excess lapses of approximately this magnitude.

13.5 CASE STUDY

Associated with this chapter is an Excel workbook, Chapter 13.xls. This workbook will be used to provide some insights into the following questions posed at the beginning of this chapter:

(1)   What cash obligations (e.g., expenses, claims, taxes) will the life insurance company have in the future?

(2)   When will these obligations occur?

(3)   What will be the amount of these obligations?

(4)   Is there a sufficient amount of assets set aside to provide for these obligations?

(5)   Are they the right types of assets (for example, will the life insurance company be able to sell the assets without incurring a loss when the investment proceeds are needed to pay for an obligation)?

The workbook makes the following simplifying assumptions:

- All positive cash flows are reinvested in six-month commercial paper with a rating of Class 2 (i.e., an S&P and Moody's rating of A)

- Negative cash flows are borrowed at a short-term rate;

- Assets are not rebalanced to maintain a certain distribution by rating class and industry;

- Statutory reserves are equal to the cash surrender values; and

- The tax rate is zero

The exercises are an important part of this case study.

3.5.1 PRODUCT DESCRIPTION

The product used in this case study is a single premium deferred annuity with the following product features:

Expense charges:	$50 policy fee deducted from the fund at the beginning of each year
Guaranteed Credited Interest:	4% for ten years and 3% thereafter

Surrender Charge:

Policy Year	Percent of Fund
1	7%
2	6
3	5
4	4
5	3
6	2
7	1
8 and later	0

Free Partial withdrawals:	10% of fund value, after first contract year
Death Benefit:	Fund value

Most of these product features are specified in the worksheet "CVA":

Contract Value Assumptions							
(1)	(2)	(3)	(4)	(5)	(6)	(7)	(8)
x	t	$RGP(t)$	$ECGP(t)$	$ECP(t)$	$^G ic(t)$	$SCFV(t)$	$RFPW(t)$
60	0	1.0000	0.0000	50.00	0.0400	0.0700	0.0000
61	1	0.0000	0.0000	50.00	0.0400	0.0600	0.1000
62	2	0.0000	0.0000	50.00	0.0400	0.0500	0.1000
63	3	0.0000	0.0000	50.00	0.0400	0.0400	0.1000
64	4	0.0000	0.0000	50.00	0.0400	0.0300	0.1000
65	5	0.0000	0.0000	50.00	0.0400	0.0200	0.1000
66	6	0.0000	0.0000	50.00	0.0400	0.1000	0.1000
67	7	0.0000	0.0000	50.00	0.0400	0.0000	0.1000
68	8	0.0000	0.0000	50.0	0.0400	0.0000	0.1000
69	9	0.0000	0.0000	50.00	0.0400	0.0000	0.1000

13.5.2 MODEL CELL

The model cell that will be analyzed is a single premium annuity contract issued on July 1, 2000 to a 60-year-old male. He is both the owner and the annuitant. The single premium paid on the issue date was $100,000. This information is captured in the worksheet "Model Cell":

	Model Cell	
Plan...		Deferred Annuity
Issue Date		7/1/2000
Number of Years to Maturity Date...............................		10 years[1]
Issue Age		60
Gender	Male	▼
Gross Premium		100,000
Premium Payment Period		1 year[1]
Initial Guaranteed Credited Interest – Rate		4.00%
– Period		10 years[1]
Scenario		0 to 0

[1] Maximum value is 10 years.

This workbook also specifies the initial interest rate guarantee. For this case study, the initial interest rate is 5 % for ten years. Finally, the "Model Cell" worksheet identifies the interest rate scenario that will be utilized by the calculation routines.

13.5.3 SCENARIOS

Interest rate scenarios are specified in the worksheet "Scenarios":

		(1)	(2)	(3)	(4)	(5)	(6)	(7)	(8)	(9)	(10)	(11)	(12)
Scenario	t	$z(t\|0)$	$z(t\|1)$	$z(t\|2)$	$z(t\|3)$	$z(t\|4)$	$z(t\|5)$	$z(t\|6)$	$z(t\|7)$	$z(t\|8)$	$z(t\|9)$	$z(t\|10)$
0	0	0.0500	0.0500	0.0500	0.0500	0.0500	0.0500	0.0500	0.0500	0.0500	0.0500	0.0500
	1	0.0500	0.0500	0.0500	0.0500	0.0500	0.0500	0.0500	0.0500	0.0500	0.0500	0.0500
	2	0.0500	0.0500	0.0500	0.0500	0.0500	0.0500	0.0500	0.0500	0.0500	0.0500	0.0500
	3	0.0500	0.0500	0.0500	0.0500	0.0500	0.0500	0.0500	0.0500	0.0500	0.0500	0.0500
	4	0.0500	0.0500	0.0500	0.0500	0.0500	0.0500	0.0500	0.0500	0.0500	0.0500	0.0500
	5	0.0500	0.0500	0.0500	0.0500	0.0500	0.0500	0.0500	0.0500	0.0500	0.0500	0.0500
	6	0.0500	0.0500	0.0500	0.0500	0.0500	0.0500	0.0500	0.0500	0.0500	0.0500	0.0500
	7	0.0500	0.0500	0.0500	0.0500	0.0500	0.0500	0.0500	0.0500	0.0500	0.0500	0.0500
	8	0.0500	0.0500	0.0500	0.0500	0.0500	0.0500	0.0500	0.0500	0.0500	0.0500	0.0500
	9	0.0500	0.0500	0.0500	0.0500	0.0500	0.0500	0.0500	0.0500	0.0500	0.0500	0.0500

The first column identifies the scenario and the second column identifies the number of years from the issue date of the contract. The remaining columns specify the spot rates for "risk-free" bonds (i.e., U.S. reasuries) for terms ranging from 0 (e.g., 6 month treasuries) to 10 years.
The following is the definition of the variables in this worksheet:

t = number of years from issue date; and

$z(t\,|\,s)$ = spot rate at time t for a zero coupon bond with a term of s years.

Since this workbook assumes the frequency of coupon payments is annual, these spot rates are effective annual interest rates.

13.5.4 ASSET FILE

The worksheet "Asset File" specifies the bonds that were purchased on the issue date:

Asset File									
Asset Class: Bonds with Fixed Coupons									
Asset ID[1]	Term (Years)	Credit Rating (1-6)	Par Value	Coupon Rate[2]	Callable? (No/Yes)	Years to First Call	Call Premium	Purchase Price[3]	YTM[3]
1	10	2	80,000	8.00%	Yes	5	1.00%	94,568	5.58%
2	7	3	20,000	8.00%	No		0.00%	19,351	8.64%

[1]Maximum number of bonds is ten
[2]A coupon rate of 0% denotes a zero coupon bond
[3]These values are calculated

The purchase price and yield-to-maturity are determined in the calculation routines. The formula for calculating the purchase price is as follows:

$$\sum_{s=1}^{nTerm(i)} \left[\frac{1}{1+z(0,s)+RP\big(s,Rating(i)\big)} \right]^{s} \cdot coupon(i)$$

$$+ ParValue(i) \cdot \left[\frac{1}{1+z\big(0,nTerm(i)\big)+RP\big(nTerm(i),Rating(i)\big)} \right]^{nTerm(i)}$$

where

$$
\begin{aligned}
nTerm(i) &= \text{term of the } i^{th} \text{ bond;} \\
RP\big(s,Rating(i)\big) &= \text{risk premium at duration s for a bond with a rating of } Rating(i); \\
Rating(i) &= \text{rating of the } i^{th} \text{ bond;} \\
coupon(i) &= \text{coupon of the } i^{th} \text{ bond; and} \\
ParValue(i) &= \text{par value (or face value) of the } i^{th} \text{ bond.}
\end{aligned}
$$

The risk premium is discussed below.

13.5.5 ASSUMPTIONS

For ease of discussion, assumptions have been grouped into two broad categories: asset assumptions and liabilities assumptions. Asset assumptions include the following:

- Bond transition matrix
- Risk premium
- Investment expense
- Loan spread

Liability assumptions include the following:

- Commission rates
- Expenses
- Inflation rate
- Partial withdrawal ratios
- Mortality rates
- Lapse rates

As noted above, taxes are ignored in this case study. In addition when a bond defaults, it is assumed that the bond will have a zero recovery value.

The worksheet "BRTM" specifies the bond rating transition matrix:

Bond Rating Transition Matrix								
	Rating Class							
	Aaa, Aa AAA,AA	A A	Baa BBB	Ba BB	B B	Caa,Ca,C CCC,CC,C	D	Recovery
Rating Class	1	2	3	4	5	6	Default	Value
1	.9564	.0417	.0013	.0005	.0001	.0000	.0000	0.0000
2	.0245	.9190	.0501	.0048	.0012	.0001	.0003	0.0000
3	.0029	.0527	.8851	.0482	.0078	.0016	.0017	0.0000
4	.0005	.0050	.0569	.8499	.0698	.0054	.0125	0.0000
5	.0004	.0013	.0043	.0663	.8315	.0315	.0647	0.0000
6	.0000	.0000	.0057	.0171	.0435	.6821	.2516	0.0000
Default	.0000	.0000	.0000	.0000	.0000	.0000	1.0000	

A bond rating transition matrix specifies the probability that a bond migrates from one rating class to another rating class after it has been purchased. The probabilities for this case study are from "*Default and Recovery rates of Corporate Bond Issues, 1920-2004*" published by Moody's Investors Service.[18]

To illustrate how these probabilities are used. Assume a bond was issued with a rating of Class 2. The second row of the above matrix means that after the first year 91.9% of Class 2 bonds remained in Class 2, 2.45% were upgraded to Class 1 and the balance were downgraded or defaulted.

The worksheet "RP" specifies the risk premium over the risk-free spot rates for the various bond terms and rating classes:

---

[18] See [17].

Risk Premiums					
Risk Premium by Asset Class					
Aaa, Aa AAA,AA	A A	Baa BBB	Ba BB	B B	Caa,Ca,C CCC,CC,C
Term	1	2	3	4	5	6
0	.0050	.0150	.0300	.0340	.0425	.4000
1	.0060	.0160	.0310	.0350	.0435	.4250
2	.0070	.0170	.0320	.0360	.0445	.4500
3	.0080	.0180	.0330	.0370	.0455	.4750
4	.0090	.0190	.0340	.0380	.0465	.5000
5	.0100	.0200	.0350	.0390	.0475	.5250
6	.0110	.0210	.0360	.0400	.0485	.5500
7	.0120	.0220	.0370	.0410	.0495	.5750
8	.0130	.0230	.0380	.0420	.0505	.6000
9	.0140	.0240	.0390	.0430	.0515	.6250
10	.0150	.0250	.0400	.0440	.0525	.6500

These risk premiums are meant to cover default risk and liquidity risk.

Finally, the worksheet "OAA" specifies the investment expense and spread over the six month spot rate that the life insurance company pays on loans.

Other Asset Assumptions		
(1)	**(2)**	**(3)**
t	$i^{expenses}(t)$	$xi^{Loan}(t)$
0	.0025	.0050
1	.0025	.0050
2	.0025	.0050
3	.0025	.0050
4	.0025	.0050
5	.0025	.0050
6	.0025	.0050
7	.0025	.0050
8	.0025	.0050
9	.0025	.0050

(1)   attained age
(2)   investment expenses per $1 of invested assets
(3)   spread over 6-month spot rate used to determine loan rate

For this case study, the lapse rates will be determined using the following formula:

$$q^w_{[x]+t} = {}^{Base}q^w_{[x]+t} + {}^{Excess}q^w_{[x]+t}$$

where $q^w_{[x]+t}$ =   lapse rate between durations t and $t+1$;

${}^{Base}q^w_{[x]+t}$ =   base lapse rate between durations t and $t+1$; and

${}^{Excess}q^w_{[x]+t}$ =   excess lapse rate between durations t and $t+1$.

The excess lapse rate is determined using the following formula:

$$\text{Excess } q^w_{[x]+t} = \frac{c}{1 + a \cdot e^{b \cdot \left[(ic_t + SC_t^{FV}) - ic_t^{Competitor} \right]}} - \frac{c}{1 + a \cdot e}$$

where $ic_t^{Competitor}$ =   competitor interest rate between durations t and $t+1$;

   = $z_{t,n} + d$

   $z_{t:n}$ =   spot for an n-year treasury at duration t; and

   d =   spread over Treasury rate.

This formula for excess lapses adjusts the base lapse rate both up and down depending on whether the credited interest rate plus the surrender charge is lower or higher than the competitor rate, respectively:

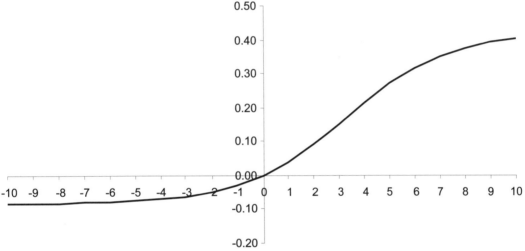

Excess Lapse Rates

Difference Between Company Rate and Competitor Rate

The parameters for this formula are specified at the top of the worksheet "LA":

									Liability Assumptions				

Excess lapse rate parameters:
a = 0.2000
b = −50.0000
c = −0.5000
d = 0.0000

(1)	(2)	(3)	(4)	(5)	(6)	(7)	(8)	(9)	(10)	(11)	(12)	(13)	(14)
x	t	$CGP(t)$	$CFV(t)$	$EAP(t)$	$EMP(t)$	$i^e(t)$	$RPW(t)$	$q^d(t)$	$^{Base}q^w(t)$	$^{Excess}q^w(t)$	$q^w(t)$	$q^m(t)$	$p(t)$
60	0	.0600	.0000	250	25	.03000	.0000	.006428	.10000	− .07840	.02160	00000	1.00000
61	1	.0000	.0025	0	25	.03000	.0000	.006933	.10000	− .07526	.02474	00000	.97198
62	2	.0000	.0025	0	25	.03000	.0000	.007520	.10000	− .07016	.02984	00000	.94119
63	3	.0000	.0025	0	25	.03000	.0000	.008207	.10000	− .06197	.03803	00000	.90602
64	4	.0000	.0025	0	25	.03000	.0000	.009008	.10000	− .04907	.05093	00000	.86413
65	5	.0000	.0025	0	25	.03000	.0000	.009940	.10000	− .02924	.07076	00000	.81234
66	6	.0000	.0025	0	25	.03000	.0000	.011016	.10000	.00000	.10000	00000	.74678
67	7	.0000	.0000	0	25	.03000	.0000	.012251	.20000	.04065	.24065	00000	.66388
68	8	.0000	.0000	0	25	.03000	.0000	.013657	.10000	.04065	.14065	00000	.49598
69	9	.0000	.0000	0	25	.03000	.0000	.015233	.10000	.04065	.14065	.84411	.41944
70	10											.00000	.00000

The exercises will explore how the parameters of this formula change the shape of this curve.

This worksheet also specifies the following liability assumptions:

- Commission rates (premium based and asset based)
- Expenses (acquisition expenses and maintenance expenses per policy)
- Inflation rate[19] (used to inflate maintenance expenses)
- Partial withdrawal ratios
- Mortality rates
- Lapse rates (base, excess and base plus excess)

The excess lapse rates and persistency factor are determined in the calculation routines.

13.5.6 CALCULATION MODULES

The primary goal of the calculation modules is to perform a yearly projection of statutory surplus utilizing the above assumptions. The following diagram is a flowchart of the calculations routines.

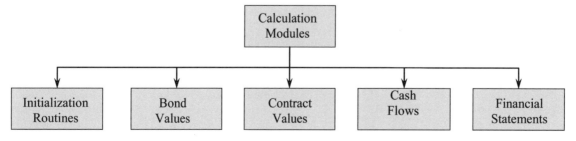

---

[19] For simplicity, the inflation rate is not linked to interest rates. In practice, this relationship should be established.

Initialization Routines

One of the primary functions of the initialization routines to select the spot rate curves for the scenario specified in the worksheet "Model Cell". The values selected are shown in the worksheet "SRC":

					Spot Rate Curves						
Scenario: 0											
(1)	(2)	(3)	(4)	(5)	(6)	(7)	(8)	(9)	(10)	(11)	(12)
t	$z(t\|0)$	$z(t\|1)$	$z(t\|2)$	$z(t\|3)$	$z(t\|4)$	$z(t\|5)$	$z(t\|6)$	$z(t\|7)$	$z(t\|8)$	$z(t\|9)$	$z(t\|10)$
0	.0500	.0500	.0500	.0500	.0500	.0500	.0500	.0500	.0500	.0500	.0500
1	.0500	.0500	.0500	.0500	.0500	.0500	.0500	.0500	.0500	.0500	.0500
2	.0500	.0500	.0500	.0500	.0500	.0500	.0500	.0500	.0500	.0500	.0500
3	.0500	.0500	.0500	.0500	.0500	.0500	.0500	.0500	.0500	.0500	.0500
4	.0500	.0500	.0500	.0500	.0500	.0500	.0500	.0500	.0500	.0500	.0500
5	.0500	.0500	.0500	.0500	.0500	.0500	.0500	.0500	.0500	.0500	.0500
6	.0500	.0500	.0500	.0500	.0500	.0500	.0500	.0500	.0500	.0500	.0500
7	.0500	.0500	.0500	.0500	.0500	.0500	.0500	.0500	.0500	.0500	.0500
8	.0500	.0500	.0500	.0500	.0500	.0500	.0500	.0500	.0500	.0500	.0500
9	.0500	.0500	.0500	.0500	.0500	.0500	.0500	.0500	.0500	.0500	.0500

Another important function performed by the initialization routines is to utilize the bond rating transition matrix to determine how the bonds in the asset file migrate from their initial rating to the other rating classes over the projection period.

The worksheet "CBRTM" contains a table showing the cumulative bond rating transition matrix for each bond in the asset file:

Cumulative Bond Rating Transition Matrix								
Scenario:	0 ▼							
Asset ID:	1 ▼							
Sum of Value	**Class ▼**							
t	1	2	3	4	5	6	Default	Grand Total
0	.00000	1.00000	.00000	.00000	.00000	.00000	.00000	1.00000
1	.02450	0.91900	.05010	.00480	.00120	.00010	.00030	1.00000
2	.04610	0.84825	.09070	.01100	.00283	.00030	.00082	1.00000
3	.06514	0.78630	.12347	.01801	.00487	.00059	.00163	1.00000
4	.08193	0.73193	.14981	.02540	.00724	.00093	.00276	1.00000
5	.00000	0.00000	.17086	.03285	.00989	.00131	.00426	0.21917
6	.00000	0.00000	.15314	.03684	.01191	.00166	.00593	0.20947
7	.00000	0.00000	.13770	.03951	.01374	.00195	.00783	0.20073
8	.00000	0.00000	.12420	.04116	.01534	.00220	.00994	0.19284
9	.00000	0.00000	.11235	.04202	.01669	.00240	.01221	0.18568
10	.00035	0.00615	.10192	.04228	.01779	.00257	.01461	0.18568

For example, the first bond in the asset file (Asset ID = 1) started with a rating in Class 2. Four years after issue ($t = 4$), 8.193% of the bonds in this cell were upgraded to Class 1, 73.193% remained as Class 2 and the balance were either downgraded or defaulted. In the fifth year, bonds in rating Class 1 and Class 2 were called.

The values in this table were calculated using the following formula:

$$CBTM(t) = \begin{cases} BTM & \text{if } t = 1 \\ CBTM(t-1) \otimes BTM & \text{if } t > 1 \end{cases}$$

where

$$
\begin{array}{rcl}
BTM & = & \text{Bond Rating Transition Matrix;} \\
CBTM(t) & = & \text{Cumulative Bond Rating Transition Matrix at duration } t; \text{ and} \\
\otimes & = & \text{matrix multiplication.}
\end{array}
$$

The values in this table are initialized to zero when a bond is called.

A third important function in the initialization routines is the determination of bond prices for the various rating classes. The values are shown in a table in the worksheet "BPM":

Bond Pricing Matrix							
Scenario:	0 ▼						
Asset ID:	1 ▼						
Sum of Value	**Class ▼**						
t ▼	1	2	3	4	5	6	Default
0	96,381	94,568	92,060	91,431	90,145	64,573	0
1	89,112	83,604	76,158	74,323	70,617	12,301	0
2	88,748	83,689	76,790	75,079	71,607	12,925	0
3	88,258	83,690	77,403	75,832	72,630	14,026	0
4	87,629	83,593	77,984	76,572	73,681	15,907	0
5	86,845	83,382	78,521	77,288	74,752	19,012	0
6	85,889	83,040	79,000	77,967	75,833	23,957	0
7	84,744	82,550	79,406	78,596	76,912	31,545	0
8	83,393	81,984	79,721	79,156	77,977	42,739	0
9	81,818	81,051	79,926	79,631	79,012	58,576	0
10	80,000	80,000	80,000	80,000	80,000	80,000	0

The values in this table were calculated using the following formula:

$$
\sum_{s=1}^{nTerm(i)-t} \left[\frac{1}{1+z(t,s)+RP\big(s,Rating(i)\big)} \right]^{s} \cdot coupon(i)
$$

$$
+ ParValue(i) \cdot \left[\frac{1}{1+z\big(t,nTerm(i)-s\big)+RP\big(nTerm(i)-t,Rating(i)\big)} \right]^{nTerm(i)-t}
$$

where

$$
\begin{array}{rcl}
nTerm(i) & = & \text{term of the } i^{th} \text{ bond;} \\
RP\big(s,Rating(i)\big) & = & \text{risk premium at duration s for a bond with a rating of } Rating(i); \\
Rating(i) & = & \text{rating of the } i^{th} \text{ bond;} \\
coupon(i) & = & \text{coupon of the } i^{th} \text{ bond; and} \\
ParValue(i) & = & \text{par value (or face value) of the } i^{th} \text{ bond.}
\end{array}
$$

Bond Value Routines

The bond value routines calculate the following values:

- Book values
- Fair values
- Bonds repaid[20] (i.e., called)
- Bonds matured
- Bond coupon payments
- Bond amortization
- Capital gains (losses)

The worksheet "BV" contains a table showing these values for each bond in the asset file:

Bond Values								
Scenario:	0	▼						
Variable:	Book Value	▼						
Asset ID:	1	▼						

Sum of Value	Class ▼							
t ▼	1	2	3	4	5	6	Default	Grand Total
0	0	94,568	0	0	0	0	0	94,568
1	2,289	85,872	4,681	449	112	9	0	93,413
2	4,252	78,251	8,367	1,015	261	28	0	92,174
3	5,927	71,548	11,235	1,639	443	53	0	90,845
4	7,346	65,630	13,433	2,277	649	83	0	89,419
5	0	0	15,081	2,900	873	116	0	18,969
6	0	0	13,291	3,197	1,033	144	0	17,665
7	0	0	11,736	3,367	1,171	166	0	16,440
8	0	0	10,380	3,440	1,282	183	0	15,286
9	0	0	9,194	3,439	1,366	197	0	14,196
10	0	0	0	0	0	0	0	0

The book values in this table were calculated using the following formula:

$$BV(t)[i,j] = CBTM(t)[i,j] \cdot \left[\sum_{s=1}^{nTerm(i)-t} \frac{coupon(i)}{\left(1+i^{YTM}(i)\right)^s} + \frac{ParValue(i)}{\left(1+i^{YTM}(i)\right)^s} \right]$$

where

$BV(t)[i,j]$ = book value of the ith bond in the jth rating class at duration t;

$CBTM(t)[i,j]$ = Cumulative Bond Rating Transition Matrix of the ith bond in the jth rating class at duration t; and

$i^{YTM}(i)$ = yield to maturity of the ith bond.

The values in this table are initialized to zero when a bond is called.

---

[20] A callable bond is called when the fair value is greater than the par value plus the call premium.

Bond Values								
Scenario: 0 ▼								
Variable: Fair Value ▼								
Asset ID: 1 ▼								

Sum of Value	Class ▼							
t ▼	1	2	3	4	5	6	Default	Grand Total
0	0	94,568	0	0	0	0	0	94,568
1	2,183	76,832	3,816	357	85	1	0	83,273
2	4,091	70,989	6,965	826	203	4	0	83,077
3	5,749	65,806	9,557	1,366	353	8	0	82,839
4	7,180	61,184	11,683	1,945	534	15	0	82,540
5	0	0	13,416	2,539	739	25	0	16,719
6	0	0	12,098	2,872	903	40	0	15,913
7	0	0	10,935	3,105	1,057	61	0	15,158
8	0	0	9,901	3,258	1,196	94	0	14,449
9	0	0	8,980	3,346	1,319	141	0	13,785
10	28	492	8,153	3,382	1,423	206	0	13,685

The fair values in this table were calculated using the following formula:

$$FV(t)[i,j] = CBTM(t)[i,j] \cdot BP(t)[i,j]$$

where

$$FV(t)[i,j] = \text{book value of the } i^{th} \text{ bond in the } j^{th} \text{ rating class at duration } t;$$
$$CBTM(t)[i,j] = \text{Cumulative Bond Rating Transition Matrix of the } i^{th} \text{ bond in the } j^{th} \text{ rating}$$
$$\text{class at duration } t; \text{ and}$$
$$BP(t)[i,j] = \text{bond price}^{21} \text{ of the } i^{th} \text{ bond in the } j^{th} \text{ rating class at duration } t.$$

The values in this table are initialized to zero when a bond is called.
The determination of the remaining bond values in this table will be left as exercises at the end of this chapter.

Contract Values Routines
Using the values in the "Model Cell" worksheet and the "CVA" worksheet, the contract value routines calculate the following values:

- Fund values
- Premium payments
- Interest credited
- Partial withdrawals
- Surrender charges
- Cash surrender value
- Death benefits

---

[21] Bond prices are from the "BP" worksheet.

The worksheet "CV" shows the results of these calculations:

Contract Values										
(1)	(2)	(3)	(4)	(5)	(6)	(7)	(8)	(9)	(10)	(11)
x	t	$FV(t)$ +	$GP(t)$ −	$EC(t)$ +	$IC(t)$ −	$PW(t)$ =	$FW(t+1)$ −	$SC(t+1)$ =	$CV(t+1)$	$DB(t+1)$
60	0	0	100,000	50	3,998	0	103,948	7,276	96,672	103,948
61	1	103,948	0	50	4,156	0	108,054	6,483	101,571	108,054
62	2	108,054	0	50	4,320	0	112,324	5,616	106,708	112,324
63	3	112,324	0	50	4,491	0	116,765	4,671	112,094	116,765
64	4	116,765	0	50	4,669	0	121,384	3,642	117,742	121,384
65	5	121,384	0	50	4,853	0	126,187	2,524	123,663	126,187
66	6	126,187	0	50	5,045	0	131,182	1,312	129,871	131,182
67	7	131,182	0	50	5,245	0	136,378	0	136,378	136,378
68	8	136,378	0	50	5,453	0	141,781	0	141,781	141,781
69	9	141,781	0	50	5,669	0	147,400	0	147,400	147,400

The formulas for these values are discussed in Chapter 10.

Cash Flow Routines

The cash flow routines calculate the following values:

- Liability cash flows; and
- Asset cash flows

The worksheet "LCF" shows the liability cash flows:

Liability Cash Flows										
	Projection Period									
	1	2	3	4	5	6	7	8	9	10
Gross Premium Collected										
First	100,000	0	0	0	0	0	0	0	0	0
Renewal	0	0	0	0	0	0	0	0	0	0
Total **gross premium income**	100,000	0	0	0	0	0	0	0	0	0
Net Investment Income										
Gross investment income[1]	6,683	6,882	7,069	7,229	7,336	6,774	6,655	6,195	4,982	4,541
Investment expenses	(200)	(208)	(216)	(223)	(228)	(388)	(385)	(423)	(381)	(366)
Total **Net investment income**	6,483	6,674	6,853	7,006	7,108	6,386	6,271	5,787	4,629	4,216
Commissions Paid										
Premium based	6,000	0	0	0	0	0	0	0	0	0
Fund or asset based	0	253	254	254	252	247	236	0	0	0
Total **commissions paid**	6,000	253	254	254	252	247	236	0	0	0
Expenses Paid										
Acquisition	250	0	0	0	0	0	0	0	0	0
Maintenance	25	25	25	25	24	24	22	20	16	14
Total **expenses paid**	275	25	25	25	24	24	22	20	16	14
Benefits Paid										
Death benefits	668	728	795	868	945	1,019	1,079	1,109	960	942
Partial withdrawals	0	0	0	0	0	0	0	0	0	0
Full withdrawals	2,088	2,443	2,997	3,862	5,182	7,108	9,699	21,788	9,891	60,884
Total **benefits paid**	2,756	3,171	3,792	4,730	6,127	8,127	10,778	22,898	10,851	61,826
Net cash from operations*	98,714	4,289	3,654	2,700	1,286	(5,728)	(8,453)	(21,947)	(9,961)	(60,995)

[1] Includes interest on cash and bond coupon payments, but excludes amortization of bonds bought at a discount or premium

The worksheet "ACF" shows the asset cash flows

Asset Cash Flows										
	Projection Period									
	1	2	3	4	5	6	7	8	9	10
Investment proceeds										
Sold	0	0	0	0	0	0	0	0	0	0
Matured	0	0	0	0	0	0	19,270	0	0	13,685
Repaid	0	0	0	0	63,091	784	706	638	578	0
Total **investment proceeds**	0	0	0	0	63,091	784	19,976	638	578	13,685
Investments acquired										
Bonds	113,919	0	0	0	0	0	0	0	0	0
Other assets	0	0	0	0	0	0	0	0	0	0
Total **investments acquired**	113,919	0	0	0	0	0	0	0	0	0
Net cash from investment activities	(113,919)	0	0	0	63,091	784	19,976	638	578	13,685

Financial Statements Routines

The financial statements routines calculate the following primary financial statements:

- Cash flow statement;
- Summary of Operations; and
- Balance Sheet.

The worksheet "CF" shows the cash flow statement:

Cash Flow										
	Projection Period									
	1	2	3	4	5	6	7	8	9	10
Cash From Operations										
Premiums collected	100,000	0	0	0	0	0	0	0	0	0
Interest on cash	(1,313)	(1,105)	(906)	(730)	(603)	3,854	3,823	4,989	3,855	3,489
Coupons	7,995	7,987	7,975	7,959	7,939	2,919	2,832	1,221	1,156	1,095
Investment expenses	(200)	(208)	(216)	(223)	(228)	(388)	(385)	(423)	(382)	(368)
Net investment income[1]	6,483	6,674	6,853	7,006	7,108	6,386	6,271	5,787	4,629	4,216
Commissions	(6,000)	(253)	(254)	(254)	(252)	(247)	(236)	0	0	0
Expenses	(275)	(25)	(25)	(25)	(24)	(24)	(22)	(20)	(16)	(14)
Benefits	(2,756)	(3,171)	(3,792)	(4,730)	(6,127)	(8,127)	(10,778)	(22,898)	(10,851)	(61,826)
Total **cash from operations**	98,714	4,289	3,654	2,700	1,286	(5,728)	(8,453)	(21,947)	9,961	(60,995)
Cash From Investment Activities										
Investment proceeds	0	0	0	0	63,091	784	19,976	638	578	13,685
Investment acquired	113,919	0	0	0	0	0	0	0	0	0
Total **cash from investment activities**	(113,919)	0	0	0	63,091	784	19,976	638	578	13,685
Cash From Financing										
Borrowed	0	0	0	0	0	0	0	0	0	0
Other	0	0	0	0	0	0	0	0	0	0
Total **cash from financing**	0	0	0	0	0	0	0	0	0	0
Reconciliation of Cash										
Net change in cash	(15,204)	4,289	3,654	2,700	64,377	(4,944)	11,523	(21,309)	(9,383)	(47,310)
Cash at beginning of year	0	(16,466)	(13,241)	(10,459)	(8,463)	55,333	54,106	69,317	52,824	47,165
Cash at end of period	(16,466)	(13,241)	(10,459)	(8,463)	55,333	54,106	69,317	52,824	47,165	3,226

The worksheet "SO" shows the summary of operations:

Summary of Operations										
	Projection Period									
	1	2	3	4	5	6	7	8	9	10
Revenues										
Premiums	100,000	0	0	0	0	0	0	0	0	0
Interest on Cash	(1,313)	(1,105)	(906)	(730)	(603)	3,854	3,823	4,898	3,855	3,489
Bond Coupons	7,995	7,987	7,975	7,959	7,939	2,919	2,832	1,221	1,156	1,095
Bond Amortization	(1,056)	(1,113)	(1,172)	(1,234)	(1,299)	(212)	(204)	(318)	(318)	(319)
Investment expenses	(200)	(208)	(216)	(223)	(228)	(388)	(385)	(423)	(382)	(368)
Net investment income[1]	5,427	5,561	5,681	5,772	5,809	6,174	6,067	5,469	4,311	3,897
Other revenue	0	0	0	0	0	0	0	0	0	0
Total **revenues**	105,427	5,561	5,681	5,772	5,809	6,174	6,067	5,469	4,311	3,897
Costs										
Benefits	2,756	3,171	3,792	4,730	6,127	8,127	10,778	22,898	10,851	61,826
Commissions	6,000	253	254	254	252	247	236	0	0	0
Expenses	275	25	25	25	24	24	22	20	16	14
Increase in reserves	93,962	1,635	1,083	185	(1,218)	(3,297)	(6,131)	(18,578)	(8,171)	(59,469)
Other costs	0	0	0	0	0	0	0	0	0	0
Total **costs**	102,933	5,083	5,154	5,195	5,185	5,100	4,904	4,340	2,696	2,371
Net Gain From Operations	2,434	478	527	528	624	1,074	1,163	1,129	1,615	1,527
Net realized capital gains	(61)	(107)	(157)	(208)	(6,089)	(350)	(365)	(198)	(193)	(192)
Net Income	2,373	371	370	369	(5,465)	724	798	931	1,422	1,335
Capital and Surplus										
Surplus at beginning of period	0	2,373	2,744	3,114	3,483	(1,982)	(1,259)	(461)	470	1,892
Net income	2,373	371	370	369	(5,465)	724	798	931	1,422	1,335
Surplus at end of period	2,373	2,744	3,114	3,483	(1,982)	(1,259)	(461)	470	1,892	3,226

[1]Includes interest on cash and bond coupon payments, plus amortization of bonds at a discount or a premium.

The worksheet "BS" shows the balance sheet:

Balance Sheet										
	Projection Period									
	1	2	3	4	5	6	7	8	9	10
Assets										
Bonds	112,802	111,582	110,253	108,810	38,331	36,985	16,440	15,286	14,196	0
Cash	(16,466)	(13,241)	(10,459)	(8,463)	55,333	54,106	69,317	52,824	46,165	3,226
Other Assets	0	0	0	0	0	0	0	0	0	0
Total **Assets**	96,335	98,341	99,793	100,347	93,664	91,091	85,757	68,110	61,361	3,226
Liabilities										
Policy reserves	93,962	95,597	96,680	96,865	95,646	92,349	86,218	67,640	59,469	0
Loans	0	0	0	0	0	0	0	0	0	0
Other Costs	0	0	0	0	0	0	0	0	0	0
Total **Liabilities**	93,962	95,597	96,680	96,865	95,646	92,349	86,218	67,640	59,469	0
Surplus	2,373	2,744	3,114	3,483	(1,982)	(1,259)	(461)	470	1,892	3,226

These financial statements are discussed in Chapter 2.

13.6 EXERCISES

13.6.1 Key Terms

moderately adverse   ASOP No. 7
cash flow analysis   cash flow testing
asset files   liability files
model validation   scenarios
deterministic   stochastic
investment strategy   policyholder behavior

13.6.2 Questions

a. What is one of the primary purposes of cash flow testing when it is used in support of a statutory annual statement filing?

b. Provide some examples of when minimum valuation standards might not be adequate.

c. What insights does a cash flow analysis provide?

d. What typically falls within the scope of a cash flow analysis?

e. What types of skills are required to perform a cash flow analysis?

f. Briefly describe the major activities involved in a cash flow analysis.

g. Utilizing the flowchart in Section 13.3, describe the five major parts of a typical cash flow process.

h. Why is it necessary to group the policy extract file? What does the actuary have to be carefull about?

i. What issues should the actuary consider when projecting asset cash flows?

j. What issues should the actuary consider when developing an understanding of the investment strategy of the life insurance company?

k. What issues should the actuary consider when projecting liability cash flows?

l. Why is model validation important?

m. What type of report should a cash flow model produce? Why?

n. What are the advantages and disadvantages of deterministic scenarios?

o. What are the advantages and disadvantages of stochastic scenarios?

p. What are some of the traits of a good interest rate model?

q. Describe some of the items the actuary and the investment officer need to consider when developing an investment strategy.

r. What are some of the items the actuary needs to consider with regards to policyholder behavior?

s. What are some of the items the actuary needs to consider when developing a lapse rate function?

14 ✧ The Valuation Actuary in Canada [1]

14.1 Introduction

Valuation standards in Canada vary markedly for the period before 1978, the period from 1978 to 1991 when the 1978 Canadian Method was in use, the period from 1992 to 2001 when the Policy Premium Method (PPM) was in use, and the current period since 2002 in which the Canadian Asset Liability Method (CALM) has been in use. It is important to note that, unlike in the U.S., each successive standard replaces the previous one. That is, the new standard applies to all in-force policies, not just new policies issued.

14.2 Before 1978

Prior to 1978, the prescription of valuation standards in Canada was similar to that in the U.S. A valuation method was acceptable as long as it could be shown to generate reserves not less than those produced by the method specified by law. Maximum interest rates were prescribed, along with several mortality tables, although higher rates of interest or other mortality tables producing weaker reserves could be used with the advance approval of the Superintendent of Insurance. Withdrawal assumptions were not required, but reserves had to be at least equal to cash values for each policy. Deficiency reserves were required for policies where the actual premium receivable was not sufficient to cover the valuation premium.

Like the current situation in the U.S., the one-sided character (reserves could be more conservative, but generally not less conservative) of these requirements was inconsistent with GAAP, as were a number of other accounting practices of life insurance companies. The auditor's report accompanying financial statements generally made it clear that the financial statements had been prepared in accordance with accounting principles prescribed by the Superintendent. Moreover, rapidly rising interest rates prompted an increasing number of individual requests to the Superintendent for approval of valuation interest assumptions greater than the maximum rates set by law.

14.3 1978 Canadian Method

Changes in the Canadian and British Insurance Companies Act (the Act) in effect for the period 1978 to 1991 placed the responsibility for policy valuation on the valuation actuary appointed by the directors of the company and recognized as such in the Act. The mandated mortality bases and maximum interest rates were removed and the valuation actuary could use any assumption considered "appropriate to the circumstances" and acceptable to the Superintendent. Any valuation method was permitted provided it produced a reserve not less, for any policy at any duration, than that produced by a method specified in the Act.

In contrast to the previous Act, the assumptions were a two-sided matter: to be appropriate, margins could be neither too large nor too small. The method, however, remained one-sided: there was no statutory upper limit to the safety that could be built into the valuation method.

---

[1] This chapter was written by Richard May, FSA, FCIA.

The method specified in the Act was a modified net premium method in which the initial acquisition cost that could have been deferred (equal to the total present value at date of issue of the excess of all renewal valuation premiums over all renewal net level premiums) was limited to the lesser of 150% of the net level premium or the actual costs incurred "in connection with the issuance of the policy."[2] The total valuation premium for benefits and for amortization of this deferred acquisition cost could not exceed the premium specified in the policy less future administration expenses and dividend expectations. This eliminated the possibility of a deficiency in the policy premium relative to the valuation premium, so that separate deficiency reserves were not required.

The valuation actuary could have taken withdrawals into account either by using withdrawal assumptions or by substituting cash values any time they exceeded reserves. In the former case, the total of all negative reserves and the total of all excesses of cash value over reserve had to be reported. The Superintendent required these amounts to be appropriated from retained earnings.

A reserve also had to be calculated (an estimate was acceptable) by the net level premium method, and the annual statement required by the Department of Insurance called for reserves determined by both methods to be shown. The difference (if any) represented the "deferred policy acquisition expenses" to be shown in the statement (Analysis of Liabilities) by deduction from the net level premium reserve to arrive at the reserve determined by the valuation actuary. If the valuation actuary did not use the method specified in the Act, the reserve determined by that method had to be shown in the balance sheet by a footnote. In addition, the reserve increase determined by the specified method had to be shown in the statement of operations and the adjustment to arrive at the increase determined by the method used by the valuation actuary was shown separately.

The company's published financial statements had to include the same reserve as in the annual statement to the Superintendent (after deduction of acquisition expenses), making the financial information from the two statements consistent. The auditor, in reporting on the financial results, could accept the reserve reported by the valuation actuary as presenting fairly the obligations of the company in respect of policies.

In 1979, the Canadian Institute of Actuaries issued its Recommendations for Life Insurance Company Financial Reporting, governing, among other things, the development of appropriate valuation assumptions. The Recommendations incorporated the following general principles regarding assumptions:

(1) An appropriate assumption was required for each contingency that materially affected the company's net income for the policies over their lifetime.

(2) Each assumption should include a margin which increased the actuarial liability, but the combined effect of all margins should be reasonable.

(3) Larger margins should be used where there was greater uncertainty.

(4) Greater care should be taken in setting assumptions regarding contingencies to which the actuarial liabilities were more sensitive.

(5) Provision should not be made for abnormal adverse deviations from expected experience, for catastrophic events, or for major unexpected alterations in mortality or morbidity.[3]

Excluding the margins, the valuation assumptions should represent rates of interest and contingencies expected in the future without bias in either direction. Therefore, the valuation assumptions in the Policy Premium Method have the effect of generating expected income each year that is determined by the margins released

---

[2] See [10].
[3] See [11].

during the year. This is the actual case if experience during the year exactly follows the assumptions without the margins. However, actual income fluctuates around the expected amount according to how actual experience compares with the assumptions excluding the margins. It is clear that a company could expect to earn more in respect of those contingencies that involved a greater degree of uncertainty, which was a desired result.

For actuarial liabilities to result in a fair presentation of net income during the year, the valuation assumptions have to be consistently applied at the beginning and end of the year. This means that if there is a material change during the year in expectations regarding a contingency, the assumption relating to that contingency should be changed. This results in a higher or lower actuarial liability and the difference affects income for the year. The change in the actuarial liability properly reflects the financial effect on the company of the changes in the contingency that were recognized during the year.

14.4 POLICY PREMIUM METHOD (PPM)

Neither the 1978 Canadian Method nor the Net Level Premium Method conformed to generally accepted accounting principles. Considerable effort was directed by both the Canadian Institute of Actuaries and the Canadian Institute of Chartered Accountants to bring statutory valuation requirements into line with GAAP. To that end, the Superintendent of Financial Institutions endorsed the Policy Premium Method (PPM) effective for the 1992 year end.

"Net" valuation methods are net with respect to expenses. Net methods tend to generate conservative reserves, since expenses are greater in the early policy years and are covered by the expense component of premiums spread over the full premium period. After the premium period, the method is not conservative enough unless future administrative expenses are provided for in some manner. Modified reserve methods tend to reduce the conservatism of the Net Level Premium Method by providing for amortization of certain acquisition expenses over the premium period. This is done by means of a modification of the net level premium to permit a greater proportion of the policy (gross) premium to be recognized in the valuation. There is usually an arbitrary limit on the amount of modification permitted, as is the case with both CRVM and the 1978 Canadian Method. If the valuation premium exceeds the policy premium, a deficiency reserve must be held for the present value of the excess.

The Policy Premium Method treated expenses explicitly and, hence, did not belong to the family of net methods referred to above, but rather was a gross premium valuation method. The method recognized all expenses expected to be incurred in the future along with all future policy obligations. Similarly, the premiums used in the valuation were the actual gross premiums collectable in the future under the policy. The Policy Premium Method thereby eliminated the following three aspects of net methods that do not conform to GAAP:

(1)   The over-provision resulting from anticipating less than the full amount of future premiums.

(2)   The under-provision resulting from ignoring future expenses when there are no future premiums to cover them.

(3)   The arbitrary upper limit on modifications.

Under PPM, the actuary made an explicit assumption about each contingency that could materially affect the policy liabilities, each assumption consisting of a combination of an expected component and a margin for adverse deviation. The Canadian Institute of Actuaries published standards with respect to the selection of these valuation margins. It should be noted that unlike U.S. GAAP, actuarial assumptions for traditional products under the Policy Premium Method are not fixed at the time of policy issue, but must be reviewed in light of emerging experience or actuarial judgment.

14.5 CANADIAN ASSET LIABILITY METHOD (CALM)

The Canadian Asset Liability Method (CALM) is an extension of the Policy Premium Method with scenario testing for interest rate risk required for all products (not just Single Premium Immediate annuities as was the case prior to 2002). Under CALM the actuary is required to project the expected future cash flows of the liabilities and the expenses needed to support them. In addition, the actuary projects the expected cash flows from future premiums and the assets supporting the liabilities. The projection of liability cash flows and asset cash flows are both subject to a number of requirements.

In forecasting the cash flow from the policy liabilities, the actuary should take account of policyholder reasonable expectations and include policyholder dividends in the cash flow for policy benefits. The actuary calculates the policy liabilities for a number of scenarios and adopts a scenario whose policy liabilities make sufficient but not excessive provision for the insurer's obligations in respect of the relevant policies.

The scenarios of interest rate assumptions should comprise a base scenario which, unless otherwise specified, assumes continuation of current reinvestment and inflation rates, and unless there is explicit reason to assume otherwise, the insurer's then current investment strategy. Additionally, a number of prescribed scenarios must be prepared in a deterministic approach (or ranges which recognize all of the prescribed scenarios in a stochastic application), plus other scenarios appropriate to the circumstances of the insurer.

The actuary usually applies the Canadian Asset Liability Method to policies in groups which reflect the insurer's asset-liability management practice for allocation of assets to liabilities and investment strategy. For a particular scenario, the actuary may use another method that may be equivalent to or approximates the Canadian Asset Liability Method.

In allocating assets to support liabilities, the actuary maintains the connection between unamortized capital gains, both realized and unrealized, and the asset segments which generated them. The value of the assets which support policy liabilities are their book value from the insurer's financial statements, taking account of accrued investment income and of adjustments for impairment, amortized unrealized capital gains and amortized realized capital gains. The actuary allocates assets to the liabilities, forecasts their cash flows, and, by trial and error, adjusts the allocated assets so that they reduce to zero at the last cash flow date. The policy liabilities are the book value of the assets so determined.

If the calculation of the scenarios is carried out by deterministic methods, then the actuary sets policy liabilities equal to those determined by a scenario at the upper part of the range of the policy liabilities for the selected scenarios. However, the policy liabilities must be at least as great as those in the prescribed scenario with the largest policy liabilities.

If the calculation of the scenarios is conducted using stochastic methods, then the actuary sets policy liabilities equal to those from a scenario that is within the range defined by the average of the policy liabilities which are above the 60th percentile of the range of the policy liabilities for the selected scenarios, and the corresponding average for the 80th percentile.

In developing the scenarios, the actuary utilizes estimate assumptions for future experience. Each assumption should include a margin for adverse deviations. The actuary needs to ensure that the application of each margin for adverse deviations results in an increase to the value of the policy liabilities and that the resulting provision is appropriate in the aggregate.

Because the future investment return and inflation rates are so conjectural, it is desirable that the calculation of policy liabilities for all insurers take account of certain common assumptions. Consequently, there is specific guidance and direction for interest rate scenarios and seven prescribed scenarios have been developed.

Every interest rate scenario contains an investment strategy, an investment rate of return for each asset, a default rate for each asset and an inflation rate consistent with the investment rates. The investment strategy defines both reinvestment and disinvestment practice for each type of asset. The assumed terms of assets would be large enough to permit assumption of changes in the shape and steepness of the yield curve. This implies a minimum of a short, a medium and a long term assumption. The plausible range of the Canadian default-free interest rates is from 3% to 10% for short term rates and from 5% to 12% for long term rates. Adjustments to these ranges are made if current rates are near or outside the ends of the ranges. The scenarios would include those in which the premiums for default risk range from 50% to 200% of the actual premiums at the balance sheet date.

The prescribed scenarios apply to debt investments acquired after the balance sheet date. For a prescribed scenario, if the net cash flow forecasted for a period is positive, then the actuary would assume its application to repay the outstanding balance, if any, of borrowing in prior years and then assume the reinvestment of any remainder in new investments. For the prescribed scenarios, the actuary must assume reinvestment in risk free investments only (for Canadian investments, coupon paying Government of Canada bonds with a term no greater than 15 years.) Conversely, if the net cash flow forecasted for a period is negative, then the actuary would assume an offsetting disinvestment or borrowing, or a mix of the two.

14.5.1 PRESCRIBED SCENARIO 1

The interest rates for investments grade from their current level to 5% in the 20th year and later.

14.5.2 PRESCRIBED SCENARIO 2

The interest rates for investments grade from their current level to 12% in the 20th year and later.

14.5.3 PRESCRIBED SCENARIO 3

The long-term default-free interest rate moves cyclically in 1% steps between 5% and 12%. At each anniversary, the long-term default free interest rate is changed to the next integral rate closer to 12%. After the long-term default free interest rate is 12%, the rates cycle between 5% and 12% in 1% steps.

The short-term default free interest rate changes uniformly over a period, usually not more than three years from the balance sheet date, to 60% of the corresponding long-term interest rate, and thereafter remains at 60% of the long-term interest rate.

14.5.4 PRESCRIBED SCENARIO 4

Same as Prescribed Scenario 3, except that the long-term interest rate is initially changed to the next integral rate closer to 5%.

14.5.5 PRESCRIBED SCENARIO 5

Same as Prescribed Scenario 3, except that the short-term interest rate is a different percentage of the long-term interest rate. That percentage moves cyclically in 20% annual steps from 40% to 120% and back. At the first anniversary, the percentage is the next step above the percentage at the balance sheet date if the actual percentage is less than 120% and otherwise is 120%. Thereafter the cycle continues regularly.

14.5.6   PRESCRIBED SCENARIO 6

Same as Prescribed Scenario 4, except that the short-term interest rate is a different percentage of the long-term interest rate. That percentage moves cyclically in 20% annual steps from 120% to 40% and back. At the first anniversary, the percentage is the next step below the percentage at the balance sheet date if the actual percentage is greater than 40% and otherwise is 40%. Thereafter the cycle continues regularly.

14.5.7   PRESCRIBED SCENARIO 7

Default-free interest rates are the forward interest rates implied by an equilibrium market yield curve at the valuation date.

In addition to the prescribed scenarios, which are common to the calculation of policy liabilities for all insurers, the actuary also selects other scenarios which are appropriate to the circumstances.

As with the Policy Premium Method, the expected income each year is determined by the margins released each year. However, actual income fluctuates depending upon how the actual experience compares to the expected assumptions and the impact of new business.

14.6 DYNAMIC CAPITAL ADEQUACY TESTING (DCAT)

In Canada, the valuation actuary completes an annual investigation of the insurer's recent and current financial position, and financial condition, as revealed by Dynamic Capital Adequacy Testing (DCAT) under various scenarios. The actuary's report identifies possible actions for dealing with any threats to a satisfactory financial condition revealed by the investigation.

The investigation reviews operations of recent years (normally at least three years) and the financial position at the end of each of those years. Dynamic capital adequacy testing examines the effect of various plausible adverse scenarios on the insurer's forecasted capital adequacy. The purpose of dynamic capital adequacy testing is to identify plausible threats to satisfactory financial condition, actions which lessen the likelihood of those threats, and actions which would mitigate a threat if it materialized. Dynamic capital adequacy testing is defensive in that it addresses threats to financial condition rather than the exploitation of opportunities.

The insurer's financial condition is satisfactory if throughout the forecast period it is able to meet all its future obligations under the base scenario and all plausible adverse scenarios, and if under the base scenario it meets the minimum regulatory capital requirement.

The forecast period begins at the most recent available fiscal year-end balance sheet date. The forecast period for a scenario would be long enough to capture the effect of its adversity and the ability of management to react. The forecast period for a typical life insurer would be five fiscal years.

The scenarios consist of a base scenario and several plausible adverse scenarios. Each scenario takes into account not only inforce policies, but also the policies assumed to be sold during the forecast period. The base scenario is a realistic set of assumptions used to forecast the insurer's financial position over the forecast period. Normally, the base scenario is consistent with the insurer's business plan.

A plausible adverse scenario is a scenario of adverse, but realistic, assumptions about matters to which the insurer's financial condition is sensitive. Plausible adverse scenarios vary among insurers and may vary over time for a particular insurer. The actuary would consider plausible adverse risks to the insurer. Scenario testing may be required for the actuary to determine the sensitivity of the insurer's capital adequacy to each risk. It is expected that the actuary would scenario test and report annually on the base scenario, and a minimum of three plausible adverse scenarios posing the greatest risk for the insurer. For life insurers, the actuary would consider threats to capital adequacy under plausible adverse scenarios that include but are not limited to the following risk categories:

- Mortality
- Morbidity
- Persistency
- Cash flow mismatch
- Deterioration of asset values
- New business
- Expense
- Reinsurance
- Government or political action
- Other issues

To help determine if a risk is material and plausible, the actuary may stress test the capital adequacy of the insurer. The actuary might determine how much a base scenario assumption needs to be changed before an adverse scenario gives rise to an unsatisfactory financial condition. The actuary can then judge whether a plausible risk or event exists for the insurer over the forecast period. In assuring consistency within each scenario, the actuary would consider "ripple" effects. Although most of the other assumptions used in the base scenario may remain appropriate under the plausible adverse scenario, some may require adjustment to reflect the interdependence of assumptions in the plausible adverse scenario.

The DCAT report contains the key assumptions of the base scenario and the plausible adverse scenarios posing the greatest risk to the satisfactory financial condition of the insurer. It also includes the plausible adverse scenarios examined which cause the insurer to fall below the minimum regulatory capital requirement. Even though the actuary may have signed a satisfactory financial condition opinion, the report would make it clear that under these scenarios the regulators may impose restrictions on the operations of the insurer, including its ability to write new business.

14.7 MISCELLANEOUS VALUATION PRACTICES IN CANADA

The actuary should exercise reasonable judgment in applying the Canadian Standards of Practice. A judgment is reasonable if it is objective and takes account of the spirit and intent of the standards, the Canadian Institute of Actuaries Guiding Principle No. 1, the rules, common sense, and constraints on time and resources. Deviation from a particular recommendation or other guidance in the standards is acceptable actuarial practice if, in the actuary's judgment, the effect of doing so is not material.

The standards describe the theoretical ideal. In practice, however, the actuary's work is constrained by available time and resources. The actuary would therefore strive for an interpretation and application of the standards which strikes a reasonable balance between the theory and the constraints.

An approximation is appropriate if it reduces the cost of, reduces the time needed for, or improves the actuary's control over, work without affecting the result. The results of applying a recommendation may differ immaterially from the result of a simpler practice requiring less time and expense. For example, the practice-specific recommendations for valuation of policy liabilities for term life insurance have little effect on an insurer whose volume of term life insurance is trivial. To ignore them in that situation is accepted actuarial practice if it helps the actuary to concentrate time and resources on material items.

The Canadian Institute of Actuaries identifies and addresses matters of practice which may require additional guidance. Educational notes are published periodically which illustrate an application (but not necessarily the only application) of the standards of practice, so there should be no conflict between them. Education notes are not binding, but they are compelling. The actuary should be familiar with them. They describe accepted practice for particular circumstances but not necessarily the only accepted practice and may not be applicable or appropriate for other circumstances. In addition, research papers and task force reports are published which may or may not be in compliance with the standards. Regardless, the educational notes, research papers and task force reports are not binding on the actuary.

The additional benefits associated with insurance policies tend to produce modest policy liabilities. Most companies in Canada apply approximate methods to generate reserves for these items. Canadian companies often use valuation practices similar to those in use by US companies for such items as Accidental Death Benefits, Guaranteed Purchase Options, Waiver of Premium Benefits and Substandard Risks.

15 ✦ THE VALUATION ACTUARY IN THE UNITED STATES

15.1 INTRODUCTION

The National Association of Insurance Commissioners amended the model Standard Valuation Law in December 1990 to incorporate the valuation actuary concept. Under these amendments, every life insurance company in the United States, unless exempted, must submit an actuarial opinion that considers not only the liabilities, but the ability of the cash flows of the assets to make sufficient provision for the obligations of the company. The 1990 amendment was based on New York Regulation 126.

In response to this 1990 amendment, the National Association of Insurance Commissioners adopted *Actuarial Opinion and Memorandum Regulation* and the Actuarial Standards Board (ASB) adopted Actuarial Standards of Practice No. 22, *Statements of Opinion Based on Asset Adequacy Analysis by Actuaries for Life or Health Insurers.* In reviewing this actuarial standard of practice, the actuary must be aware of the Actuarial Standards Board's approach to setting standards. This approach is probably best characterized by statements made by Harold G. Ingraham, Jr., former president of the Society of Actuaries, at the April 30 - May 1, 1990 meeting of the Society:

"The ASB also has made it plain that it won't permit the setting of rigid standards. Its members believe that standards of practice must be conceptualized and worded in such a way that they don't unnecessarily circumscribe an actuary's creativity in approaching new problems. In other words, the ASB endorses what it refers to as the 'disclosed defendable deviation' approach. And the ASB has specifically instructed its operating committees 'to avoid being overly prescriptive and to allow the actuary to deviate when he or she has justification'."

The following provides a brief overview of the provisions of the model Standard Valuation Law amendments and the associated model regulation and actuarial standard of practice.

15.2 MODEL STANDARD VALUATION LAW[1]

Section 3 of the model Standard Valuation Law sets forth the requirements adopted in December 1990 by the National Association of Insurance Commissioners that incorporate the valuation actuary concept.

---

[1] See [4].

15.2.1 GENERAL REQUIREMENT

Section 3 begins with the following general statement:

> *"Every life insurance company doing business in this state shall annually submit the opinion of a qualified actuary as to whether the reserves and related actuarial items held in support of the policies and contracts specified by the commissioner by regulation are computed appropriately, are based on assumptions that satisfy contractual provisions, are consistent with prior reported amounts and comply with applicable laws of this state. The commissioner shall define by regulation the specifics of this opinion and add any other items deemed to be necessary to its scope."*

This statement not only requires an actuarial analysis of reserves and assets held in support of these reserves, but it also requires the appointment of a qualified actuary who must issue a statement of actuarial opinion with regards to this asset adequacy analysis.

15.2.2 APPOINTED ACTUARY

For purposes of the model Standard Valuation Law, an ***appointed actuary*** is a qualified actuary who is appointed or retained by the board of directors of the company to prepare the statement of actuarial opinion. A qualified actuary is a member in good standing of the American Academy of Actuaries, who is qualified to sign statements of actuarial opinion for life and health insurance companies in accordance with the Academy's qualification standards, and who also meets certain requirements set forth by the commissioner.

15.2.3 ACTUARIAL OPINION OF RESERVES

The appointed actuary must submit annually a ***Statement of Actuarial Opinion*** as to whether the reserves and related actuarial items are computed appropriately, are based on assumptions which satisfy contractual provisions, are consistent with prior reported amounts, and comply with applicable laws of the state. The opinion applies to all business in force including individual and group plans and is subject to standards adopted from time to time by the Actuarial Standards Board. The commissioner may, by regulation, prescribe other standards.

15.2.4 PROFESSIONAL LIABILITY

Other than in cases of fraud or willful misconduct, the appointed actuary, according to the model Standard Valuation Law, shall not be liable for damages to any person other than the insurance company and the commissioner for any act, error, omission, decision, or conduct, with respect to the actuary's opinion. The model Standard Valuation Law thus attempts to exempt the actuary from "third party liability."

The model Standard Valuation Law has been adopted with some variations on a state-by-state basis. For example, in some states the actuary is not specifically exempted from third party liability.

15.2.5 SUPPORTING MEMORANDUM

Section 3 of the model Standard Valuation Law also requires that an ***actuarial memorandum*** be prepared in support of the actuarial opinion. If the company fails to provide a supporting memorandum, the commissioner may engage a qualified actuary at the expense of the company. The supporting memorandum is a confidential document.

15.3 ACTUARIAL OPINION AND MEMORANDUM MODEL REGULATION[2]

The primary purpose of this model regulation is to prescribe:

(a) requirements for statements of actuarial opinion that are submitted to comply with Section 3 of the model Standard Valuation Law;

(b) requirements for the actuarial memorandum prepared in support of the actuarial opinion;

(c) rules governing the appointment of the appointed actuary; and

(d) guidance as to the meaning of "adequacy of reserves."

The next several sections gives a brief description of these items.

15.3.1 ACTUARIAL OPINION REQUIREMENTS

The statement of actuarial opinion must be included or attached to page one of the statutory annual statement submitted to the state insurance department. This opinion must comply with Section 6 of the Actuarial Opinion and Memorandum Model Regulation.

Section 6 requires that the statement of actuarial opinion shall consist of:

(a) a paragraph identifying the appointed actuary and his or her qualifications;

(b) the scope of the appointed actuary's opinion, including a tabulation of the reserves that have been analyzed for asset adequacy, the method of analysis and the reserves covered by the opinion that have not been so analyzed;

(c) the extent to which the appointed actuary has relied upon other individuals;

(d) the appointed actuary's opinion with respect to the adequacy of the assets held in support of the liabilities; and

(e) one or more additional paragraphs if needed to qualify his or her opinion, to disclose any inconsistencies, to disclose if additional reserves established in a prior opinion are being released in the current period and to briefly describe any assumptions on which the opinion is based.

With regards Item (c), it is important that the appointed actuary document whether he or she has relied on other individuals in developing data, procedures or assumptions. If so, these individuals must sign a statement. This statement must comply with Subsection E of this model regulation. Finally, Section B of Section 6 contains recommended language for this opinion.

15.3.2 ACTUARIAL MEMORANDUM REQUIREMENTS

The appointed actuary must prepare a memorandum to the company describing the asset adequacy analysis done in support of his or her opinion. Some states require that this memorandum be available for examination by the insurance commissioner. Other states require that this memorandum be filed on a confidential basis with the state insurance department.

---

[2] See [4].

The memorandum must comply with Section 7 of the Actuarial Opinion and Memorandum Model Regulation. Specifically, the memorandum must include six sections:

(1) Liability section,

(2) Asset section,

(3) Analysis section,

(4) Summary of material changes,

(5) Summary of results, and

(6) Conclusion.

The liability section must include the following information about the liabilities:

(a) a description of each product including marketing, underwriting and other aspects deemed significant by the appointed actuary;

(b) the source for the liabilities in force;

(c) the policy reserve valuation methods and assumptions;

(d) investment reserves;

(e) reinsurance agreements;

(f) identification of any explicit or implicit guarantees made by the general account in support of benefits provided thorough a separate account; and

(g) documentation of assumptions used in the asset adequacy analysis.

Similarly, the asset section must include the following information about the assets:

(a) a description of asset portfolios, including a risk profile on quality, distribution and type of assets;

(b) the source for the assets held in support of the liabilities;

(c) assumptions about future purchase and sales;

(d) the bases of asset valuation;

(e) documentation of assumptions

With regards to the documentation of assumptions for both liabilities and assets, it should be in sufficient detail that an actuary reviewing the actuarial memorandum could determine that the assumptions were reasonable.

The analysis section of the memorandum must describe:

(a) the methodology used to perform the asset adequacy analysis;

(b) the rationale for inclusion or exclusion of different blocks of business;

(c) the rationale for the degree of rigor in analyzing different blocks of business;

(d) the criteria for determining asset adequacy;

(e) how reinsurance was handled; and

(f) whether the impact of federal income taxes was considered.

The summary of material changes should describe any changes in methods, procedures, or assumptions from the prior year's asset adequacy analysis.

Finally, the memorandum must include the following statement:

> "*Actuarial methods, considerations and analysis used in the preparation of this memorandum conform to the appropriate Standards of Practice as promulgated by the Actuarial Standards Board, which standards form the basis for this memorandum.*"

The most important Standard of Practice with regard to an asset adequacy analysis is Actuarial Standards of Practice No. 22, *Statements of Opinion Based on Asset Adequacy Analysis by Actuaries for Life or Health Insurers.* In addition, the life Valuation Subcommittee of the American Academy of Actuaries has prepared *Asset Adequacy Analysis Practice Note.*

15.4 ACTUARIAL STANDARDS OF PRACTICE NO. 22[3]

Actuarial Standards of Practice No. 22 provides "guidance to actuaries when serving as an appointed actuary or a qualified actuary in providing a statement of actuarial opinion relating to asset adequacy analysis of a life or health insurer, when such opinion is prepared pursuant to applicable law such as the following:

(a) applicable law based on the model Standard Valuation Law as amended by the National Association of Insurance Commissioners (NAIC) in 1990, in conjunction with the model Actuarial Opinion and Memorandum Regulation (AOMR) adopted by the NAIC in 1991 and subsequently amended;

(b) applicable law based on the NAIC's Synthetic Guaranteed Investment Contracts Model Regulation;

(c) applicable law based on the NAIC's Separate Accounts Funding Guaranteed Minimum Benefits Under Group Contracts Model Regulation; or

(d) other applicable laws requiring an actuary to opine on the adequacy of a life or health insurer's reserves and other liabilities in light of supporting assets."

Actuarial Standards of Practice No. 22 requires the actuary to exercise considerable judgment in determining whether or not cash flow testing is required. The items the actuary should consider in making this judgment include the following:

(1) The sensitivity of liability cash flows to changing investment environments.

(2) The composition of assets supporting reserves. (Do they contain liberal call provisions or prepayment options?)

(3) Any significant reinvestment risk to which the liabilities expose the company.

Actuarial Standards of Practice No. 22 makes it clear that cash flow testing is not always necessary. However, it is up to the actuary to make that judgment. Actuarial Standards of Practice No. 22 does provide some examples of situations where cash flow testing may not be necessary, including the following:

---

[3] See [2].

(1) Situations where a gross premium valuation or a prior cash flow analysis has shown the results to be relatively insensitive to economic changes;

(2) Situations where the valuation actuary can demonstrate that experience will almost certainly be less severe than provided for in the reserves;

(3) Products where the cash flows are relatively insensitive to changes in economic conditions due to design feature or investment strategy;

(4) Short-term products.

The need for cash flow analysis should be considered in almost every aspect of the actuary's work. If, however, the actuary feels sufficiently confident that the results will not be sensitive to such analysis, the analysis need not be performed. Often it would be difficult to make such a statement without first performing at least a limited analysis.

15.5 REQUIRED ANALYSIS

The model regulation no longer prescribes cash flow testing using seven specific scenarios that were similar to those used in New York Regulation 126. However, most actuaries continue this practice.[4] In 2004, New York Regulation 126 required the following interest scenarios:

Scenario	Description
1	Level
2	Uniformly increasing 0.5% over 10 years and then level
3	Uniformly increasing 1% over 5 years, then uniformly decreasing 1% over next 5 years and then level
4	A 3% pop-up and then level
5	Uniformly decreasing 0.5% over 10 years and then level
6	Uniformly decreasing 0.5% over 5 years, then uniformly increasing 0.5% over next 5 years and then level
7	A 3% pop-down and then level.

All rates in the above scenarios are subject to a minimum interest rate.

New York Regulation 126 indicates that beginning interest rates may be based on interest rates on new investments close to the valuation date that are comparable to those being purchased to support the product liabilities being tested, or may be based on an outside index, such as Treasury yields, of assets of the appropriate length on a date close to the valuation date. The beginning yield curve and associated interest rates should be consistent in all seven interest rate scenarios.

15.5.1 ADDITIONAL ANALYSIS

In addition to the seven "New York" scenarios, additional analysis may be deemed necessary by the appointed actuary. The tests should cover as many alternative interest rate scenarios as the valuation actuary deems necessary to generate an understanding of the dynamics between the insurance and investment cash flows. In line with this objective, consideration should be given to supplemental testing based on a set of stochastic interest rate scenarios.

---

[4] New York Regulation 126 stills prescribes seven scenarios.

15.5.2 CONSIDERATIONS

In developing the required set of seven interest rate scenarios, consideration must be given to the following items:

(1) The point in time or period over which the starting rates are based.

(2) The shape of the ultimate yield curve.

(3) The application of the minimum rate constraint.

The starting rates should be based on applicable investment yields close to the valuation date. For Treasury yields, reasonable choices are (a) the rate on the last reported day closest to the valuation date, (b) the average of rates for the last full week closest to the valuation date, or (c) the average of rates for the last full month closest to the valuation date. Referring to Regulation 126, the New York Insurance Department has indicated a preference for using the last reported day closest to the valuation date.

With respect to the second item, a decision must be made either to maintain the shape of the starting yield curve in all future years or to assume that a more "normal" shape of the yield curve ultimately applies. Under Regulation 126, the New York Insurance Department has indicated that either approach is acceptable regarding the shape of the ultimate yield curve. However, New York mentioned in their most recent annual "Special Considerations" memorandum that the yield curve should not be normalized.

Maintaining the shape of the starting yield curve might be supported by the following reasoning:

(1) The selection of the shape of the ultimate yield curve would be somewhat arbitrary.

(2) The shape of the yield curve may be dependent on the level of rates which would suggest selecting not one but a multitude of curves.

(3) The desire for simplicity.

With respect to the minimum rate constraint, it would seem to make sense to apply the minimum rate constraint to each rate after first having determined what the rates would be without such minimum.

Under each of the seven scenarios, and as many other as the actuary deems necessary to form an opinion, the actuary must examine the cash flow characteristics of the business. This analysis involves the development of assumptions regarding policyholder and corporate behavior described in Chapter 14.

There are currently no regulatory or professional standards which identify either precisely the number of scenarios that should be tested or the number of scenarios that a company must pass in order that reserves are deemed adequate. However, Actuarial Standards of Practice No. 22 does state:

"In the event that the supporting assets are insufficient to meet the reserves and other liabilities under a scenario, the actuary may determine that further analysis is required. However, this situation does not necessarily mandate additional reserves or liabilities. Further analysis may indicate that current reserves and other liabilities are adequate. For example, if a large number of scenarios were run, the failure of a small percentage of them may not indicate the need for additional reserves or liabilities. The basis of any such judgment should be documented in the supporting memorandum."

16 ✧ RISK-BASED CAPITAL

16.1 INTRODUCTION[1]

An important measure of the financial soundness of a life insurance company is the amount of statutory surplus it holds in relation to the profile of the company. In order to attract new policyholders, retain existing policyholders, borrow and raise capital, management must demonstrate to policyholders, insurance regulators, rating agencies and banks that the life insurance company has an appropriate amount of surplus for the types of risks it has underwritten.

But what is the appropriate amount of surplus? This is a difficult question to answer. In the 1970's, a valuation task force developed a broad framework to assist with the answer to this question. It classified the risks of a life insurance company into four categories:

(1)   Asset risk;

(2)   Pricing risk;

(3)   Interest rate risk; and

(4)   General business risk.

The answer to this question received added attention in the late 1980's when the Savings and Loans industry experienced a significant number of insolvencies. These insolvencies led to the development by bank regulators of minimum capital requirements that are based on the types of risks a bank has assumed.

Concern that a similar "crisis" might develop in the life insurance industry provided a catalyst for similar risk-based capital requirements for the life insurance industry. On December 6, 1992, the NAIC responded by adopting the *Risk-Based Capital (RBC) for Life and Health Insurers* Model Act. This act significantly increased the minimum capital requirements for most life insurance companies and increased state regulators' authority over life insurance companies whose financial conditions deteriorate.

This chapter discusses the RBC formula and the various regulatory action levels contained in the RBC Model Act. It also discusses the new changes to the formula for variable products with guarantees, known as RBC C-3 Phase II. Finally, an example of how risk-based capital is calculated for a life insurance company is illustrated as the various components of the RBC formula are discussed.

16.2 GOAL OF RISK-BASED CAPITAL

It was mentioned in Chapter 2 that with almost $3 trillion of invested assets under management[2], the life insurance industry performs an important role as a financial intermediary and provides financial security to

---

[1] This discussion of risk-based capital ignores taxes and health risks. For taxes, many risk-based capital requirements are reduced by an assumed 35% tax rate.

[2] *2006 Life Insurers Fact Book,* Table 2.1 [7].

hundreds of millions of policyholders. It was also mentioned that insurance regulators are primarily concerned with the ability of the life insurance company to satisfy their contractual obligations with policyholders. In other words, regulators are concerned with the solvency of a life insurance company and would like to know as early as possible when a life insurance company might not be able to honor its commitments. One of the primary goals of the Risk-Based Capital Model Act is to minimize the risk of insolvency and the cost of insolvency when it does occur.

16.2.1 INSOLVENCY RISK[3]

It may take several years before the financial results of poor underwriting or an inappropriate product design surface. Accordingly, the determination of when a life insurance company is no longer financially sound is based on concepts that are different than those for most other industries.

To illustrate this point, consider a company whose primary business is publishing books and magazines. If this company does not have sufficient cash from operations and can not raise cash from the financial markets to pay its current obligations, then the company is financially insolvent and most likely will declare bankruptcy. For most industries, financial insolvency results when cash inflows are insufficient to cover cash outflows. In other words, financial insolvency is primarily based on a current cash flow concept.

Financial insolvency of a life insurance company is based on a different concept. Even if a life insurance company can pay for its current obligations, it may be considered financially impaired and require regulatory intervention[4]. This is because insolvency of a life insurance company is determined on a balance sheet basis using statutory accounting principles (i.e., the life insurance company does not a have a sufficient amount of reported surplus to meet its future obligations). In particular, the RBC Model act determines a minimum amount of capital a life insurance company must have and requires various levels of regulatory action if reported surplus of a life insurance company falls below certain threshold amounts.

16.2.2 RISK-BASED CAPITAL DEFINED

The 2004 NAIC Life Risk-Based Capital Report defines *risk-based capital* as "a method of measuring the minimum amount of capital appropriate for an insurance company to support its overall business operations in consideration of its size and risk profile."[5] It is the primary measure used by insurance regulators to determine the financial soundness of a life insurance company. Prior to the RBC Model act, regulators generally required a life insurance company to maintain as little as $5 million of capital, regardless of the company's size and risk profile. The RBC formula in this model act determines a "minimum" capital level. In most circumstances, the Risk-Based Capital requirement is significantly higher than the minimum capital requirements prior to the adoption of the RBC Model act.

16.2.3 TARGET SURPLUS

Most life insurance companies have their own target surplus goal. Usually, this goal is to have reported surplus more than two to three times the minimum risk-based capital amount. If reported surplus falls below this target surplus amount, most life insurance companies have the flexibility to take action to restore surplus above their target amount such as:

- Emphasize products that have low risk-based capital requirements and deemphasize products with high risk-based capital requirements

---

[3] Some of the concepts in this chapter are from the publication Risk-Based Capital by Life Office Management Association [16].

[4] For example, even though Executive Life had a significant portfolio of liquid, high quality securities (primarily government bonds) to cover current cash flow demands, it was declared financially insolvent when its large below investment grade securities suddenly decreased significantly in value.

[5] *2004 NAIC Life Risk-Based Capital Report,* page i [20].

- Redesign products to lower the risk-based capital requirements
- Increase the profitability by lowering expenses, exiting unprofitable lines of business and/or increasing prices
- Reduce asset risk by buying assets with low risk-based capital requirements and selling assets with high risk-based capital requirements
- Reduce liability risks by entering into reinsurance agreements or selling certain product lines
- Reorganize the legal structure of the life insurance company by moving certain subsidiaries to a holding company
- Raise capital by issuing surplus notes or issuing equity securities

If the situation becomes more severe, the life insurance company may have to stop selling new business[6] or merge with another company.

16.3 RBC FORMULA

The instructions[7] to the RBC Model act contain a detailed formula, called the **RBC formula** that is used to determine Risk-Based capital. This formula centers on the classification of a life insurance company's risks into five major risk categories:

Risk Category	Description
C-0	Asset Risk – Affiliates
C-1	Asset Risk – Other
C-2	Insurance Risk
C-3	Interest Rate Risk, Health Risk and Market Risk
C-4	Business Risk

The RBC formula applies RBC factors to various annual statement entries to determine the RBC requirement for that particular entry. For example, assume a life insurance company had $1 billion invested in bonds with a Class 2 NAIC Asset Classification. The RBC requirement for these bonds would be determined by multiplying the RBC factor for Class 2 bonds (which is 0.013) times the stated value of these bonds in the statutory annual statement. In particular, the risk-based capital requirement for these bonds would be determined as follows:

$$
\begin{aligned}
RBC \ requirement &= RBC \ factor \times Statement \ Value \\
&= 0.013 \times 1,000,000,000 \\
&= 13,000,000
\end{aligned}
$$

The RBC factors reflect the riskiness of invested assets and the type of insurance products that companies underwrite. The factor is higher for those entries with greater underlying risk and lower for those entries with less underlying risk. For example, a corporate bond with the highest quality rating (i.e., NAIC Asset Class 1) would have a factor of 0.004 and a corporate bond with a lower quality rating (i.e., NAIC Asset Class 5) would have a factor of 0.23. This reflects the fact that a bond in Asset Class 1 is less likely to default than a bond in Asset Class 5.

---

[6] In 2002, Allmerica stopped selling life insurance policies and annuity contracts when its surplus decreased significantly relative to its risk-based capital requirements.

[7] The National Association of Insurance Commissioner updates these instructions each year.

16.3.1 Asset Risk – Affiliates (C-0)

Asset Risk – Affiliates (C-0) is intended to cover the risks of affiliated investments. Life insurance companies, property and casualty insurance companies, health insurance companies and investment companies have risk-based capital requirements. Accordingly, the risk-based capital requirement for these affiliated investments is the subsidiary's risk-based capital requirement.

The RBC factors for other types of subsidiaries that do not have risk-based capital requirements vary from 30% to 100% of the book value of the subsidiary as reported in the statutory annual statement.

16.3.2 Asset Risk – Other(C-1)

Asset Risk-Other(C-1) is the risk of loss due to asset defaults on debt-type investments or fluctuations in the fair value of equity type investments. It is important to note that the loss in this definition is measured on a statutory accounting basis. For example, bonds and mortgages in good standing[8] are recorded in the balance sheet at amortized cost. A statutory loss is recorded on a bond or mortgage in the accounting period when "it goes into default" (i.e., when it is determined to be other than temporarily impaired). The loss is the difference between the amortized cost and an estimate of the value of the bond or mortgage at the time of default. Common stock is recorded on the balance sheet at fair value. The decline in the fair value of common stock investments is the risk covered by Asset Risk-Other(C-1).

The major categories of RBC factors within Asset Risk-Other(C-1) are:

(1)   bonds

(2)   mortgages

(3)   preferred stock and common stock

(4)   real estate

(5)   assets reported in Schedule BA

(6)   separate accounts

The next several paragraphs give a description of the RBC factors for these major asset categories.

Bonds

The RBC factors for bonds vary from 0% to 30% and depend on their NAIC asset class designation:

Asset class	Meaning	Factor
Exempt obligations	Government and certain exempt issuers	0.000
Class 1	Highest quality	0.004
Class 2	High quality	0.013
Class 3	Medium quality	0.046
Class 4	Low quality	0.100
Class 5	Lower quality	0.230
Class 6	In or near default	0.300

---

[8] A bond or mortgage is in good standing if the interest and principal payments have been made within 90 days of the due date.

The Risk-Based Capital Task Force spent a significant amount of effort developing and updating the factors used in the RBC formulas, as evidenced by following excerpt from the *2004 NAIC Life Risk-Based Capital Report*:[9]

> "The bond factors are based on cash flow modeling using historically adjusted default rates for each bond category. For each of 2,000 trials, annual economic conditions were generated for the ten-year modeling period. Each bond of a 400-bond portfolio was annually tested for default (based on a "roll of the dice") where the default probability varies by rating category and that year's economic environment. When a default takes place, the actual loss considers the expected principal loss by category, the time the sale actually occurs and the assumed tax consequences.
>
> Actual surplus needs are reduced by incorporating anticipated annual contributions to the Asset Valuation Reserve (AVR) as offsetting cash flow. Required surplus for a given trial is calculated as the amount of initial surplus funds needed so that the accumulation with interest of this initial amount and subsequent cash flows will not become negative at any point throughout the modeling period. The factors chosen for the proposed formula produce a level of surplus at least as much as needed in 92 percent of the trials by category and a 96 percent level for the entire portfolio."

This excerpt also provides insight into the adequacy of the RBC requirements that the task force is striving to achieve. The bond factors were developed to determine a capital requirement that is adequate 96 percent of the time under various economic conditions over a ten year time horizon.

The risk of loss due to bond defaults decreases as the number of bond issues in a portfolio of a given size increases. Accordingly, the above factors are multiplied by a size adjustment that is developed using the following table:

Issuers[10]	Number of Issuers ·	Size Factor =	Weighted Issuers
First 50		2.500	
Next 50		1.300	
Next 300		1.000	
Over 400		0.900	
Total Number of Issuers			
Total Weighted Issuers			
Size Factor			

Note that the size adjustment is based on the number of issuers and not the number of bonds. For example, assume a life insurance company had 2,000 bonds that were issued by 1,000 different issuers (excluding government and other exempt issuers). The size factor would be determined as follows:

Issuers	Number of Issuers ·	Size Factor =	Weighted Issuers
First 50	50	2.500	125
Next 50	50	1.300	65
Next 300	300	1.000	300
Over 400	600	0.900	540
Total Number of Issuers	1,000		
Total Weighted Issuers			1,030
Size Factor			1.03

---

[9] See [20], page 1.

[10] Excludes government issues and certain other exempt issues.

The size factor in the above example was determined as follows:

Weighted Issuers	1,030
Total Number of Issuers	÷ 1,000
Size Factor	1.030

Mortgages

The RBC factors for mortgages depend on the standing (in good standing, 90 days overdue or in process of foreclosure), the type of mortgage (farm, residential or commercial) and whether or not the mortgage is insured or guaranteed. As the following table shows, RBC factors before adjustment vary from 0.14% to 23% based on these criteria:

Standing	Type	Insured or Guarantee	Factor[11]
Good standing	Farm	All	0.0260
	Residential	Insured or guaranteed	0.0014
		All other	0.0068
	Commercial	Insured or guaranteed	0.0014
		All other	0.0260
90 days overdue	Farm	All	0.1800
	Residential	Insured or guaranteed	0.0027
		All other	0.0140
	Commercial	Insured or guaranteed	0.0027
		All other	0.1800
In foreclosure	Farm	All	0.2300
	Residential	Insured or guaranteed	0.0054
		All other	0.2300
	Commercial	Insured or guaranteed	0.0054
		All other	0.2300

These factors were based on the default experience of the life insurance industry. To reflect the underwriting skills of the life insurance company relative to the life insurance industry, the above factors are adjusted by a Mortgage Experience Adjustment Factor. This factor is determined by dividing (A) by (B), where:

(A)   is the rolling average of the actual mortgage default experience of the life insurance company over the past eight quarters; and

(B)   is the rolling average of the actual mortgage default experience of the life insurance industry over the past eight quarters.

The Mortgage Experience Adjustment Factor can not be less than 0.50 or greater than 3.5 for mortgages in good standing. Other limits apply for mortgages that are not in good standing.

Preferred Stock

The RBC factors for preferred stock depend on whether the preferred stock was issued by an affiliated or unaffiliated company. The RBC requirement for affiliated preferred stock is determined using the requirements discussed for Asset Risk-Affiliates (C-0). For unaffiliated preferred stock, the RBC factors are the same as the RBC factors for bonds. In other words, it varies by the NAIC asset classification:

---

[11] These factors do not reflect the mortgage experience adjustment factor.

Asset class	Meaning	Factor
Class 1	Highest quality	0.004
Class 2	High quality	0.013
Class 3	Medium quality	0.046
Class 4	Low quality	0.100
Class 5	Lower quality	0.230
Class 6	In or near default	0.300

However, unlike bonds, there is no size adjustment applied to these factors.

Common Stock

Similarly, the RBC factors for common stock depend on whether or not the common stock was issued by an affiliated or unaffiliated company. For unaffiliated common stock, the RBC factor is 30 percent. This factor was based on studies conducted at two large life insurance companies with common stock portfolios similar in composition to the Standard and Poors 500. The factor was developed to determine the amount of capital needed to cover approximately 95 percent of the losses over a two-year time horizon[12].

Two adjustments are made to the 30 percent factor to take into account the common stock portfolio of a life insurance company that is different in composition from the Standard and Poors 500. First, the factor applied to publicly traded unaffiliated common stock is adjusted up or down by the weighted average beta[13] of the common stock portfolio of the life insurance company. The beta adjusted factor is subject to a maximum of 45 percent and a minimum of 22.5 percent. Second, a common stock concentration component is calculated, adding an additional requirement of 50 percent of the beta adjusted basic requirement for the five largest holdings of common stock in the common stock portfolio of the life insurance company.

Real Estate

The RBC factor for real estate is 15 percent for both real estate occupied by the company and for investment real estate. For foreclosed real estate and real estate in Schedule BA, the RBC factor is 23 percent[14].

Schedule BA Assets

Schedule BA contains a variety of assets. Some of these assets have low risk and others have high risk. Accordingly, the RBC factors vary from 0 percent to 30 percent, depending on the type of asset and its risk.

Separate Accounts

The RBC factors for separate accounts depend on whether it is a separate account with guarantees or a separate account without guarantees. Since the explanation is rather technical, the reader should refer to *2004 NAIC Life Risk-Based Capital Report*.[15]

---

[12] *2004 NAIC Life Risk-Based Capital Report,* page 8 [20].

[13] ***Beta*** measures the systematic (or non-diversifiable) risk of a stock (i.e., the variability of the return of a stock return relative to the variability of the return of the S&P 500) . It is determined by dividing (a) by (b), where (a) is the covariance of the monthly return of a stock with the monthly return of the S&P 500 and (b) is the variance of the monthly return of the S&P 500. For example, if a stock has a beta of 0.9 and the variability of the S&P 500 over the measurement period is 20%, then that variability of return of the stock is 18% (= 0.9 * 20%).

[14] Additional RBC is required for real estate with encumbrances.

[15] See [20], page 9.

Asset Concentration Factor

To reflect the additional risk of high concentrations in a single asset holding, an asset concentration factor doubles the risk-based capital requirements for the ten largest holdings, excluding various low risk categories and categories that already have a high risk factor.

16.3.3 INSURANCE RISK (C-2)

Insurance Risk (C-2) is intended to cover such risks as underestimating liabilities on business already underwritten or inadequate pricing on business to be written in the coming year. The RBC factor for life insurance is based on the net amount at risk and amount of business inforce:

	Net Amount at Risk ·	Factor =	RBC Requirement
First 500 million		0.0023	
Next 4,500 million		0.0015	
Next 20,000 million		0.0012	
Over 25,000 million		0.0009	
Total RBC requirement			

In the above table, net amount at risk is determined by subtracting the policy reserve for ordinary life in Exhibit 5 from the amount of insurance inforce for ordinary life in the Exhibit of Life Insurance.

For life insurance, the RBC factors chosen represent the surplus needed to provide for excess claims due to random fluctuations and inadequate pricing. The above factors are based on a Monte Carlo simulation of 10,000, 100,000 and one million insured lives. The probability of death reflects both normal and excess claims. The present value of the claims generated by this process, less expected claims, is the amount of surplus needed. The above factors were chosen so that 95 percent of the time the level of surplus resulting from these factors would cover the excess claims.

16.3.4 INTEREST RATE RISK, HEALTH RISK AND MARKET RISK (C-3)

Interest Rate Risk, Health Risk and Market Risk (C-3) is intended to cover three types of losses:

(1)   Interest rate risk: the risk of loss due to changes in the level of interest rates;

(2)   Market risk: The risk of loss on variable products with guarantees (e.g., variable annuities and variable life with living benefits and guaranteed minimum death benefits) due to changes in market returns; and

(3)   Health risk: The risk of loss from health benefits prepaid to providers that may again become the obligation of the health provider[16].

The first type of loss occurs when a life insurance company must reinvest cash flows when the levels of interest rates have fallen below the level guaranteed to policyholders. This type of loss also includes losses that occur when the life insurance company must sell assets when the level of interest rates has risen above the rates at the time the assets were purchased (and hence the current market price of the asset is below the value reported in the statutory annual statement).

The second type of loss occurs when the financial markets have declined and the life insurance company has guaranteed a minimum benefit amount above the market value of this benefit without a minimum guarantee. For example, a life insurance company that sells variable annuities with minimum death benefit guarantees may have to pay claims in excess of the account balance on the date of death.

---

[16] The third type of risk applies to health providers and will not be discussed further in this book.

The risk of losses due to the change in the level of interest rates depends to some extent upon the withdrawal provisions contained in the contract. The risk is higher for those contracts that do not contain, or provide minimal protections to the life insurance company against this type of risk than for those contracts that adjust the withdrawal benefit to reflect the level of interest rates at the time of withdrawal. Accordingly, the RBC factors for interest rate risk vary by three risk categories:

(1)   Low risk

(2)   Medium risk; and

(3)   High risk

The RBC factors were developed based on the assumption that assets and liabilities are well matched (i.e., the duration[17] of assets is within 0.125 years of the duration of the liabilities). The RBC factors are increased by 50% if the assets and liabilities are not well matched. The life insurance company must submit an unqualified opinion based on an asset adequacy test to avoid increasing the RBC factors by 50%.

Low Risk Category

The low risk category includes the following:

- the reserves for life insurance policies net of policy loans;
- the reserves for annuity contracts that do not provide withdrawal benefits;
- the reserves for annuity contracts with a market value adjustment; and
- the reserves for life contingent payout annuities.

The RBC factor for this category is 0.77% if the life insurance company submits an unqualified opinion based on an asset adequacy testing. If it issues a qualified opinion or no opinion, then the RBC factor is 1.15%.

Medium Risk Category

The medium risk category includes the following:

- the reserves for annuity contracts with a book value withdrawal less a surrender charge that is 5% or higher;
- the reserves for structured settlements;
- the reserves for supplementary contracts without life contingencies;
- the reserve for dividend accumulations; and
- any additional reserves established as a result of cash flow testing.

The RBC factor for this category is 1.54% if the life insurance company submits an unqualified opinion based on an asset adequacy testing. If it issues a qualified opinion or no opinion, then the RBC factor is 2.31%.

High Risk Category

The high risk category includes the following:

- the reserves for annuity contracts with a book value withdrawal, less a surrender charge that is less than 5%; and
- the reserves for annuity contracts with a book value withdrawal and no surrender charge.

The RBC factor for this category is 3.08% if the life insurance company submits an unqualified opinion based on an asset adequacy testing. If it issues a qualified opinion or no opinion, then the RBC factors is 4.62%.

---

[17] **Duration** measures the approximate change in the value of an asset or liability due to a change in interest rates.

Cash Flow Testing

If the life insurance company performed cash flow testing for interest rate risk, the valuation actuary may have determined that an additional risk-based capital amount should be established. If so, this additional amount would be included in this section of the RBC formula[18].

16.3.5 BUSINESS RISK (C-4)

Business Risk (C-4) is intended to cover general business risks such as losses due to fraud, mismanagement and litigation. The RBC factor for business risk is based on premium income, annuity considerations and separate account liabilities. For life insurance and annuities, the RBC factor is 3.08% of the life premiums and annuity considerations appearing in Schedule T of the statutory annual statement. Deposit-type funds shown in Schedule T are not included in the determination of Risk-Based Capital. For separate account business, the RBC factor is 0.08% of separate account liabilities. Similar to deposit-type funds, variable life insurance premiums and variable annuity considerations are not included in the 3.08% factor mentioned above.

16.3.6 OTHER RISKS

There is a risk that the life insurance company may not be able to recover amounts due from a reinsurer because the reinsurer is insolvent. Accordingly, there is an RBC requirement for reinsurance. The RBC factor is 0.8% times the amount due from the reinsurer. To avoid an over-statement of Risk-Based capital, the formula gives a 0.8% credit for reinsurance with non-authorized reinsurers, reinsurance with affiliated companies, reinsurance with funds withheld and reinsurance involving policy loans.

Another risk is the risk of loss from off-balance items. Not surprisingly, off-balance sheet items are assets and liabilities that are not recorded on the balance sheet. For example, a life insurance company may make certain guarantees on behalf of an affiliated company. The RBC factor for these off-balance sheet items is 1.3%.

The RBC requirements for reinsurance and off-balance sheet items are included in Asset Risk – Other (C-1).

16.4   RBC RATIO

Once the Risk-Based Capital of the life insurance company has been determined using the RBC formula, an RBC ratio is calculated. The *RBC ratio* is (A) divided by (B), where

(A)   is the total adjusted capital of the life insurance company; and

(B)   is the authorized control level Risk-Based Capital of the life insurance company resulting from the formula.

If this RBC ratio falls below a specified level, certain "action levels" are triggered, ranging from a "mandatory control level" where the insurance commissioner must seize control of the company, to a "trend test level" where the company must perform an additional test to determine trends in the RBC ratios.

16.4.1 CALCULATION OF TOTAL ADJUSTED CAPITAL

In the determination of the RBC ratio, statutory surplus is adjusted to reflect that certain RBC factors were developed without recognizing that a portion of the risk is covered by a specific liability. For example, the Asset Valuation Reserve (AVR) is a reserve for future expected loss on invested assets due to defaults and fluctuation in market values. The RBC factors used in the determination of Asset Risk – Other (C-1) do not

---

[18] If a life insurance company has a low RBC ratio or significant C-3 component, then it may have to perform cash flow testing. This testing is described further in Section 16.5.1.

recognize that the Asset Valuation Reserve would absorb these specific types of losses up to the amount of the reserve. Therefore, the Asset Valuation Reserve is counted as capital for purposes of determining the RBC ratio, even though it is a liability and not available for general business purposes.

Similarly, the policyholder dividend liability provides a general cushion against potentially adverse future experience. Accordingly, 50 percent of the liability is counted as capital for the purpose of determining the RBC ratio.

16.4.2 COVARIANCE ADJUSTMENT

The denominator in the RBC ratio is not simply the sum of the Risk-Based Capital requirements for the various risks. Instead, recognition is given to the correlation between certain risk categories. This adjustment is called the *covariance adjustment*.

The sum of the Risk-Based Capital requirements for the various risk categories adjusted for covariance is called *Authorized Control Level Risk-Based Capital*. It is determined using the following formula:

$$0.50 \cdot \left[C_0 + C_{4a} + \sqrt{(C_{1a} + C_{3a})^2 + C_{1cs}^2 + C_2^2} \right]$$

where

$$
\begin{aligned}
C_0 &= \textit{Asset Risk} - \textit{Affilates} \\
C_{1a} &= \textit{Asset Risk} - \textit{Other (excluding common stock)} \\
C_{1cs} &= \textit{Asset Risk} - \textit{Other (common stock)} \\
C_2 &= \textit{Insurance Risk} \\
C_{3a} &= \textit{Interest Risk} \\
C_{3c} &= \textit{Market Risk} \\
C_{4a} &= \textit{Business Risk}
\end{aligned}
$$

This formula essentially assumes that certain risks are correlated, while other risks are independent.

16.4.3 REGULATORY ACTION LEVELS

As noted above, when the RBC ratio falls below a specified level, certain "action levels" are triggered. There are five levels and they are:

Level	RBC Ratio	Action
Trend Test Corridor	200% ≤ ratio < 250%	The life insurance company must perform a trend test.
Company Action Level	150% ≤ ratio < 200%	The life insurance company must prepare and submit an RBC Plan to the commissioner of the state of domicile.
Regulatory Action Level	100% ≤ ratio < 150%	The life insurance company must submit an RBC Plan, or if applicable, a revised RBC Plan to the commissioner. After examination or analysis, the commissioner will issue an order specifying corrective actions to be taken.
Authorized Control Level	70% ≤ ratio < 100%	Authorizes the commissioner of the state of domicile to take whatever regulatory actions considered necessary to protect the best interest of the policyholders and creditors.
Mandatory Control Level	ratio < 70%	Requires the commissioner of the state of domicile to take actions necessary to place the company under regulatory control (i.e., rehabilitation or liquidation).

16.5 PRINCIPLE-BASED RISK-BASED CAPITAL

The determination of reserves and risk-based capital is evolving from "formula-based" to "principle-based". This evolution reflects the increasing complexity of life insurance and annuity products since the initial development of the Standard Valuation Law.

The principles in the early versions of the Standard Valuation Law reflected that whole life was the primary product sold by the life insurance industry. Compared to the life insurance and annuity products sold today, whole life has a relatively simple design. Given this simple design, coupled with the limitations of computer technology at the time, the determination of reserves using factors developed from prescribed formulas was appropriate. The RBC formula discussed above used this same factor-based approach, although significant testing was performed to develop the factors.

In the 1980's, recognition was given to the notion that a formula based reserve does not adequately reflect all the assumptions on which a liability should be established. It also does not reflect the volatility of some of these assumptions. The shortcomings of a formula-based reserve led to the development of the valuation actuary concept. Specifically, the valuation actuary must consider whether or not reserves make good and sufficient provisions for future obligations, not only under expected experience, but also under a range of scenarios.

16.5.1 CASH FLOW TESTING FOR C-3 RBC (PHASE I)

In the late 1990's, the Risk-Based Capital Working Group of the National Association of Insurance Commissioners requested that the American Academy of Actuaries determine whether a practical method of incorporating cash flow testing into the C-3 component of the Risk-Based Capital formulas was possible.

In October 1999, the American Academy of Actuaries issued a report, known as RBC C-3 Phase I, recommending that Risk-Based Capital requirements for interest sensitive products (e.g., annuities and single premium life) be determined by scenario testing. The National Association of Insurance Commissioners adopted this recommendation and it became effective in December 31, 2000.

The life insurance company may have to perform an asset adequacy analysis for annuities and single premium life using cash flow testing. The testing is done using the same cash flow models, assets and assumptions used in support of the actuarial memorandum but with a different set of interest rate scenarios. A weighted average subset of the results of the scenario testing is used to determine the C-3 RBC requirement.

Appendix I of the American Academy of Actuaries' RBC C-3 Phase I report contains the following general approach for determining this RBC requirement:

(1)   Use the same asset and liability model(s) as used for year-end Asset Adequacy Analysis cash flow testing, or a consistent model.

(2)   Run the scenarios (12 or 50) produced from the interest-rate scenario generator[19]. These scenarios come from a randomly generated set of 200 scenarios and were selected because they have the greatest likelihood of producing a C-3 result at least as great as that determined by using all 200 scenarios. The other scenarios can be characterized as more "level" and less volatile than the selected set.

---

[19] A Microsoft Excel spreadsheet is posted at the National Association of Insurance Commissioners website (NAIC.org). By entering the Treasury yield curve as of the date of the cash flow testing, it will generate 50 or 12 interest rate scenarios. The life insurance company can use either the standard 50 scenarios or the alternative, but more conservative, 12 scenarios.

(3) The statutory surplus result, $S(T)$, should be captured for every scenario for each calendar year-end of the testing period. The surplus result is equal to statutory assets less statutory liabilities for the portfolio.

(4) For each scenario, the C-3 measure is the most negative of the series of present values $S(t) \times pv(t)$, where $pv(t)$ is the accumulated discount factor for t years using 105% of the after-tax one-year Treasury rates for that scenario. In other words:

$$pv(t) = \prod_{s=1}^{t} \frac{1}{(1+i_s)}$$

(5) Rank the scenario-specific C-3 measures in descending order; that is, from the largest need for capital to the smallest. The scenario ranked number one measures the largest amount of capital needed to eliminate the very worst present value result.

(6) The final C-3 requirement is calculated as the weighted average of a subset of the ranked scenario specific C-3 results.

(a) For the 50 scenario set, the C-3 results are multiplied by the following series of weights:

Weighting Table													
Scenario Rank	17	16	15	14	13	12	11	10	9	8	7	6	5
Weight	.02	.04	.06	.08	.10	.12	.16	.12	.10	.08	.06	.04	.02

The sum of these products is the C-3 requirement for this product. This weighting is centered on the scenario considered to be the 95th percentile, as the 50 scenarios are considered the most extreme of the full 200 scenario set.

(b) For the 12 scenario set, the C-3 requirement is calculated as the average of the C-3 results for the scenarios ranked 2 and 3, but cannot be less than half the worst scenario result.

A life insurance company is exempted from this cash flow testing if the following two conditions are satisfied:

(1) **C-3 Significance Test**: This test determines whether interest rate risk is a significant risk of the life insurance company. This determination is done by calculating the ratio of (A) divided by (B), where:

(A) is the interest rate risk component of C-3 risk-based capital requirements; and

(B) is the sum of the risk-based capital requirements for C-0, C-1, C-2, C-3 and C-4.

If this ratio is less than 40%, then the first condition is satisfied.

(2) **C-3 Stress Test**: This test determines interest rate risk under a stress condition. This determination is done by calculating the ratio of (A) divided by (B), where:

(A) Total Adjusted Capital; and

(B) Risk-Based Capital after covariance with RBC interest rate risk requirement for annuity multiplied by 7.5.

If this ratio is greater than 100%, then the second condition is satisfied.

16.5.2   CASH FLOW TESTING FOR C-3 RBC (PHASE II)

RBC C-3 Phase I excluded equity-related risk in variable products with guarantees. In December 2002, the American Academy of Actuaries issued a second report, known as RBC C-3 Phase II. This report recommends the cash flow testing requirements for interest rate risk in Phase I be expanded to include products with equity risk. This recommendation was adopted by the National Association of Insurance Commissioners on October 14, 2005. To assist in implementing these new requirements, a work group of the American Academy of Actuaries has developed a practice note.

This was a major undertaking and signifies a significant shift from "formula-based" to "principle-based." In particular, Appendix 7 of a preliminary draft of the American Academy of Actuaries' Report states "The projection methodology used to calculate the ***Total Asset Requirement*** ("TAR"), as well as the approach used to determine the Alternative Methodology, is based on the following set of principles."[20] These principles should be followed when applying the methodology in these recommendations and analyzing the resulting TAR:

Principle 1
The objective of the approach used to determine the TAR is to quantify the amount of statutory capital needed by the insurer to be able to meet contractual obligations in light of the risks to which the company is exposed.

Principle 2
The calculation of TAR is based on the results derived from an analysis of asset and liability cash flows produced by the application of a stochastic cash flow model to equity return and interest rate scenarios. For each scenario the greatest present value of accumulated statutory deficiencies is calculated. The analysis reflects Prudent Best Estimate (see the definition of Prudent Best Estimate in the Glossary of this Report) assumptions for deterministic variables and is performed in aggregate (subject to limitations related to contractual provisions)[21] to allow the natural offset of risks within a given scenario. The methodology utilizes a projected total statutory balance sheet approach by including all projected income, benefit, and expense items related to the business in the model and sets the TAR at a degree of confidence using the conditional tail expectation measure applied to the set of scenario specific greatest present values of accumulated statutory deficiencies that is consistent with the quantification of other risks in the NAIC Life RBC formula.

Principle 3
The implementation of a model involves decisions about the experience assumptions and the modeling techniques to be used in measuring the risks to which the company is exposed. Generally, assumptions are to be based on the conservative end of the actuary's confidence interval. The choice of a conservative estimate for each assumption may result in a distorted measure of the total risk. Conceptually, the choice of assumptions and the modeling decisions should be made so that the final result approximates what would be obtained for the Conditional Tail Expectation Amount at the required CTE level if it were possible to calculate results over the joint distribution of all future outcomes. In applying this concept to the actual calculation of the Conditional Tail Expectation Amount, the actuary should be guided by evolving practice and expanding knowledge base in the measurement and management of risk.

Principle 4
While a stochastic cash flow model attempts to include all real world risks relevant to the objective of the stochastic cash flow model and relationships among the risks, it will still contain limitations because it is only a model. The calculation of TAR is based on the results derived from the application of the stochastic cash flow model to scenarios while the actual capital needs of the company arise from the risks to which the company is (or will be) exposed in reality.

---

[20] See [6].
[21] Ibid.

Principle 5

Neither a cash flow scenario model nor a method based on factors calibrated to the results of a cash flow scenario model, can completely quantify an insurer's exposure to risk. A model attempts to represent reality, but will always remain an approximation thereto and hence uncertainty in future experience is an important consideration when quantifying the TAR using the AAA recommendations. Therefore, the use of assumptions, methods, models, risk management strategies (e.g., hedging), derivative instruments, structured investments or any other risk transfer arrangements (such as reinsurance) that serve solely to reduce the calculated TAR without also reducing risk on scenarios similar to those used in the actual cash flow modeling is inconsistent with these principles. The use of assumptions and risk management strategies should be appropriate to the business and not merely constructed to exploit 'foreknowledge' of the components of the required methodology.

The approach recommended by this report is as follows:

(1)   Perform a stochastic simulation using prudent best estimate assumptions and probability distribution functions for equity returns that have been calibrated.

(2)   Calculate the required capital for each scenario using the following formula:

$$RC_i = Max\left\{v^t \cdot S(t) \mid 0 \le t \le n\right\}$$

where

$$\begin{aligned}
i &= i^{th} \text{ scenario;} \\
RC_i &= \text{required capital for the } i^{th} \text{ scenario;} \\
t &= t^{th} \text{ projection year;} \\
n &= \text{length of projection period} \\
v &= \textit{discount factor; and} \\
S(t) &= \text{the negative of accumulated surplus in the } t^{th} \text{ projection year.}
\end{aligned}$$

(3)   Sort the required capital for each scenario determined in Step 2.

(4)   Calculate the **Additional Asset Requirement** (AAR) which is the Conditional Tail Expectation at the 90th percentile (CTE 90) of the sorted capital requirements for Step 3. The Total Asset Requirement is equal to the AAR plus the starting assets.

(5)   The Risk-Based Capital requirement is the Total Asset Requirement less the statutory reserve for variable products with guarantees.

The *Conditional Tail Expectation* at the 90th percentile is the average of the required capital for the 10% of the scenarios with the highest capital requirements. As stated in the American Academy of Actuaries' RBC C-3 Phase II report:

> *"Conditional Tail Expectation is a statistical risk measure that provides enhanced information about the tail of a distribution above that provided by the traditional use of percentiles. Instead of only identifying a value at the 95th percentile (for example) and ignoring possibly exponentially increasing values in the tail, CTE provides the average over all remaining values in the tail. Thus for many "traditional" loss distributions that are near normal CTE(90) will approximate the 95th percentile, but for distributions with "fat tails" from low probability, high impact events, the use of CTE will provide a higher, more revealing (and conservative) measure than the traditional percentile counterpart."[22]*

Given the complexity of the types of products sold by the life insurance industry, RBC C-3 Phase II is a necessary and important change to the determination of Risk-Based Capital. The approach assesses a much wider range of financial economic risks and will be a valuable early warning mechanism if used appropriately. However, it is a complex regulation and will require a significant amount of education and

---

[22] See [6].

training. Furthermore, the types of risk being measured are inherently volatile, and individuals may draw the wrong conclusion in reaction to significant changes in Risk-Based Capital requirements from one reporting period to the next. It will likely take several years to understand how this regulation will work in practice and it will definitely place considerable responsibility on the valuation actuary.

16.6 EXAMPLE

The Excel workbook, Chapter 16.xls, illustrates the calculation of the Risk-Based Capital and the RBC ratio for a life insurance company[23]. This sample life insurance company sells participating life insurance, term insurance and annuities. The first worksheet, Data, is the data needed to determine the Risk-Based Capital:

Information for Calculation of Risk-Based Capital	
Bonds	
Class 1	10,000,000,000
Class 2	8,000,000,000
Class 3	1,000,000,000
Class 4	900,000,000
Class 5	90,000,000
Class 6	10,000,000
Number of bond issuers	5,000
Mortgages	
Commercial Mortgages in Good Standing	900,000,000
Commercial Mortgages more than 90 days overdue	90,000,000
Commercial Mortgages in foreclosure	10,000,000
Preferred Stock (assumed to all belong to Class 2)	200,000,000
Common Stock	1,000,000,000
Real Estate	100,000,000
BA Assets	1,000,000,000
Policy Loans	5,000,000,000
Ordinary Life Insurance Inforce	200,000,000,000
Aggregate Reserves	
Ordinary Life	20,000,000,000
Annuity contracts with market value adjustment	5,000,000,000
Annuity contracts with book value withdrawals less a surrender of 5% or higher	7,000,000,000
Annuity contracts with book value withdrawals less a surrender of less than 5%	5,000,000,000
Annuity contracts with book value withdrawals and no surrender charge	3,000,000,000
Life contingent payout annuities	1,000,000,000
Supplementary contracts with life contingencies	100,000,000
Supplementary contracts without life contingencies	100,000,000
Dividend accumulations	200,000,000
Life Premiums and Annuity Considerations	2,500,000,000
Separate Account Liabilities	25,000,000,000
Statutory Surplus	2,000,000,000
Asset Valuation Reserve (AVR)	500,000,000
Policyholder Dividend Liability	750,000,000

---

[23] In actual practice, the determination of the Risk-Based Capital and the RBC ratio is considerably more complicated.

Using the asset information from the first worksheet, the worksheet called Asset Risk (C-1) determines the required capital for Asset Risk – Other (C-1):

Asset Risk (C-1)			
	(1)	(2)	(3)
Asset Type	Annual Statement Value	RBC Factor	RBC Requirement
Bonds			
Government and exempt issuers	0	0.0000	0
Class 1	10,000,000,000	0.0040	40,000,000
Class 2	8,000,000,000	0.0130	104,000,000
Class 3	1,000,000,000	0.0460	46,000,000
Class 4	900,000,000	0.1000	90,000,000
Class 5	90,000,000	0.2300	20,700,000
Class 6	10,000,000	0.3000	3,000,000
RBC for bonds before bond size adjustment			303,700,000
Bonds Size Adjustment (see Bond Size worksheet)			0.9260
Total **RBC for Bonds**			**281,226,200**
Mortgages			
Commercial mortgages in good standing	900,000,000	0.0260	23,400,000
Commercial mortgages more than 90 days overdue	90,000,000	0.1800	16,200,000
Commercial mortgages in foreclosure	10,000,000	0.2300	2,300,000
Total **RBC for Mortgages**			**41,900,000**
Preferred Stock			
Class 1	0	0.0040	0
Class 2	200,000,000	0.0130	2,600,000
Class 3	0	0.0460	0
Class 4	0	0.1000	0
Class 5	0	0.2300	0
Class 6	0	0.3000	0
Total **RBC for Preferred Stock**			**2,600,000**
Common Stock	1,000,000,000	0.3000	300,000,000
Real Estate	100,000,000	0.1500	15,000,000
BA Assets	1,000,000,000	0.3000	300,000,000
Asset Concentration Factor (see Concentration worksheet)			9,775,000
Total Asset Risk (C-1)			**950,501,200**

The Bond Size Adjustment is determined in the worksheet called Bond Size Factor:

Bond Size Factor				
Issuers	Number of Issuers	× Size Factor	=	Weighted Issuers
First 50	50	2.500		125
Next 50	50	1.300		65
Next 300	300	1.000		300
Over 400	4,600	0.900		4,140
Total Number of Issuers*	5,000			
Total Weighted Issuers				4,630
Size Factor				0.9260

*Excludes government issues

Similarly, the asset concentration factor is determined in the worksheet, Asset Concentration Factor:

Asset Concentration Factor		(1)	(2)	(3)
10 Largest Holdings	Asset Class	Annual Statement Value	· RBC Factor =	Additional RBC
First	Bond (Class 2)	25,000,000	0.0130	325,000
Second	Bond (Class 2)	25,000,000	0.0130	325,000
Third	Bond (Class 2)	25,000,000	0.0130	325,000
Fourth	Bond (Class 3)	25,000,000	0.0460	1,150,000
Fifth	Bond (Class 3)	25,000,000	0.0460	1,150,000
Sixth	Mortgage (in good standing)	50,000,000	0.0260	1,300,000
Seventh	Mortgage (in good standing)	50,000,000	0.0260	1,300,000
Eighth	Mortgage (in good standing)	50,000,000	0.0260	1,300,000
Ninth	Mortgage (in good standing)	50,000,000	0.0260	1,300,000
Tenth	Mortgage (in good standing)	50,000,000	0.0260	1,300,000
				9,775,000

The worksheet, Insurance Risk (C-2), determines the required capital for Insurance Risk (C-2):

Insurance Risk (C-2)	(1)	(2)	(3)
Assets Type	Annual Statement Value ·	RBC Factor =	RBC Requirement
Individual Life Insurance			
Ordinary Life Insurance Inforce (from Exhibit of Life Insurance)	200,000,000,000		
less Aggregate Reserve for Ordinary Life	20,000,000,000		
Total Net Amount at Risk	180,000,000,000		
First 500 million	500,000,000	0.0023	1,150,000
Next 4,500 million	4,500,000,000	0.0015	6,750,000
Next 20,000 million	20,000,000,000	0.0012	24,000,000
Over 25,000 million	155,000,000,000	0.0009	139,500,000
Total **RBC for Individual Life Insurance**			171,400,000
RBC for Other Insurance Risks			0
Total Insurance Risk (C-2)			**171,400,000**

The worksheet, Interest Rate Risk (C-3), determines the required capital Interest Rate Risk, Health Risk and Market Risk (C-3):

Interest Rate Risk, Health Risk, and Market Risk (C-3)			
	(1)	(2)	(3)
Assets Type	Annual Statement Value	RBC Factor	RBC Requirement
Low Risk			
Life insurance reserves net of policy loans	15,000,000,000	0.0077	115,500,000
Reserve for annuity contracts with no withdrawal feature	0	0.0077	0
Reserve for annuity contracts with market value adjustment	5,000,000,000	0.0077	38,500,000
Reserve for life contingent payout annuities	1,000,000,000	0.0077	7,700,000
Reserve for supplementary contracts with life contingencies	100,000,000	0.0077	770,000
Total **RBC for Low Risk**			7,700,000
Medium Risk			
Reserve for annuity contract with book value withdrawals less a surrender of 5% or higher	7,000,000,000	0.0154	107,800,000
Reserve for structure settlements	0	0.0154	0
Reserve for supplementary contracts without life contingencies	100,000,000	0.0154	1,540,000
Reserve for dividend accumulations	200,000,000	0.0154	3,080,000
Additional reserves established as a result of cash flow testing	0	0.0154	0
Total **RBC for Medium Risk**			112,420,000
High Risk			
Reserve for annuity contracts with book value withdrawals less a surrender of less than 5%	5,000,000,000	0.0308	154,000,000
Reserve for annuity contracts with book value withdrawals and no surrender charge	3,000,000,000	0.0308	92,400,000
Total **RBC for High Risk**			246,400,000
Additional RBC as the result of Cash Flow Testing			0
Total Interest Rate Risk, Health Risk and Market Risk (C-3)			366,520,000

Finally, the worksheet, Business Risk (C-4), determines the required capital Interest Business Risk (C-4):

Business Risk (C-4)			
	(1)	(2)	(3)
Assets Type	Annual Statement Value	RBC Factor	RBC Requirement
Life Premiums & Annuity Considerations	2,500,000,000	0.0308	77,000,000
Separate Account Liabilities	25,000,000,000	0.0008	20,000,000
Total (C-4)			97,000,000

Using the information from these worksheets, the final worksheet, Risk-Based Capital Ratio, determines the Total Authorized Control Level Risk-Based Capital and the RBC ratio for the life insurance company:

Risk-Based Capital Ratio	
Asset Risk (C-1)	950,501,200
+ Insurance Risk (C-2)	171,400,000
+ Interest Rate Risk, Health Risk and Market Risk (C-3)	366,520,000
+ Business Risk (C-4)	97,000,000
− Covariance adjustment (see covariance adjustment worksheet)	544,239,625
= Total Authorized Control Level Risk-Based Capital	1,041,181,575
Total Adjusted Capital	2,875,000,000
Risk-Based Capital Ratio (Total Adjusted Capital/Total Risked Based Capital)	276.1%

16.7 EXERCISES

16.7.1 Key Terms

Insolvency risk	risk-based capital
Target surplus	RBC formula
Asset Risk – Affiliates (C-0)	Asset Risk – Other (C-1)
Insurance Risk (C-2)	Interest Rate Risk, Health Risk and Market Risk(C-3)
Business Risk (C-4)	RBC Ratio
Total Adjusted Surplus	covariance adjustment
Regulatory Action Levels	Authorized Control Level Risk-Based Capital
Total Asset Requirement	Conditional Tail Expectation

16.7.2 Questions

a. Who are the primary constituencies interested in whether a company has the appropriate amount of surplus? Why?

b. What is the appropriate amount of surplus?

c. What were the two most important implications to life insurance companies when the NAIC adopted the Risk-Based Capital (RBC) for Life and Health Insurers Model Act in 1992?

d. What is insolvency risk?
How is it different for a life insurance company as compared to a typical manufacturing company?

e. What is target surplus? How is it different from Risk-Based Capital?

f. What actions can the managers of a life insurance company take to increase the surplus of the company relative to its risk-based capital requirements?

g. What are the five major risk categories that the RBC formula centers around?

h. Briefly describe how the RBC formula utilizes RBC factors to determine the RBC requirement.

i. How are these RBC factors determined?

j. What are some of the advantages of using RBC factors?
What are some of the disadvantages?

k. What is Asset Risk Other (C-1)?
What are the major categories of RBC factors for Asset Risk Other (C-1)?

l. Why does the formula for Asset Risk Other (C-1) have a size adjustment factor?

m. Briefly describe the rationale of the Mortgage Experience Adjustment Factor.

n. What are the two adjustments made to the 30% RBC factor for common stock?
What is the rationale for the adjustment?

o. Briefly describe the rationale of the asset concentration factor.

p. What is Insurance Risk (C-2)?
    Why is the RBC factor for life insurance based on net amount at risk as opposed to total face amount?

q. What types of losses are Interest Rate Risk, Health Risk and Market Risk (C-3) intended to cover?

r. What are the three risk categories for interest rate risk?

s. Why is it necessary to incorporate cash flow testing into the determination of RBC?

t. What types of losses are Business Risk (C-4) intended to cover?

u. What is the formula for the RBC ratio?

v. What is the rationale for using total adjusted capital in the RBC ratio as opposed to statutory surplus?

w. Briefly describe the rationale behind the covariance adjustment.

x. What are the regulatory action levels?

y. Why are the regulatory requirements evolving toward principle based capitol requirement?
    What are the advantages? What are the disadvantages?

z. Briefly describe RBC Phase I and RBC Phase II.

 APPENDIX

A.1 PRODUCT DESCRIPTIONS

A.1.1 WHOLE LIFE CONTRACTS

Whole life contracts provide a fixed amount of insurance coverage over the life of the insured and the related benefits are normally payable only upon the insured's death. Premiums are paid over various periods as allowed by the terms of the policy contract. Whole life insurance contracts provide for nonforfeiture values, some common types being reduced paid up insurance, extended term insurance, and cash values and some provide for the payment of policy dividends. A level premium is usually paid for policies of this type, and the premium may be paid in annual or more frequent modes. An ordinary life (straight-life) policy stipulates that premiums are to be paid during the life of the insured.

A.1.2 ENDOWMENT CONTRACTS

Endowment contracts are principally savings contracts which incorporate an element of life insurance protection. Endowment insurance contracts provide a benefit if the insured survives the endowment period or the amount is paid to a beneficiary if the insured does not survive. A pure endowment contract only provides a benefit to the insured if he/she survives the endowment period. Endowment policies mature at a specified attained age of the insured or at the end of a specified period. Premium payments for endowment contracts are made over a specified period, but may also be made under a single premium or limited-payment plan. Both whole life and endowment policies contain nonforfeiture or similar clauses which provide for cash or some other form of insurance to be available in the event of failure to continue the required premiums.

A.1.3 TERM LIFE CONTRACTS

Term life contracts provide insurance over a specified period of time. If the insured dies during this term, the face amount of the policy will be paid to the beneficiary. Policies for term insurance which are written for relatively short periods of time commonly grant the policyholder the right to renew for an additional period or periods up to a maximum age, such as 60 or 65, without requiring additional evidence of insurability. Such policies do not usually provide nonforfeiture values.

A.1.4 SUPPLEMENTARY CONTRACTS

Supplementary contracts with life contingencies are agreements between the insurance company and either the insured or the beneficiary, usually to provide for full or partial settlement of the amount payable upon the termination of an original contract. Generally, the proceeds are paid over the lifetime of one or more beneficiaries. This differs from a *supplementary contract without life contingencies* under which the proceeds are paid over a definite period without regard to the life of the beneficiary.

A.1.5 UNIVERSAL LIFE AND VARIABLE LIFE CONTRACTS

Universal life and variable life contracts include those contracts which have terms that are not fixed and guaranteed relative to premium amounts, expense assessments, or benefits accruing to the policyholder. These contracts generally provide for death benefits and nonforfeiture values and may be issued on a fixed premium basis or on a flexible premium basis where the premiums are paid at the insured's discretion.

A.1.6 LIMITED-PAYMENT CONTRACTS

Limited-payment contracts are contracts with terms that are fixed and guaranteed and for which premiums are paid over a specified number of years or to a specified age. The insurance coverage continues for the remainder of the insured's life. A single-premium policy requires a lump-sum payment at the inception of the policy.

A.1.7 ANNUITY CONTRACTS

An *annuity contract* is an arrangement whereby an annuitant is guaranteed to receive a series of stipulated amounts commencing either immediately or at some future date. A contract with a purchase rate guarantee represents a life contingency that would require an annuity contract to be classified as a life contract. The main types of annuity contracts with life contingencies are discussed below.

A *deferred annuity* provides for the accumulation of funds to be applied at some future period designated by the policyholder. Premium payments can be made in a lump sum amount (single premium deferred annuity), or periodically (flexible or fixed premium deferred annuity) as allowed by the policy contract. At the end of the accumulation period, the policyholder may elect to receive a lump sum distribution or may elect to receive periodic payments for life, or over a specific period, or some combination thereof.

A *variable annuity* is an annuity that includes a provision for benefit payments which vary in accordance with the rate of return of the underlying investment portfolio selected by the policyholder. The considerations for a variable annuity are usually invested in a separate account in which the value of the contract share varies according to the performance of the separate account, both before the commencement of annuity payments as well as after. Premium payments can be made in lump sum amounts or periodically as allowed by the policy contract. A minimum death benefit is often guaranteed during the annuity consideration accumulation period and these contracts are, therefore, classified as life contracts.

A *straight-life annuity* provides for periodic payments to the annuitant as long as the annuitant lives. Death of the annuitant constitutes completion of the contract and no further payments are made by the insurance company.

A *life annuity with a period certain* works essentially the same way as the straight-life annuity as the annuitant receives periodic payments for as long as the annuitant lives. However, if the annuitant dies before the end of the specified "certain" period, payments are continued to a beneficiary until the specified number of "certain" payments (i.e, .the specified period in the contract) is completed.

A *refund annuity* is similar to the life annuity with a period certain in which the annuitant receives periodic payments for as long as the annuitant lives. There are two variants of this type of annuity. Under the cash refund annuity, a lump-sum payment is made at the death of the annuitant equal to the excess, if any, of the purchase price of the annuity over the sum of the annuity payments made to the date of death. The installment refund annuity provides that annuity payments are to continue to a beneficiary after the death of the annuitant until the sum of all payments made equals the purchase price.

A *joint and survivorship annuity* provides for the continuation of payments after the death of one of the annuitants during the lifetime of the surviving annuitant.

A.2 VARIABLE ANNUITY LIVING BENEFITS

A.2.1 GUARANTEED MINIMUM ACCUMULATED BENEFIT (GMAB)

Guaranteed Minimum Accumulation Benefit (GMAB) provides a guarantee that deposits less withdrawals will accumulate to a specified amount by a given contract year (e.g., 10 years).

A.2.2 GUARANTEED MINIMUM INCOME BENEFIT (GMIB)

Guaranteed Minimum Income Benefit (GMIB) provides that a minimum fund value will be available for annuitization after the contract has been inforce a specified number of years. In other words, it guarantees a minimum income benefit, since the contract guarantees purchase rates as well.

A.2.3 GUARANTEED MINIMUM WITHDRAWAL BENEFIT (GMWB)

Guaranteed Minimum Withdrawal Benefit (GMWB) guarantees that the contractholder will be able to withdraw a specified percentage (e.g., 5%) of the fund each year, regardless of market conditions, until they have received the amount deposited into the contract.

A.2.4 GUARANTEED PAYOUT ANNUITY FLOOR (GPAF)

The income benefit of a variable payout annuity will increase or decrease depending on how the fund performs relative to the assumed interest rate. Guaranteed Payout Annuity Floor (GPAF) guarantees that the income benefit will not decrease below a specified amount.

A.3 VARIABLE ANNUITY MINIMUM DEATH BENEFIT GUARANTEES

A.3.1 RETURN OF PREMIUM

The death benefit is the larger of the account balance on the date of death or the sum of premium deposits less partial withdrawals since inception of the contract.

A.3.2 RESET

The minimum death benefit is the larger of the account balance on the date of death or the account balance after a pre-set number of years have elapsed (e.g., every three, five or seven years) plus the sum of premium deposits less partial withdrawals since the last reset date.

A.3.3 ROLL-UP

The death benefit is the larger of the account balance on the date of death or the accumulation of premium deposits less partial withdrawals accumulated at a specified interest rate (e.g. 5%) up to a specified age (e.g., attained age 80).

A.3.4 ONE-YEAR RATCHET

The death benefit is the larger of the current account balance or the highest account balance on any previous contract anniversary date adjusted to reflect any premium deposits and partial withdrawals since the anniversary date with the highest account balance.

✧ BIBLIOGRAPHY

1. Actuarial Standards Board, Actuarial Standard of Practice No. 7, *Analysis of Life, Health, or Property/Casualty Insurer Cash Flows.* Washington, D.C.: American Academy of Actuaries, 2002.

2. Actuarial Standards Board, Actuarial Standard of Practice No. 22, *Statements of Opinion Based on Asset Adequacy Analysis by Actuaries for Life and Health Insurers.* Washington, D.C.: American Academy of Actuaries, 2001.

3. Ahlgrim, K., S. D'Arcy, and R. Gorvett, "Report on Modeling of Economic Series Coordinated with Interest Rate Scenarios." Casualty Actuarial Society and Society of Actuaries, July 2004.

4. American Academy of Actuaries, *Life and Health Valuation Law Manual.* Washington, D.C.: American Academy of Actuaries, 2005.

5. American Academy of Actuaries, "Principle-Based Risk-Based Capital Report," December 2002.

6. American Academy of Actuaries, "Recommended Approach for Setting Regulatory Risk-Based Capital for Variable Products with Guarantees (Excluding Index Guarantees)," September 2003.

7. American Council of Life Insurers, *2006 Life Insurers Fact Book.* Washington, D.C.: ACLI, 2006.

8. American Institute of Certified Public Accountants, *AICPA Audit and Accounting Guide for Life and Health Insurance Entities.* New York: AICPA, 2000.

9. Brealey, Richard A., Stewart C. Myers and Franklin Allen, *Principles of Corporate Finance.* New York: McGraw-Hill, 2006.

10. "Canadian and British Insurance Companies Act." 1978.

11. Canadian Institute of Actuaries, *Recommendations for Life Insurance Company Financial Reporting.*

12. Financial Accounting Standards Board, *Proposed Statement of Financial Accounting Standards Fair Value Measurement.* Norwalk: FASB, 2004.

13. Frasier, William M., "Second to Die Joint Life Cash Values and Reserves," *The Actuary.* Society of Actuaries, March 1978.

14. Ibbotson Associates, *Stocks, Bonds, Bills, and Inflation, Valuation Edition 2005 Yearbook.* Chicago: Ibbotson Associates, 2005.

15. International Accounting Standards Board Mission Statement, www.iasb.org.

16. Life Office Management Association, "Risk-Based Capital in the Life Insurance Industry." LOMA, 1994.

17. Moody's Investors Service, "Default and Recovery Rates of Corporate Bond Issuers, 1920-2004." New York: Moody's Investors Service, January 2005.

18. National Association of Insurance Commissioners, *Accounting Practices and Procedures Manual.* Kansas City: NAIC, 2005.

19. National Association of Insurance Commissioners, Constitution. www.naic.org

20. National Association of Insurance Commissioners, "Life Risk-Based Capital Report," 2004.

21. National Association of Insurance Commissioners, *Model Laws, Regulations, and Guidelines.* Kansas City: NAIC, 2005.

22. New York Insurance Law. Albany: New York Insurance Department.

23. Scher, Edward, "Relationships among the Fully Continuous, the Discounted Continuous, and the Semicontinuous Reserve Bases for Ordinary Life Insurance," *Transactions XXVI, Part I.* Schaumburg: Society of Actuaries, 1974.

INDEX